READINGS ON
ACCOUNTING DEVELOPMENT

THE DEVELOPMENT OF CONTEMPORARY ACCOUNTING THOUGHT

Advisory Editor
Richard P. Brief

Editorial Board
Gary John Previts
Basil S. Yamey
Stephen A. Zeff

*See last pages of this volume
for a complete list of titles.*

READINGS ON
ACCOUNTING DEVELOPMENT

Edited by
S. Paul Garner and Marilynn Hughes

ARNO PRESS
A New York Times Company
New York ● 1978

**Publisher's Note: This book has been reproduced
from the best available copy.**

Editorial Supervision: LUCILLE MAIORCA

———◆———

Reprint Edition 1978 by Arno Press Inc.

Arrangement and compilation copyright © 1978
      by Arno Press Inc.

THE DEVELOPMENT OF CONTEMPORARY ACCOUNTING THOUGHT
ISBN for complete set: 0-405-10891-5
See last pages of this volume for titles.

Manufactured in the United States of America

———◆———

Library of Congress Cataloging in Publication Data

Main entry under title:

Readings on accounting development.

  (The Development of contemporary accounting thought)
  Reprint of articles published between 1912 and 1977 by
various publishers in various journals.
  Includes bibliographical references.
  1. Accounting--History--Addresses, essays, lectures.
I. Garner, Samuel Paul, 1910-   II. Hughes, Marilynn.
III. Series.
HF5605.R4   657'.09   77-87313
ISBN 0-405-10926-1

ACKNOWLEDGMENTS

"Initial Development of Accountancy" by Calvin C. Potter was reprinted with permission from CAmagazine, published by The Canadian Institute of Chartered Accountants, Toronto, Canada.

"The Financial Organisation of the Manor" by A. E. Levett was reprinted by permission of the *Economic History Review*.

"Evolution of the Integration of the Cost and Financial Records" by S. Paul Garner was reprinted by permission of the University of Alabama Press.

"Goodwill—The Company's 'Ultimate Asset'" by Hugh P. Hughes was reprinted by permission of the *Atlanta Economic Review*.

All other articles were reprinted by permission of the American Accounting Association.

ACKNOWLEDGMENTS

INTRODUCTION

The idea for this book of readings on accounting evolution originated over ten years ago between the late Dr. H. Peter Hain of Australia and Dr. S. Paul Garner, now Dean Emeritus of the Graduate School of Business at the University of Alabama. Since Dr. Hain's death, the book has been completed by Dr. Garner and Dr. Marilynn L. Hughes, a graduate of the University of Alabama and Professor of Accounting at Morehouse College in Atlanta, Georgia. The intent of the book was and is to present a wide range of subject matter on the evolution of accounting as supplementary material for background reading by accounting majors in advanced theory and seminar courses and as a library reference work.

Dr. Garner has had a long-time interest and enthusiasm for writing and research in the field of accounting history and evolution and is a noted authority in this field. He has given some forty years' attention to accounting evolution, and his sizeable volume <u>Evolution of Cost Accounting to 1925</u> has been distributed throughout the world.

Dr. Hain, also a noted authority in the field of accounting history and evolution, was a prominent member of the Accounting Department at the University of Melbourne in Australia. He was educated in Austria at the famous University of Vienna where he developed much original material on accounting history, and he had extensive experience in both European and Commonwealth countries.

Dr. Hughes' interest in the field stems from her experience as a graduate student at the University of Alabama, the accounting curriculum of which strongly emphasizes accounting history and evolution, and her contact with accounting professors themselves interested in history.

SECTIONS

Introduction

The introductory articles illustrate the importance of studying accounting development and evolution as a basis for understanding the present state of the art. Richard Homburger emphasizes the meaning and purpose a knowledge of accounting history has for students intending to become C.P.A.s, and he suggests the inclusion of history in the traditional accounting courses as well as a separate history course. H. Thomas Johnson takes a broader view and discusses the role accounting history has in the study of modern business enterprises, pointing out its unique contributions which are not found, for example, in the research of economic historians primarily due to the need for familiarity with highly complex modern accounting techniques.

Accounting in Antiquity

Accounting in Antiquity stresses the origin and development of accounting before Pacioli with evidence of the existence of financial records and through relating accounting development to the highly developed commercial activities of the ancients.

Orville Keister presents translations of ancient Mesopotamian tablets used in commercial recordkeeping as evidence of the origins of accounting in antiquity and notes the related use of a monetary unit, a high degree of mathematical accuracy, the presence of negotiable records of indebtedness including the concept of interest, and the employment of allowances and expense accounts.

H. P. Hain discusses the 1915 discovered Zenon Papyri which provide evidence of elaborate accounting systems and audits developed in Ancient Greece. Like Keister, he relates accounting evolution to commercial development.

Max Teichmann cites evidence of the origin of accounting in ancient governmental units levying taxes which necessitated formal records kept in terms of a monetary unit.

Orville Keister's second article describes a simple but interesting counting device known as the Quipu used by ancient Incan recordkeepers.

Beginning of a New Era

The beginning of a new era focuses on medieval records which reveal the development of partnership, mercantile, and manorial accounting. Additional speculations on the origin of double-entry bookkeeping also are offered.

Raymond de Roover bases his explanations of the origin of double-entry bookkeeping on recently discovered medieval Italian account books, and he discusses the existence of textile industries with their effect on the development of industrial accounting.

Calvin Potter summarizes the origins and assumptions of bookkeeping, then correlates bookkeeping to prevailing social conditions as a first step of an investigation into criticism of accountancy to satisfactorily portray financial position and results of operations.

Basil Yamey examines single-entry and agency bookkeeping, earlier developments in recordkeeping, as an explanation that the origin of double-entry bookkeeping was a part of an evolutionary process of development rather than a discovery.

A. E. Lovett uses manorial accounts as a means to understanding the dynamic facts of agrarian evolution in the Middle Ages.

Early Achievements

Early achievements in the development of accounting mainly occurred in the general use of accounting for management or control purposes and in handling technically difficult problems such as those of foreign exchange.

Kenneth Most outlines the lengthy and difficult articles on Sombart's propositions regarding the role accounting played in the rise of capitalism and Basil Yamey's criticisms of Sombart. He then presents his own interpretation of the evidence which they adduce to bring Sombart up to date.

Raymond de Roover explains how medieval bankers determined profit on foreign exchange transactions, an interesting disclosure considering the current interest this topic has generated among accountants and in particular with the Financial Accounting Standards Board.

The Holding Period to 1800

The holding period of the seventeenth and eighteenth centuries provided few innovations in the development of accounting, but records and textbooks of that era do give some insight to the accounting practices which developed, for example, in profit calculation, inventory valuation, and depreciation treatment.

W. T. Baxter studies colonial American economic conditions and bookkeeping as possible clues to medieval practice and the possibility of drawing conclusions about medieval bookkeeping based on an analogy with this simple economy.

A. C. Littleton traces the history of the use of "cost or market" to show it developed as a result of special circumstances not applicable in current accounting practice and concludes this method should, at best, be only an exception to the rule in valuing inventories.

Lawrence Vance refutes Littleton's contention that the lower-of-cost-or-market rule was a result of expediency and convenience, citing historical references to prove it developed in response to the needs of businessmen.

H. R. Hatfield presents examples of accounting practices developed in the past which continue to be followed out of custom rather from need.

Perry Mason covers the development of depreciation treatments from 1675 to 1867 in Europe and America.

Revival in the 19th Century

The second half of the nineteenth century and later periods saw developments occurring in accounting in response to the development of joint-stock companies and general limited liability.

Elmer Hartzell relates developments in accounting with changes in science and political organizations to indicate these areas had a significant effect on accounting as did commerce and industry.

Paul Crossman demonstrates the long period of growth and refinement in cost control by tracing several centuries of writings in which the authors urged accounting records be useful to management in controlling and thereby reducing costs through detailed cost analysis and classification.

Basil Yamey reviews Edward Jones' book, English System of Bookkeeping, to point out his influence on the art of accounting and the concern of writers of the time with fraud prevention through adequate accounting records.

Stanley Howard translates and interprets the spirit of Thomas Turner's book, An Epitome of Book-keeping by Double Entry, one of the earliest American textbooks on commercial subjects valuable for its contribution to knowledge of history, economics, and accounting.

Emerging Specialization

Specialization emerged fairly early in the evolution of accounting in areas such as cost accounting, budgeting, auditing, and executorship accounting.

Edwin Theiss examines conditions leading to the development of budgeting from its beginning in England during the eighteenth century to its use in the United States in municipal accounting and business, its inclusion in university instruction, and its appearance in accounting literature.

S. Paul Garner, in tracing the evolution of integrating cost and financial records, discusses major contributors and indicates, in relation to present practices, the retention and modification of techniques developed during the period from the 1880's to the 1920's.

Leon Hay focuses on examples of executorship accounting in Rome, England, and America as it developed from ancient times to the present.

Leonard Hein reviews the British Companies Acts and their control of auditing to draw conclusions about the segments of society pressuring for control, the needs for control, and the effects of control on the development of auditing theory and practice.

C. A. Moyer describes changes in American auditing as a contribution to understanding present occurrences and predicting future trends.

Hugh Hughes' article is a capsule history of problems surrounding accounting for goodwill. In it he also discusses the problems associated with the pooling/purchase controversy and its effect on the Accounting Principles Board.

CONTENTS

I INTRODUCTION
Homburger, Richard H.
STUDY OF HISTORY—GATEWAY TO PERSPECTIVE (Reprinted from
The Accounting Review) Menasha, Wis., July, 1958

Johnson, H. Thomas
THE ROLE OF ACCOUNTING HISTORY IN THE STUDY OF MODERN
BUSINESS ENTERPRISE (Reprinted from *The Accounting Review*)
Menasha, Wis., July, 1975

II ACCOUNTING IN ANTIQUITY
Keister, Orville R.
COMMERCIAL RECORD-KEEPING IN ANCIENT MESOPOTAMIA
(Reprinted from *The Accounting Review*) Menasha, Wis., April, 1963

Hain, H. P.
ACCOUNTING CONTROL IN THE ZENON PAPYRI (Reprinted from
The Accounting Review) Menasha, Wis., October, 1966

Teichmann, Max
A SKETCH OF ACCOUNTANCY (Reprinted from *The Journal of Accountancy*)
New York, June, 1912

Keister, Orville R.
THE INCAN QUIPU (Reprinted from *The Accounting Review*) Menasha, Wis.,
April, 1964

III BEGINNING OF A NEW ERA
de Roover, Raymond
CHARACTERISTICS OF BOOKKEEPING BEFORE PACIOLO (Reprinted
from *The Accounting Review*) Menasha, Wis., June, 1938

Potter, Calvin C.
INITIAL DEVELOPMENT OF ACCOUNTANCY (Reprinted from *The
Canadian Chartered Accountant*) Toronto, January, 1952

Yamey, Basil S.
NOTES ON THE ORIGIN OF DOUBLE-ENTRY BOOKKEEPING
(Reprinted from *The Accounting Review*) Menasha, Wis., July, 1947

Levett, A. E.
THE FINANCIAL ORGANIZATION OF THE MANOR (Reprinted from
The Economic History Review) London, January, 1927

IV   EARLY ACHIEVEMENTS
Most, Kenneth S.
SOMBART'S PROPOSITIONS REVISITED (Reprinted from *The Accounting
Review*) Menasha, Wis., October, 1972

de Roover, Raymond
EARLY ACCOUNTING PROBLEMS OF FOREIGN EXCHANGE
(Reprinted from *The Accounting Review*) Menasha, Wis., October, 1944

V   THE HOLDING PERIOD TO 1800
Baxter, W[illiam] T.
CREDIT, BILLS, AND BOOKKEEPING IN A SIMPLE ECONOMY
(Reprinted from *The Accounting Review*) Menasha, Wis., April, 1946

Littleton, A. C.
A GENEALOGY FOR "COST OR MARKET" (Reprinted from *The Accounting
Review*, Vol. XVI, No. 2) Menasha, Wis., June, 1941

Vance, Lawrence L.
THE AUTHORITY OF HISTORY IN INVENTORY VALUATION (Reprinted
from *The Accounting Review*, Vol. XVIII, No. 3) Menasha, Wis., July, 1943

Hatfield, Henry Rand
THE ACCOUNTING TRIVIA (Reprinted from *The Accounting Review*,
Vol. XV, No. 3) Menasha, Wis., September, 1940

Mason, Perry
ILLUSTRATIONS OF THE EARLY TREATMENT OF DEPRECIATION
(Reprinted from *The Accounting Review*) Menasha, Wis., September, 1933

VI   REVIVAL IN THE 19TH CENTURY
Hartzel, Elmer
THE BACKGROUND OF ACCOUNTING (Reprinted from *The Accounting
Review*) Menasha, Wis., June, 1934

Crossman, Paul
THE GENESIS OF COST CONTROL (Reprinted from *The Accounting Review*,
Vol. XXVIII, No. 4) Menasha, Wis., October, 1953

Yamey, Basil S.
EDWARD JONES'S "ENGLISH SYSTEM OF BOOKKEEPING" (Reprinted
from *The Accounting Review*) Menasha, Wis., October, 1944

Howard, Stanley E.
CHARGE AND DISCHARGE (Reprinted from *The Accounting Review*)
Menasha, Wis., March, 1931

VII   EMERGING SPECIALIZATION
Theiss, Edwin L.
THE BEGINNINGS OF BUSINESS BUDGETING (Reprinted from
The Accounting Review) Menasha, Wis., March, 1937

[Garner, S. Paul]
EVOLUTION OF THE INTEGRATION OF THE COST AND FINANCIAL
RECORDS (Reprinted from *Evolution of Cost Accounting to 1925*, Chapter VI)
Tuscaloosa, Alabama, 1954

Hay, Leon E.
EXECUTORSHIP REPORTING—SOME HISTORICAL NOTES (Reprinted
from *The Accounting Review*) Menasha, Wis., January, 1961

Hein, Leonard W.
THE AUDITOR AND THE BRITISH COMPANIES ACTS (Reprinted from
The Accounting Review) Menasha, Wis., July, 1963

Moyer, C. A.
EARLY DEVELOPMENTS IN AMERICAN AUDITING (Reprinted from
The Accounting Review, Vol. XXVI, No. 1) Menasha, Wis., January, 1951

Hughes, Hugh P.
GOODWILL—THE COMPANY'S 'ULTIMATE ASSET' (Reprinted from
Atlanta Economic Review) Atlanta, Georgia, March-April, 1977

VIII   TABLES AND BIBLIOGRAPHIES
Abs, George et al.
HISTORICAL DATES IN ACCOUNTING (Reprinted from *The Accounting
Review*) Menasha, Wis., July, 1954

Hatfield, H. R. and A. C. Littleton
A CHECK-LIST OF EARLY BOOKKEEPING TEXTS (Reprinted from
The Accounting Review) Menasha, Wis., September, 1932

STUDY OF HISTORY—
GATEWAY TO PERSPECTIVE

Richard H. Homburger

STUDY OF HISTORY—GATEWAY TO PERSPECTIVE

Richard H. Homburger
University of Wichita

The rapid development of graduate study programs in accounting in recent years has brought about an increasing number of course offerings in Accounting History, a field of instruction which had been largely neglected by the majority of standard accounting curricula in this country during the earlier period. The traditional neglect of history in accounting instruction, as compared with instruction in other fields of the social sciences, such as economics and law, can be explained by two major factors. It may be maintained that modern accounting practice, geared to the legal requirements of the SEC and the Internal Revenue Code and guided by the most recent recommendations of the AICPA, draws only to a very small extent upon its historical heritage. Furthermore, many feel that accounting is primarily a professional skill to which historical research contributes little, if anything.

What, then, is the reason for the increasing popularity of history courses within the last few years? In a superficial way, the course in Accounting History is thought of as a graduate "background" course designed to promote the student's insight into and understanding of the underlying factors and problems of his major field of study. It is assumed that a review of historical foundations and developments always deepens appreciation and understanding of modern conditions, regardless of the area of study. It is felt that graduate education in accounting should be of the same quality and depth as that offered in the other areas of the social science field.

While this may be well as a precept, it must not be forgotten that most graduate students in accounting are practitioners or future practitioners concerned primarily with the improvement of their skills to deal more competently with the problems of modern accounting practice. For many, the CPA examination still looms as the major goal to achieve. To have meaning and purpose for those students, the history course must be much more than a study of historical data. Even a mere comparison of past and present practices will not do. In approach and content the course must be designed to evaluate critically, by way of comparison, past and present theories and procedures in the light of the requirements set by the social and economic conditions of each period and each country. The primary objective of this approach must be the improvement of the professional competence and judgment of the modern accountant.

The study of history can help to improve judgment and competence by bringing present-day theories, conventions, and practices into perspective, by awakening the student's consciousness of their relationship to our economic and legal environment. A few examples will serve to illustrate this point.

In modern elementary and intermediate accounting instruction the two primary financial statements, the balance sheet and the income statement, are presented to the student as the logical basis and ultimate objective of double-entry bookkeeping and accounting. This is educationally sound and largely in line with our present-day needs. But it makes it somewhat difficult to appreciate a possible need for a double entry set of records without the use of formal financial statements as one may find in personal or household bookkeeping, or the need for a limited set of single entry records for special situations. A look at pre-Pacioli accounting history shows that certain forms of single entry records served a useful purpose before the advent of double entry, and that double entry itself was appreciated for its control aspects before financial statements meeting the modern requirements of form and classification were developed or even desired. The student may also find that certain approaches to modern accounting which to him are advanced subject matter, such as tracing the flow of invested funds, and the charge-discharge approach characteristic

for fiduciary accounting, have earlier origins in history than the balancing balance sheet—presumably because they meet more basic needs of society.

The principles of asset valuation—namely cost as the primary valuation basis, with a lower market value as a ceiling being applied only to current assets, and a systematic depreciation adjustment on some theoretical basis applicable to plant and equipment are, again, doctrines to which the modern accounting student is exposed very early in his course of study. At this point, lower of cost or market, where it applies, is usually explained by the need for conservatism. As the student's understanding of accounting procedures matures, he becomes more aware of the technical interrelationship between income statement and balance sheet, and of the problems of income measurement. Then, in the more advanced courses, he meets the rather unpopular doctrines which recognize asset valuation at market, and which he learns to know as an undesirable by-product of rising prices and high income taxes. On the other hand, an objective look at accounting history will show "market" as the originally preferred basis of valuation for current assets, especially inventories, as well as fixed or equipment assets in terms of measuring the periodic depreciation adjustment. And the student will thus be better able to understand the mutual influence which tax legislation and accounting doctrines have exercised upon each other, and the limitations to which any method of establishing accounting values must necessarily be subjected. He will come to realize that our modern concepts of operating income, accrual accounting, and systematic write-offs of unamortized costs are tools that evolved slowly to serve the specific needs of our modern economy.

Such a "perspective" view of the accounting concepts and procedures of the past as well as of the present is difficult to achieve by a systematically chronological presentation of available historical material, beginning with the ancient civilizations and ending with the recognized procedures of our time. Most European texts on accounting history, dating back to the turn of the century and earlier, have taken this approach. Aside from the lack of continuity in the development of accounting institutions throughout the world, lack of reliable information on many important periods and areas, even today, makes this a difficult path to follow. Furthermore, the contact between the past and the present is lost too easily if certain periods of history are made subjects of study for their own sake. Alternative approaches used by modern writers include those where certain concepts or institutions, such as depreciation or by-product accounting, are traced from their earliest origins to the present time, and those where certain outstanding episodes of accounting history are selected for isolated and detailed study. While all of these methods of presentation have merit, it is fortunate that in the classroom a certain degree of flexibility and informality is feasible and even desirable. Therefore, the first half of the course may well lay a foundation upon which further specialized study can be built. This first part will then include a survey of the socio-economic conditions found during the earlier periods of history, and of the legal, financial, and accounting practices evolved under those conditions, as far as we know them. The evolution of double-entry procedure in Pacioli's time should conclude this basic survey. If the known accounting practices of this earlier period are closely aligned with its economic, financial, and legal history, a preliminary comparison with modern conditions as to causes, objectives, and results can be achieved without too much effort. On the other hand it seems quite impractical to trace the development of modern accounting in its many ramifications as a single unit, step by step. Evolution of the

public accounting and auditing profession was one distinct development, that of industrial cost finding and cost analysis was another. The same is true of governmental accounting procedure. Each one of the various phases of accounting activity had its own origins, motivation, and pioneering activity. It also appears that each of a number of basic theoretical concepts, such as income or depreciation, has had its own historical development. For these reasons, tracing the various strands of modern accounting development separately and, perhaps, attempting to tie them together at the final class meeting, viewing them as distinct consequences of one primary cause, namely modern industrial development, will aid the student toward the broader perspective which he seeks. If, furthermore, each student is asked to do some individual research in any specific area of modern accounting development, and to submit his findings to class discussion, this will stimulate his own interest as well as that of the rest of the class.

The course in Accounting History is now fairly well established as an essential part of the graduate curriculum in accounting. With the increased emphasis now being placed on the *why* rather than the *how* in elementary accounting instruction, one may ask whether a bit more historical perspective should not be injected into our undergraduate courses as well. Since the terms *debit* and *credit* are introduced at the very beginning of our accounting training program, they could perhaps be explained in their original meaning by way of a modified and modernized version of "account personification." And if we chose to include a discussion of cost or market *valuation* concepts in our elementary texts, we might, perhaps, make use of two time-tested concepts of *income*, namely that of increase in wealth on one hand, and that of fruit of our efforts on the other, to help explain their significance.

THE ROLE OF ACCOUNTING HISTORY IN THE STUDY OF MODERN BUSINESS ENTERPRISE

H. Thomas Johnson

The Role of Accounting History in the Study of Modern Business Enterprise

H. Thomas Johnson

IT is a truism to observe that one major objective of accounting history is a "better understanding of economic . . . history" (American Accounting Association, 1970, p. 53). Works by accounting historians have long been acknowledged as indispensable to the investigations of economic historians studying Europe and North America from the medieval era to approximately 1850. Indeed, accounting historians and economic historians concentrating upon these early periods often consult the same research materials and ask questions strikingly similar in nature.

This intimate relationship seldom obtains, however, when accounting and economic historians examine the modern age. Economic historians assessing developments from 1850 to the present rarely weigh the findings of accounting historians. Certainly one explanation of the economic historian's indifference to modern accounting history is the increasing sophistication of accounting practices. Only highly trained accounting historians are able to deal with these practices gracefully and perceptively. Although economic historians are capable of recognizing and discussing elementary accounting principles common before the nineteenth century, they are seldom familiar with those complex accounting techniques current since the late 1800's. The work of the economic historian studying the modern era usually ignores, then, the issues and conclusions which would naturally occur to the ac-

counting historian concentrating upon modern history. At times the two fields appear to be as unrelated as C. P. Snow's two cultures. Although the economist and the accountant may not single out the same modern issues and problems for their attention, and although they may not acknowledge the possibility that their modern studies can merge, nevertheless I believe that they can work together effectively to explain the development of American large-scale business firms between 1850 and 1930. The need for cooperative investigation becomes evident if one considers how the typical manufacturing firm of the mid-nineteenth century evolved into those vertically integrated industrial firms that appeared in great numbers during the merger wave of 1897–1903.

It is well known, of course, that typical manufacturing firms of the mid-nineteenth century specialized mainly in one activity: that of transforming raw materials into finished products. These manufacturing firms necessarily relied for nonmanufacturing services upon outside companies that specialized, as did they, primarily in one operation (Chandler and Redlich, 1961). For example, the manufacturer depended upon wholesale suppliers and commission merchants to provide raw materials and to sell finished goods to the

H. Thomas Johnson is Associate Professor, Department of Economics, University of Western Ontario, Canada.

final customer. In that world of specialized firms, "the impersonal forces of supply and demand [governed] the coordination of the flow of goods from the original producer to the final consumer" (Chandler, 1970, p. 56). The vertically integrated industrial firm is quite unlike a mid-nineteenth century firm. The vertically integrated industrial combined into one centrally managed enterprise each specialized activity formerly carried out separately by independent firms. However, in order to control and coordinate these combined activities, the vertically integrated industrial firm had to develop new organizational methods. It is these methods, or structures, which are of particular interest to both the accounting and economic historian.

One new method for controlling and coordinating company procedure was an innovation commonly called "the unitary form of organization." This innovation entailed the creation of independent departments and of one central office to manage both the departments and the entire firm (Williamson, 1970, pp. 10 and 110–12; Chandler, 1966, pp. 43–50). The unitary form of organization also involved the design of complex accounting systems to carry out assessment, operations, and planning throughout the firm. Were accounting historians to conduct extensive analyses of these complicated accounting systems, they would undoubtedly contribute enormously to the economic historian's interpretation of the evolution of America's giant industrial firms. A brief look at the evolution of the E. I. du Pont de Nemours Powder Company suggests how the expertise of the accounting historian is needed to complement the economic historian's work on the development of modern industry since about 1850.

The Du Pont Powder Company exemplifies the early use of accounting data for management control in vertically integrated industrial firms. In order to assess the development of the accounting practices which enabled management to govern the complex operation of this integrated firm, it is useful to know something of the company's background (Chandler and Salsbury, 1971, passim). Since 1804 E. I. du Pont de Nemours and Company had engaged primarily in one economic function, the manufacture of explosives. In 1903, however, when three Du Pont cousins purchased this company's assets, thus founding the E. I. du Pont de Nemours Powder Company, they vertically integrated the new firm. After 1903, then, the Du Pont Powder Company was a centrally managed enterprise coordinating through its own departments most of the activities formerly conducted by scores of firms which specialized only in a single operation.

As one might anticipate, a centralized accounting system was indispensable to the Du Pont Powder Company's complex structure (Johnson, 1975). This centralized accounting system needed to accomplish two major objectives: to enable top management to control, coordinate, and assess the horizontal flow of operations among the company's three main departments—manufacturing, sales, and purchasing; and to enable top management to plan the company's long-range development. The first of these objectives was achieved in part because the centralized accounting system coordinated activities among departments by transmitting routine data and instructions. This coordination among departments was complemented by top management control; such control was streamlined as a result of certain accounting procedures. These accounting procedures affected control, for example, by making possible the delegation of responsibility for decisions and daily operations and by generating profit incentives among lower-level management and staff. The centralized accounting system permitted more, however, than the control and coordination of activities within the various departments. It also provided routine data which allowed top management to assess each department's operations in terms of management's basic objective—maximum return on investment.

Because the centralized accounting system permitted the coordination, control, and assessment of operations within and among the company's departments, it alleviated the need of time-consuming, demanding attention of top management to daily operations. Once freed from the necessity of making short-term operating decisions, the Powder Company's top management could concentrate on a task relatively unknown in nineteenth century enterprise, the task of planning long-range development. Such planning involved two fundamental activities: the allocation of new investment among competing uses and the financing of new capital requirements. These activities could not be executed without data supplied by the centralized accounting system. This system made available return-on-investment information, cash forecasts, and earnings forecasts. Having established in very general terms the major objectives of the Du Pont Powder Company's centralized accounting system, let us now consider in more detail how this system facilitated short-term operations and long-term planning.

An examination of the uses made of accounting data in the manufacturing, sales, and purchasing departments indicates ways in which the centralized accounting system affected administration of the Powder Company's day-to-day operations. A cost system was the main accounting device that enabled top management to control and assess manufacturing, the largest and most complex of the Powder

Company's operations, involving over forty geographically dispersed mills. Maintained in the home office in Wilmington, Delaware, the centralized cost accounting system compiled full financial information on the cost of goods manufactured. This information was derived in part from home office accounting records and in part from records kept at each mill. Home office payroll and purchasing records supplied wages and raw material costs, while mill production control records provided information on labor, quantities of materials used, and quantities of output produced. Drawing upon all these data, the home office cost department issued separate monthly reports not only for top management, but for each mill superintendent as well.

The monthly reports to superintendents pertained to the physical efficiency of production processes and showed the quantities of raw materials, the dollar costs of labor, and the dollar costs of all other inputs (except administrative overhead) used in every stage of production in each mill. Clearly such data allowed mill superintendents to assume responsibility for daily operational decisions. This responsibility was more limited, however, than would have been the case had the data described the full financial cost of goods manufactured. For example, because their information was only partial, mill superintendents could not make informed "buy or make" decisions.[1] The monthly reports to mill superintendents did encourage them, however, to compete against their own past performance records and those of other mills.

The monthly reports sent by the home office cost department to top management did contain, as one might expect, complete

---

[1] This problem certainly perplexed at least one of the Powder Company's vice-presidents, who felt that mill superintendents should weigh the benefits of purchasing such inputs as acids and wood pulp, products traditionally manufactured by the company.

financial descriptions of product and mill costs. These data enabled top management to make decisions about mill operations in full knowledge of the effect their decisions would have on company profits and return on investment.

Just as centralized accounting procedures were indispensable to the administration of the manufacturing department, so were these procedures essential to the conduct of operations within the Du Pont Powder Company's sales department. Before 1903, the marketing activities of the American explosives industry had been conducted primarily by many independent agents and commission salesmen. Instead of depending upon such decentralized market methods, the Du Pont Powder Company established a large network of branch sales offices across the United States and trained salaried salesmen to move almost all company products. This highly integrated sales department was able to execute its responsibilities successfully—responsibilities which began when goods were finished in the mills and lasted until their delivery to the customer—only because of an effective centralized accounting system. This system provided for control of customer balances, timely appraisal of market trends, and coordination of customer orders with mill production schedules.

Based in part upon the accounting practices of early nineteenth century firms, the Du Pont Company's centralized accounting system, particularly as it affected the sales department, entailed several innovations. One of the most important of these enabled top management to set minimum prices guaranteeing a target rate of return on investment for each product.[2] Because top management was able to fix minimum prices, it could entrust further pricing almost entirely to branch office sales managers. The Du Pont Powder Company's centralized accounting system, in other words, made it possible for top management to delegate some of the responsibility of making decisions about pricing; thus it minimized considerably what had been, prior to 1903, one of management's major tasks in the explosives industry. Branch office managers were encouraged to set actual prices to customers at levels which, while low enough to discourage new entrants into the industry, were sufficient to allow maximization of total revenue. Indeed, branch managers and their salesmen understood that, if they should bring in a total revenue exceeding that earned merely by selling the required volume at the set minimum price, they would receive a bonus. A bonus incentive system was made available to members of the sales staff, then, as an indirect consequence of the accounting system.

Accounting procedures also aided the administration of daily operations in the purchasing department. Rather than rely upon separate mills to purchase their raw materials, the Powder Company relegated all purchasing of materials to one central purchasing department. A centralized accounts payable voucher system made such an arrangement possible, for it enabled control of the ordering, receiving, and expensing of all raw material purchases. Eventually top management concluded that total reliance upon outside suppliers was ill advised and decided instead to invest capital in the ownership and manufacture of materials required by their company. This decision was based upon careful analysis of expected return from such investment. An investment of this sort (in an outside supply source) was deemed advisable if it seemed likely to yield at least 15% per annum, the return normally earned by the Powder Company's most

[2] These minimum prices were based, of course, on an expected level of output and expected range of input prices; if either the volume or the cost factor changed, then the minimum price changed accordingly.

profitable production activity, dynamite making.

The Powder Company's centralized accounting system did more than provide for the control, coordination, and assessment of short-run operations within the manufacturing, sales, and purchasing departments. In addition, it assisted top management with the task of long-term planning. Long-term planning involved two phases: allocation and financing. Allocation of new investment among competing uses was conducted according to the principle that there "be no expenditures for additions to the earning equipment if the same amount of money could be applied to some better purpose in another branch of the company's business . . . " (Johnson, 1975, p. 4). Return on investment was used to evaluate investment alternatives. Because the centralized accounting system routinely provided information both on net earnings and total investment for each product line and each mill, top management could allocate new investment funds to those products and to those mills that earned the highest return. The Du Pont Powder Company's accounting system enabled top management to carry out another phase of long-term planning, that of financing, by providing monthly forecasts of the company's net earnings and cash position for a year in advance. Since it was the policy of the Du Pont Powder Company to finance its development primarily from retained earnings and sale of common stock, top management required reliable forecasts of net earnings. These forecasts permitted them to determine how much capital would be forthcoming to finance future growth. New long-term capital was needed primarily to construct plant and equipment. An elaborate construction appropriation system advised top management each month for one year in advance of the amounts that would be necessary to cover building outlays. This construction appropriation system and the forecast of net earnings provided the essential information for cash forecasts.

Certainly present-day management accountants are well acquainted with the use of accounting data to plan long-term development and to coordinate, control, and assess short-run operations. When the Du Pont Powder Company followed these practices, however, it was being highly innovative. The uniqueness of the Powder Company's centralized accounting system becomes apparent if one considers some of the most obvious features of accounting systems employed by typical manufacturing firms prior to 1900 (Chandler, 1970, pp. 45–54; Johnson, 1972; Litterer, 1963). Before 1900, routine accounting information seldom guided long-term planning in business firms. On the contrary, the Du Pont Powder Company may well have been the first industrial enterprise to develop an accounting procedure which regularly provided forecasts and other financial information essential to informed long-term planning.

The typical manufacturing firm operating before 1900 apparently expected its accounting system simply to provide information on short-run operations. Cost accounting records were the basic and most highly developed source of such information. Developed first by railroads and textile manufacturers in the 1850's, by the 1890's such cost systems had become quite sophisticated. For example, the little research that has been done on the accounting records of large firms active during the late 1890's in the steel, traction, machine making, and chemical industries suggests that such firms used their relatively advanced cost systems almost exclusively to monitor material and labor costs at the factory level. This emphasis on shop and factory efficiency reflects, of course, the bias of such industrial engineers as Frederick W. Taylor, who designed many of the complex cost systems used by large manufacturing firms during the late nineteenth century.

What is noteworthy in this necessarily brief description of accounting practices in typical manufacturing firms prior to 1900 is the fact that such firms evidently did not concentrate upon commercial efficiency and assessment of overall company performance. Clearly the centralized accounting system of the vertically integrated Du Pont Powder Company was, then, far more sophisticated than accounting procedures adhered to in other firms. The Du Pont Powder Company's system was unique in three fundamental respects: (1) it enabled top management to monitor total financial costs of operations in relation to the company's total performance; (2) it made possible assessment of both operations and overall performance in relation to total investment in productive assets; and (3) it assisted long-term planning decisions.

These remarks about the centralized accounting system employed by the Du Pont Powder Company indicate, I hope, that accounting historians can contribute significantly to the understanding of the development of big business. Accounting historians can very profitably examine the accounting procedures of firms which participated in the merger wave of 1897–1903 and were transformed from executing primarily only one activity, such as manufacturing, to integrating a number of operations. There are two major reasons for encouraging such an investigation. First, the inquiry would indicate how giant enterprises, vertically integrated, are able to function effectively. Many people in the early 1900's believed that large firms such as the Du Pont Powder Company would either topple from the weight of internal inefficiency or would abuse their market power and pass the costs of bureaucratic inefficiency on to the consumer. The record of the past seventy years has disproved this gloomy prediction. Giant enterprise is quite capable of efficient and acceptable behavior. Accounting historians can explain in detail one possible cause of this efficiency.[3] A second reason for the accounting historian's analysis is that, should he help to reveal why large firms operate effectively, he will ultimately provide valuable insight into the relationship between the growth of productivity in the American economy and innovations in the organization of big business.

Economic historians have yet to explain the contribution that innovations in business organization have made both to the growth and to the level of national income per capita in the United States during the past century. Although economists usually agree that improved organizational methods in the business sector of the economy have been responsible for much of the productivity growth in the United States, none has carefully explained these organizational methods (Denison, 1967, pp. 340 and 344; Reynolds, 1973, p. 301). Undoubtedly accounting historians who study the evolution of accounting procedures in large corporations will be able to illuminate the relationship between improved organizational methods and economic growth in this country.

[3] It is obvious that accounting systems are part of the administrative structure which affects an organization's efficiency. Although the following works give only cursory treatment to accounting systems *per se*, the relationship between enterprise efficiency and organizational structure is brilliantly analyzed in Chandler, 1966; Chandler and Redlich, 1961; and Williamson, 1970. I believe that accounting historians can add greatly to the understanding of the problems discussed by these authors.

REFERENCES

American Accounting Association, Committee on Accounting History, "Report of the Committee on Accounting History," THE ACCOUNTING REVIEW, Supplement to Vol. XLV (1970), pp. 53–64.

Chandler, Alfred D., Jr., *Strategy and Structure: Chapters in the History of the Industrial Enterprise* (The M.I.T. Press, 1966).
———, *The United States: Evolution of Enterprise* (unpublished ms., September 30, 1970).
——— and Fritz Redlich, "Recent Developments in American Business Administration and Their Conceptualization," *Business History Review* (Spring 1961), pp. 1–31.
——— and Stephen Salsbury, *Pierre S. Du Pont and the Making of the Modern Corporation* (Harper and Row, 1971).
Denison, Edward F., *Why Growth Rates Differ: Postwar Experience in Nine Western Countries* (The Brookings Institution, 1967).
Johnson, H. Thomas, "Early Cost Accounting for Internal Management Control: Lyman Mills in the 1850's," *Business History Review* (Winter 1972), pp. 466–74.
———, "Management Accounting in an Early Integrated Industrial: E. I. du Pont de Nemours Powder Company, 1903–1912," *Business History Review*, XLIX (Summer 1975), pp. 1–28. Page numbers cited refer to the typescript edition which is available from the author on request.
Litterer, Joseph A., "Systematic Management: Design for Organizational Recoupling in American Manufacturing Firms," *Business History Review* (Winter 1963), pp. 369–91.
Reynolds, Lloyd G., *Macroeconomics: Analysis and Policy* (Irwin, 1973).
Williamson, Oliver E., *Corporate Control and Business Behavior: An Inquiry into the Effects of Organization Form on Enterprise Behavior* (Prentice-Hall, 1970).

ACKNOWLEDGMENT

This paper was presented to the Fifty-eighth Anniversary Convention of the American Accounting Association in New Orleans, Louisiana on August 19, 1974. I am grateful to Fred Bateman (Indiana University) and Richard B. Du Boff (Bryn Mawr College) for presenting formal comments on this paper to the Convention. I also wish to thank Alfred Chandler (Harvard Business School), Elaine Bowe Johnson (Huron College), and Richard Keehn (University of Wisconsin–Parkside) for helpful comments. Inaccuracies, inconsistencies, and other errors are, of course, my responsibllity.

ACCOUNTING IN ANTIQUITY

COMMERCIAL RECORD-KEEPING
IN ANCIENT MESOPOTAMIA

Orville R. Keister

COMMERCIAL RECORD-KEEPING IN ANCIENT MESOPOTAMIA

Orville R. Keister*

IN THE Mesopotamian Valley, between the Tigris and the Euphrates Rivers, the Assyrian, Chaldaean-Babylonian, and Sumerian civilizations flourished from at least as far back as 4500 B.C. to approximately 500 B.C. On the present-day map, the Mesopotamian Valley falls mostly within the boundaries of Iraq, with small peripheral areas in Syria and Iran. The geographical area was small, but the historical impact made by these countries was most extraordinary.

The Tigris-Euphrates River Valley was an extremely fertile area due to periodic floodings, and, just as in Nile-enriched Egypt, the farmers had bountiful harvests every year—sometimes three or four overflowing harvests per year. In the cities there were many businesses, such as brick-making, barbering, weaving, carpentry, and banking. The products of both the farms and the businesses were traded back and forth within the empires, and much was traded with civilizations quite some distance away. In fact, the language used by the Babylonians became the language of the immediate commercial and political world, and Babylon became the center of the oriental commercial network. In addition to this type of commercial activity, the religious temples owned and accounted for land, buildings, and herds; they sent representatives to distant cities on temple business; and they were the recipients of sacrifices, taxes, and services.

It would be preposterous to suppose that this extensive scale of trading operations and temple activities could have been carried on without a rather elaborate accompanying record-keeping system. However, students of accounting history have been somewhat engrossed with post-Paciolian developments and have almost completely neglected this period of accounting history. Probably the reason for this lack of interest is the general belief that surely the embryonic records used by those ancient people four to six thousand years ago have all been lost or destroyed, so any attempt to reconstruct the accounting system then existing would be rather useless. By referring to archeological texts and journals, however, one soon discovers that archeologists have recovered and translated thousands of these ancient records which are in the form of clay tablets of all shapes and sizes and are of widely varying subject content. It is possible to find, for example, four-thousand-year-old tablets of receipts, disbursements, inventories, loans, purchases, sales, leases, partnership formations and dissolutions, guarantees, etc. Although these records do not much resemble modern accounting records, they *are* commercial records and they constitute adequate evidence that commercial record-keeping enjoyed its infancy in these civilizations.

The purpose of this article is to present a much abbreviated summary of the types of records kept by the ancient Mesopotamian people. This purpose will be accomplished by the presentation of appropriate tablet translations. Admittedly, much faith has been placed in the translating skill of archeological experts, but the writer has painstakingly compared hundreds of translations and only the typical, semi-standard ones are presented here.

* Orville R. Keister is Lecturer in Accounting at The Pennsylvania State University, University Park. He is a Ph.D. candidate at the University of Illinois.

The ancient Mesopotamian record-keeping system was a very simple system based mostly upon receipts, expenditures, listings, and contracts. Receipts tablets had to be prepared whenever any money or goods were received in the temple, in the palace, or in private businesses, even if it meant going to the expense of calling in a public scribe to record a single, small transaction. Internal movements and inventories of these items had to be duly recorded, as did the final use or expenditure. All obligations had to be recorded in clay and witnessed. Simple tablet records had to be made of work done and of payments made to employees. Commercial contracts recorded partnership formation and dissolution, rents, sales, and even marriages, which were commercial purchases by nature and illegal if not correctly recorded. The all-inclusiveness of the simple system was amazing—very few commercial transactions or commodity movements of any kind went unrecorded.

A functional approach, rather than a chronological approach, is necessary in the analysis of the records kept by Mesopotamians, because there were almost no significant changes in these records between the years 4000 B. C. and 538 B. C., the date that the second Babylonian empire fell to the Persians. The word "silver" was used more as this metal became more important in the exchange process, the passage of years saw more particulars entered on the records, the totals were less frequently incorrect, information known to everyone was not written down as often, and the dating system became more precise and accurate, but, other than these relatively unimportant changes, the records remained quite unchanged. Most of the development occurred in the Pre-Sargonic Period, and after that the Mesopotamian economy changed so little that no improvements in the record-keeping function were really required.[1] There-fore, the following illustrative tablet translations are not dated, but they all fall within the period 4000 B. C. to 538 B. C.

Probably the most numerous type of commerical record prepared by the Mesopotamians was the receipts tablet. Literally thousands of these tablets have been found by archeologists. A record of this nature was prepared upon the receipt of practically anything—from a barge full of grain to a dead fowl. The latter item is not an exaggeration, as several tablets have been found recording the receipt of dead animals, and these tablets are one of the best indications available of the completeness and the meticulosity with which the record-keeping function was performed. The following translation of a receipts table shows the standard form then in use.

> 1 goat with wool
> 1 suckling kid with wool
> 1 suckling she-kid (of) Magan
> slaughtered;
> (on the) eighth day
> from Axuni
> Urnigingar
> has received.
> (In the) month (of the) festival (of) Anna
> (in the) year (when) Urbilum
> was laid waste.[2]

This very typical translation shows the standard receipts tablet form, which was: (1) the amount and the kind of money, goods, etc. received; (2) the name of the person from whom they came; (3) the name of the recipient; and (4) the date.

Despite the fact that most tablets recording obligations were broken or otherwise disposed of as soon as the debts were paid, archeologists have found many of this type of record in their excavations. Although there is less of a standard schema evident in these Mesopotamian debt records, a number of different particulars in

[1] See Federigo Melis, *Storia della Ragioneria* (Bologna: Cesare Zuffi, 1950), pp. 235-236.
[2] William M. Nesbit, *Sumerian Records from Drehem* (New York: Columbia University Press, 1914), pp. 29-30.

somewhat the same order are usually found in most of the tablets, except the very simplest. These information items are: (1) the amount and the nature of the commodity or the money loaned; (2) the rate of interest, if any; (3) the name of the debtor; (4) the name of the creditor; (5) the time of repayment; (6) specifications regarding the method or return; (7) witnesses; and (8) the date. The following simple obligation tablet is typical.

½ mina of silver
its interest (shall be) a meal,
Apil-ilisu
took
from Samas.
At harvest time
in the month Saddutum
he will (re)pay the silver.
Before Ili-u-Samas,
son of Iddin-Bunene,
before Ipiq-Aya, son of Adidum.
Month Abum, 12th day,
year (when) Samsu-iluna (became king).[3]

One of the most interesting features of these tablet records of indebtedness is the fact that sometimes they were negotiable, which is contrary to the popular theory that the concept of negotiability was introduced to commerce sometime after 1100 A. D. On this subject A. H. Pruessner made an extremely scholarly study which proves that payment of principal and interest in Bablyonia was sometimes made to the holder or bearer of the debt tablet. The earliest negotiable tablet that he found was dated *circa* 2090 B. C., and it was translated as follows:

Five shekels of refined silver, at the interest rate of Samas temple, Sa from Samas and Idiniatum, Idin-Adad, the son of Samas-mutabbil, and Hamtani have borrowed. When seen at the city wall they shall pay the silver and interest to the bearer of their tablet. (Three witnesses.) Month of Elul, year 35 of Hammurabi.[4]

Practically no purchases were accomplished in Mesopotamia without the preparation of a purchase tablet. Most of these records contain the following infor-

mation: (1) a description of the nature and the location of what was purchased; (2) the purchaser; (3) the seller; (4) that which was given in payment; (5) an agreement regarding the future claims concerning the purchased object; (6) the witnesses; and (7) the date. The following translation is typical.

7½ Gin improved property, adjoining the house of Ali-Akhati, with the long side facing the street, the house of Adad-rabi, son of Ur-Innanna, from Adad-rabi, son of Ur-Innanna, Apil-Sin, son of Bulalum, has bought. As its price in full 2½ shekels and 15 She of silver he weighed out. For all times, Adad-rabi shall not make any claim on the house. In the name of the king he has sworn an oath: before Sin-Gamil, son of Gubbani-dug, Elali, son of Nabi-ilishʌ, Ur-Ningishzida, son of Nurum, (and) Azag-Nannar (as) the scribe. Month of Gan-gan-e, in the year when King Sin-ikisham made a statue of gold and silver.[5]

A large number of tablets recording rentals or leases have been recovered by archeologists, indicating that this commercial procedure was much used by the Mesopotamians. Most of these tablets were rather detailed and lengthy. However, no matter what the tablet size, the standard structure of rental records appears to have included: (1) a rather complete description of what was being rented; (2) the lessor and the lessee; (3) the payment; (4) other provisions, such as time limits, special payment methods, etc.; (5) the witnesses; and (6) the date. The following translation is one of the simplest examples available.

The house of Damu-ribam, from Damu-ribam, Sinidinnam, the commercial agent (or merchant), has rented as a dwelling and possession at a

---

[3] Albrecht Goetz, "Old Babylonian Documents from Sippar in the Collection of the Catholic University of America," *Journal of Cuneiform Studies,* Vol. XI, No. 1 (1957), p. 17.

[4] A. H. Pruessner, "The Earliest Traces of Negotiable Instruments," *The American Journal of Semitic Languages and Literatures,* Vol. XLIV, No. 2 (January, 1928), p. 92.

[5] Morris Jastrow, *The Civilization of Babylonia and Assyria* (Philadelphia: J. B. Lippincott Company, 1915), p. 327.

yearly rental of ⅓ of a shekel of silver. In the presence of Sin-magir, son of Zibu'a, (and) Ina-ckur-rabi, the scribe. First day of the month Shu-Kul, in the year when King Samsu-iluna, in accordance with the oracle of Enlil. . . .[6]

The expenditure tablets take a great variety of forms. Most of them are simple listings of money or goods released from one's control for one reason or another, so it is important to realize that the word "expenditure" here does not carry with it all of the more modern connotations of the word and it does not suggest that the Mesopotamians had an entirely crystallized concept of revenue, expense, and net income. Expenditure tablets were prepared often to summarize reductions in money, goods, or animals resulting from purchases, sacrifices, internal usage, loss, etc. For example, the following translation is from a tablet recording money paid for various articles. Probably it is a periodic compilation from a number of smaller documents.

5 shekels of silver of the silver of the income
for the wood of the house of Rab-bani;
2½ shekels for the doors
of the weavers' house; Total, 7½ shekels of silver
to Nabu-shum-lishir, the son of
Nabu-makin-zer, and Gimillu,
the son of Ardia are given.
1½ shekels, his food of the month Marchesvan,
Zeria, the son of Ahe-sa,
½ shekel for ⅚ mina of lead
to Liblut, the blacksmith, is given.
1 shekel to Balatsu, the son of Ardi-Nabu,
and the soldiers, who with him to the presence
of the administrator went, is given.
The 25th day of Marchesvan
of Nebuchadrezzar, king of Babylon.[7]

This tablet records the expenditure of money; others record the expenditure or distribution of goods.

1 qa of beverage from the plant . . .
10 qa of coarse (?) flour,
10 qa of bean (?) flour,
3 qa of . . . flour
2 qa of rice (?) flour
to the temple of Raman-
10 qa of coarse (?) flour,

10 qa of bean flour,
10 qa of . . . flour,
5 qa of rice flour,
to the Antashurra (temple)
. . .
has expended.
Month: She-il-la.[8]

Evidently an expenditure or distribution sooner or later was always recorded on a tablet of this nature. Since these tablets were prepared solely for the use of the person or the office distributing or paying the goods or the money, there was no need to mention the name of the person or the office on the tablet. Basically, these commercial records are uncomplicated listings.

A very interesting variation of the expenditure tablet is the allowance record. The palace, the temple, and most of the large business firms had many men traveling to distant parts of the country and even to foreign countries. For example, the palace had traveling tax collectors. All of these men needed certain supplies and incurred certain expenditures for which they would later be reimbursed, and the allowance tablets are equivalent to the modern expense account record. For example, one of the simplist illustrations is the following translation recording an advance of fifty shekels for a specific purpose—to purchase a donkey and some flour.

50 shekels of silver for
1 road donkey
and his flour
to Nabu-mushetig-urra,
the son of Ishtar-nadin-ahi,
who to the land of Tema
is sent, are given.
The fifth day of Adar, the fifth year
of Nabonidus, king of Babylon.[9]

---

[6] Jastrow, *loc. cit.*
[7] Raymond P. Daugherty, *Archives from Erech, Time of Nebuchadrezzar and Nabonidus* (New Haven: Yale University Press, 1923), p. 27.
[8] Robert Julius Lau, *Old Babylonian Temple Records* (New York: The Columbia University Press, 1906), pp. 11–12.
[9] Daugherty, *op. cit.*, pp. 34–35.

At times the expenditure tablets served as cost records showing how much food it took to feed the herds, how much seed it took to sow a field, etc.

> 200 sheep at 1½ qa each
> total grain, 1 gur
> to Ninkalla (shepherd).
> 160 sheep at 1½ qa each
> total grain 240 qa;
> 160 sheep at 1½ qa each
> total grain 240 qa;
> 200 sheep at 1½ qa each
> total grain 1 gur
> to Sin-lishir (shepherd).
> 100 oxen at 8 qa each
> 9 oxen at 6 qa each
> 6 rams (he-goats) at 2 qa each
> total grain 146 qa
> to Urki-Gula (shepherd).
> Month She-il-la
> the 5th day.[10]

An expenditure tablet variation similar to the above is the pay list tablet, a record recording the pay of the workers. There was relatively little structural uniformity in pay list tablet preparation, but the following tablet is an example of one frequently found type.

> 16 women . . .
> 2 women helpers at 10 qa each,
> 93 women helpers at 10 qa each,
> 42 women at 30 qa each,
> 8 women helpers at 10 qa of flour,
> 6 old women helpers at 20 qa, each
> 38 boys at 20 qa each,
> 28 boys at 15 qa of flour,
> 19 boys at 10 qa each,
> total of grain rations 26 gur 180 qa.
> . . .[11]

Accurate records were also kept of incomes and of what was produced. The income tablets usually included the following information: (1) what was received as income; (2) from whom it was received; (3) the reason for its receipt; and (4) the date.

> 120 (qa) of grain, best quality,
> from Ur-Kal, son of Kalam-il;
> 120 (qa) from Lu-Ningirau,
> son of Limmashu-
> the grain is rent, income;
> from the storehouse of the field Higal-

from the priest of the god Ninmar
per tablet of Lukani,
son of Ur-Bau.
The year in which Bur-Sin became king.[12]

Sometimes the tablets recording production were very short, simple lists, such as the following:

> 6 dyed princely garments; 6 men's cloaks; 20 weaver's cloaks; for Gudea, the chief of the storehouse has had made. Akara (?)-nisaga has taken them away.[13]

A very strict account was kept of all possessions, but special care was taken in accounting for the large herds owned by the palace and the temple. Periodically the officials in charge of these herds had to submit reports showing how many animals were present, how many were given out for food, sacrifices, etc., and how many were lost. The following translation illustrates the basic structure of this type of inventory record.

> 12 ewes
> . . . .
> 2 mature sheep
> 3 weaned lambs exchanged for ewes
> 6 sucking lambs
> 1 weaned kid
> 8 weaned lambs exchanged for mature sheep
> were present.
> . . . ewes 1 mature sheep
> expended.
> Lost were 22 sheep . . .
> Total: 1 expended.
> Total: 22 lost.
> Total: 32 present.
> Ur-Nintur, shepherd
> Tikabba
> Two years after (the king) devastated Kimosh.[14]

Some of the most interesting records kept by the Mesopotamians are the account tablets—records reporting a beginning

---

[10] Lau, *op. cit.*, pp. 16–17.
[11] *Ibid.*, p. 18.
[12] *Ibid.*, p. 21.
[13] Theophilus G. Pinches, *The Babylonian Tablets of the Berens Collection* (London: Royal Asiatic Society, 1915), p. 66.
[14] Hugo Randau, *Early Babylonian History* (New York: Oxford University Press, American Branch, 1900), p. 357.

balance, additions to or subtractions from this balance, and the ending balance. To illustrate, the following tablet records some type of royal examination or audit.

Royal inspection:
2997 kor 3 Pi 5 seah and 7 qa of sesame were the initial amount.
1461 kor 3 Pi 3 seah and 9 qa of sesame were the transfer to the grain magazine.
The surplus balance is 1536 kor 1 sut and 8 qa of sesame.
Complete account for one year,
(namely) the year Sin-iddinam king.
(In) the town of the . . .
. . . [15]

Many other types of records were kept by the Mesopotamians. The translations above are merely illustrative, not exhaustive. Although they are the least complex and involved translations available and although they are only the more common types, they show that the Mesopotamian people had a record-keeping system that was quite adequate for their needs—a system which, unfortunately, most modern accountants do not even know existed.

[15] Albrecht Goetz, "Sin-iddinam of Larsa. New Tablets from his Reign," *Journal of Cuneiform Studies*, Vol. IV, No. 2 (1950), p. 83.

ACCOUNTING CONTROL IN THE ZENON PAPYRI

H. P. Hain

Accounting Control in the Zenon Papyri

H. P. Hain

EGYPTIAN peasants, in 1915, digging for antiquities in the Fayum discovered a horde of inscribed rolls which later-became known as the Zenon papyri. Many of them have since been reconstructed, translated, and evaluated. Taken as a whole they have thrown important light on the accounting system not only of Ptolemaic Egypt, but also of Greece by which it was inspired. Under Alexander the Great, Egypt had been a Greek province; and although the country regained its independence under the native dynasty of the Ptolemies, Greek influence persisted in practically every aspect of public administration and business organization.

The Zenon papyri, a collection of more than one thousand documents, are mainly concerned with the private estate of Apollonios, who was the chief financial minister (*dioiketos*) of Ptolemy Philadelphos but also conducted a variety of business activities on his own account. The estate was situated in a recently-drained area near the new city of Philadelphia and was still in the process of development. The accounts therefore reflect construction projects as well as current agricultural and business operations. They span a period of approximately thirty years during the third century B.C.

The Zenon papyri give evidence of a surprisingly elaborate accounting system which had been used in Greece since the fifth century B.C. and which, in the wake of Greek trade or conquest, gradually spread throughout the Eastern Mediterranean and the Middle East. When these areas became part of the Roman Empire, the Romans adopted the system with some modifications, and it thus became the official method of both public and private administration which persisted until the Barbarian and the Islamic invasions. Although we are relatively well informed on the systems and procedures used,[1] very few actual records have survived since they were mostly kept on wax tablets and other impermanent writing material. The discovery of the Zenon papyri was therefore both fortunate and significant, because they comprise a mass of minor detail that would not normally have been preserved over a long period. Moreover, the papyri reflect a variety of economic activities and show the hand of a most capable and efficient organizer.

[1] Cf. Beigel, *Rechnungswesen und Buchführung der Römer* (Karlsruhe, 1904). The abbreviations used for the papyri quoted follows the accepted system of numeration. P. (papyrus) indicates the nature of the manuscript, the following group of letters denotes the location of the document, followed by the inventory or catalogue number. (S.I. = Società Italiana, Col. = Columbia University, Cornell = Cornell University, Wis. = University of Wisconsin, Mich. = University of Michigan).

H. P. Hain is a member of the faculty in the Department of Accounting, University of Melbourne, Victoria, Australia.

Zenon, a Greek, was Apollonios' chief executive. He must have been a man of exceptional administrative ability, for he controlled the diverse enterprises of his principal with remarkable skill. Several letters (or probably copies of letters) to his subordinates contain inquiries and reprimands which indicate that he was intimately familiar with their work and reserved major decisions for himself.

When he took charge of the administration in 256 B.C., Zenon reorganized the accounting system that had given rise to complaints under his predecessor.[2] He introduced a clearly defined structure of responsibility accounting. Each section of the estate—the farms, vineyards, herds of livestock, grain stores, household units, and administrative offices—was managed by a supervisor who had to render account daily or at frequent intervals. The same applied to capital projects such as the clearing of land, building of irrigation systems, and the erection of buildings.

Written documents were prepared for every transaction, many of them taking the form of accounts rendered for money and other assets received by the heads of departments. Although these documents were essentially lists of cash expenditure and records of various assets (grain, oil, livestock, building material, clothing, etc.) issued by way of loan,[3] they were organized in a systematic manner. Items of a similar nature were summarized in paragraphs and only the totals extended, so that a pre-classification was taking place even in the originating documents. Each of these records had to be approved by Zenon himself or a subordinate, and was then carefully tagged and filed for future reference.

Departmental vouchers were regularly summarized in a number of accounts. Most important were the money accounts (*argyrikoi logoi*) and the grain accounts (*sitikoi logoi*) which recorded the largest number of transactions. In addition, accounts existed for oil, wine, livestock, imported merchandise, and various building materials. There was also a personal account (*idios logos*) of Apollonios' for wages paid to his household employees and other personal expenses unconnected with the estate.[4] The name of the account was always stated at the top of the sheet. Where the name is not legible, the nature of the account can usually be determined by the cross references to originating documents. In some accounts, acquisitions and disposals of assets were added and deducted as they occurred, so as to arrive at a new balance after every transaction.[5] Other accounts were written up from daily summaries (*ephemerides*) recording receipts and disbursements of cash and goods; they may have been prepared only periodically.[6]

At the time of the Ptolemies, coined money was still a relatively recent introduction and was not available in sufficient quantities to supply all needs of the economy.[7] Services of employees were remunerated both in coined money and in staple goods—grain, lighting oil, material for clothing, etc.—and were reflected in the accounts, where the various issues were recorded in detail. Several long wage

[2] In P.S.I. IV. 502 Apollonios, an exacting master, accused him of neglecting his duties. No complaints of any significance were recorded during Zenon's period of office.

[3] Seed grain, farm animals for breeding, and other items advanced to tenants.

[4] P.Cairo Zenon III 59355. On one occasion a copy of this account was sent to the head office accountant Pyron for purposes of reconciliation (P.Cairo Zen. 59253, 3–8).

[5] E.g., the money account P.Cairo Zen. II 59176.

[6] E.g., P.Cairo Zen. II 59292; P.Cairo Zen. IV 59787 and III 59326; P.Col. Zen. 5.

[7] There were two distinct monetary systems, one for payment in cash and one in kind with occasional exchange transfers between them. For instance taxes were paid partly in cash to the royal treasury (*basilikon*) and partly in produce to the royal granaries (*thesauroi*). Cf. Wilcken, Schmoller's *Jahrbuch* XLV (1921), pp. 80–81, 89–90.

sheets included in the Zenon papyri were posted to the money as well as to the grain, oil, and materials accounts.[8] Similarly, the farmers of the estate required loans in money, seed grain, and breeding stock; these loans and their ultimate repayment also appeared on the respective asset accounts.[9] Taxes, usually one sixth of the net surplus, were paid in produce and recorded as outgoings.

All accounts were audited, as evidenced by a sloping downstroke or a heavy dot in front of each figure. There are numerous corrections and marginal notes in a different hand, usually relating to discrepancies, omissions, and overdue accounts.[10]

The position of the accounts clerk does not appear to have been privileged, for his remuneration was not much higher than that of a tradesman.[11] Evidently his skill was not in short supply, as it was possible to recruit additional staff or temporary clerical assistants at short notice. It appears that working hours extended into the night, for lighting oil was issued on most working days,[12] and there are records of additional issues for extended overtime work—on one occasion for three nights in succession.[13] When Apollonios traveled, members of his accounting staff accompanied him, as is shown in statements of traveling expenses.[14] Even then his clerks were kept busily occupied and continued burning the midnight oil, for when he traveled Apollonios remained in constant touch with his numerous business interests.

Record-keeping in Egypt was greatly facilitated by the abundance of cheap writing material. One of the documents in the collection reveals that on the average ten to thirteen rolls of papyrus were issued daily to an office employing three clerks and that some of it was used for wrapping purposes.[15] The fact that it was economically possible to originate permanent written

memoranda, incorporating even minor detail, permitted a degree of accounting control that was not emulated elsewhere for more than two thousand years.

It is true that Zenon's accounting control was concentrated on assets—receivables, produce, merchandise, and raw materials. It did not extend to profitability although it might well have been concerned with operational efficiency.[16] All expenditure was closely supervised, and any dishonesty was promptly reprimanded.[17] However, his main purpose appears to have been to conserve the substance of his master's estate.

The Zenon papyri include several monthly, annual, and even triennial summaries of accounting transactions.[18] It is interesting to speculate on Zenon's reasons for preparing these reports. They must have required considerable clerical effort; and yet they appear to have been a regular feature of the accounting system.

[8] P.Col. Inv. No. 249; P.Col. Inv. No. 211 and others.
[9] Grain account P.Mich. Zen. 119 contains lists of cultivators who received loans of wheat. Some of these loans became overdue and had to be repaid at the penalty rate of 150% of the quantity received.
[10] E.g., P.Cairo Zen. I 59008, an agent's account of bran used for feeding animals is corrected by an accountant or auditor. Also, P.Cairo Zen. I 59013, III 59326, 51–52, P.Col. Zen. 5, and others.
[11] By contrast, the office manager received more than twice as much as his clerks and in addition obtained "fringe benefits" like a free lease of land, free seed grain, and traveling allowances (P.Mich. Zen. 46).
[12] Cf., P.Cornell 1.
[13] P.Cornell 1, 95–99, 115–117, 123–125.
[14] Cf. P.Cairo Zen. I 59087. There is also a notification of additional papyrus rolls being shipped to Apollonios' traveling accounting office (P.Mich. Zen. 22).
[15] P.Col. Zen. 4, 10–11.
[16] In a predominantly agricultural community, standards of performance under given circumstances are common knowledge. It seems more than likely that a capable administrator like Zenon would have policed the performance of his various departments at least to that extent.
[17] An example is P.Cairo Zen. III 59499, which deals with the embezzlement of an accountable amount by the stonecutter Herieus. The supervisor who detected the fraud promptly reports it to Zenon and asks him to make sure that a similar situation does not arise again.
[18] Cf. P.Col. Inv. No. 249 (expenditure and receipts for one year) and P.Cairo Zen. II 59293 (wheat and barley issued during three years).

One possible explanation is the evidence of taxes payable in cash and kind required by government officials[19] and state bankers.[20] Another reason may be that these summaries provided management information that could not be obtained from the detailed records of individual transactions. Both Zenon and Apollonios were well versed in interpreting accounting data, and it can be inferred that they obtained useful information from the perusal of accounting reports.[21] On several occasions there is evidence of management action—for example, changes in personnel, introduction of new departments and discontinuation of existing ones, modification of procedures[22]—and some of these decisions may have been based on accounting statements.

It would be misleading, of course, to attribute modern concepts of management to an age whose sense of values and basic philosophies were substantially different from our own. But the Zenon papyri reveal surprising similarities between Greco-Ptolemaic and modern accounting practices, some of which were not commonly applied in European accounting until well into the nineteenth century. Zenon used a departmental structure with periodical reports from the heads of departments, all of which were fully responsible for their sections. Transactions were individually documented as they occurred and progressively condensed in monthly and yearly reports. The various types of accounting records were clearly defined and their sequence and interdependence observed. An accounting terminology of nearly one hundred specific terms and phrases was consistently applied throughout the organization.

Most remarkable, however, is the high degree of accounting control and the businesslike efficiency of central management. To some extent this may have been due to the particular genius of Zenon, which was not attained by either his predecessor or his successor. Yet the system as it is reflected in the Zenon papyri was not the work of one man. It was the result of an administrative tradition and a high level of clerical literacy that was lost almost entirely and had to be painfully re-created after the fall of the Roman Empire. Considering that no Greek or Roman accounting records of a commercial nature have been preserved in the original, the historical importance of the Zenon papyri can hardly be overemphasized. They are the only coherent body of accounting documents known to exist prior to the thirteenth century A.D. They far exceed the early Italian ledgers in detail and completeness, particularly as far as originating documents and subsidiary records are concerned.

The work of reconstructing and translating the majority of the scrolls is still in progress, and as it can only be carried out by small teams of experts, the completion of the task is not in sight. Most of the documents are located in Cairo, but several have been acquired by universities, museums, and private collections. Although this has helped to accelerate the processing of the material, it has also disrupted the co-ordination of related records, as many of the papyri are jealously guarded, and access to them is difficult even for scientific workers. As a further complication, classical scholars are rarely familiar with the principles of accounting and thus have experienced difficulties where a trained accountant might have found the solution. Some of the published translations leave

---

[19] In P.Col. Zen. 42 Apollonios instructs Zenon to render account for collections from beer and other concessions.

[20] According to P.Wis. Inv. No. 1 the state bank at Philadelphia prepared an annual assessment of taxes based on Apollonios' accounts.

[21] P.Col. Zen. 59 is a long check-list of accounts and individual entries which Zenon wished to have investigated before the preparation of the annual summary.

[22] For example, in P.Cornell 1 the daily issue of castor oil for lighting was changed to only one issue of an entire month's supply.

the lingering suspicion that such a man would have translated certain passages quite differently.

The final processing and evaluation of the Zenon papyri will give us a knowledge of Greek and, indirectly, Roman accounting which seemed unattainable before they were discovered. But even the relatively small part of the material that has so far been made available to the general public commands respect and invites modesty on the part of those who tend to overstress the achievements of recent generations. The example of Zenon shows that men of managerial ability have lived long before our times and that even in those days their efforts were greatly enhanced by the intelligent use of an effective system of organized records.

BIBLIOGRAPHY

R. Beigel, *Rechnungswesen und Buchführung der Römer* (Karlsruhe, 1904).

C. C. Edgar, *Zenon Papyri in the University of Michigan Collection* (University of Michigan Press, 1931).

E. Grier, *Accounting in the Zenon Papyri* (New York: Columbia University Press, 1934).

E. Grier, "Wages Paid in Kind in the Zenon Papyri," *Transactions of the American Philological Association*, 1932, pp. 230–244.

M. Rostovtseff, *A Large Estate in Egypt in the Third Century B.C.* (University of Wisconsin Studies in the Social Sciences and History No. 6, 1922).

W. Spiegelberg, *Die demotischen Urkunden des Zenon-Archivs* (Leipzig, 1929).

A. Steiner, *Der Fiskus der Ptolomäer* (Berlin, 1914).

M. Voigt, "Über die Bankiers und die Buchführung der Römer," *Abhandlung der Sächsischen Gesellschaft der Wissenschaften*, X (1888), pp. 517–577.

A SKETCH OF ACCOUNTANCY

Max Teichmann

A Sketch of Accountancy*

By Max Teichmann, C. P. A.

The word "Accountancy" relates in the first place to the science of accounts. The science of accounts is a knowledge of the expression or manifestation of accounting, while bookkeeping is an art involving the practical application of the principles and methods of accounts to the record of business transactions. Thus the exponent of the science is the professional accountant, while the exponent of the art is the bookkeeper.

The science of accounts means the ability to converge all transactions of a business or industry, or those of municipalities and governments, to a focus, embracing the whole, and permitting of their proper comprehension and classification—the faculty of so systematizing accounting methods that the best results shall be obtained with the least labor and expense and the least possibility of error or fraud.

Accountancy thinks out, and thus finds out, the condition of affairs of any business enterprise with logical and mathematical accuracy. Accountancy gives account not only of employers' affairs but of its own accounts so that one in possession or in authority may know how matters stand, may render in turn the same intelligent account to any third party, and may keep a complete surveillance over all the accountable agents of the enterprise.

Accountancy is the element that has kept our ever broadening and increasing commercial and financial relations from hopeless confusion and has maintained in harmonious relations the numberless values of our economic life, and as accountancy, as a profession, is brought into a very close touch and relationship with other important departments of business activity, the distinction between it and one and another of these is not always clear to popular apprehension.

The terms "accountant" and "bookkeeper" are often used interchangeably as being one and the same, when as a matter of fact the functions of each are distinct and the lines of demarcation very sharply drawn.

---

* A paper read at the annual meeting of the Maryland Association of Certified Public Accountants of Baltimore City, February, 1912.

The accountant does not do the recording of the transactions of a business, industry, municipality or government. He is not the bookkeeper of the concern, but a bookkeeper in the sense that he thoroughly understands the ins and outs of that art.

The work of the bookkeeper is synthetical. He compiles the history of acts performed. The work of the accountant is analytical. He analyzes the record, proves its correctness, searches for causes and inquires into methods. The work of the two is not identical, and yet they may have kindred purposes.

The accountant's confidential relation is with his client, whether proprietor, manager, administrator, director or stockholder, and it is only as the representative, the advisor or helper of his client that he has to do with others. He critically examines the books, accounts, records and all other related matters in order that he may give to his employer a scientific and true showing of the financial and other conditions of the enterprise, point out defects or more serious matters in connection therewith and make such suggestions as will tend to improve or remedy things. So that in his advisory capacity, not as a legal practitioner, but as knowing what is allowable or not in certain cases, the professional accountant must have a full knowledge of commercial law to assist his client in steering clear of litigations and of complications that may result in financial ruin.

The development of the science of accounting, as we know it, has been gradual and slow. Mankind has always traded, necessitating records, and as accounting is so closely allied to mathematics there is every reason to believe it of the most ancient origin.

The development of social life and especially the formation of states or sovereignties levying any form of taxation necessitated, in addition to a knowledge of numbers, a power of holding count and reckoning. In this we find the origin of the science of accounting. It ante-dated the stating of accounts as we know them, since that could not take place until some monetary standard had been adopted in which the items composing an account could be expressed in terms of equality. In the earliest of such states some kind of organization must have been necessary to collect and account for the public revenues. We can look back on civilized communities existing more than 5,000 years before

Christ. The Chaldean-Babylonian Empire is said to have been the first regularly organized government of the world. As far back as 4500 B. C., civilization in Babylonia had already reached a high point, presupposing unknown ages of previous development. Among the most notable evidences of the wonderful civilization of Babylonia is the monument discovered at Susa, on which is inscribed the code of laws promulgated by Hammurabi—a contemporary of Abraham—who reigned in Babylon from 2285 to 2242 B. C. This code contains a number of enactments dealing with commerce, finance and accounting.

One of the earliest actual traces of accounting for receipts and disbursements has been found in the Assyrian tablets discovered by Sir Henry Rawlinson. The first record of a sale in exchange for money appears to be the sale of the field and cave of Machpelah to Abraham for four hundred pieces of silver and there is no doubt that all the great ancient trading nations from Babylon to Rome had more or less elaborate systems of accounting.

Evidences of the Babylonian accounting are on view in the British Museum in London. They consist of tablets, each set being contained in a separate jar, probably so that they could be balanced separately and errors easily located. (Each may be regarded as a ledger.)

Large numbers of business and accounting records have come down to us from the period beginning about 2600 B. C., dealing with sales, letting, hiring, money-lending, partnership and the like. The medium employed by the scribe in preparing these records was clay. He wrote with a stylus on a small slab, sufficiently moist to receive an impression easily, and sufficiently firm to prevent the impression from becoming blurred or effaced, and then he made the record permanent by baking or sun-drying the slab.

Among these tablets are the records of two banking firms, the Sons of Egibi of Babylon and the Marashu Sons of Nippur. The Egibi carried on business from an unknown period to about the fourth century before Christ. The tablets recording their transactions and accounting vary in size, are usually covered with writing on both sides and sometimes on the edges as well. The more important transactions were copied on larger tablets with great care and elaboration of details and usually contained impressions from cylindrical seals with nail and fingermarks, which were considered to be a man's natural seal.

A room at Nippur, excavated by the expedition of the University of Pennsylvania, contained 730 tablets recording and accounting for the transactions of Marashu Sons, who flourished in the times of Artaxerxes I (464 to 424 B. C.) and Darius II (423 to 405 B. C.) in whose reigns the documents are dated.

The provinces of this vast empire were administered by satraps, one of whose principal duties it was to receive the tribute in money or in kind, for which purpose each satrap was assisted by a superintendent of the revenue and numerous other officials. The business of the central administration was carried out by the scribes who seem to have combined the functions of counsel, attorney and accountant of the present day. A carefully prepared register served as a state record of the titles to estates and also as a basis for the imposition of taxes. The system of storehouses for the custody of taxes paid in kind seems to have been similar to that of Egypt.

The offerings to the gods were treated by the priests, according to Maspero, as articles of commerce.

"We have to look upon the temple and the industrial establishments of the rich citizens as factories. We have a number of certificates which show how the raw materials were delivered into the establishments and how the finished products were delivered from them. These indicate how long the laborers worked and what wages they received. From the temple archives of the sun god have been derived a great mass of tablets, which, after the fashion of commercial accounting, record the temple revenues in money and other commodities, the expenses in salaries, wages, etc., and the investment and employment of the temple property in loans, real estate, rents, etc."

The valley of the Nile boasts of a civilization only less ancient than that of Mesopotamia. According to Manetho the dynasties of the Egyptian kings go back to 5004 B. C. The pictures on the walls of Memphite tombs of the fourth and fifth dynasties show large square-sailed barks floating on the Nile, employed in a commerce which everything proves to have been most extensive.

The scribe, as in Babylonia, was the mainspring of the administrative machinery. The scribes were present on all occasions. They prepared their accounting on papyrus with a calamus. "They squatted on the ground, with deed box or the case for the papyrus rolls by them, a pen behind their ear and the strip of papyrus on which they were writing in their hand." Nothing was given out of the Treasury without a written order. Peculation was prevented by the records of one official checking the other.

Some interesting accounts belonging to the end of the second or early part of the first century before Christ were found a few years ago in a strange resting place—the mummies of crocodiles.

Other ancient peoples among which methods of accounting were more or less developed, were the Persians, the Phœnicians and Carthagenians with their extensive commerce and their colonies, and the Rhodians, with their navigation laws which were adopted by the Romans.

In the case of the Israelites the Bible furnishes us with a number of references to matters of accounting. Joseph in Egypt was certainly an up-to-date scientific accountant as exemplified by his providing for an accumulation of a sufficiently large surplus with which to pay dividends during unprofitable or bad periods. After the Egyptian the next nation of whose methods of accounting we have any real information is the Grecian. The public economy of the Athenians shows a highly developed system of accounting. The public accounts were thoroughly scrutinized at the expiration of every term of office and "no person who had not rendered his account could go abroad, consecrate his property to a god, or even dedicate a sacred offering, nor could he make a will, or be adopted from one family to another."

While there was no lack of well-conceived and strict regulations, the spirit of the administration was bad. All officers of finance were sworn to administer without peculation the money entrusted to them, but Polybius says: "If in Greece the State entrusted to anyone only a talent, and if it had ten checking-clerks, and as many seals and twice as many witnesses, it could not ensure his honesty."

For purposes of publicity the accounts of public officials were engraved on stone and exposed in public. Some of these accounts still exist and specimens of them are among the Elgin marbles in the British Museum.

The Romans possessed the genius of administration as well as jurisprudence. Their system of financial administration and accounting, which began with the simple arrangements required under the kings and the Republic, developed into the elaborate and complicated organization of the enormous Empire, spreading like a network over the greater part of the known world.

In the original constitution of Rome there was no regular direct taxation nor was there any direct regular state expenditure. The state gave no recompense for service in the army nor for the public service generally. If there was any recompense at all it was given to the person who performed the service by the district concerned, or by the person who could not or would not perform the service himself. The king managed the finances and the receipts consisted chiefly of port dues, income from domain lands, cattle fines and confiscations and the gains of war. A special tax was sometimes imposed, but was repaid when circumstances permitted.

It is under the Republic that we first see the idea of a treasury of the Roman people, governed by the senate, administered by the consuls, and managed by the quæstors. These were the first elements of the financial organization created for a municipality.

The system of recording the state accounting in Rome was based on the system practised in private life from very early times. The father of the Roman family entered in a sort of waste book (*adversaria*) all the receipts and payments of his household. He posted these monthly to a carefully kept register of receipts and disbursements (*codex accepti et depensi*), in which an entry, made with the consent of the debtor, was considered as a good ground of civil obligation. Bankers—of whom there were many in Rome—and merchants used similar registers down to the time of Justinian. Bankers appear also to have kept a third kind of register, called the book of accounts (*rationes, liber rationum*), probably arranged in alphabetical order, in which an account was kept for each customer. The accounts were balanced at certain agreed-on times, the banker being required to render an account and to produce an extract of the same before the prætor. When the balance was to the credit of the customer, the banker had to pay the amount unless authorized to retain it for the new business. Usually the father of a rich family paid his debts by means of a sort of cheque on his banker.

The scribes of the Roman treasury, under the order of the quæstors recorded the transactions in *tabulae publicae*, a species of journal. A monthly register was also kept, resembling the *codex accepti et depensi*, in which the receipts and payments were entered separately and regularly, with particulars of the dates, the names of persons paying or receiving, the nature of the transaction and the balance of each account at the end of the month. There was also a register of debts (*calendarium*) and special registers for the current accounts between the treasury and the military cashiers, who exchanged letters of credit with the quæstors of the provinces.

The quæstors on quitting office rendered an accounting to their successors of the state of the funds and of the condition of the registers, and they also submitted accounts of their administration to the senate, the meetings of which body they attended for the purpose of advising about the general financial business. These and other various regulations rendered fraud very difficult; their observance being under the supervision not only of the senate, but of the censors, consuls, and each member of the college of quæstors.

From the sixth century of Rome financial abuses began. The organization of Rome, suitable for a municipality, was ill-adapted to the requirements of a great state. The governors, all-powerful outside the precincts of the city and exempt from all local supervision, respected as little the rights of the treasury as the feeble guarantees of the provincial constitution. The generals, not content with enriching themselves at the expense of the enemy, adopted also in their turn independent and almost kingly state.

With the Empire, in spite of the official maintenance of the national sovereignty, public government assumed a dual form, that of the senate and that of the emperor. The provinces and the magistratures were divided into senatorial and imperial, the treasury into the treasuries of the people, of the emperor and of the army. While republican forms were at first retained, all authority became concentrated more and more in the hands of the emperor until the last trace of representative government disappeared.

Under Hadrian, the man invested with the department of finances received the title of *procurator a rationibus* with the rank of *perfectissimus.* The finance minister in the third century received the name of *rationalis,* which title was extended later by custom to the fiscal procurators of the provinces. The central accounting office was called *tabularium,* where the work was carried on by the *tabularii,* the *approximi* and the assistants. Every accounting official had to render an account of his administration to his superior, the chief minister accounting to the emperor.

After the fall of the Western Empire (dating that event from the election of Odoacer as patrician in Italy), while elaborate methods of accounting were continued in the Eastern Empire, Roman accounting traditions were continued for a time in Italy by Odoacer and Theodoric, the Ostrogoth, and in later years in the ecclesiastical organization. In the year 1001 we find a high official on the papal staff, called *logotheta,* whose duties were those of an accountant.

Before leaving the dark ages we may pause for a moment to refer to the enlightened arrangements established by Charlemagne in the Frankish Empire, which are especially remarkable in view of the barbarism prevailing elsewhere. An ordinance of that emperor of the year 812 contains elaborate instructions for the management of the imperial estates. It prescribes that accounts of income and expenditure shall be kept and rendered. Every *judex* was required to report yearly, at Christmas, separately, distinctly and in order, what he had out of his administration, rents, duties, fines, farm produce, etc., and he says very politely: "In all the foregoing, let it not seem harsh to our judices that we require these accounts, for we wish that they, in like manner, count with their subordinates, without offense."

In Italy we find the first traces of professional accountants. As early as 831 a document is signed by Garefrit Rationatari, accountant, Milan. The ducal court and the commune of Milan each employed an accountant in 1164; and in 1387, also in Milan, an accountant and revisor of accounts was appointed. That the accountants of that time were held in high esteem is evidenced by the fact that in the settlement of accounts those authenticated by accountants were accepted as decisive by all parties.

In Venice and other Italian cities accountants flourished from very early times. The fees were well regulated and later it was the custom for the examiners of accounts to receive a percentage of the mistakes and frauds which they discovered.

The first association of accountants of which we find any record, the *Collegio dei Raxonati,* was founded in Venice in 1581. By the year 1669 the influence of this association or college had become so powerful that nobody could practice the profession unless he was a member of the college, whose officials watched over the members and had power to exclude the incapable and the unworthy. Membership in the present accountants' associations of Italy is open to persons who have obtained the *Diploma di Ragioniere* of one of the sixty royal technical institutes.

There are *Bücher-Revisoren* in all important cities in Germany (a majority of whom are sworn in by courts of justice), who are admitted and act as sworn experts for commercial matters in civil and criminal actions at courts of law. They are appointed after due inquiry by the respective chambers of commerce concerning their standing, training, experience and capabilities, and enjoy the special confidence of all German authorities by virtue of their position as sworn experts, in which capacity they are usually called upon to audit the accounts of public and private corporations and companies and to make up balance sheets and statements of affairs of public and private concerns.

Professional accountants now practise in all climes and countries. But, while the name and the business of the accountant are at least of respectable antiquity, it must be admitted that the profession, as now and here understood, is to a very large extent the creation of the last fifty or sixty years.

It is unnecessary to refer to the enormous advance which has taken place in every department of human thought and energy. Everyone is familiar with the great strides in the domain of scientific invention and discovery. These have been accompanied by a steady and rapid growth of commerce, both in regard to volume and the complicity of business affairs. No business nor profession has remained untouched by these changes and the accountant can fairly claim that the development of his profession has not been incommensurate with the progress in other departments.

The first organization of modern accountants was perfected in Scotland and a royal charter granted it in 1854. Since then the movement has spread over the world and the American certified public accountant and his associations stand today at the head of the procession.

Not so many years ago, business in this country was conducted upon a mere speculative basis. The country was young, in possession of apparently inexhaustible resources, with no competition to speak of and large profits, so that the business man was satisfied when the year rolled around that he had been not only able to pay his expenses, but could live in comparative luxury and boast of an increased bank-balance at the end of the year. Accounting was loose and primitive, considered of no value, except as memoranda to refresh one's mind. The bookkeeper was the worst paid, most abused and most overworked employee in the whole establishment. Under such conditions waste and leaks were the rule rather than the exception—without any possible detection, unless by accident.

Now, in the face of keen competition it is an absolute necessity to conduct business upon a strictly scientific basis and where formerly the professional accountant had been called in as an undertaker, he now enjoys the duties of a business nurse and doctor. As the architect prepares his plans for a structure so must the accountant lay out a system suitable for a particular business concern, in each case according to the special requirements and needs. He must see that there is a proper foundation and on that foundation he must build; all details must be so arranged that they give the best results, that they can be easily seen, compared, supervised and regulated, and that the system as a whole is not top-heavy. The same applies to cost accounting.

Some years ago, when a delegation, selected by chambers of commerce for the purpose, called on Andrew Carnegie at Pittsburg to see his wonderful arrangement and management of his shops, yielding enormous profits, he took them to an office instead and said: "Here is where I make my money." It was the cost accounting department.

New methods are constantly found to illustrate or demonstrate the importance of saving small things. For instance, in the case of a railroad, for a two-cent postage stamp needlessly used the company must haul a ton of freight 3½ miles. Other similar examples are lead pencil, 2 miles; one track spike, 2 miles; one lamp chimney, 10½ miles; one station broom, 35 miles; one lantern, 100 miles; one track shovel, 90 miles; one hundred pounds of coal, 20 miles, one gallon of engine oil, 50 miles.

In the last few years it has been realized that municipalities have been clinging to accounting methods that have long been discarded by private enterprises. Disorganization, decentralization, overlapping and short-reaching archaic methods and inefficiency were generally found by investigators. The feeling has grown that cities and other municipalities or governments should adopt up-to-date systems and methods. The reorganization schemes, however, are difficult to effect, because the various administrations regard this work as antagonistic rather than sympathetic.

As far as the accounting systems and methods of our national government are concerned, it is astonishing that up to about four years ago the double entry system was practically unknown and that millions of dollars were annually wasted, because of inefficiency and other causes. President Taft deserves great credit for taking the matter in hand. His economy and efficiency board has already accomplished much, but as many of the changes cannot be put into effect by executive order, it is up to Congress to enact suitable laws.

THE INCAN QUIPU

Orville R. Keister

THE INCAN QUIPU

ORVILLE R. KEISTER*

ONE of the more interesting old civilizations in the Western Hemisphere was that of the Inca Indians, who inhabited Peru from *circa* 3000 B.C. to the Spanish conquest near the middle of the sixteenth century.[1] The quipu,[2] a record keeping device used by the Incas, provides one with another fascinating story of the development of accounting. The modern accountant, surrounded with his electronic equipment, needs the perspective provided by an awareness of the simple tools used by record-keepers of the past. The present is often much more meaningful when one understands the past.

The presence of electronic equipment especially is more thought provoking when considered in the light of the quipu, a simple Incan counting device of knotted strings widely used less than five hundred years ago. This knot record consisted of a main cord to which were attached knotted pendent cords. The knots on the hanging strings recorded, for example, the number of people in a village or the inventory in a storehouse. Many writers have suggested that the quipu had a narrative character which permitted the recording of poems and descriptions of battles, but more recent research suggests that the device was mainly a mnemonic and mathematical tool.[3] Other writers have suggested that the quipu was used as a calculating instrument; others flatly deny this possibility.[4] It is rather evident that there is still much archaeological work to be done on the quipu, but even at this stage of historical research, an accountant may profitably study this early tool.

It appears that the main cord (which was usually of cotton or wool) varied in length from a few inches to more than a yard.[5] After preparing this main cord, more strings would be spun twice the desired length, doubled, twisted together, looped over the main rope much as a gift tag string is attached to the ribbon, drawn taut, and knotted at the free end.[6] At this stage then, there would be a main cord from which would be hanging varying numbers of strings. Sometimes there was only one of these pendent strings; some-

* Orville R. Keister is Assistant Professor of Accounting at The Pennsylvania State University at University Park. He has published previously in THE ACCOUNTING REVIEW.

[1] Maria Jolas, *The Incas; The Royal Commentaries of the Inca Garcilaso de la Vega 1539-1616* (New York: The Orion Press, 1961), p. 419 and Henry S. Lucas, *A Short History of Civilization* (New York: McGraw-Hill Book Company, Inc., 1943), pp. 562-563.

[2] Pronounced kē'poo. From the Quichua Indian word meaning knot.

[3] For example, about four hundred years ago, Cieza de Leon reported that the Jesuit José de Acosta said "the ancient Peruvians, by their combinations of larger and smaller threads, double and single knots, green, blue, white, black, and red colours, could express meanings and ideas as innumerable as we can by the different combinations of our twenty-four letters." From Pedro de Cieza de Leon, *Parte Primera de la Chronica del Peru* quoted in L. Leland Locke, *The Ancient Quipu or Peruvian Knot-Record* (New York: The American Museum of Natural History, 1923), p. 33. Locke made what is probably the most exhaustive archaeological study of the quipu, and he came to the conclusion that "the quipu was used primarily for recording numbers." See pages 31 and 32 of his book quoted above. See also Philip Ainsworth Means, *Ancient Civilizations of the Andes* (New York: Charles Scribner's Sons, 1931), p. 326.

[4] For example, Means wrote: "We may be sure, therefore, that, in spite of its humble and primitive appearances, the quipu was a really efficient mathematical and statistical instrument, fully on a par with the abacus, and, in well-trained hands, almost equal to the modern slide ruler." Means, *op. cit.*, p. 327. Locke refuted this: "The quipu was not adapted to calculation. For this purpose, small pebbles and grains of maize were used." Locke, *op. cit.*, p. 32. See also Jolas, *op. cit.*, p. 44.

[5] Locke, *op. cit.*, p. 13.

[6] "These People Kept Track of Themselves by Tying Knots," *The Literary Digest*, Vol. LXI, No. 4 (April 26, 1919), p. 90.

times there were more than one hundred. Apparently, they seldom exceeded one-half yard in length.[7]

On these pendent cords, knots would be made, and these knots represented differ-ent numbers, their value depending mostly upon their distance from the main cord. A single overhand knot at the bottom of the string, or farthest from the main cord, represented the unit one.[8] Two overhand knots in the same position represented the unit two. A single knot in a position some-what closer to the main cord represented ten, and a single knot in a position still higher or closer to the main cord repre-sented one hundred. On some quipus, there have been found knots representing hundred thousands.[9] Usually the knots were arranged in fairly systematic rows across the quipu, so the unit knot on one cord . would usually fairly approximate the unit knots on the other cords in the quipu.[10] This placement of the knots indi-cates an early awareness of the decimal system. In fact, authorities at the Ameri-can Museum of Natural History have stated that the quipu system probably represents the earliest decimal system of notation of the Western world.[11] Inter-estingly enough, the Inca Indians evi-dently had some grasp of the zero concept, a rather important part of the decimal system, because some authorities have re-ported the presence of many empty spaces or intervals without knots. It appears that a space with no knot represented nought.[12] It would seem that this development was indeed an important step taken by these early people.

Sometimes different colored cords were used to indicate the counts of different things.[13] For example, cords of one color might be the tally of men in a village; cords of another color, the tally of women, and cords of a third color the tally of children.[14] Another interesting variation was the fre-quent attachment of short subsidiary

strings to the pendent cords. These supple-mentary knotted strings represented num-bers outside the main count.[15] To continue the above example, to the knotted string of a certain color recording the number of adult males living in a particular village, a subsidiary cord might be attached to re-cord the number of adult male deaths that occurred during the year.

The people skilled in preparing and reading the quipus were called quipua-mayus.[16] The skill was often passed down from father to son and, in addition, youths of the ruling caste sudied quipus in the third year of their four-year course at the "Teaching House."[17] Those record-keepers were quite important in the Inca civiliza-tion. Prescott's discussion of them is one of the best available. He said:

[The] quipucamayus . . . were required to furnish the government with information on various important matters. One had charge of the reve-nues, reported the quantity of raw materials dis-tributed among the labourers, the quality and quantity of the fabrics made from it, and the amount of stores, of various kinds, paid into the royal magazines. Another exhibited the register of births and deaths, the marriages, the number of those qualified to bear arms, and the like details in reference to the population of the kingdom. These returns were annually forwarded to the

[7] Locke, *loc. cit.*
[8] For an excellent analysis of the number values, see the description provided by the American Museum of Natural History in New York City.
[9] Jolas, *op. cit.*, p. 159.
[10] Locke, *op. cit.*, p. 15.
[11] *The Literary Digest, op. cit.*, p. 92.
[12] Louis Baudin, *Daily Life in Peru* (London: George Allen & Unwin, Ltd., 1961), p. 100.
[13] Archaeologists recognize the probability that oc-casionally the use of different colored strings was a mat-ter of individual whim or practical convenience.
[14] *The Literary Digest, op. cit.*, p. 90.
[15] *Ibid.*, p. 80 and Locke, *loc. cit.*
[16] In a recent book, Louis Baudin wrote that con-tinued proficiency in handling quipus was ensured by the quipucamayus being punished by instant death for the least fault or omission. See Baudin, *op. cit.*, p. 101. This practice seems somewhat radical and the present writer was unable to verify it with another authority, but its interest deserves at least a passing mention.
[17] Philip Ainsworth Means, "The Incas: Empire Builders of the Andes," *The National Geographic Maga-zine*, Vol. LXIII, No. 2 (February, 1938), p. 258.

capital. . . . The government was thus provided with a valuable mass of statistical information.[18]

It is interesting to note that the Incan record-keepers had some concept of internal control. A sixteenth century writer who lived with the Inca Indians while their empire was falling reported that each village had several quipucamayus—the larger the village, the more record-keepers required to live there. However, no matter how small the village, at least four skilled quipukeepers were required so that each would act as a check upon the others. In the words of that writer, "where there were so many, all must be at fault or none."[19]

The record-keepers of this civilization developed the quipu system to a fairly high level of perfection. One needs only to see an old quipu record to recognize this fact.[20] However, the fine art was apparently lost after the fall of the Inca Empire, although even today simple, less advanced forms of the quipu are used in various places in Peru. For instance, a recent traveler to Q'eros, a village in a barren part of southern Peru, saw the quipu being used to count the number of llamas in the community flocks. He wrote:

> The quipu as it survives at Q'eros today is an extremely simple device. The knots no longer follow the complex ancient variations from one to nine; size, rather than position, is the clue to higher numeral values. Perhaps its simplicity and continued usefulness is the secret of this quipu's survival.[21]

Pedro de Cieza de Leon, a sixteenth century historian, summarized the story of the quipu rather well. "Although to us it may seem strange and awkward, it is a fine way of counting."[22]

[18] William H. Prescott, *History of the Conquest of Peru* (London: George Allen & Unwin, Ltd., 1935), p. 57.

[19] Garcio Lasso de la Vega, *Los Commentarios Reales que tratan del Origin de los Yncas* quoted in Locke, *op. cit.*, p. 40. See also Jolas, *op. cit.*, p. 159.

[20] Persons who are unable to view the fine collection of quipus in the American Museum of Natural History in New York City or other comparable collections, will be interested in the excellent pictures of the quipu found in Locke's book already cited and in "The Fine Art of the Quipu," *Natural History*, Vol. LXVI, No. 9 (November, 1957), pp. 490–491.

[21] John Cohen, "Q'eros: A Study in Survival," *Natural History*, Vol. LXVI, No. 9 (November, 1957), pp. 489 and 492.

[22] Harriet de Onis, *The Incas of Pedro de Cieza de Leon* (Norman, Oklahoma: University of Oklahoma Press, 1959), p. 105.

BEGINNING OF A NEW ERA

CHARACTERISTICS OF BOOKKEEPING BEFORE PACIOLO

Raymond de Roover

CHARACTERISTICS OF BOOKKEEPING BEFORE PACIOLO

RAYMOND DE ROOVER

IT IS now generally accepted that double-entry bookkeeping is by no means the invention of one man nor the product of a single generation, but that it is the result of a long evolution.[1] Even today, we see that it progresses under the spur of actual needs, and its development is the result of a persistent effort to adapt the account methods to the growing requirements of business enterprise. As we shall see, its evolution in the past has been dominated by the same commanding necessity of adaptation.

There is, however, still one dark spot in the history of accounting. Although we can perceive fairly well how the double-entry system developed, once the basic principle of duality and equilibrium was laid down, it is hard to understand how it came into being. As a matter of fact, the specialists of the history of bookkeeping have all tried to solve the problem and to offer some satisfactory explanation. Owing to a lack of source material, these solutions, however, are based mainly on conjectural reasoning rather than on factual evidence.

As you probably know, double-entry bookkeeping originated in Italy and the first example of it is found in Genoese records of the year 1340. It arose from the economic conditions which prevailed in the Italian commercial cities at the end of the Middle Ages. We have, therefore, to look towards Italy, if we want to find the clue to our problem. Fortunately, many excerpts or full texts of medieval Italian account books, which were unknown to former historians, have been published in recent years. These publications seem to throw some light on the stages which led to the emergence of double-entry bookkeeping. On the basis of this new material, I shall venture an explanation of the crucial problem. I am fully aware that the explanation which will be offered is not entirely satisfactory, but it seems to me that it points towards an acceptable solution. This is, I believe, its chief and its only merit.

[1] A. C. Littleton, *Accounting Evolution to 1900* (New York, 1933), p. 22.

It is not possible here to support any statement by quotations from the documents on which it is based. Therefore, I have to restrict myself to the conclusions called for by the recent publications of source material. Those who want to go further into the subject will kindly refer to my recent study in a French review.[2]

Three factors seem to have contributed to the development of accounting: credit, partnership, and agency. Let us deal with credit first, because it gave rise to the earliest and most rudimentary accounting records. Before the commercial revival of the twelfth century, the peddler or traveling merchant did not feel the need of keeping any records. Most of his dealings consisted of cash and barter transactions which were settled as soon as they were concluded. Moreover, the peddler's business could be managed without resorting to any clerical work. This ceased to be true at a little higher stage, when merchants began to extend credit to their fellow merchants or to customers. It did not take long before they discovered that memory was too treacherous to be relied upon. As a result of some deceiving experience, they began to write down all transactions which involved credit, so as to keep track of amounts outstanding. At this early stage in the development of bookkeeping, there is no question of forming real accounts. Each transaction was recorded separately, leaving a small blank in order to indicate how the settlement took place. In many cases such indication is even lacking and the original entry is simply cancelled with a stroke across.

As account books could not yet be used as evidence before the courts, the entries frequently mention the name of one or two witnesses in the presence of whom the transactions were concluded. This was ob-

viously done to have legal witnesses in case the debtor contested the claim. Sometimes, the debtor wrote and signed a promise to pay in the account book of the creditor. In general, transactions were recorded as they occurred. In order to economize paper, they were, however, often entered wherever spare space was left among other entries of an earlier date. It should also be stressed that, at this stage, all transactions were registered in one and the same account book.

But economic life does not stand still. Partnerships, at first formed only for the duration of a single venture, began to assume a more permanent character and were no longer occasional agreements. At the same time, the sedentary merchant resorted more and more to agents who looked after his interests abroad and in other cities. These new developments involved new problems. The formation of partnerships called for better methods of record-making in order to ascertain the profits and to determine the share of each partner. This aim could only be achieved in following up all the changes which the common equity of the partners underwent in the normal course of business. Almost the same problem faced the agent who had to render the account to his principal of all the goods which were entrusted to him. As these changes came along, and as business, even outside of partnerships and agencies, extended more and more, it became apparent that the single account book kept hitherto was a source of confusion and entirely inadequate to meet the new requirements. Obviously, some more appropriate method of classification had to be contrived.

We are here on the eve of a very important development, and I think it is worthwhile to pause a moment and to consider why classification is so important. I am greatly indebted to Professor A. C. Littleton, who discussed the matter with me and

[2] Raymond de Roover, "Aux origines d'une technique intellectuelle: La Formation et l'Expansion de la Comptabilité à partie double," *Annales d'Histoire économique et sociale,* IX (1937), 171–193, 270–298.

who pointed out that classification is the very essence of bookkeeping. Even the basic principles of duality, which is at the root of the double-entry system, is not so essential as one is inclined to think. Accounting is largely a means of classifying entries into their proper pigeonholes, which are called accounts. Double-entry was born when people came to see that you could not take something out of one pigeonhole without putting it into another. Apparently, this is simple, but it took a long time before the mechanics of it were fully understood.

Let us now examine how, in the Middle Ages, a better method of classification was gradually achieved. In my opinion, improvement was the result of progress in three different directions, namely:

(1) a constant improvement in the presentation of the individual accounts and, finally, the adoption of the bilateral form;

(2) the replacement of the single memorandum by a set of several books, each book serving a different purpose;

(3) the integration of personal and impersonal accounts into a cohesive system.

As to the first objective, real accounts began to take shape with the growing tendency of grouping together all items relating to the same person. This result was attained by leaving more space to provide for subsequent entries. No attempt was made in the beginning to segregate debit and credit entries. The exact nature of each entry had to be inferred from the text.

Some further improvement was made by dividing the ledger into two sections: one for the accounts receivable and another for the accounts payable. Under each initial credit or debit entry, some space was left blank in order to enter the payments made or received. This form of presentation is called by the Italians *a sezioni sovrapposte*, because the accounts are divided into horizontal compartments,

one placed above the other.[3] This system was only practical in so far as each account did not record too many transactions. If more space was needed than had been anticipated, there was still some danger that the debit would run into the credit or vice versa.

To obviate these defects, the next step taken was to establish a clearcut division between the debit and the credit entries. For that purpose, the ledger remained divided into two sections but the first half was reserved for all items involving a debit and the rear for all those involving a credit. Thus, the debit of any account was placed in the front section and the credit, in the rear of the ledger.[4] By doing this much confusion was evidently avoided. The system, nevertheless, was still rather unhandy and cumbersome. The individual accounts were in a certain sense disrupted, as debit and credit were found at different places in the ledger. To close and balance an account was not a simple matter: the debit and the credit had to be added separately and the lower total of the two had to be transferred from one section of the ledger to the other, and then subtracted from the higher one. This procedure was greatly simplified, when people finally found it more convenient to place the debit and the credit of each account opposite each other. This form is generally known as the bilateral form. With its in-

[3] This system seems to have been less scarce than I have assumed on page 180, note 2, of my above-mentioned article. It is found in a ledger for the years 1431–34 (MS. 496) of the Selfridge Collection of Medici documents at Harvard, which I have had an opportunity to examine thoroughly, since my arrival in this country. Cf. Florence Edler, *Glossary of Mediaeval Terms of Business: Italian Series, 1200–1600* (Cambridge, 1934), pp. 351 f.

[4] This form is found in the ledgers of Francesco Datini, an Italian merchant of the late fourteenth century. A good example is given by Enrico Bensa in his *Francesco di Marco da Prato* (Milan, 1928), pp. 409–411. Cf. Gaetano Corsani, *I fondaci e i banchi di un mercanto pratese del Trecento* (Prato, 1922), p. 71 and R. de Roover, *op. cit.*, p. 274. Even earlier examples are given in the appendices of Armando Sapori's book on the Del Bene Company, *Una Compagnia di Calimala ai primi del Trecento* (Florence, 1932), pp. 362–378.

troduction, the account took a form which it has retained up to now. We are, however, getting away from the bilateral form, as accounts kept by a machine have a third column giving the balance after each new entry.

As we have seen before, the single memorandum was in danger of becoming a hodgepodge of the worst sort. The medieval bookkeepers, therefore, looked for some way of substituting order for chaos. They solved the problem by replacing the single memorandum with several books. Different books were kept for different purposes, thus affording an easy means of classification.

As early as 1277, a company of Sienese merchants kept simultaneously at least six or seven books among which were a ledger, a cash book, and a *libro dei chapitali* (book of capitals) which contained the accounts of the partners and the principal employees.[5] The Peruzzi, a company of merchant-bankers, who had a network of branches all over Western Europe and the Near East and went bankrupt in 1343, kept a great number of books, both in the central office and in the various branches. At the top of the whole structure were a *libro dell'asse* or general ledger and a *libro segreto* which contained the accounts of the partners and the branch managers. These two books were the only ones that escaped destruction owing to their value for the settlement of the bankruptcy.[6] The number of books is also quite conspicuous in the Florentine woolen industry. The Medici account books preserved at the Harvard School of Business Administration, for instance, show that the fifteenth-century cloth manufacturers used various books, namely a ledger, a journal, a wage ledger, and several wage books.[7]

[5] Guido Astuti, *Il libro dell'entrata e dell'uscita di una compagnia mercantile senese del secolo XIII, 1277–1282* (Turin, 1934), pp. x–xii.
[6] Armando Sapori, *I libri di commercio dei Peruzzi* (Milan, 1934), xxiv–xxx.
[7] Edler, *op. cit.*, p. 355.

Some of the numerous books in use before the introduction of double entry overlap to a certain extent. I have the feeling that their number could have been reduced appreciably by a more systematic organization. In my opinion, the use of empirical methods is largely responsible for the considerable amount of duplication in the medieval records, as is, also, the fact that the single-entry system does not provide any check on the accuracy of the accounts.

The spread of double-entry bookkeeping, in the fifteenth century, introduced a better and more accurate method of classification. It entailed a great deal of simplification and a number of books dropped out. The cash book, for instance, was superseded by the cash account, the *libro segreto* was rendered superfluous by the proprietorship accounts in the ledger, while the journal took care of the transactions formerly dispersed in miscellaneous notebooks. It should, however, be observed that for obvious reasons the reduction in the number of books was far greater in the mercantile than in the industrial enterprises.

As for the third point, the integration of personal and impersonal accounts into a cohesive system, personal accounts for receivables and payables were in the beginning the only accounts known. As partnerships and agencies grew, the necessity was felt to keep also records of goods and expenses. Records of that kind make at first only a casual appearance in the account books under the form of simple annotations. As time goes on, these records are encountered more frequently and take the form of real accounts. This evolution can best be followed in the account books of Francesco Datini, a fourteenth-century merchant, who started out with books kept by single entry, but who adopted the double-entry system at the end of his career. In the first account books, only a few impersonal accounts are found, but they grow rapidly in number. After a few years, the account books contain, besides accounts for payables and receivables, capital accounts representing the money invested in the business and impersonal accounts for goods and expenses. Each entry refers to a counterpart in another account. The transition from single to double entry is thus accomplished by the gradual building-up of a cohesive system of accounts and the concentration in the ledger of formerly scattered material.

There are two other characteristics of medieval bookkeeping which I wish to stress. It has often been contended that financial statements of some sort or another were unknown in the Middle Ages. This is not entirely true. Most of such statements were written on loose sheets of paper and consequently have been lost. A few, however, have survived both in Italy and in other countries. These examples show that the practice of making up financial statements was more common than has been suspected hitherto.[8] In partnerships, of course, it was often indispensable to draw up some kind of a statement in order to apportion the profits to the different partners or to determine their equity in case of dissolution. Agents, too, were often required to send reports to their principals concerning their management. Some good examples are found in the Datini documents. The branches which Francisco Datini had founded in Spain and Southern France, were expected to send every year a copy of their inventory and later of their balance sheets to the headquarters in Prato (Italy). In 1400, the branch in Palma on the island of Majorca even added a profit and loss account to its balance sheet.[9]

There is, nevertheless, a fundamental difference between modern and medieval practice. In the Middle Ages financial statements were generally not drafted every year, but at irregular intervals, when, for instance, the ledger was full and a new one was started, or when a partnership was dissolved.

The second point which I want to discuss refers to the development of industrial accounting in medieval Italy. As early as the fourteenth century, the textile industry in Florence, Lucca, and other Italian cities, was already organized on a capitalistic basis. Of course, the factory system which we know today, did not yet exist. The industry was under the control of industrial entrepreneurs who owned the materials and gave them out to artisans working at home. This system is commonly called the putting-out or wholesale handicraft system.

Some of the books of Florentine clothiers have come down to us. The most remarkable group is the Selfridge Collection of Medici business records. This material shows that the Medici in their capacity as industrial entrepreneurs used a quite elaborate system of bookkeeping. Besides the usual books, they had several registers for their accounts with artisans: wool-washers, spinners, weavers, dyers, and cloth-finishers. These records did not constitute a cost-finding system, but were primarily intended to keep track of the raw materials and to provide a basis for the computation of the wages. I cannot emphasize strongly enough that this complicated system of accounting control was imposed upon the clothiers by the organization of their industry. It seems to have been so common that it has left traces in the gild regulations and is decribed in a contemporary treatise on the silk industry, which was organized along the same lines as the woolen industry.[10]

---

[8] R. de Roover, *op. cit.*, p. 192.
[9] Corsani, *op. cit.*, pp. 157 f. and appendix no. 7, pp. 175–178.

[10] Girolamo Gargiolli, ed., *L'Arte della seta in Firenze: trattato del secolo XV* (Florence, 1868), pp. 113–124.

Attempts to go beyond a mere control of the use of raw materials do appear, however, at an early date. In an account book of 1395, belonging to a cloth-manufacturing firm in which Francesco Datini was a partner, an effort was made to determine the cost of each bolt of cloth. Besides direct expenses, allowances are made to cover rent, costs of apprentices, and other indirect charges; the value of the residual material is also deducted. One of these cost records is reproduced here in a summarized and modernized form:

2 Bolts of Cloth made of Minorca Wool,
Lot no. 8+[11]

COST OF RAW MATERIAL (wool).........		£16.14. 3
COST OF PROCESSING:		
Cleansing, carding, combing, etc................	£ 6. 8. 2	
Spinning................	5. 6. 3	
Weaving................	4.12. 1	
Finishing................	11. 1. 0	
Dyeing.................	8. 5. 8	
Supplies................	3. 8. 0	39. 1. 2
ALLOWANCE FOR OVERHEAD:		
Rent, cost of apprentices, etc....................	£2.10. 0	
Petty expenses..........	0.18. 0	3. 8. 0
		£59. 3. 5
LESS:		
Value of residual material.............		− 0. 9. 0
Total cost.......................		£58.14. 5

[11] Corsani, *op. cit.*, Appendix 3, pp. 163–165.

This sketch shows that the bookkeeping of the medieval merchants was entirely adequate for their purpose and attained a high degree of flexibility. The merchants sought to adapt it to the increasing requirements of business and succeeded fairly well by improving their modes of classification. Major steps in this direction were the adoption of the bilateral form, the use of more than one book and the addition of impersonal to the existing personal accounts. All these changes culminated finally in the adoption of the double-entry system of bookkeeping which brought with it a certain degree of simplification and constituted a self-controlling system.

The treatise of Paciolo dated 1494, in which the double-entry system is first described in print, is, it should be remembered, only a copy of a contemporary manuscript circulating in the schools of Venice. It is, therefore, a general work which does not give an accurate picture of actual practice as it entirely neglects, for instance, to discuss how industrial enterprises kept their books. In many ways, practice in the fifteenth century was far ahead of theory. Indeed, the more one delves in the past, the more modern the Middle Ages appear to be.

INITIAL DEVELOPMENT OF ACCOUNTANCY

Calvin C. Potter

Initial Development
Of Accountancy

By Calvin C. Potter, M. Com. (Econ.)

A summary of the origins and
assumption of double-entry bookkeeping

THE ALMOST CONTINUOUS RISE in the level of prices during the last decade has been paralleled by an increase in the amount of space accorded by accounting journals to examinations of the inadequacies of traditional accounting methods and procedures. This dissatisfaction with the results of financial accounting, and criticism of its correctness and significance, is not restricted to the accounting rebels, such as George O. May and associates, but is also reflected in the writings and actions of national income analysts[1], business corporations[2], and trade union leaders.

The implication of the criticism from within and without the profession is that accountancy has ceased to portray accurately the facts of reality and, as a result, its use as a guide to policy may not only be misleading, it may also be disastrous.

Such a serious accusation calls for a thorough investigation into how accountancy has come to misrepresent the financial position and results of accounting

[1] For statement of accounting inadequacies see "Measurement of National Income and the Construction of Social Accounts", United Nations, p. 106.
[2] See the revaluation of assets and the Directors' Report, ICI, May 1951.

entities, and how that misrepresentation percolated through the economy to thwart and distort national economic policies. This article, the first step in such an investigation, will attempt to summarize the origins and assumptions of double-entry bookkeeping and correlate them with the conditions of the then prevailing social reality.

Requirements for Accountancy

The purpose of accountancy is to aid human judgment by providing financial data of past transactions in qualitative and quantitative terms of sort and size. To furnish such aid, it is essential that, first, some form of systematic record be maintained to ensure accuracy, and, second, if the transactions are numerous, that a methodical manner of treating the content of the records be adhered to in order to achieve consistency.

Since accounting records act as *prima facie* evidence of the rights and responsibilities of real and imaginary persons in their contractual relations with other members of the social group, accuracy is the major standard of measurement for judging the adequacy of any system of accountancy. Any form that systematically records all data will satisfactorily perform this standard, as is reflected in the earliest form of accountancy, which is as old as the art of doing business, where "business transactions along with other social or political events were entered on what might be described as a diary".[3] While such a form is accurate, with any considerable degree of activity it tends to be inefficient, and some are of the opinion that during the Phoenician, Greek, and Roman eras of commercial supremacy, the considerable trading activity gave rise to a need for an efficient and consistent method of classifying the type and magnitude of contractual responsibilities, and thereby forced the surrender of the earlier diary method for the more efficient method of double-entry. If such was the case, all trace of it was lost during the Dark Ages, when the need for systematic records was eliminated. In that period, credit for production and exchange was non-existent, and the prevailing transportation difficulties and closed local economies restricted the limited trade to local markets where there was little scope for the forces of demand and supply, and where transactions were concluded at a customary price and on a cash basis.

Three Essential Conditions

The introduction of double-entry during eras of commercial activity and its disappearance upon stagnation indicates that there is a minimum of three essential conditions that must be present before a system of accountancy will develop beyond the diary stage. First, there must be a series of contractual relationships, and the duties and privileges of the real and imaginary persons must arise directly as a result of exchange, and not as a product of social custom or traditional practice. Second, there must be a knowledge of writing so that the contract can be classified according to type and category. Third, there must be a knowledge of the

principles of counting so that the magnitude of the exchange can be described.

We have noted the absence of the first condition during the Dark Ages, when sparsity of trade and transactions at a customary cash price were the rule. The Crusades period that followed the Dark Ages initiated a redistribution of wealth and a revival of commerce that encouraged and facilitated the introduction of the advance guards of an embryonic price economy, including the extension of credit to the processes of production and exchange.

The redistribution of property and the introduction of credit made it a matter of good business practice for merchants to keep a memorandum as an *aide-de-memoire* concerning the disposition of their property and their relations with creditors and debtors. The description in the *aide-de-memoire* classified the items into some pre-existing class or group, and accompanied it by a notation indicating its quantitative magnitude. The quantitative magnitude involved the process of counting, since relative size is determined by the ordinal principle of ordered succession until a collection is exhausted and absolute size by the cardinal principle that each number corresponds with a collection and determines its plurality. But because the quantities in the notation were expressed in terms of the Roman numeral system, which is based upon the alphabet, the numerals in the notation were by themselves incapable of providing a means of counting, and mechanical aids, such as the abacus or *jetons*, had to be introduced to do the computations.

Development of Systematic Records

The earliest known surviving accounting memorandum is an Italian account book for the year 1211.[4] It recorded all

---

[3] E. Peragallo, "The Origins and Evolution of Double-Entry Bookkeeping", p

[4] R. DeRoover, "La Comptabilité à Partie Double", *Annales d'Histoire Economique et Sociale*, Vol. 9, 1937, p. 176.

Mr. Calvin C. Potter, M. Com. (Econ.), was graduated from Sir George Williams College in 1948 as a Bachelor of Science in Commerce. He then did post-graduate work at McGill University where he obtained the degree of Master of Commerce in 1950. In 1950-51 he studied at Glasgow University on a McGill-Glasgow Exchange Fellowship and now is completing his doctorate studies at McGill.

transactions in chronological order, with an accompanying description and a space to be filled in later when the account was settled. The settlement was indicated by a stroke through the entry. By the first half of the fourteenth century there had been an improvement over the rudimentary accounts payable and receivable ledger in that the debits and credits were separated, the book divided into two equal sections and all the debits put into the first section and all the credits into the second section. This meant that each account was subdivided and appeared in both sections of the books, making it necessary to total the debits and credits, transfer the lesser to the greater section, and subtract, when one wished to establish a balance. This cumbrous procedure was improved towards the latter half of the century by the Venetians, who perfected a "bilateral form" of account where the debits and credits were entered in the same account. This innovation was the introduction of the contemporary form of double-entry bookkeeping.

Development of Double-Entry Content

Because of poor communications and restricted markets, the medieval trade of the Italian cities in which double-entry first developed had two main characteristics: namely, the practice of joint-venture trading and the lack of special-ization.[5] The practice of joint-ventures was due not only to the fact that the merchant wished to diversify his risks, but also because of a custom that buyers inspected personally the quality of the goods offered for sale. The prevalence of the custom forced the merchant to find an outlet for his merchandise by forming a venture or "limited partnership" with an agent or representative for each particular voyage or enterprise. The agent was usually another merchant, who carried from 10 to 20 separate ventures, sold the merchandise at the best price obtainable, accounted for each venture separately, and generally, for his enterprise, obtained a commission of 25% on the profits of each venture. Obviously, this was merely agency-selling on a consignment basis. The merchant (known as the *commendator*) who provided the capital in the form of goods took no part in the management, and his liability was restricted to his capital contribution. The travelling agent or representative who was responsible for the management was called a *tractator,* and the arrangement itself was termed a *commenda.*[6]

For the agents to report intelligently, and the *commendators* to appraise knowingly the personal (debt) accounts ledger that was already in extensive use had to be extended to include impersonal (goods) accounts recording sales and expenses, and possibly a "master's account" into which the others would be closed upon termination.[7]

As the *tractators* accumulated capital of their own, their position as contact men enabled them, by contributing part of the capital, to become the equivalent of proprietors of a business making use

---

[5] R. DeRoover, "The Medici Bank", p. 40.

[6] W. J. Ashley, *"English Economic History and Theory",* p. 413-5.

[7] A. C. Littleton, "Social Origins of Modern Accountancy", *Journal of Accountancy,* 1933, p. 265.

of capital from home merchants. The fact that both the *commendator* and *tractator* now assumed the risks of loss changed the nature of the association from one of a limited partnership, where the liabilities of the partners who took no part in management were limited to their contributions, to that of the nature of a *societas,* where personal liability was unlimited.

Up to this stage businesses had generally been run by families as social units, and the introduction of *tractators* from outside the family into the rights of proprietorship required a clearer statement of what was a legitimate offset to the master's account than had been the case when the business was a purely family affair. Now, the problems of periodical divisions of profits or losses and dissolution or liquidation of the partnership called for a clearer delineation of what constituted capital contributed, and what and who was eligible for withdrawals. The final outcome was that household and personal expenses were excluded from the business accounts and a specified money capital was allocated to the business, represented by the capital account, and the business was treated for accounting purposes as an entity separate from the identity of its owners.

Spread of Double-Entry System

With the development of systematic records and the creation of personal, impersonal, and capital accounts, there remained two important factors which blocked the wide-spread adoption of the double-entry system. First, the Roman numeral system was a handicap in that it was incapable of creating an arithmetic within the intellectual means of an average man, and consequently, it restricted the art of reckoning to a small and privileged class.[8] From the eleventh to the fifteenth centuries the Arabic columnar system, which had been invented by the Hindus and came to Europe via the Arabs during the time of the Crusades, had struggled for recognition in official and commercial documents. At one time it was banned from all official documents, at another the art was prohibited altogether, and even when the notational system was finally accepted around the beginning of the fifteenth century, Roman numerals were still used for making entries in the account books after the computation had been calculated with Arabic figures, because of a fear that Arabic numerals could be easily falsified. Second, until the thirteenth century, while the unit-of-account was expressed in pounds which contained 20 sous of 12 pence each, the denominations did not have the direct association with specific coins as is now the case, the pound and sou not being represented by coins.

In the thirteenth century gold coinage was introduced and attempts were made to establish coins for each of the denominations of accounts. In Florence a gold coin, the florin, was designed to represent the pound, a large silver coin was issued to represent the sou, and a smaller coin to represent the penny. However, the symmetrical balance of this system was of short duration, because of the instability of the ratio between gold and silver, and the Florentines soon had the choice of changing the weight of their florin or reckoning it at a different value in the unit-of-account. They preferred the latter choice, and although it was still possible for them to express the

---

[8] It is interesting to note that insofar as accuracy was an aim, the notational system that superseded the Roman numerals was no better, since the frequency of errors with the Roman system was no greater than it is today with Arabic numerals. R. DeRoover's well documented conclusions on this matter contrast very favorably with the assertion of Max Weber "that the Florentine literal notation was frequently wrong to the extent of three or four fifths". (*General Economic History*, p. 224).

values of the coins in terms of a new series of units of accounts, the long established habit of counting in terms of pounds, sous, and pennies prevailed, with the result that each denomination was used as a counting system with each coin as a base. Accordingly, depending upon convenience, Florentine accounts used either florins, grossi, or pennies, as the unit-of-account, and because of the instability in the gold-silver ratio, they had two bases for reckoning the value of each of the units-of-account: the denominational basis, where the florin was taken at its original value of one lira or 20 *solidi a oro,* and the mint basis, where one lira was equal to 29 *solidi affiorino.* The latter was described in the unit-of-account as one *lira affiorino* equals 20 *solidi affiorino* equals 240 *deniers affiorino*[0].

Towards the end of the fourteenth century this conversion procedure was simplified, and the basis laid for a greater degree of comparability when a common gold unit-of-account was adopted by the seven "greater" crafts, and a vellon[10] unit-of-account by the fourteen "lesser" crafts; and the coins used as the actual means of payment were rated in both denominations[11].

By the fifteenth century, as we have seen, the Arab notational system had superseded Roman numerals in the calculation of accounts, the concept of business having an identity distinct from that of its owners had been accepted, and a stable and standard monetary unit had been established. This provided a realistic basis for the two basic assumptions in bookkeeping: namely, that the undertaking can be treated as an entity distinct from the identity of its owners, and that the unit-of-account is sufficiently stable to justify the neglect of minor fluctuations. On the basis of these two assumptions the double-entry system was developed and firmly established in the books of *commendas* and *societas* in the three cities of Genoa, Venice, and Florence.

In Genoa, the books, which were entered in perfect double-entry form[12], comprised a ledger for impersonal accounts, accounts payable and receivable ledgers for personal accounts, and capital accounts for partners. Genoa at this period was at the height of her wealth and power, commerce having flourished for a long time on the exploitation of the lucrative Levantine trade.

At this same period, the Venetian system of double-entry, which otherwise was very similar to the Genoese system, effected co-ordination of the bookkeeping system by the introduction of the journal. The journal entries were arranged in chronological order, formerly classified into debits and credits with full explanations, and then posted to the ledger.

Mercantile Accounting

In both cities it was customary to open an account for each venture in the books of the partnership. The account was charged with the purchase of the commodity and all its incidental expenses, and credited with the proceeds from sales. The difference between debits and credits on conclusion of the venture represented a profit or loss and was transferred to a Profit and Loss on Merchandise Account[13]. It is to be noted that this system of venture accounting precluded any necessity for annual inventory valuations and closing of the books.

---

[9] A. P. Usher, "The Early History of Deposit Banking in Mediterranean Europe", p. 206.

[10] A base alloy of silver and copper, in which the silver was designed to give intrinsic value to fractional coins.

[11] A. P. Usher, "The Early History of Deposit Banking in Mediterranean Europe", p. 207.

[12] R. DeRoover, *Annales* etc., p. 180.

[13] R. DeRoover, "The Medici Bank", p. 44.

Industrial Accounting

As contrasted with the commercial growth of Genoa and Venice, the development of Florence's cloth manufactures, and her establishment as the foremost banking centre of Europe, compelled the adoption of accounting methods peculiar to herself. Her great commercial achievement was the development of the partnership contract to a high degree of perfection. The contracts clearly stated the capital of all the separate partners, made provisions for the division of profits and losses, clearly defined the rights and duties of each partner, and, finally, provided for the dissolution of the partnership. This high perfection of contract entailed an equally advanced concept of partnership accounting, and of the financial statement necessary to show each partner's interest. The statement used for determining profits and losses was called a *bilancio*. Its construction was relatively simple. At each year end the book assets were listed and totalled, the liabilities and partners' capital were listed and totalled below the assets, and the difference between the two totals was the net profit for the period[14].

The essential difference between the mercantile accounting of Genoa and Venice, and the industrial accounting of Florence, was that the Florentine type of activity did not lend itself to accounting on a venture basis, because some of the services consumed in the textile and banking activities were derived from durable assets that had useful life expectations beyond the normal period of waiting involved in venture accounting. The problem of durable assets was solved by the adoption of the third basic assumption that is implicit in double-entry bookkeeping, the assumption of continuity in the affairs of the accounting entity. Acceptance of the assumption permitted the apportionment, on the basis of past experience, of the present and future services to be derived from the assets of the entity. Thus it was possible for interim reports to be issued during, as well as after, the life of durable assets.

From an early date the Florentines were aware of the requirement for such interim statements, as is illustrated by Dr. DeRoover's comments on the books of the firm of Alberto del Guidice de Florence (1304-1322). "The inventory of the company was prepared with particular care. The stock on hand, furniture, and fixtures, were evaluated by experts appointed by the banking house of Bardi. The valuation of stock was made at current market price, and not cost, while in determining that for furniture and fixtures, consideration was given to depreciation due to usage."[15]

In the foregoing summary we have traced the development of the five categories of account that were essential for entity bookkeeping. The first three categories: the personal accounts, or those accounts which recorded the relations with debtors and creditors (other than on capital account), the impersonal (or operating) accounts pertaining to revenues, and the impersonal (or operating) accounts relating to the costs involved in obtaining the revenues, simply recorded a series of contractual relationships through time, and the only essential conditions for the existence of these records were that there be contractual relationships based upon exchange, that there existed a knowledge of writing, and that use was made of the principles of counting.

Of the two remaining categories, the profit and loss account was used in the manipulation and disposal of impersonal accounts, and as we have noted, the validity of its results was dependent upon how accurately the assumptions of con-

---

[14] E. Peragallo, "The Origin and Evolution of Double-Entry Bookkeeping", p. 136.

[15] *Annales* etc., p. 179.

tinuity and stability in the unit-of-account were reflected in the actual conditions of social reality. On the other hand, while the capital account was not dependent upon the assumption of continuity, the significance and validity of its total was dependent upon the assumption of stability in the unit-of-account being realistic, and upon the fact that if the household accounts were eliminated and the resources contributed by the proprietors quantitatively evaluated in one account, then the undertaking itself could be considered an imaginary person for accounting purposes and treated as an entity distinctly separate from that of its owners.

NOTES ON THE ORIGIN
OF DOUBLE-ENTRY BOOKKEEPING

Basil S. Yamey

NOTES ON THE ORIGIN OF DOUBLE-ENTRY BOOKKEEPING

BASIL S. YAMEY

THE FACT THAT THE origin of double-entry bookkeeping remains shrouded in mystery does not detract from the merits of the valuable researches into the early history of accounting made by several scholars. In the nature of things attempts to probe the origins of the technique are at best intelligent guesses or inferences. The search provides an interesting pursuit for the historian even if he knows that the spoor will disappear, sooner or later, in a confused tangle of speculation and conjecture, with the scent of red herring always present. The following notes deal with one of the possible trails to the unknown origin; or rather, a possible trail provides a tenuous central theme about which some observations are presented.

A POSSIBLE LINE OF APPROACH

Accounting resembles crafts in so far as it consists of techniques designed to serve certain practical ends. The methods and instruments of crafts generally undergo a continual though often almost imperceptible process of change. The discovery of new media,[1] the influence of particular craftsmen,[2] chance circumstances, or the coercive urge of unfilled requirements, may be the cause of these changes. Rarely, one would imagine, are the changes so radical that the continuity of the development is broken. Inertia and the belief in the sanctity of earlier procedures often lead to the adherence to earlier practices long after they have ceased to serve any useful purpose.[3] It is likely that the majority of changes, when they do occur, take the form of variations on the existing practice, by omission, simplification, addition or adaptation: the newly-evolved techniques closely resemble the ones previously used, and their character is largely determined by them.

Is it not possible or likely that mercantile accounting has evolved along the lines sketched in the previous paragraph? And that the appearance of double-entry bookkeeping is to be explained as one event, albeit a momentous one, in a gradual evolutionary process of development? Row Fogo has expressed this view that bookkeeping "is neither a discovery . . . nor the inspiration of a happy moment, but the outcome of continued efforts to meet the necessities of trade as they gradually developed."[4] Elsewhere I have queried this thesis that double-entry developed in direct response to some particular business need(s), which was not adequately served by earlier methods of accounting.[5] But

---

[1] As an example of a new medium, the possible effects of the introduction of Arabic numerals upon bookkeeping technique may be mentioned. The view has even been expressed that Arabic numerals are indispensable for systematised bookkeeping, since the earlier Roman numerals were, allegedly, unsuitable for tabular recording and computations. On this view Spain, where the use of Arabic numerals was first introduced to Europe by the Moors, has been claimed as the birthplace of double-entry. (See Theodor Drapala: *Die Buchhaltungskunde in ihrer wissenschaftlichen Pflege*, 1889, p. 68.) That this view is scarcely plausible may be gathered from the fact that Roman numerals were used in double-entry records for some time after the adoption of the Arabic system of numeration, apparently in order to make the fraudulent alteration of records more difficult.

[2] Thus the use of the "opening balance account," which "has since become a regular feature of the bookkeeping methods of practically the whole of Continental Europe" has been ascribed to Alvise Casanova

in his *Spechio lucidissimo* (1558). (P. Kats: "James Peele's Maner and Fourme" in *The Accountant*, Vol. LXXXII, 1930.)

[3] Professor H. R. Hatfield has collected some of the "folk-lore" of double-entry bookkeeping, procedures still practised for no other reason than the magical influence of custom, in his article, "Accounting Trivia," in *Accounting Review*, September, 1940.

[4] In Brown's *A History of Accounting and Accountants*, 1905, p. 93.

[5] In *The Functional Development of Double-Entry Bookkeeping*, Publication No. 7 of the Accounting Research Association, 1940, reprinted in *The Accountant*, November 2, 1940.

even if my doubts are accepted as valid, the possibility of the emergence of double-entry as the product of a gradual process of change still remains open; for changes in the technique of a craft are not necessarily nor solely caused by the stimulus of novel problems awaiting solution. At the other extreme changes may be initiated almost by accident.

Here two sorts of bookkeeping, which it is reasonably certain were practised before the appearance of double-entry, will be examined to throw light on the question whether it is possible that double-entry developed as an improvement or expansion of them, taking over some of their basic features but representing a further stage in the process of adaptation and change. The two sorts of bookkeeping are single-entry and agency or factors' bookkeeping, the main emphasis being placed on the second.

SINGLE-ENTRY AND DOUBLE-ENTRY

It seems as if, before double-entry appeared, accounting records of proprietorships, whether single or multiple, were confined to records of dealings involving the granting or receiving of credit. The records assumed various forms and often the "books of account" were mere scraps of paper. Sometimes there were entries in diaries or journals, where the settlement of debts was indicated by the effective though untidy method of deletion. Sometimes the entries in the journal were reclassified into accounts, the beginnings of the modern ledger.

Though there is evidence that other transactions were sporadically recorded, the scope of the early bookkeeping efforts was very similar to that of what is now known as single-entry bookkeeping. But as the records were in no way systematized, it is perhaps incorrect to describe them as single-entry, which term today implies the presence of some system in the

records. Indeed, single-entry as a *system* is more likely to have been a development from double-entry.

Dr. Jäger has stated that single-entry, *as a system*, developed out of double-entry through the gradual omission of all impersonal accounts.[6] Schmalenbach says that "there existed in Germany, particularly in the Hanseatic towns and in the South German trade centers, before the adoption of the Italian bookkeeping, a system of commercial accounting with a fairly well-developed technique and nomenclature." He continues that double-entry considerably influenced this native brand, "so that the single-entry bookkeeping methods of today have the appearance of being stunted versions of double-entry bookkeeping."[7] Also Flügel in his text, *Der getreue und aufrichtige Wegweiser* (1741) states: "Here I have purposely described double-entry first, because this is the chief source from whence single-entry has sprung."

Professor Hügli disagrees with this opinion that single-entry as a system is derived from double-entry by a process of attenuation. It is his view that "single-entry is no mere fragment, but in form and for its purpose a complete and satisfactory whole," and that "the natural development can indeed have been no other than that double-entry grew out of single-entry after the latter had matured into a complete system."[8] A subsidiary argument of Hügli's is that Luca Pacioli mentioned by name both single- and double-entry in the thirteenth chapter of his *Particularis*, the first printed work treating of accounting, thereby indicating at least the co-existence of the two systems at an early date. However, it is clear that in the chapter concerned Pacioli was merely referring to two

---

[6] *Altes und Neues aus der Buchhaltung*, 1889, p. 3.
[7] *Dynamische Bilanz*, 5th. edition, p. 56.
[8] "*Ueber die Geschichte der Buchhaltung in Italien*" in *Zeitschrift für Buchhaltung*, 1894.

sorts of registers or indexes to the ledger, and not to two sorts of bookkeeping.[9]

But even if a system of single-entry bookkeeping had existed before the emergence of double-entry, there is still a very wide gap between the two methods both in scope and technique. The latter contains nominal and real accounts which the former does not. The cohesion of the accounts in the latter is without counterpart in the former. It would require the introduction of *deus ex machina* of considerable proportions to explain how the two widely dissimilar systems are actually successive stages in the evolution of accounting methods. Professor Littleton has suggested one way in which the gap may have been crossed: the automatic, unreasoned extension of the practice of making dual entries for some transactions to all transactions. If a cash account is kept in conjunction with the personal accounts in a system of single-entry, then the receipt or payment of cash in settlement of debts would require two entries. Similarly, even in the absence of the cash account, the substitution of one debtor or creditor for another would require two entries in the personal accounts. In Professor Littleton's words: "Once the practice of dual entries upon opposing sides of bilateral accounts had become established, it would not be difficult to extend it by analogy to new accounts. No one would have to stop and reason out the philosophy of the matter first."[10]

AGENCY BOOKKEEPING

It is the contention of Dr. de Waal, supported to some extent by the views of Professor Littleton and Mr. Kats,[11] that "factor" or agency bookkeeping played a significant part in the emergence of double-entry. Briefly, the view appears to be that agents had to keep accounts to show thei. indebtedness to their principals; that these accounts assumed a distinctive form; and, that double-entry is a lineal descendant of that system.

The bookkeeping aspects of agency may be summarized by saying that the agent must be able at all times to show to what extent and for what reasons he is indebted to his principal, or vice versa. The bookkeeping technique amounts to the keeping of a personal account in the name of the principal, debiting it with all expenses incurred by the agent on the principal's behalf, and crediting it with all the proceeds of the agency business received by the agent. There would be no profit calculation, partly because the agent would not necessarily know all the relevant facts (e.g., the cost of the goods he may receive from the principal), and partly because the profit calculation would be irrelevant from the agent's point of view. The receipt of goods from the principal would not give rise to an entry in the principal's account until the sale of the goods. The agent would find a stores book with details of *quantity*, disposal instructions, etc., useful to keep track of different consignments. He would also find it useful to keep accounts of his cash transactions and credit dealings in connection with the agency.

Dr. Mickwitz in an interesting study has shown[12] that this type of agency accounting is most suited for another type of trading, which appears to have been common among the traders in the Hanseatic towns. He has described the practice as it prevailed in Reval in the fifteenth and sixteenth centuries. The form of trading was a type of partnership between two

---

[9] See Kheil's *"Ueber einige Bearbeitungen des Buchhaltungs-Tractates von Luca Pacioli"* in *Zeitschrift für Buchhaltung*, 1895.

[10] *Accounting Evolution to 1900*, 1933, pp. 38–39. An interesting conjecture on similar lines is put forward in the article on Bookkeeping in McCulloch's *Commercial Dictionary* (New Edition, 1859).

[11] P. G. A. de Waal: *De Leer van het Boekhouden in de Nederlanden tijdens de Zestiende Eeuw*, 1927. A. C.

Littleton: *op. cit.* P. Kats: "Early History of Bookkeeping" in *Journal of Accountancy*, Vol. XLVII, 1929.

[12] *Aus Revaler Handelsbüchern*, 1938.

merchants, each in a different town, and each sending goods to the other to be disposed of at the best price, profits being shared in a pre-arranged ratio. In such circumstances each partner was virtually the factor for the partnership. There was no single centralized set of books, but each partner kept records of partnership transactions in which he had taken part. Each partner kept records of his expenses on account of the partnership, and his receipts from the partnership business. A balance of receipts over payments would be of almost the same significance as the excess of an agent's receipts over his payments, viz., indebtedness to an external entity. The only difference would be that the partner-factor had an interest in the profits made by the external entity, which was calculated periodically by combining the separate records of the two partners. Undoubtedly the bookkeeping adopted resembles that of agents, and Dr. Mickwitz objects to the name "agents' bookkeeping" as a description of the common system, as being incorrectly restrictive in its title.

Whether or not agency bookkeeping has been a stage in the evolution of double-entry has been made by Dr. de Waal to depend largely, but by no means exclusively, upon the interpretation given to the works of Valentin Mennher von Kempten, who wrote several texts on accounting published in Antwerp between the years 1550 and 1565. But before discussing these works it is useful to go back to the works of the earliest German writers on bookkeeping, Heinrich Schreiber and Johann Gottlieb. It has been variously suggested by some historians that the system described in their volumes antedates the Venetian double-entry method, and is quite independent of it; that their work describe agency bookkeeping, and that Mennher borrowed from them.[13]

---

[13] For opinions about these early works, see: Mickwitz: *op. cit.*, p. 200; Kats: *op. cit.*, p. 12; Row Fogo in

SCHREIBER AND GOTTLIEB

Schreiber's *Ayn new kunstlich Buech*, published in Nürnberg in 1518, is the earliest known book on bookkeeping in German, and the earliest treatise in any language devoted solely to bookkeeping. It describes a system of accounts that requires three main books: a journal (*Zornal*), a ledger (*Schuldtbuch*), and goods-book (*Kaps*). All transactions are first recorded in the journal. The ledger contains only personal accounts and a cash account. The goods accounts, one for each type of merchandise, are placed in the goods-book. For each transaction a double entry is made, though each of the two entries may be made in a different book. On the purchase, say, of wine for cash, two entries would be made, one in the cash account in the ledger, and the other in the wine account in the *Kaps*. The entries are made in a peculiar way, because the receipt of goods would be entered on the right-hand side of the goods account, while the payment of cash would be recorded on the right-hand side of the cash account—so that the purchase of goods would give rise to two entries, both "credits" to modern eyes.

To verify the accuracy of the books, a "Proof of the Bookkeeping" (*Proba*) has to be carried out. The total profit has to be calculated in the goods-book, by summating the profits on each goods account, after introducing the closing stocks. Then "add together the cash receipts, what others owe you, and the goods on hand; and from the total subtract the cash payments, and what you owe others; and then if the balance equals the profit, it is correct." Schreiber did not illustrate the *Proba* or the closing of the books. But if the journal

---

Brown: *op. cit.*, p. 123; A. H. Woolf: *A Short History of accountants and accountancy*, 1913, pp. 124–125; B. Penndorf: *Geschichte der Buchhaltung in Deutschland*, 1913, p. 113; de Waal: *op. cit.*, pp. 77–78; Jäger: *op. cit.*, p. 71; D. Murray: *Chapters in the History of Bookkeeping*, 1930, p. 207.

entries in his example are correctly posted (there are several typographical errors in the 1544 edition), the proof naturally holds.

Schreiber's system is certainly based on the double entry for each transaction, though the arrangement of the books is strange (about which there are some comments below). The *Proba* is based on the fact that the increase in the net assets is equal to the profits. In Schreiber's example there is no opening capital, so that the closing net assets equal the profits. His equation:

Receipts +Debtors +Goods − Payments
− Creditors = Profits

may be transcribed as:

Cash balance +Debtors +Goods − Creditors
= Profits
or, Net Assets   = Profits
or, Increase in Net Assets = Profits (where there is no opening capital).

The last equation is of course one of the fundamental equations of double-entry bookkeeping.[14]

Gottlieb's *Ein Teutsch verstendig Buchhalten* (1531) and *Buchhalten* (1546) describe a system very much akin to that of Schreiber. The same three books are used. In the 1531 volume the closing of the books is not described, because Gottlieb believed that it was advisable to give oral instruction on that difficult subject. In the later work this omission is rectified. The profit-and-loss calculation is appended to the goods-book, just as in the case of Schreiber's system. The proof of the accuracy of

the books is the proof provided by double-entry bookkeeping. The increase in the net assets is calculated and is checked against the profit as calculated in the rear of the goods-book.

It appears quite clearly that Schreiber and Gottlieb had come into contact with double-entry bookkeeping, but that they had given imperfect and confusing renderings of it. Their system is based on the dual entry for each transaction. The profit is calculated in two ways from the entries made; but the two calculations are not linked together as in double-entry bookkeeping. Dr. De Waal's contention that the system is single-entry is incorrect, because impersonal accounts have no place in single-entry.[15] Penndorf's judgment that it is neither single-entry nor double-entry is nearer the mark, though its double-entry basis should be stressed.[16]

As both Schreiber and Gottlieb appear to have described some modified form of double-entry proprietorship bookkeeping, complete with a profit calculation, it is difficult to see how their system can be referred to as agency bookkeeping. The confusion may have arisen because in the 1546 volume Gottlieb gives two worked examples, one for a single proprietor and one for an agent. As the system is exactly the same in both cases, and identical with that described in the 1531 volume, which was expressly intended for "masters and partners," it seems, if anything, that the modified double-entry had been adapted for agency bookkeeping, and not the other way about. The works of Schreiber and Gottlieb appear to be interesting historical curiosities, without any great significance for the emergence, development, or spread[17]

---

[14] Proofs of the accuracy of accounts kept on a double-entry basis have taken a fascinating variety of forms. Here it may be of interest to mention one other variation on the basic theme, that of J. Sedger in *An Introduction to Merchants' Accounts* (1807–08). His formula is:
 Opening assets +profits balances +closing liabilities = Opening liabilities +loss balances +closing assets.
Of this Proof Sedger says: "Note—That this kind of Proof, which is most concise, has not been observed before, except by an intimation in my former production." He also gives "The usual Proof of Book-keeping": opening "neat estate" plus profit equals closing "neat estate."

[15] *Op. cit.*, pp. 77–78.
[16] *Op. cit.*, p. 113.
[17] The main influences which spread the knowledge and use of the Italian bookkeeping to Germany seem to have been: (i) The commercial contacts between German merchants (and their subordinates) and merchants in the Italian cities and the Low Countries. Matthäus Schwarz, the head bookkeeper of the Fuggers, spent

of double-entry bookkeeping.

Before leaving Schreiber and Gottlieb, some comments on their treatment of goods accounts by segregating them in a separate "ledger" (the *Kaps*) may be of interest. The exclusion of goods accounts from the general ledger seems to have been a common practice in parts of Germany, difficult to eradicate and therefore probably a relic of earlier methods.[18] Gottlieb, though not abolishing it, does not approve of the practice. He likens the split ledger to a room which is divided in two for no reason. He shows how it makes posting and cross-reference difficult, and that it requires two indexes. Also, "many books, many errors." Both Kaltenbrunner in *Ein newgestellt kunstlich Rechenbüchlein* (1565) and Schultz in *Arithmetica oder Rechenbuch* (1611) maintain the division of the ledger in two parts, *Schuldtbuch* and *Kaps*.

It is possible that this practice was borrowed from agency bookkeeping, except for the important difference that in agency bookkeeping it is unlikely that the agent would have recorded monetary values in his "goods book," if he kept one, as did Mennher's "agent" (*infra*). An agent would have greater need of detailed merchandise records than the owner of a business, since the agent is accountable to another for the disposal of the merchandise entrusted to his care. At the same time he would have no need to keep his merchandise records on the same basis as his cash or personal accounts, as his interest in the merchandise, until sold, is confined to quantitative control. Hence it is likely that merchandise records in agency bookkeeping may have preceded merchandise accounts in proprietorship bookkeeping; and that a separate account-book for detailed merchandise records may have been one feature of agency bookkeeping, taken over in double-entry bookkeeping.[19]

VALENTIN MENNHER VON KEMPTEN[20]

Mennher's first work on accounting, his *Practique briefue pour cyfrer et tenir Liures de Compte*, was published in 1550 in Antwerp, and his later work, *Practicque pour brievement apprendre a Ciffrer, & tenir Liure de Comptes*, in the same city in 1565. A Spanish translation by Antich Rocha appeared in Barcelona in 1565, and German editions were published in Antwerp in 1560 and 1563. An important work in Dutch, Pietersz' *Practicque Omte Leeren Rekenen Cypheren ende Boeckhouwen* (1596) is a version of Mennhers edition of 1565; and in turn the English *Pathway to Knowledge* by "W.P." (1596) is a translation of Pietersz' work.

Mennher explains why he wrote his books, and in so doing expresses sentiments, for the first time I believe, which have often been repeated quite independently by writers of later manuals, either by way of prefatory explanation or of advertisement. He says he wrote his books

---

some time in Venice, and on his return brought out an unpublished manuscript on double-entry, which may have been influential, (ii) The publication of German text-books, of which Schweicker's *Zweifach Buchhalten*, (1549), based on Manzoni's *Quaderno Doppio* (1540), was the first satisfactory exposition of double-entry. (iii) Joachim Rademann in *Der Wehrt-geschätzte Handels-Mann* . . . (1714) traces the practice of double-entry in Germany to the merchants of Brabant who were forced to flee to Germany when expelled by the Duke of Alva. One of these refugees, Passchier Goessens, wrote a book, *Buchhalten fein kurtz zusammen gefasst* . . . (1594), which had considerable influence.

[18] See Woolf: *op. cit.*, p. 124.

[19] A further speculation arises out of these observations. The suggested influence of agency bookkeeping may explain why in the early practice of double-entry there were no single aggregated purchases, sales, and "unsold merchandise" accounts, but instead a number of separate "trading accounts" for each type or lot or parcel of goods, each "trading account" combining the purchase, sales, unsold stocks, and profit or loss for the batch concerned. This practice appears to have died out, in Britain at least, somewhere in the nineteenth century.

[20] Discussions on Mennher's works may be found in the works of de Waal and Kats cited in footnote 11, and in articles by Berliner and Kheil in the *Zeitschrift für Buchhaltung*, 1895 and 1898, resp. An at times acrimonious controversy between Berliner and Kheil is in the latter volume of the *Zeitschrift*.

"because many books have been written about the noble art of arithmetic and about the way accounts are kept, by persons without practical experience in business, and who consequently use many examples and illustrations which are of little value, and are more diverting than useful."

Both Professor Volmer, who edited a re-issue of Mennher's first work, and Dr. de Waal, regard the system described in that work as agency bookkeeping, anterior in point of time to Italian double-entry bookkeeping. Dr. de Waal is of the opinion that the agency bookkeeping described by Mennher is "a remarkable and indispensable link necessary for a thorough understanding of the development of the system of double-entry." He has taken the historians, Penndorf and Kheil, to task for having paid insufficient attention to agency bookkeeping in the history of accounting, and for having regarded Mennher "rather 'as a peculiar, than as an important, writer."[21]

Mennher himself points out that his work is *"a la guise et mainiere italiana,"* thus suggesting Italian influence. Dr. de Waal attempts to explain this away by his assertion that Mennher followed one of the many methods other than double-entry which existed in Italy; and, by way of substantiation, he refers to Johann Gottlieb's remark that he knew of 40 varieties of bookkeeping. But this reference is unfortunate. In his 1531 volume, Gottlieb says:

"As there are different kinds of business, so there are different kinds of bookkeeping (of which I have met with some forty varieties); however, all are grounded on the same principle. If one knows this fundamental principle of bookkeeping, then not only does one understand all kinds of bookkeeping, but one is also able to adapt the bookkeeping to each kind of business and as the circumstances require; like a piece of wax, which allows itself to be moulded into any shape."

[21] *Op. cit.*, p. 140, note.

A similar remark appears in George Thomas Flügel's *Der getreue und aufrichtige Wegweiser* (1741):" One will find as many kinds of bookkeeping as there are counting-houses: but actually in the keeping of the books one uses not more than two methods, namely, single-entry and double-entry." It should be clear that Gottlieb was indicating the possibility of various ways of arranging the accounting records, all based, however, on double-entry.

In the 1550 edition Mennher advises the uses of three main books: a journal, a ledger containing personal accounts, and a goods-book containing details of consignments bought and sold. The resemblance to the system described by Schreiber and Gottlieb is striking; but an important difference is that Mennher's goods-book does not contain any "value" entries but only details of *quantities* bought and sold.

In the worked example the business and the bookkeeping is conducted by Pierre du Mot on behalf of his principal or master (*mon maistre*), Nicolas de Reo. There is an account in the latter's name.

The entries concerned with the handling of goods are of special interest. When goods are received by du Mot from de Reo, only a quantitative entry on the debit side of the appropriate goods account in the goods-book is made. When goods are sold, cash or the purchaser's personal account is debited, and the account of de Reo is credited. In addition, the goods account is credited with the quantity sold.

When a debtor goes bankrupt, his account is credited and the account of de Reo is debited. When expenses are paid, cash is credited and the master's account is debited. A similar double entry represents the payment of a salary to du Mot.

The entries for the various transactions suggest agency bookkeeping in no uncertain manner. The omission of "money" for goods, unless du Mot pays for them or received money for them, is characteristic of agency bookkeeping. The booking of expenses paid against the principal's account is also a typical procedure. The account of de Reo at any time *before the closing of the books* shows what du Mot owes him. There is no profit calculation.

On the closing of the books the cash balance and all the personal account balances are closed into the account of de Reo. As every transaction that has been recorded in the ledger has given rise to two entries in ledger accounts, one in the debit and the other in the credit, it follows that de Reo's account will be in equilibrium.[22] Its contents, after closing, are:

Debits

Opening creditors
Cash purchases ⎫incurred by
Credit purchases⎭ du Mot
Expenses paid
Closing debtors
Closing cash balance

Credits

Opening debtors
Opening cash balance
Cash sales
Credit sales
Interest receipts
Closing creditors

As this account stands, it is very confusing and almost meaningless. (It is certainly meaningless in the context of agency accounts.) It was apparently not intended as a statement to be submitted to de Reo, because Mennher gives instructions for drawing up two statements, one showing the amount of the indebtedness to de Reo and the other the quantities of goods on hand, which together would have been an admirable, brief account of de Reo's position at the date of balancing. The reason for the curious balancing method is ob-

scure; but it does suggest that Mennher, who probably was well-versed in agency bookkeeping, had come into contact with double-entry bookkeeping and had attempted to graft the idea of balancing on to the former system, and in doing so robbed it of much of its clarity.

In his later volume of 1565 Mennher describes full-fledged, double-entry bookkeeping, with a profit and loss account and balance account. In the example the books are still kept by an "agent," Jacques le Beau, for his principal. Kheil convincingly explains the introduction of a bookkeeper apparently acting as agent for the proprietor as a common expository device, employed both by Ympyn (*Nieuwe Instructie*, 1543) and Wolffgang Schweicker (*Zweifach Buchhalten*, 1549) in their works dealing with double-entry. Having regard to the closing entries in the 1550 work, to the subsequent exposition of double-entry in 1565, and to Kheil's explanation, it does not seem as if Mennher's work can be used as strong support for the thesis linking agency bookkeeping with the development of double-entry. Mennher, even if he set out to describe agency bookkeeping in 1550, was already influenced by double-entry. And as Kheil points out in his detailed and knowledgeable study, there is reason to doubt whether he ever intended his work as a hand-book for agents, his view being that the 1550 work was intended as an elucidation of double-entry, and not a very successful one.[23]

AGENCY AND DOUBLE-ENTRY BOOKKEEPING

The conclusions reached as regards Mennher's works do not, of course, imply that there cannot be any truth in the the-

---

[22] This shows some similarity with the closing of the accounts in Manzoni's *Quaderno Doppio* (1540).

[23] Berliner (see footnote 20) has stated his view that Mennher in 1550 was dealing with agency bookkeeping. He regards the changes introduced in 1565 as evidence "that Mennher has taken a step out of the real world into the realm of theory, where one has to deal with speculative possibilities, whereas the merchant rejects all theories which produce no practical results."

sis that agency bookkeeping is an indispensable link in the process of change in accounting technique eventuating in the appearance of double-entry bookkeeping. It merely implies that some of the evidence advanced in support of this view appears to be faulty. Indeed, an analysis of some of the characteristics of agency bookkeeping alone suggests that there may be some validity in the thesis.

One may quite reasonably assume that some form of agency accounting, incorporating the essentials of the modern method, existed before the emergence of double-entry bookkeeping. The relationship of principal and agent was well-known in Western commerce from an early date; and where the relationship exists there is a pressing need for some form of detailed accounting—a much more urgent need for systematic records than in the case of single proprietorships or even partnerships. The earliest known proprietorship accounting records reveal a rudimentary "system," confined to credit transactions. An agent would have required more detailed records; and almost certainly records of all transactions, whether cash or credit, would have been necessary. A well-developed system of agency bookkeeping may have been in existence side by side with a rudimentary system of proprietorship accounting. Even if there were no pressing need for improvements, there would have been a tendency for the more "advanced" form to influence the "backward" practice.

Moreover, if there is a cash account in the agency bookkeeping alongside of the personal accounts, each transaction would give rise to two entries. This would arise because the principal is the debtor or creditor of the agent. Every expense or item of revenue, whether in cash or on credit, decreases or increases the debt due to the principal, and also necessitates an entry in the cash account or a personal

account. Hence, one of the formal characteristics of double-entry may have existed in the earliest systems of agency accounting.

Double-entry bookkeeping may have developed through the slavish adoption of agency bookkeeping technique by proprietary business concerns. Following the analogy of the agent's records, each expense would be debited to the proprietor's (capital) account, and each item of revenue would be credited to the proprietor's account, would contain all revenues and expenditures as credits and debits, and the profit—here the analogy ends—would be reflected in an increase in the balance on capital account, allowing, of course, for capital additions and withdrawals. In other words, the owner of the business would be regarded as being outside the firm, a principal for whom the business was being conducted. (Here, incidentally, is one possible explanation of how the proprietor, in double-entry, came to be treated, formally, as a creditor of the firm.) Gradually it would become apparent that it would be useful to show each type of expense and revenue separately (or more realistically, in view of the facts, to show the expenses and revenues of each trading event separately). These separate revenues and expenses would be collected periodically in the profit-and-loss account to be closed in total to the capital account.

It may be argued that the idea of slavish adoption, followed by transformation, is not plausible. Both Dr. de Waal and Professor Littleton have suggested other ways which may be more acceptable. Dr. de Waal shows how the application and broadening of agency bookkeeping may have taken place if the agent became his principal's bookkeeper.

The agent, who has now entered the service of his master as bookkeeper, will have to deal not only with a part but with the whole of the proprietor's possession. The account of the principal would in this way acquire the characteristics of a capital account.[24]

Professor Littleton postulates a change in the nature of trading organization. He suggests that the distinguishing features of double-entry bookkeeping "would grow quite naturally out of these 'agency' relations, as trading partnerships of more permanent nature replaced single ventures or occasional agreements."[25]

A 'HAPPY MOMENT'?

These theories can account for the development of double-entry out of agency bookkeeping, though the necessary assumptions are large. Some, doubtlessly, will find the differences between double-entry bookkeeping and agency bookkeeping (and even more so, single-entry bookkeeping) too great to make the gradual bridging of the gap between them seem likely or plausible. Perhaps, it may be hazarded, it would be more realistic to regard the appearance of double-entry as a more or less complete break in the development of accounting methods, noting, however, that double-entry may have taken over many features of earlier techniques.

The latter consideration points to the suggestion that double-entry bookkeeping may have been the "inspiration of a happy moment." Augspurg has expressed this more romantic view that double-entry is the product of one man's brain. His view is based upon "the definite conclusion, which will be reached by every competent judge after a thorough examination, that the scientific system based on mathematical principles could have had no other source than the genius of one individual (and he a mathematician well acquainted with commerce) from whose pen it must have flowed forth in one gush."[26] This theory poses the interesting questions of how and why the system was adopted by others, and who the mathematician was. Augspurg identified Luca Pacioli as the genius; but Pacioli himself disclaimed the honour, and there is evidence of double-entry records before 1494, and that Pacioli's work is a recension of an earlier Venetian manuscript. But whether or not double-entry is the brain-child of some mathematician, it is at least certain that double-entry was nurtured and encouraged in the high places of mathematical learning.

And so the probings into the origins of double-entry bookkeeping lead from one speculation to another. The true story is likely to remain as much of a mystery as double-entry itself must be to the uninitiated.

---

[24] *Op. cit.*, p. 282.
[25] *Op. cit.*, p. 38.

[26] "Die Irrthümer in den neuerlich verbreiteten Ansichten über die Erfindung der Doppelbuchführung und ihre Berechtigung" in *Zeitschrift für Buchhaltung*, 1897

THE FINANCIAL ORGANIZATION
OF THE MANOR

A. E. Levett

THE FINANCIAL ORGANIZATION OF
THE MANOR

THE work of the writer on mediæval economic history can only be compared with that of the old Saxon *Gerefa :*[1] " it is toilsome to recount all that he who holds this office ought to think of; he ought never to neglect anything that may prove useful, not even a mouse-trap, nor even, what is less, a peg for a hasp." His only consolation is that " ever as he becomes more diligent will he be more valued, if he observes a course like that of a wise man." Yet diligence alone will not make him more than a statistician. He has " fields upon his hands," and his unpretentious toil must have behind it some sympathy with, some insight into the real life of the people; some hidden sense that

> " She is not any common Earth,
> Water, or wood, or air ";

that the fields and the woods have a history and a meaning which sympathy and diligence may unravel.

" Manorial Accounts " sounds a barren enough subject: actually it is a most effective means to an end. There are always two methods of approaching agrarian problems—the doctrinaire and the practical; the one impervious to facts, the other only too apt to be impervious to ideas. The land may be treated as a more or less constant factor, which may be valued at a given moment, and the valuation used as a basis of policy for considerable periods. In the Middle Ages, this static aspect of the land is reflected in Domesday Book, though the value of that great record is enormously enhanced by the fact that it quotes figures for three dates, differing by some twenty years, and so gives a strong lead as to " tendencies." It is this stationary aspect which we find in the customals and cartularies of the twelfth and thirteenth centuries, or again in the extents, the *inquisitiones post mortem*, or the Hundred Rolls; and it is this type of evidence which has received, perhaps, most attention in the past. It is obvious that the material on which this static picture is built up should be subjected to close scrutiny, and that the utmost care is necessary to avoid transferring to one century what may have been true of the last.

[1] Liebermann, *Gesetze*, i., 453-5.

There is no heresy about the Middle Ages quite so pernicious as the theory that they were unchanging. The second method of regarding the land is concerned rather with evolution, with tendencies, with change or progress, and it requires evidence of a different type. This dynamic aspect of agrarian questions seems to belong chiefly to the later centuries, the thirteenth, fourteenth, and fifteenth, but this is largely a matter of the available records. The regular book-keeping of the manor begins in the thirteenth century, in the Court Rolls and the Ministers' Accounts. It is a nice question whether the records were produced by the changes, or whether they merely record, for the first time, changes similar to those of past centuries. In any case, these documents definitely record a state of movement, of change: they are therefore worthy of the closest study from the economic point of view, while they may at times throw considerable light upon legal problems. If their technique is understood, they can hardly lead us astray, since they are, in a unique degree, free from interested motives. Apart from official records there is some literature, more or less idealistic, on the subject of the mediæval land-system—the legal text-book and the agricultural treatise—which, like the extents and surveys, takes up a stationary view-point, but is far less satisfactory in its accuracy. The lawyer only too often seems to be divorced from reality, as he describes a kind of paradise for landlords, while the villein either suffers from impossible restrictions, or, at times, seems to occupy " acres in Utopia." Walter of Henley or the author of the *Dite de Hosbandrie*, again, describe what they hope rather than what they expect to see; and their calculations often need considerable checking by the accounts of work actually done. Thus Mr. Ballard pointed out that the crops of wheat, oats and barley grown at Witney between 1340 and 1349 seldom reached more than half the yield which is demanded in the *Dite de Hosbandrie*, while the threefold rotation of crops would seem to have been a vain imagination; wheat might apparently be sown on the same field seven or eight years in succession. Again, he has shown how the rents actually received seriously exceeded the estimates given in the Hundred Rolls.[1] A strong case may thus be made out for a more thorough and complete use of compotus rolls, or ministers' accounts, whenever they have survived in a reasonably good sequence: the isolated roll is, of course, not particularly illuminating. These accounts are, of all the manorial records we possess, the most closely in touch with facts, and the least influenced by extraneous circumstances, since they were only intended for private use. It seems true to say that they are less influenced by prejudice or by personality than any other type of material, while,

---

[1] *Oxford Studies in Social and Legal History* (ed. Vinogradoff), v., 186, 192.

nevertheless, they give some real glimpses of corporate organizations and communities.

The manorial and agrarian history of England appears to need rewriting almost every ten years, as new material comes to light or fresh investigators work over the old ground, seeking some new cause which shall explain the break-up of villeinage. The fashionable explanation is sometimes the Black Death, sometimes assarts and enclosures, or the statutes of labourers, or, as in a recent essay, soil exhaustion followed by a necessary throw-back to pasture. The explanations are various, but the data used are generally the same, or at least of the same class. For this reason it is particularly desirable to make sure of the precise meaning of the terms used in the compotus rolls. I have therefore endeavoured to make a slight comparative study of some account-rolls of Battle Abbey, Merton College, the Priory of St. Swithin's, Winchester, and of other isolated manors in Southern England, and have compared them constantly with the accounts of the Bishop of Winchester and with the economic conditions of the St. Albans Abbey estates. There are two broad lines of comparison: the actual economic conditions, and the technical construction and presentation of the account. Under the second heading is included a discussion of the nature and significance of assized rents, and the method of presenting and balancing the receipts and expenses—purely technical points which may nevertheless prove useful.

A brief but suggestive introduction to the study of manorial accounts has been recently furnished by Mr. H. S. Bennett, in an article mainly concerned with the position of the reeve.[1] The genesis of the account-roll lies in the responsibility of the reeve; its elaboration arises from the methods of estate-management developed by absentee landlords. There are comparatively few good sets of accounts dealing with a single manor whose lord resided at the hall; the accounts of Wellow, in Somerset, belonging to Sir Walter Hungerford, are among the few exceptions which prove the rule.[2] In some of the accounts we can trace the weekly or monthly reckonings by the reeve, who thus kept track of the labour services, the rents, the stock, the expenditure of corn, the expenses of the lord or his agents. The primitive system of tallies served him well. The shepherds or the haywards would bring in their own tallies, kept up to date with the scrupulous care and unfailing memory of the illiterate. The reeve probably needed no written record for himself, but when the seneschal or the cellarer or the bishop's clerks and auditors came upon their rounds of supervision a more intelligible medium might be required. Hence among the

[1] *English Historical Review*, July, 1926, pp. 358-365.
[2] P.R.O. Ministers' Accounts, 974/20-25.

Winchester account-rolls we find here and there scraps of parchment only an inch or two square, on which are entered the numbers of the stock, the names of men eligible as reeve, or a note of the imposition of labour services: similar notes may be found among the Merton College account-rolls. There is very little to show whether the reeve was capable of writing these notes with his own hand or not. The full account would seem to have been always the work of a professional scribe, the fee for whom was often included in the account. With the tallies thus translated the scribe would proceed to make out the final account. To help him in this task, several model accounts and formularies, or brief treatises on the keeping of the accounts, were written.[1] Both Dr. Cunningham and Mr. Bennett have made use of these models, though neither of them has noted the confusion and repetition into which the model itself sometimes falls, furnishing no very infallible guide to an inexperienced reeve. Moreover, the model sometimes quotes figures which, though they may have been possible locally, are very far from being generally applicable. An entry fine of £10 as early as the thirteenth century is not incredible, but great would have been the outcry if it had been exacted in some districts. It might have been expected that the famous St. Albans Formulary Book,[2] which furnishes a model for almost every piece of ecclesiastical or temporal business in which the Abbey was likely to engage, would also have included a model of a St. Albans account. This would have been specially welcome, in view of the almost complete lack of any such accounts for this Abbey's estates. An account-roll there is, certainly, in the Formulary Book, but it proves to be one from the manor of Wolaston, which obviously belonged to a lay landlord, since a large sum is paid *de auxilio nativorum ad filiam domini primogenitam maritandam*. However, this account is obviously intended to be used as a model, and therefore probably represents the St. Albans practice sufficiently faithfully.

The normal form and subdivision of an account-roll are well known. What is by no means clear is how the common form was evolved. Probably the Winchester Rolls[3] were the earliest to be systematized, under the inspiration of Exchequer methods, and their classifications and subdivisions imposed themselves as a logical necessity. Rents, corn, stock, miscellaneous produce, labour services and judicial profits form the inevitable framework. Two points, however, have not always been noted: first, that almost any item or any piece of information

---

[1] Cambridge University Library, Dd, vii. 6, f. 58b; Ee, i. 1, f. 221 and f. 231b.
[2] *Ibid.*, Ee, iv. 20.
[3] *The Pipe Roll of the Bishopric of Winchester*, 1208-9 (ed. H. Hall); and *Oxford Studies in Social and Legal History* (ed. Vinogradoff), v.

may be found under any heading, and the investigator who expects a mediæval scribe to be as methodical as he undertook to be is likely to be sorely deceived; secondly, items which do not involve money payments are apt not to be recorded, if the lord has reasonable confidence in his reeve; hence the account of the labour services is frequently not entered in full. The ordinary week-work in winter, which involved no meals and no expenditure, was hardly worth recording. Harvest works, on the other hand, are carefully and separately described. Thus the lists of "works" on the back of the rolls are often missing; on the Winchester Pipe Roll they are not transcribed (even if they were available on the separate manorial accounts) except for one group of manors round Taunton, and very imperfectly for one manor in Hampshire. Nevertheless the services were being steadily performed. There is no apparent reason for this variation, but it is a strong argument against relying too much upon the non-appearance of any expected item. Another consideration was suggested by the late Mr. Ballard. It is evident that the receipts of a manor will be partly agricultural, and partly seigneurial. To get any clear idea of agrarian evolution, the seigneurial dues ought to be excluded; this involves separating almost all the profits of the courts, except the entry fines, or *ingressums*, which are of the nature of rent; but the separation cannot be complete, since the rents themselves are largely seigneurial rather than economic. In the fourteenth century, however, the real problem lies in the economic results of demesne farming, and these can be arrived at more or less accurately by merely subtracting the whole profits of the courts, and all the older rents, and balancing the rest of the receipts and expenses. Whether the landlord himself ever made this analysis is not very clear, but it is indisputable that, where seigneurial dues were heavy, an account which shows a large total balance might readily cover a net loss on the demesne, while the contrary could not happen unless abnormal expenses—for example, for building—were included. Again the moral is that strict scrutiny and analysis is necessary if manorial statistics are to be really significant. The framework of the account-roll survived in proportion to the learning and conservatism of the system behind it. On the smaller manors by the middle of the fifteenth century the use of Latin had almost died out, and the accounts took on a modern shape. At Wigsell, Salehurst,[1] in 1463, we find: "Also paid for a day carriage of gret sawe logg' with a drage and 12 beasts 1s. and for three men a day to help lode the same logges . . . xiid. Also payd Morys Sawyer for fellynge and cuttynge of timber 21d." The entries are hardly distinguishable, even to the names, from the day-books or yearly accounts of a farm at the end of the nineteenth century. The

[1] British Museum, Harl. Roll, Cc, 26-27.

Winchester accounts,[1] on the other hand, though they change their material form after 1455, and become books instead of rolls, yet retain almost all their traditional classifications through the sixteenth century, and in some respects down to the beginning of the eighteenth century, though by the latter date the grouping is an empty form. The use of Latin survives until the seventeenth century.

One final reason for urging the study of manorial account-rolls, apart from their essential economic value, is that, like all accounts, they form an unrivalled field for the picking up of " unconsidered trifles," which elude us in all the more likely sources of information. Thus from two manorial accounts we may gather that the expenses of the clerical proctors in Parliament were charged upon certain manors —*e.g.*, at Gamlingay (Merton College)[2] in 1322-23, and at Wootton[3] (St. Swithin's Priory) in 1338. The latter entry appears among the miscellaneous and irregular expenses. Again, in the sixteenth century Winchester rent books may be traced the cessation of the collection of Peter's Pence, while a very early mention of the Mayor of London is found in the roll for 1213. In a St. Albans manor, Abbots Langley, it is clear that the expense of providing the *panis benedictus* had been transformed into a rent.[4] None of these facts are what the historian naturally seeks in manorial accounts, but by some lucky chance they are there, and may provide just the clue by which other unrelated facts may be given their due significance.

Perhaps the best way of illustrating the comparative method of dealing with accounts is to pass at once to the technical questions already mentioned—the rents of assize, and the final balance of the account: hence it will be easy to return to more general considerations. One of the items in a manorial account to which the closest scrutiny should be given is the *Redditus Assisus*, or *Redditus Assisæ*—fixed rents, or rents of the " Great Fixing " or assize, as one might perhaps translate the latter form. These rents are sometimes contrasted by

[1] Eccles. Comm., Various, 159270-159445, deposited in the Public Record Office. The Rent Books, from 1458 onwards, are numbered Ecclesiastical Commission, Various, 155784. The original Compotus Rolls, from which the Pipe Roll was made up, are Ecclesiastical Commission, Various, Bundles 56-117.

[2] Merton College Archives, Ministers' Accounts, 5376: Item procuratori cleri pro parliamento apud Ebor, viii d. ob.

[3] Compotus Roll of Wootton in *The Manor of Manydown* (ed. Kitchin: Hampshire Record Society), 149: *In solutis procuratori existenti pro clero ad Parliamentum domini regis*, xv d. How far this was part of a general system I cannot ascertain, but this question of the expenses of the clerical proctors is one on which Professor Pollard has as yet thrown no light.

[4] Court Rolls of Abbots Langley, 9 Ed. III. in Sidney Sussex College, Cambridge, Library, ⌂ i. 1. Cf. A. E. Levett, *The Courts and Court Rolls of St. Albans Abbey* in *Trans. Royal Hist. Soc.*, N.S. vol. vii., 1924.

historians with the labour services still performed and with the wages and other payments made to hired servants. Exact mathematical comparisons have been worked out by one or two writers, as if the rents were a precise equivalent of earlier services. Now if this contrast be sound, if we have here a genuine standard of comparison, then it is desirable to collect as much information as possible under these heads, and to extend the available statistics as widely as may be. But if it be unsound, if there is no ascertainable relationship between the two, then the sooner a misleading type of investigation is abandoned the better. That there is normally no such relationship is what I would seek to prove.

It is perhaps unfortunate that Miss Neilson, in her usually exhaustive study of *Customary Rents*,[1] has not given a very emphatic definition of rents of assize, nor has she used the evidence of the Winchester pipe rolls on this point as fully as it deserves. Nevertheless her definition should invite caution: " The fixed rents, of whatever kind, agreed upon by the lord and the villein or freeholder for the holding of certain tenements, whether of assart land, demesne land, or land in the fields of the village, rents which, however originating, were regulated not by the custom of the manor, but by agreements depending upon the nature of the land, and the advantage to the persons concerned. It should be stated, however, that the term *redditus assisœ* has sometimes a broader application." It is not possible or necessary to follow Miss Neilson's further analysis of the different classes of rents, but enough has been quoted to show that no single or simple definition of rents of assize is of any use to the historian or the statistician. Any manor or group of manors may be working on a definition of its own. Account-rolls must be scrutinized with the utmost care if they are to give up their secrets of methods of book-keeping.

The Winchester pipe rolls, or ministers' accounts, have a peculiar value, in that they are the earliest as yet discovered, probably the earliest to be compiled. In the first extant roll (1208–09) the various mentions of fixed rents with which each account begins are sometimes given under the name of *gabulum*, or *gabulum assisum*, sometimes of *redditus assisus*. *Land-gabulum* is carefully distinguished from *burgabulum*. Comparison with later accounts where the word *gabulum* dies out makes it perfectly clear that *gabulum assisum* is identical with *redditus assisus*.[2] Now *gabulum* is *gafol*, the old Saxon payments de-

---

[1] *Oxford Studies in Social and Legal History* (ed. Vinogradoff), vol. ii.

[2] The term *Gabulum* survives till the sixteenth century on one or two of the Winchester manors; for example, at Meon we find in 1530 a *Prepositus operum*, and a *Prepositus gabuli*. At the end of the fifteenth century, at Cheriton, there

scribed in the *Rectitudines Singularum Personarum*, itself probably a West Saxon document—and *gafol* was a money payment for land, customary at least a century before Domesday Book, and customary alongside of labour services. There seems to be no possibility of regarding *gafol* as commuted labour services. It may possibly have been an original money rent, of the nature of a tribute or tax, or, more probably, it was the commutation of dues in kind.[1] Later evidence would seem to support the latter suggestion, since the assized rents are evidently in part a commutation of payments in kind, and in other districts the term *gabulum* is associated with specific dues in kind. It can be indubitably proved that on the Winchester estates there is absolutely no connection between rents of assize and commutation of services. This has been said before, but it is worth while to say it again with all possible emphasis. The rents quoted in the pipe rolls, though they rise rapidly in some cases in the thirteenth century, are almost stationary for periods of fifty or a hundred years in the fourteenth or fifteenth centuries. Moreover, each " increment " is carefully noted and accounted for. In nearly every case it is due to an " assart " or " purprestura," enclosed with the lord's permission, for which a small fine is paid and a small additional rent is added to the total. Or it may be expressly due to a commutation of dues in kind. After one year's mention it is merged in the total *redditus assisus*. It is therefore impossible to determine the composition of the rents of assize, or the reasons for the thirteenth-century increases, without close examination of a large number of rolls. The Battle Abbey manors[2] show assized rents which hardly vary by a penny during the fourteenth century: the same is true of some of the Merton College manors: while the manors of Ramsey Abbey vary in the most erratic fashion. At Wistow[3] the assized rents of 4s. 6d. are unchanged from 1297 to 1380, while at Elton and elsewhere they vary in a manner perfectly inexplicable, unless the variations are merely caused by differences of classification. Mr. Tawney has quoted from various sources a number of examples of these stationary rents of assize for periods previous to the sixteenth century.[4] There are none quite so striking as those of Winchester, but the moral to be drawn is the same.

---

is a clear distinction between *Terra Gavellata* and *Terra Budell* (? illegible). I have not found this term *Gavellata* in the earlier records. *Cf.* Eccles. Comm., Various, 155874/1.

[1] *Cf.* Liebermann, *Gesetze*, ii., s.v. *Pastung*.

[2] P.R.O. Ministers' Accounts, Crowmarsh, Bundle 958; Brightwaltham, Bundles 742 and 753; Appledram, Bundle 1016; Ansty, Bundle 978/3.

[3] P.R.O., Bundles 879, 882, 877. I owe these references to Mrs. C. B. Buckland's kindness.

[4] Tawney, *Agrarian Revolt in the Sixteenth Century*, 115-117.

If the rents represented commutation of services, they would not be stationary in the fourteenth and fifteenth centuries. Moreover, on the Winchester estates the actual commutations are entered, either in a special entry *venditio operum*, some items of which are unchanged for at least a century, or they may be hidden away under the heading " Issues of the Manor," together with sales of timber, or eels, or refuse wool. The same arrangement is found elsewhere: the accounts for Woolstone, Berks,[1] clearly state: " exits of the manor, with commuted services "; West Wittenham[2] enters commuted services under the heading *capitagium*, an arrangement I have found nowhere else. Obviously, therefore, the burden of proof lies with those who would contend that rents of assize represent labour services: in individual cases they may be able to prove the point, but the great bulk of evidence tells in the other direction.

We return, then, to the question of the relationship, if any, between *gabulum* and assized rents and labour services. It is not easy to discover the total obligation of a virgater on a Winchester manor, since there are no extents available; it is not easy to ascertain whether the same individual both paid *gabulum* and rendered services for the land. Evidently a man who held office as shepherd or other manorial servant had 5s. per virgate remitted to him: this may have been his whole rent of assize. More definite evidence is forthcoming from adjacent manors belonging to the Priory of St. Swithin's. In a rental of the manor of Crondall,[3] dated 1287, we find that the first cottar tenant named pays as much as 8s. *gabulum* for a holding of 15 acres, while performing a tolerably full complement of services—week-work. harvest-works, and carrying services—and rendering at least some dues in kind—for example, cocks and hens as church scot. Smaller tenants—for instance, of 10 acres—paid exactly the same, and performed the same services, with very slight variations in the dues in kind, while the holder of a full virgate (24 acres) pays annually 2s. 9d. as *gabulum*, and performs specific services (no week-work) to the extent of about one day in the week, at irregular times. Another virgate estimated at 39 acres pays 5s. *gabulum*, and one of 34 acres pays only 2s. 9d. This high rate of 8s. for the cottar is the more remarkable since in many districts, notably in the Thames Valley near Oxford,[4] the whole works of a virgate were commuted at 7s. per annum, or occasionally 10s. Hence 8s. from a *cotagium* of 15 or 16 acres, in addition to full services, seems to be an unusually heavy money obligation. It is noteworthy that a hide of 106 acres only pays

---

[1] P.R.O. Ministers' Accounts, Bundle 756/1, etc.   [2] *Ibid.*, Bundle 756/2.
[3] *Crondall Records* (Hampshire Record Society), 84 *seq.*
[4] Eynsham Cartulary, ed. Salter: Oxford Hist. Soc., 1908.

12s. 8d., while half a hide (39 acres) pays 2s. 6d.: another hide pays
20s. The word "hide" is used indiscriminately for free and villein
tenements. The only conclusion to be drawn is that the assessment
of *gabulum* depended upon status rather than acreage, and that the
wealthier members of the manors enjoyed a very "beneficent" assessment. It is not easy to establish a connection between the *gabulum*
of 1208 or of 1287 and the pre-Conquest *gafol*. Speaking generally,
however, it may be asserted that the Winchester manors rendered
very few dues in kind, compared with the long, strange lists discover-
able elsewhere, notably on the Ramsey estates.[1] Nor were the Bishop's
tenants burdened with the petty personal services characteristic of
Ramsey, and perhaps of most monastic estates. A few odd pounds of
cumin, or of pepper, or a red rose, or a bunch of arrows, or horse-
shoes or ploughshares are found here and there, but very infrequently.
They represent, probably, an irregular survival of freeholders' symbolic
dues, rather than a genuine render in kind. It seems reasonable,
therefore, to suppose that in Hampshire at least *gafol* represented
an early commutation of dues in kind, probably dating back long
before the Norman Conquest. These dues must have constituted a
substantial burden, and, as has been shown, the burden would seem
to have been personal instead of, or as well as, territorial in its basis.

A point which may be worth noticing is that the Winchester assized
rents were normally paid at the four quarter days, in equal sums—
a fact which probably points to a single definite commutation at a
fixed date. This, however, is not quite an unvarying custom. At
Havant,[2] as late as 1530, the assized rents were payable on twelve
festivals throughout the year, in irregular sums. The newer rents, on
all the manors, in the fifteenth and sixteenth centuries, are entered
separately under various names, and payable once, twice or four times
a year at regular dates. Elsewhere we may find the greatest irregularity. On the St. Swithin's Priory estates[3] the assized rents are
paid at various dates—eight or ten festivals scattered through the
year. The sums payable at each, of which hardly two are alike, vary
from £4 17s. 4d. down to 8s. Again, at Wye[4] in Kent, where there
is an almost complete absence of labour services, the rents are paid
at twelve different festivals, nearly but not quite regularly one in
each month—surely an ancient assessment This irregularity evidently
suggests that a considerable proportion of the rents must represent
commutations of the eggs and hens at Easter, or the Christmas cake,

---

[1] Neilson, *Economic Conditions of the Manors of Ramsey Abbey.*
[2] Eccles. Comm. Various, 155874/1.
[3] *The Manor of Manydown* (Hampshire Record Society), 143.
[4] P.R.O. Ministers' Accounts, 899/1.

or the yule-log, or the young and able lamb at St. John's tide. More-over, in many cases it is expressly stated that certain old customary rents have been included under the heading " assized rents." At Crondall are included ploughshares, pond-penny and sheriff's aid.[1] At Bray (Battle Abbey) the rents include free rents, villein rents, increments, ploughshares, horseshoes, red silver, pond-penny, church-scot, corn, salt, *auxilium* and ward-silver.[2] At Cookham (Battle Abbey) the list is similar—free rents, villein rents, ploughshares, horse-shoes, pond-penny, *auxilium*, merssgavel, mircre, fifpenny, eels, cocks and hens.[3] At Cheddington (Merton College) rents of assize include cocks and hens, pepper, hidage, *secta, veteri placiti* (?) and tithing-penny.[4] At Ansty, in Hampshire (Battle Abbey), on the other hand, in 1401, assized rents only cover free rents, villein rents and new rents[5]—the latter a very unusual item to be merged in the assized rents. Abbots Langley (St. Albans Abbey) numbers among its rents not only sheriff's aid, cocks and hens, and some commuted labour services, but also a yearly $2\frac{1}{4}$d. *pro pane benedicto*—apparently a parochial obligation converted into a rent.[6] In only one case known to me does it seem clear that rents of assize consisted in large measure of commuted services, or new rents. On the manor of Wellow, Somerset, the assized rents rise from £4 to £17, between 1342 and 1365. The most rapid rise is between 1348 and 1352, when large numbers of leases are granted. The exception strengthens the plea for close scrutiny or caution.[7]

As regards freeholders' rents it is almost impossible, in early accounts, to differentiate them from the rents of villeins. By the early fifteenth century they are often, but not invariably, distinguished. The proportion of freeholders to villeins varied in different districts, and constitutes another element of uncertainty. Mr. Ballard believed that a large proportion of the assized rents usually consisted of free-holders' rents.[8] It is just possible that some lines of distinction in the composition of assized rents as between different types of owners might emerge if investigation could be carried far enough. Even in a cursory study of two or three of the older Benedictine monasteries, some points of general interest arise. Ramsey Abbey, and, in lesser degree, St. Albans Abbey, were remarkable for an immense variety of rents, which are clearly commutations either of dues in kind or of

[1] *Crondall Records* (Hampshire Record Society), 51.
[2] P.R.O. Ministers' Accounts, Bundles 742/5 and 13.   [3] *Ibid.*, Bundle 742/6.
[4] Merton College Archives, Court Rolls, 5576.
[5] P.R.O. Ministers' Accounts, 978/3.
[6] Sidney Sussex College, Cambridge. Library, Δ i. 1.
[7] In a model account-roll (Cambridge University Library, Ee i. 1, f. 231b) "forensic rents " is glossed as assized rents, *tam de bondis quam de cotariis.*
[8] From a private letter.

trifling miscellaneous services—not the normal labour by which the agriculture of the manor was maintained, but the petty services exacted by a resident lord and a soulless corporation. An abbot, and perhaps especially a Benedictine abbot of one of the older foundations, was particularly likely to maintain the memory of these archaic personal services and marks of servitude. Hence perhaps the prominence of these older houses in the risings of the fourteenth century. Battle Abbey, on the other hand, with its scattered estates, granted after the Conquest, and often in districts where the orthodox three-field system was not customary, was obliged to evolve new methods. The rents of assize on these manors are even more stationary than elsewhere. Brightwaltham[1] on the Berkshire Downs has rents which only vary by 1s. 2d. in fifty years: at Crowmarsh[2] (Oxon) the rents of assize are absolutely stationary between 1323 and 1392, save that in the latter year a rise of about 7s. has taken place. At Hutton[3] (Essex) the rents increase by less than £1 between 1341 and 1367, and the increase is clearly not due to commutation. The point of interest on most of the Battle Abbey manors lies in the *stipendia*, or wages paid to regular and permanent manorial servants; the system was evidently developed very early on the Battle manors. Appledram[4] in Sussex, chiefly engaged in corn-growing, had twenty-three regular servants as early as 1286, and paid for all harvest labour at 2d. per day. But the development of this wage-system, as has been shown, leaves no trace upon the assized rents.[5]

Almost every worker on manorial history could provide innumerable examples of the varying relationship between rents and services; but it is worth while to emphasize the fact that students of documents, or compilers of statistics, in which the term " rents of assize " is used, are dealing with a double ambiguity. In the precise account-keeping of a manor it is often impossible to analyze the exact meaning of *redditus assisus*, and historians have hardly attempted the task. On the other hand, in general statements such as extents or *inquisitiones post mortem*, it is always possible that the figures given bear the same relation to the actual revenues as an income tax return bears to income received, or an assessment for rates to the actual yearly value of a property. In either case the only sound motto is *caveat eclor*. In all the history of land problems there is no sin like the sin of generalization. Wherever the two types of records—the official

---

[1] P.R.O. Ministers' Accounts, Bundles 742 and 753.

[2] *Ibid.*, Bundle 958.

[3] *Ibid.*, Bundles 844/22-28. *Cf.* K. G. Feiling in *English Historical Review*, April, 1911.　　　　　　　　　　　[4] *Ibid.*, Bundle 1016.

[5] I have not examined in detail the account-rolls of any great Cistercian house; a set of these ought to provide some very interesting comparisons.

statement and the private book-keeping—disagree, the balance of probability always lies with the private accounts, though the latter unfortunately are the least likely to have survived.

Another technical point in the scrutiny of account rolls is the presentation of the balance at the end of the roll. In collecting statistics to cover a long period, there is always a tendency merely to accept the balance as stated without further scrutiny. There are at least two different methods of presenting the account which may easily be confused, and in that case will produce very misleading results. The two crucial entries are " forensic expenses " and *Liberatio denariorum*. In some accounts " forensic expenses " cover only what one might expect—sums of money allotted here and there for special purposes, as the lord of the manor might direct. They normally have no connection with the economic working of the estate, and ought to be included in profits. For example, on the Winchester manors this heading may cover sums sent from one manor to another, to pay part of the cost of special building operations; or it may cover the expenses of some of the Bishop's household, over and above the normal charges. The *Liberatio denariorum* covers the whole of the cash actually paid direct into the Bishop's treasury. Normally, it appears true to say that on the Winchester accounts the " forensic expenses " are unimportant, and the *Liberatio* represents, with reasonable accuracy, the year's profits. It ought, of course, always to be scrutinized in connection with the arrears, which are occasionally very large, and throw our statistics into confusion. Many estates, among which may be noted Merton College, had a peculiarly confusing system. The " forensic expenses " might contain considerable sums of money paid direct to the warden or the lord, while the *Liberatio denariorum*, which represents the main profits of the year, is added to the general " expenses," and this combined *Liberatio et expensa*, under the title of *Summa omnium expensarum*, is deducted from the receipts, leaving a small but entirely misleading net balance of two or three pounds, occasionally rising to £10 or £12. Thus to arrive at the actual profit on a manor we must add the *Liberatio* to the spurious net balance (*et debet*), and probably part of the " forensic expenses " as well.

To contrast the two methods in tabular form may make the difference clearer.

MERTON COLLEGE.

	£
Receipts	70
Expenses	32
[Forensic Expenses]:	
Liberatio	35
Expensa et Liberationes	67 Profits = £35 + 3.
(or Summa Expensarum)	
Et debet	3

WINCHESTER PIPE ROLL.

					£	s.	d.	
Summa totius receptæ	..	..	..	..	61	7	3¾	
,, ,, expensæ	..	..	..	..	12	19	10¼	
Et sic debet	..	..	..	..	48	7	5½	=Profits.
In liberatione domino	..	..	..	..	23	0	0	
Et sic debet de claro	..	..	..	..	25	7	5½	

The meaning of the second account is absolutely clear, the profits stand out, self-evident, without further analysis. The Winchester pipe roll, however, only reached this clarity after a slow process of change and experiment. In 1213 and in 1235, and apparently up to 1264, the form ran thus:

					£	s.	d.
Summa totius receptæ	..	.	..	..	..	87	6	0¾
,, ,, expensæ	..	..	..	..	..	6	17	0
,, ,, liberationis	..	..	..	..	..	78	4	3¾
,, exp' et lib'	..	..	.	..	..	..	85	1	3¾
Et debet..	..	..	..	..	..	..	2	4	9

This method is at least clearer than the Merton system, since the " expenses " are given separately, and a simple calculation will supply the actual profit; between 1264 and 1283, however, the change is made to the form of statement first quoted, which permits the investigator to ignore all the complications of the " delivery " into the Treasury. Confusion is not very likely when the united items are described as *Expensa et Liberationes*, but when they are disguised under the title *Summa omnium expensarum*, a mistake is extremely easy. The worker on account-rolls will be wise to give careful attention to this point, if he hopes to compile sound statistics.

It would be unwise to assert, categorically, that Thorold Rogers was misled by this method of accounting followed by Merton College; indeed, in one case he clearly allows for it; but at least some of his statements as to the fall or disappearance of profits after 1349 would seem to have been coloured by it—if one may assume, as I think is not unjust, that he examined in detail only two or three of the long and consecutive series of Merton accounts.[1] For example, at Ibstone the *Liberatio*, which had stood at £9, or £5 before the Black Death, ran down to £2 in 1347–48, and up to £10 in 1348–49; at Cheddington the *Liberatio* of £10 rises in 1348–49 to £18, and falls afterwards to £2 and £4, but by 1357 and in later years it is up again to £6, £14, £10, and £12. This does not suggest the greatly decreased profits and very narrow margin of which Rogers speaks. If, however, he had accidentally followed what we have called the " spurious net balance," his pessimistic conclusions could readily be explained. The following diagrams have put the two methods into the form of graphs—rather for the sake

[1] Not only do his quotations suggest this very limited use of the records, but quite recently the bursar's clerk at Merton was able to point out the exact rolls used by Rogers.

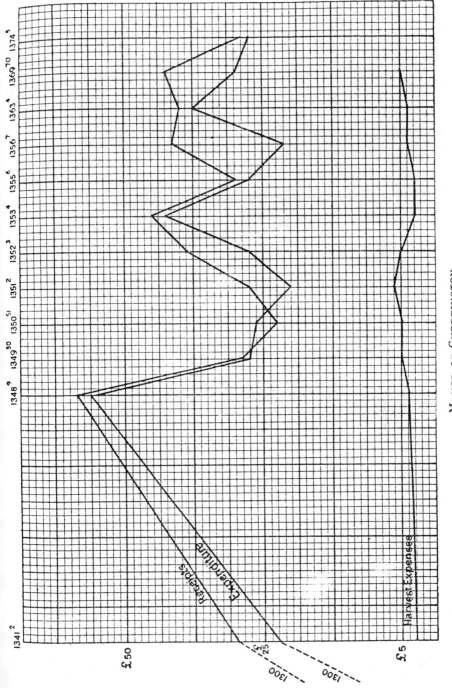

Manor of Cheddington.
To Merton College.
(Note: *Liberatio* is included with "Expenses.")

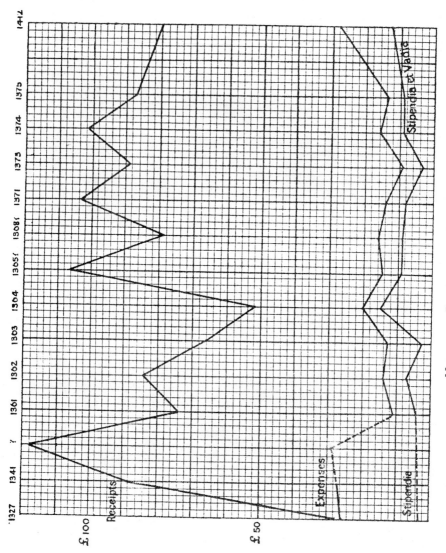

MANOR OF LULLINGTON, SUSSEX.
To Battle Abbey.

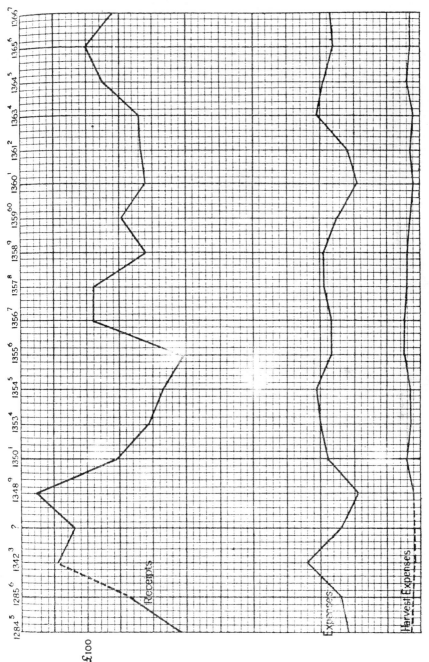

MANOR OF APPLEDRAM, SUSSEX.
To Battle Abbey.

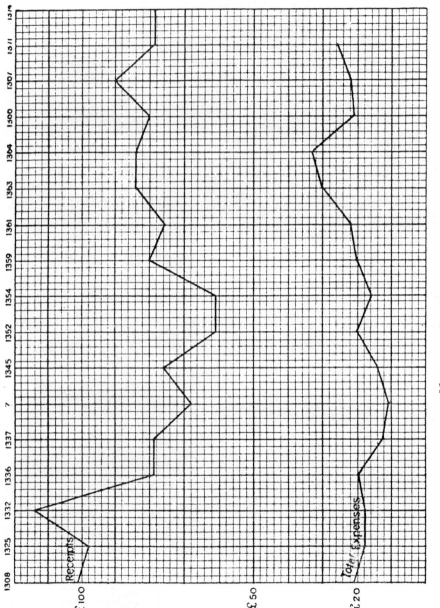

MANOR OF WOOLSTON, BERKS.
To the Priory of St. Swithin, Winchester.

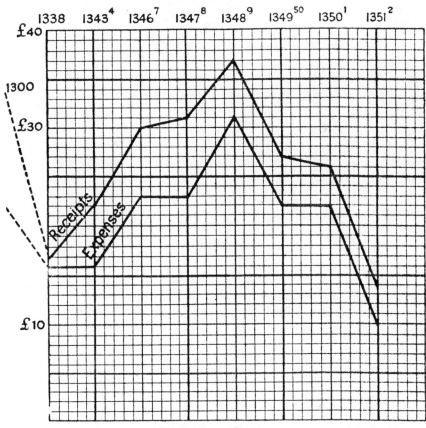

M A N O R   O F   I B S T O N E.
To Merton College.

of indicating the relationship between receipts and expenses than to labour unduly the question of the Merton system. They provide an ocular demonstration of the stability of profits on some manors, while the close correspondence between the expenses and the receipts on the diagram for Cheddington would suggest the need for some explanation, even if the details of the account were not forthcoming. Several of the Battle Abbey manors, from whose accounts two of these graphs were drawn,[1] possessed a highly developed wage system from an early date; they represent very different geographical districts, yet all those which have been examined show a margin of profit so large that the doubling or trebling of harvest expenses would hardly have touched the owners, and if the total expenses of all kinds had been doubled, a profit would have been left. The same is even more true of the Winchester manors: Crawley, one of an average group with receipts under £100, could have seen its expenses doubled

---

[1] And several others which it is impossible to reproduce here.

in each year between 1346 and 1353 without losing its whole balance; in 1351 and 1353 expenses might safely have been multiplied by three. On this manor seigneurial dues played a very small part in producing a profit; the balance is purely agricultural. On most of the Winchester manors, however, the seigneurial payments are a very important item, ranging from £20 to £100 and sometimes more. On the Battle Abbey and the Merton College estates the seigneurial payments through the courts are almost negligible; they rarely rose above £1 or £2, and might sink to 1s., and obviously did not pay the expenses of the seneschal's visit. The St. Albans Abbey courts, though so carefully held, could only have produced comparatively small sums. It is evident that we have here an interesting line of differentiation, which may supply one of the many reasons for the disastrous decay of the courts in the fifteenth century.

Apart from technical points, indeed, one of the most striking differences between the accounts of various groups of manors is the wide divergence in the average incomes to be expected. Obviously the size of the manor, as well as its fertility and prosperity, would be an important factor. But the cleavage seems to go deeper and to suggest very real differences of burdens, of method and of success. Apparently none of the St. Albans Abbey manors within the " liberty " produced as much as £30 per annum, while the greater number of them produced less than £20; the total revenue of the abbot from within the " liberty " is calculated at £315, while the revenues of all the Obedientiaries amounted to £324; property outside the "liberty " accounts for £163 more. This sum of something under £900 includes some "farms" and "pittances" to the various Obedientiaries, and the revenues due from many churches. These figures are drawn from an elaborate statement in the St. Albans Formulary Book,[1] and they are somewhat unsafe, in that no date is assigned to them. However, the Formulary Book was compiled in and after 1382 (apparently in a moment of panic after the wholesale burnings of 1381), and it would seem safe to assume that the calculations belong to the second half of the fourteenth century. Since this account includes all the profits of the courts, and we know how very strictly and regularly the courts were kept, it is obvious that the dues exacted must have been comparatively low. St. Albans, of course, ranked as a rich abbey, but evidently its wealth did not depend only upon its estates. A hasty comparison with the revenues of the Bishop of Winchester suggests a very sharp difference. The manorial revenues alone of the bishop, as recorded in his pipe roll, reached the sum of £2,730 as early as 1209. By the middle of the fourteenth century

---

[1] Cambridge University Library, Ee iv. 20, f. 215a.

five manors together would produce over £1,000 profits, without including Taunton, which showed a net balance of £700. The total receipts in 1316 were between £5,000 and £6,000.[1] Only the Hampshire and Somerset manors show such large figures. The average receipts would seem to have been well over £70, while only a small minority sink below £30. The contrast is remarkable and helps to form something like a standard of comparison. That is, any two of the six wealthiest of the Winchester manors would have equalled the whole manorial revenue of the abbot of St. Albans, while the remaining four of these six would have more than balanced the revenues of the Obedientiaries. Some such scale of payments and values must be borne in mind whenever a landlord is to be summed up as lenient or oppressive. Turning again to the Merton manors, we find that Ibstone, one of those most frequently quoted by Thorold Rogers, has total receipts ranging from £17 up to £31 and down again to £14, between 1338 and 1352. The serious cause of variation is always the sale of corn. At Cheddington, between 1341 and 1375, the receipts vary between £29 and £41; at Cuxham the limits would seem to be £50 and £26, while Gamlingay, which shows sharper variations, from £15 to £75, has its accounts complicated by heavy rectorial tithe. The perquisites of the court at Ibstone dropped to 1s. 1d., or 3d., both before and after the Black Death; Cheddington has 6d. before the pestilence and 3d. after, with 4s. as a maximum. Hence it is not surprising to find that in 1375 no courts were held. Comparing again with Winchester, we find that the profits of the court of one of the bishop's manors in 1208 would equal the total receipts of several of the Merton manors in 1340 or 1380. Hence it is at least clear that the evidence from the Merton manors is purely economic and agricultural; no question of the emoluments of justice is involved. No satisfactory reason can be suggested for the very marked differences in the seigneurial dues: it is not entirely a matter of geography, as the Merton estates are in some cases reasonably near to the outlying Winchester manors, as are also some of the Battle Abbey manors. The generalization may be hazarded that, wherever a group of estates had been consolidated at an early period, perhaps a pre-Conquest period, the courts tended to be better and more strictly organized, and the dues heavier and the profits larger. This may be an entirely fallacious argument, but at least a consideration of the Winchester, St. Albans, and Ramsey estates, over against those of Battle Abbey and Merton College, would seem to lend it some probability.[2]

[1] The bishopric was valued in 1293 for Pope Nicholas' Taxation at £2,977, and in 1535 at £5,885.

[2] Colleges, of course, started late in the acquisition of estates, as compared with bishoprics and abbeys, and they had few, if any, special officials for the

The great disadvantage of working in such voluminous material as account-rolls is that even the most careful of historians lays himself open to contradiction by almost any other worker in parallel fields. Contrary results can always be obtained by a deliberate or even by an accidental choice. It is well, therefore, to remember that in some cases the original cause of difference will be personal, not economic. Even the account-rolls may show indirect results of temperament. The contrasted economic types, which remain even to this day to complicate most social problems, are remarkably well illustrated by a little-known fourteenth-century poem entitled *A good short Debate between Winner and Waster*.[1] Its vivid dialogue may perhaps provide the clue for reconciling many of the divergent conclusions reached by more prosaic writers of economic history.

A. E. LEVETT.

---

maintenance of manorial economy. Their estates were scattered over many counties, and they had little, if any, connection with local justice.

[1] Edited by Sir Israel Gollancz (1920). Its date lies between September, 1352, and March, 1353.

EARLY ACHIEVEMENTS

SOMBART'S PROPOSITIONS REVISITED

Kenneth S. Most

Sombart's Propositions Revisited

Kenneth S. Most

Accounting scholars have given little attention to the hypothesis that accounting is first and foremost a conceptual framework used for planning economic activities, and that its function as a control instrument is a derived one. A similar proposition, or set of propositions, was formulated by Sombart, whose erudition in this field has not been challenged.[1] We shall outline Sombart's position and Yamey's criticisms of it, and show how we differ from both Sombart and Yamey in our interpretation of the evidence which they adduce, and on which we also rely in great measure. Brief comments on accounting contained in the earlier work of Sombart were subsequently expanded and more fully documented by Sombart in a work which does not appear to have received translation into English.[2]

SOMBART AND THE RISE OF CAPITALISM

The Origins of Capitalism

Sombart attempts to trace several causal factors which led eventually to the emergence of a capitalist civilization. He defines capitalism thus:

By "capitalism" we mean a particular economic system, recognizable as an organization of trade, consisting invariably of two collaborating sections of population, the owners of the means of production, who also manage them, and propertyless workers, bound to the markets which they serve; which displays the two dominant principles of wealth creation and economic rationalism.[3]

The essential features are the profit motive and rationality; an exchange economy, in which the material requirements of several trades are satisfied by free exchanges of equivalent goods or money, may be either artisanal or capitalistic.[4]

Sombart takes as his point of departure a precapitalistic feudal society in early medieval Europe when a sufficiency for existence was the goal of every man. He then poses the question: by what means was society transformed into a different one, in which the profit motive replaced the satisfaction of basic wants as man's main driving force?

The spirit of enterprise manifests itself in personalities like the "freebooter," the "speculator" and the "projector" who rely on robbery of economic surpluses created by others to form the capital necessary for their undertakings. Such men can be found throughout history, but the qualities of the bourgeois capitalist are not so common; they include an organizing ability, a facility for rapid calculation, and the art of

[1] Werner Sombart, *Der Bourgeois* (Munich and Leipzig: Duncker & Humblot, 1913), transl., by M. Epstein as *The Quintessence of Capitalism* (E. P. Dutton & Co., 1915).

[2] Werner Sombart, *Der Moderne Kapitalismus* (Munich and Leipzig: Duncker & Humblot, 1919). Because of the significance of the relevant passages of this work for the ideas developed in this paper, a fairly complete translation of Sombart's comments on accounting and the growth of scientific business management has been prepared by this author, a copy of which will be sent to any interested scholar on request.

[3] *Ibid.*, Vol. I, 1, p. 319 (our transl.).

[4] *Ibid.*, pp. 92–93.

Kenneth S. Most is Professor and Head of the Department of Accounting at Texas A & M University.

planning outlays.[5] What turns the crafts-
man into a manufacturer? In two words,
he must be able to calculate and to save.[6]
Sombart sees the transition as a function of
mental or spiritual changes which resulted
in man ceasing to see himself as the center
of his universe, and replacing himself with
the institutions and material objects of a
capitalistic society. This change in attitudes was dependent upon, if not actually
caused by, the mensuration process.

Thought in economic activities, then becomes
more definite and conscious, in other words, more

individual economic actions, and leads a
life of its own extending beyond the lives
of the persons concerned."[8]

Such entities had existed previously, but
always tied to a named group of partners,
family or villagers. The new concept of
"the business" effectively separated the
economic relations from the persons; property rights were depersonalized, permitting
"it" to pursue profit without regard to any
other goals.

Three causal factors contributed to the
independence of the capitalistic enterprise:

1. The law
2. Business management techniques } leading { "Firma" (the firm)
3. The market   to   { "Ratio" (the account)
                                              "Ditta" (credit)

rational, and modern technical science has
tended to make it so. But it has also helped to
make it more exact and punctual, by providing
the necessary machinery for measuring time.

Clocks have played a very important part in
the mental history of the business man. Pendu-
lum clocks are said to have been invented in the
10th century, while the first clock worked by
wheels was that made by Heinrich von Wick, in
Paris in 1364, for King Charles V. . . . Now, the
exact measurement of time became possible only
when the necessary instruments were available,
just as the exact calculations in terms of money
became possible only when technical progress
was able to provide a reliable currency.[7]

The two elements are combined suc-
cinctly in Benjamin Franklin's dictum:
time is money.

The ability to calculate can create
wealth when combined with the requisite
institution: The capitalistic enterprise. In
Der Moderne Kapitalismus, Sombart describes the special features of this institution: ". . . the complete independence of
the business; raising an independent economic organization above the individual
economic men involved in it; the combination of all concurrent and successive business operations into a conceptual entity
which then appears as the performer of the

That is to say, the business could be
viewed as a legal entity, an accounting
entity and a credit entity. We are concerned here with the business as accounting entity.

The Business as Accounting Entity[9]

The invention of accounting was vital
to the development of the capitalistic
enterprise. In particular, double-entry
bookkeeping permitted the full representa-
tion of the flow of capital through a business: ". . . from the capital account to the
transaction accounts through the profit
and loss account and back into the capital
account."

This facilitated concentration on the
idea of creating wealth; the "wealth producing sum," or amount invested for the
purpose of obtaining profits, was separated
from all want-satisfaction objectives of the
persons involved. In double-entry book-

[5] Sombart, *Quintessence*, p. 102.
[6] *Ibid.*, pp. 201-202.
[7] *Ibid.*, p. 326.
[8] Sombart, *Der Moderne Kapitalismus*, Vol. II, 1,
Chapter X, p. 101 (our transl.).
[9] The following is a summary of the Sombartian
views on accounting referred to at the beginning of this
article.

keeping there was only one objective: the increase of a sum of money.

The concept of "capital" could only be formulated under these conditions; prior to double-entry bookkeeping there was no "capital;" thus, capital could be defined as the property of wealth represented in a double-entry system of accounts. Double-entry bookkeeping also led directly to the principle of economic rationality. Since the bookkeeper recognized no economic processes outside the books of account, and nothing could be recorded in these unless it was capable of expression in monetary terms, production and consumption could be reduced to calculation.

Economic rationality went hand in hand with planning and control, the accounting system permitted the analysis of business operations and the establishment of plans for their progressive and systematic improvement. In this way did the invention of double-entry bookkeeping create the necessary conditions for the essential principles of capitalism to develop. Further, it created the conceptual framework which was required in order to grasp the nature of a capitalistic economy, by means of concepts such as the classification of assets into fixed and circulating, the ascertainment of costs of production, and so on. The scientific equipment of economic theory, insofar as it related to capitalist economics, was taken from double-entry bookkeeping.[10]

Finally, since the separation of the business from its owners was a necessary feature of the capitalistic enterprise, systematic bookkeeping gave material aid to the creation of the capitalistic enterprise. The business replaced the entrepreneur; the firm, represented by its capital, appeared as an accounting entity and the person of the entrepreneur was clearly shown to be a separate entity, more like a creditor than an owner.

Sombart did not claim to produce evidence that this theoretical argument can be empirically verified; indeed, he complains on several occasions of the paucity of historical materials available to him. He did claim to be able to see the slow development of double-entry bookkeeping taking place side by side with the growth of juridical concepts of the firm as a separate entity, and that these changes coincided with what he termed "the period of early capitalism;" he also referred to parallel developments in a number of European countries as evidence of a tendency. Further, the rise of capitalism took place unevenly, so that artisanal and other pre-capitalistic features could be discerned in the business enterprises of the period. The organized and systematized business management which accounting made possible was perhaps an ideal type represented by only a few outstanding examples, while the majority of businesses remained rooted in traditional inefficiencies; nevertheless, he concluded with conviction that, starting in Italy in the fourteenth century, new principles of business management were adopted and their application depended upon accounting systems based on double-entry bookkeeping.

Yamey and the Sombart Propositions

Sombart's work has been assimilated into the mainstream of economic history and his view of the nature and origins of double-entry bookkeeping into accounting theory.[11] However, in two papers published at an interval of fourteen years, Yamey has expressed criticism of what he calls "the Sombart propositions" relating to the connection between double-entry bookkeeping and the rise of capitalism.[12]

[10] Echoing Proud'hon: "La comptabilité est toute l'économie politique et le comptable le véritable économiste à qui une coterie de faux litterateurs à volé son nom."

[11] See W. W. Cooper, "Social Accounting: An Invitation to the Accounting Profession," THE ACCOUNTING REVIEW (July 1949), p. 233.

[12] B. S. Yamey, "Scientific Bookkeeping and the Rise of Capitalism," Economic History Review, second series, Vol. I (1949), pp. 99–113, repr. W. T. Baxter, ed.,

In the first of these papers, Yamey denies that the management objectives identified by Sombart—clarity of contractual relationships and economy of expenditures—can be pursued only through double-entry bookkeeping; he suggests that single-entry will do as well. As to the origins of the former, while he harbors some confidence in the assertion that double-entry bookkeeping had its origins in medieval Italy, he says: "But in the nature of things we are on less sure ground when trying to explain the process whereby earlier collections of incomplete and unorganized commercial accounting records become transformed into a systematized and simple yet elegant arrangement of interlocking accounts."

He puts forward four possible hypotheses: (1) the single inventor, (2) the spirit of the Renaissance, (3) the result of chance or accidental influence, and (4) the necessary outcome of a purposive evolution.

Yamey is unwilling to subscribe to any of these; while he is prepared to see some utility in accounts, he finds that evidence of *how* they were used is missing. In his view, "narrow" bookkeeping purposes predominated, involving comprehensive and orderly records of past transactions, and checks on accuracy and completeness. Financial statements of profit and loss or of capital, assets and liabilities were relatively unimportant.

In the second paper Yamey addresses himself again to the refutation of the Sombart propositions that bookkeeping aided the rise of capitalism and that double-entry bookkeeping made possible the separation of the business from its owners. He examines ". . . the simple question provoked by the thesis, namely, the contribution of double-entry accounting to the solution of problems in business organization and administration." He would show that the contribution was small, and "not made by those features of the system or in solving those business

problems particularly emphasized by Sombart . . . I also suggest, incidentally, that in the context of the solution of business problems, double-entry bookkeeping was not greatly superior to less elaborate methods of accounting."

Yamey expresses the strange view (strange, that is, for an economist) that abstraction may lead to less successful decision-making, since the decision-maker " . . . would have had to view the complexities and detail of reality through the drastically simplifying and possibly distorting screen of his accounts." He finds little or no evidence that accounts were used in the decision processes of seventeenth and eighteenth century entrepreneurs whose books of account he has examined, and, indeed, would be surprised to find any, since "steps in the dark" lie at the heart of capitalistic entrepreneurship. "Thus, when the businessman expresses himself most emphatically as entrepreneur he is necessarily without benefit of accounting records pertaining to past events and experiences." "Insofar as the early centuries of capitalism can be described as a period of dynamic change from a static base—itself a dangerous simplification—one would have to discount heavily the contribution made by systematic accounting or accounting calculation."

He also draws upon the evidence provided by the accounts of partnerships and joint stock companies to show that the business could be, and was, treated as distinct from its proprietors even in the absence of a double-entry bookkeeping system complete with capital and profit and loss accounts.

Yamey commences his paper with the statement that "Sombart's work gave prominence and prestige to the humble art of accounting by ascribing to it wide eco-

---

Studies in Accounting (London: Sweet and Maxwell, 1950), pp. 13–30; and B. S. Yamey, "Accounting and the Rise of Capitalism: Further Notes on a Theme by Sombart," *Journal of Accounting Research* (Autumn 1964), pp. 117–36.

nomic significance." He concludes that "In the achievement of other aspects of successful enterprise . . . accounting records and accounting systems have only a humble, but nevertheless interesting, contribution to make."

In taking a position on these arguments we shall concentrate on the later paper. It will be apparent that we agree generally with Yamey's criticism of the Sombart propositions, particularly insofar as we see no special significance in double-entry bookkeeping other than that it permits accounting functions to be performed efficiently.

It is undoubtedly true that the mechanics of double-entry bookkeeping cannot be observed before the fourteenth century, but we may remark that, when observed, the system is so well formed that it is unlikely to have been a new invention. The accounts of Pope Nicholas for the year 1279–80 and the expenditure book of Florence for the year 1303 are fairly complex examples of simple bookkeeping, but the books of the City of Genoa for 1340 display a double-entry structure which must have been long in the making. In this respect we tend to agree with Sombart that the method must have been ". . . well established for a long time."[13]

Nevertheless, Yamey's claim that single-entry will do as much reveals that he has overlooked Sombart's remark, admittedly expressed in a bibliographical note, that Pacioli's double-entry did not grow out of single-entry bookkeeping, the latter being a "crippled" version of the former, and of later date.[14] Business accounts of the early Middle Ages were quite different in form; Sombart calls them "sparse and confused" collections of notes.

This point acquires some significance in relation to the arguments of the second paper. They begin with this statement:

. . . knowledge of the *total* profit of an enterprise for a period, either absolutely or in relation to the amount of capital in the enterprise, is rarely necessary or useful for business decision-making within that enterprise. In a continuing enterprise, knowledge of the total or aggregated profitability or rate of return on capital is not relevant to current decisions which are concerned with changes in the use of part of the resources at the firm's disposal; and these, in turn, are related to the expected profitability of the various separable activities constituting the firm's total activity and of other activities under consideration.[15]

There is obviously a valuation problem here. If the immediate past use of capital is a continuing alternative, the past rate of return constitutes the opportunity cost of capital and is a necessary element of a decision model. Generally speaking, one cannot change direction rationally without knowing where one happens to be, and the relevance for the future of the profit of past periods is a question of fact in each case. Perhaps the view of the entrepreneur as Janus is obscured by a tendency to read "year" for "period," a natural result of the preoccupation with financial journalism; a declining trend of weekly profits would certainly not be irrelevant to a baker or brewer.

We must agree with Yamey's statement (p. 120) that calculations of profit or of total capital can be made independently of a system of double-entry bookkeeping since "profit" and "capital" may be defined in such a way that it must be true. The proprietor of a "small business" (such as Marshall's locksmith employing thirty hands or a motel with twenty rooms) may be able to accumulate data under his hat, but the emergence of a hierarchical structure in a business automatically separates the entrepreneur from the source of his data and renders formal record-keeping obligatory. Double-entry bookkeeping, in out view, is simply an efficient and widely-accepted method of doing this, in both simple and complex business situations.

[13] Sombart, *Quintessence*, p. 128.
[14] Sombart, *Der Moderne Kapitalismus*, Vol. II, 1, p. 115.
[15] Yamey, "Further Notes," p. 119.

We must also consider the possibility that the single-entry bookkeeping systems referred to by Yamey were in fact truncated double-entry systems like the one popularized in the eighteenth century by the indefatigable Jones of Bristol. The use of aggregates is common to both single and double-entry bookkeeping, and it is not essential in the latter system for each individual entry to be made twice, once on each side of an account. The basic equation of double-entry bookkeeping, Assets = Liabilities + Proprietors' Capital, leaves to the individual accountant the task of determining how these aggregates are to be derived; the number of possible solutions to this problem is infinite. As long as a balance sheet and profit and loss account dovetail into one another through the profit (or loss) figure, the equation can be established. It is fairly common to find double-entry accounts which have not been formally completed by writing up a balance sheet and profit and loss account in the ledger, although the continental European tradition would see such a deficiency as more grave than it appears in the United States or in Britain. In such systems, these accounts can be seen as loose-leaf parts and are no different in kind from the loose-leaf sales account (composed of copies of the sales invoices) or the somewhat bizarre bits and pieces of an electronic data processing accounting routine. Yamey himself refers to the possibility that these incomplete, or single-entry, systems were completed in an informal manner, one less likely to leave traces than the bound books which contained the transaction accounts.

Further, Yamey admits that ". . . it is generally impossible to deduce from the records (or textbook discussions) precisely what was intended or achieved by the procedures in question."[16] We may therefore conclude that the way is still open to the acceptance of the Sombart hypothesis, that double-entry bookkeeping as-

sisted the rise of capitalism by providing the capitalist with a powerful instrument for the management of a business.[17]

The assertion that double-entry bookkeeping was not a necessary condition for the separation of finance from production, which occurred during this period of early capitalism, is also debatable. It will be appreciated that the only accounts affected by the ownership of a firm are those relating to capital and profit. The only way in which accounting could have aided the creation of independent enterprises, therefore, is by techniques of accounting for capital and profit. If such accounts were not made up, as Yamey suggests, then his assertion is obviously true. Again, where the enterprise was not separate from its proprietor, as in the cases he mentions, these accounts would not have been called upon to perform any special function.

Early forms of corporate enterprise were of a temporary or "joint venture" kind. Trading operations, consisting very often of voyages by land or on sea, were treated as separate cycles, and on their conclusion the assets of the venture were divided among the participants in proportion to their investments. The dividend liquidated the firm. Maintenance of capital and measurement of profit were of little significance to plural owners of this kind, although highly important to owners of banks and factories, as the accounts of the Medici, Datini, Fuggers and others demonstrate clearly.

With the growth of continuing businesses, however, such as the chartered companies in Britain, the problem of separate persons of owners and managers mani-

[16] Ibid., p. 126, fn. 17.
[17] Quoting Sombart, and also H. M. Robertson, "Cambridge Studies in Economic History," *Aspects of the Rise of Economic Individualism* (The University Press, 1939) (which appears to be a bowdlerized version of Sombart). Yamey's n. 25, p. 128 of "Further Notes" appears to confuse Sombart's planning hypothesis with the conceptually distinct hypothesis that accounting assisted businessmen to prepare decisions scientifically. See *Der Moderne Kapitalismus*, Vol. II, 1, p. 121.

fested itself. The maintenance of the firm's capital could no longer be the direct responsibility of the individual proprietor, and he came to rely more and more upon a balance sheet presentation to satisfy him on the condition of his investment. More important than this, however, and resulting from the fact of a changing body of shareholders, the profit and loss account begins to take on a different function from the one mentioned by Yamey, of reviewing overall business results (p. 119). It becomes necessary to ascertain "a" profit figure in order to treat equitably successive groups of shareholders. The profit of the firm is a jointly owned residue and must be apportioned between periods, a feature which underlies all problems of profit measurement.

The point Yamey makes is that some seventeenth and eighteenth century companies whose records have survived did not keep capital and profit and loss accounts, and therefore these accounts cannot have been necessary for the separation of the business from its owners. The evidence is inconclusive, however; on the other hand, it is hard to believe that the separation of the business from its owners could continue for any length of time without the latter requesting that accounts be rendered, and one of the matters on which they would wish to be informed would certainly be the state of their capital and the reason for any increase or decrease. The spectacle of a succession of British companies acts in the nineteenth century, each of which placed great importance on financial reporting and auditing, and the fact that this was done in order to protect financial investors in companies, is highly suggestive, to say the least.

It is only fair to point out that in his "Introduction" to *Studies in the History of Accounting*,[18] Yamey took some pains to emphasize that he was concerned only with criticizing the tendency to exaggerate

the economic significance of double-entry bookkeeping rather than accounting generally.

THE SOMBART HYPOTHESIS BROUGHT UP TO DATE

Sombart's Assumptions Criticized

Although we have failed to find much substance in Yamey's detailed criticisms of "the Sombart propositions," we do not accept Sombart's views as they stand, and some distance separates our thesis from his. It will be found, however, that this separation does not lead to conclusions which are diametrically opposed.

Sombart was undistinguished as a forecaster. Writing shortly before World War I he predicted an end to large-scale wars, a declining world population and the impending disappearance of capitalism. Besides a defective telescopic vision, however, he also displayed attenuated historical perspective, attributable in some measure to the paucity of source material then at his disposal. Another reason for his failure was methodological. In the preface to the second edition of his work on the rise of capitalism, he confessed to a tendency not always to distinguish clearly between the empirical and the theoretical, a trait which had been brought to his attention, in the friendliest manner, by Max Weber.

On the other hand, we cannot ignore his great contribution to the subject which is the field covered by this study. In the first place, Sombart was one of the first modern socio-economic theorists, attempting to weave together threads from several disciplines in order to create his tapestry of the origins of modern capitalism. Second, and with one exception which will be noted later, he carefully examined all the source materials then available to him, and did not hesitate to draw conclusions from

[18] A. C. Littleton and B. S. Yamey (eds.), *Studies in the History of Accounting* (Richard D. Irwin, Inc., 1956), pp. 1–13.

them even if these contradicted the conventional wisdom of his time. Third, the manner in which he integrated his knowledge of accounting into his socio-economic framework is far more sophisticated than any other attempt which has been made to combine accounting with economics for purposes of evaluation, and eventually, prediction. One can only speculate on the progress of social accounting if Fisher, Hicks or Stone had possessed a comparable grasp of accounting theory.

It is significant, however, that Sombart made no mention of Niebuhr's claim to have discovered, in the Vatican fragments of the oration *Pro Fonteio*, evidence that the Roman *quaestors* used double-entry bookkeeping, invention of which could not, therefore, be attributed to the Lombards.[19] This claim has been denied by other historians[20] but refutation had not been made when Sombart wrote. On the other hand, it is hard to believe that he, with his great erudition, was unaware of the contents of Niebuhr's German language masterpiece, particularly since it was nearly one hundred years old at the time he wrote *Der Moderne Kapitalismus*. The evidence would, of course, have been fatal to his thesis that double-entry bookkeeping was a creation of the period of early capitalism, although it might not have destroyed the validity of his wider propositions. Interestingly enough, de Ste. Croix in his lengthy treatise arguing against the view that double-entry bookkeeping was known to the Greeks or Romans, makes only one brief reference to *Pro Fonteio*, in another connection altogether.

How, then, do we differ from Sombart? Like him we have chosen a tribological[21] approach to our subject matter, but during the intervening sixty years his appeals for additional historical materials have been answered in large measure. Not only have accounting historians such as Melis, de Roover, Yamey and Mommen contributed

to our knowledge of this field, but also archaeologists (Woolley), antiquaries (de Ste. Croix, Elizabeth Grier), students of the administration of medieval manors (Hudson) and of Roman Law (Jolowicz, de Zulueta). We may also refer here to Schumpeter's important contribution of a theory of economic development[22] and to the many investigators of the history of scientific thought, who have taught us to be wary of the very idea of "invention." As a result of these researchers' efforts we can no longer see the rise of capitalism in the same historical light.

Mandeville, in his *Fable of the Bees, or Private Vices, Publick Benefits*,[23] pointed out that the prosperity of a nation depends upon the acquisitive efforts of its citizens, and ultimately on such immoral qualities as ambition and a desire for power and luxury. The social problem is, and always has been, to reconcile this with justice, charity and equality. The Roman triumvirate of Pompey, Crassus and Caesar, taking for themselves the spoils of the Mithradatic War, may be classed as speculators, or even as robbers, but the Roman colonists who settled Africa were as strongly motivated to create wealth and by economic rationality as any late medieval capitalist. The history of Carthage shows that, prior to its destruction, large-scale manufacture of furniture, beds, mattresses and pillows was undertaken for the Roman market, and problems of organization and management no doubt arose. Although we can never be certain, from the evidence

[19] B. G. Niebuhr, *History of Rome*, trans. by Charles Hare and Connop Thirlwall (Thomas Wardle, 1835), Vol. II, p. 448, n. 19.
[20] The principal reference is G. E. M. de Ste. Croix, "Greek and Roman Accounting," in *Studies in the History of Accounting*, pp. 14–74.
[21] Tribology is the technology of interacting surfaces. The term "interface" in cybernetics has a related meaning.
[22] J. A. Schumpeter, *The Theory of Economic Development* (Oxford University Press, 1961) (first German ed. 1911).
[23] John Mandeville, *Fable of the Bees, or Private Vices, Publick Benefits* (Oxford, 1924).

now available to us it would appear that the capitalist-entrepreneur has been known at all periods of human history. Those socioeconomic studies (Huberman's *Man's Worldly Goods*[24] is another example) which start with the concept of a medieval pre-capitalistic society, ignore the fact that there were earlier periods when a "sufficiency for existence" was not the goal of every man, ages when the dominant sectors of society pursued the aim of increased wealth through production and distribution by means of trade, rather than through robbery and speculation.

Nor can we accept Sombart's psychological assumption that man occupied the central place in human thought in pre-capitalist times, but was ousted by institutions and material things in the period of early capitalism. It was in this latter period, after all, that Pope wrote: "An honest man's the noblest work of God"[25] and echoed Charron's dictum: "The proper Science and Subject for Man's Contemplation is *Man* himself."[26] Although Maine's view of history as a movement from status to contract no longer seems irreversible,[27] the statement still rings true of the period under consideration, and it was not until the twentieth century that Sweeney replaced Samson *agonistes*.

The humanitarian social initiatives of the nineteenth century would have been unthinkable in the eleventh or twelfth, but we are not on that account entitled to conclude that people then were somehow different, emotionally or psychologically. We must assume from the great mass of historical evidence that, in respect of all relevant characteristics, human beings have not changed during the past thousand years.

The spirit of undertaking, Sombart points out, combines the qualities of the conqueror, the organizer and the trader: ". . . he must by peaceful means influence masses of people whom he does not know

so to shape their conduct that he will derive benefits from it."[28] Sombart connects the freebooter with the birth of capitalism, but the freebooter was primarily a species of robber, not one who operates by peaceful means. Consider also Sombart's view of speculation as the noncalculatory approach to business, the attempt to participate in an "inherent and qualitative" manner in processes which are essentially quantitative and rational.[29] We rather see speculation at one extreme in the spectrum of calculatory activities, lying immediately beside games of chance, which are easily accommodated in the calculus of probabilities.

He quotes with approval Heine's words in *Englische Fragmente* "Were it possible for the Irish by a sudden *coup de main* to attain to the enjoyment of wealth they would seize upon it with alacrity. But ask them to get rich slowly by cultivating double-entry, sitting over miserable accounts until they are round-shouldered, and they cannot do it."[30] When the time came, however, the Irish chose the Sweepstakes, which is almost entirely carried out by "sitting over miserable accounts."

Finally, we reject Sombart's assumption that the concept of capital resulted solely from the abstraction of a process of wealth creation (profit), since it is clear that "capital" was ascertainable separately from market transactions involving the purchase or sale of a business, or a share in one. As we have already attempted to make clear, this rationalization of Som-

---

[24] Leo Huberman, *Man's Worldly Goods* (Monthly Review Press, 1952).
[25] Alexander Pope, *Essay on Man* (Yale, 1951), Ep. IV, 1.248.
[26] Pierre Charron, *of Wisdom* (Stanhope's translation, London: R. Bonwick and J. Tonson, 1707, Bk. I, Ch. I. See Pope, *Essay on Man*, Ep. I. 1.57.
[27] Sir Henry Maine, *Ancient Law* (E. P. Dutton and Co., 1917), p. 182.
[28] Sombart, *Quintessence*, pp. 52–54.
[29] *Ibid.*, p. 312.
[30] Heinrich Heine, *Englische Fragmente* (Hamburg: Hoffman and Campe, 1867), pp. 35–36.

bart's hangs together with his assumption that systematic accounting and double-entry bookkeeping are the same, and we do not subscribe to this viewpoint.

An Alternative Hypothesis

We shall pose two historical questions:

1. How does a Lebanese money-changer become an international banker, or an Iowa farm boy construct an enterprise big enough to put the world on wheels?
2. Why are occurrences of this phenomenon increasingly apparent in Europe, starting with Italy in the fourteenth century and culminating in the great entrepreneurial explosion of the twentieth century?

Only by keeping these two questions separate are we likely to throw light on the subject of our debate.

In Sombart's view, "projectors" such as Tonti, Caratto and Cagliostro turn into "promoters" of the order of a Law, de Lesseps, Rockefeller or Mond, through the invention of a conceptual framework which permits them to discriminate between ideas for wealth of the order of fantasies, and profitable plans which are capable of execution. This conceptual framework is a combination of double-entry bookkeeping and commercial arithmetic. We subscribe to a similar hypothesis except that we attribute its origins to multiple causes and a much earlier period in time; we do not regard the assumption that the plans must be profitable to be a necessary one; and we view accounting as a self-contained conceptual framework different from, although clearly related to, the models of commercial arithmetic.

We assume that the human mind seeks certainty and creates rationalizations in order to displace the unbearable idea of a purely stochastic environment.[31] All conceptual frameworks are designed to this

end; prediction, planning and control are the essence of rationalism and by their means we liberate ourselves from the tyranny of birth, copulation and death. This desire for a certainty of the mind is often aggravated by religious, political and social upheavals, so that the individual, robbed of one haven, seeks refuge in another. Sombart relates the observation that the United States represents the apogee of economic rationality to the uprooting of its immigrants, and the strangeness of their environment.

We would replace the Sombartian hypothesis of profit motivation with the Keynesian view that: ". . . it is probable that the actual average results of investments, even during periods of progress and prosperity, have disappointed the hopes which prompted them. . . . If human nature felt no temptation to take a chance, no satisfaction (profit apart) in constructing a factory, a railway, a mine or a farm, there might not be much investment merely as a result of cold calculation."[32]

The desire to create a capitalistic enterprise arises out of a desire to bring goods and services to those who do not now enjoy them, and the basic problem faced by the entrepreneur is how to finance his enterprise, that is, how to acquire capital in order to bridge the time gap between investment, or the allocation of scarce resources for production, and realization, or the receipt of payment in some form from the market to be served. The creation of wealth and the recognition of profit are separate phenomena, although related; Böhm-Bawerk first pointed out that lapse of time in the production process was one of the factors permitting profit to arise, and Knight confirmed this observation: "Profit arises out of the inherent, absolute

[31] For a similar statement, see Schumpeter, p. 85.
[32] J. M. Keynes, *The General Theory of Employment, Interest and Money*, Harcourt, Brace & World, Inc., 1965), p. 150 (first pub. 1936).

unpredictability of things, out of the sheer brute fact that the results of human activity cannot be anticipated and then only insofar as even a probability calculation in regard to them is impossible and meaningless."[33]

If the entrepreneur does not face this critical financing problem, he may select whatever conceptual framework seems to him appropriate; not having any necessity to communicate his plans to others he may formulate them in any way he chooses. Business history is full of examples of achievers who failed at the moment when it was necessary for them to exteriorize their systems. The historical novelist, Zoe Oldenburg, describes a feudal lord planning to build a road through his estate, presumably to bring its economic surplus to a market; he would not have needed accounts to convince a banker of the soundness of his project.

It seems to us, as indeed to Sombart, that the use of mathematics in the scientific preparation of decisions is a quite separate phenomenon from the development of a conceptual framework which will enable financial plans to be communicated to financiers and others. The techniques of "commercial arithmetic" were all known to, and used by, the Romans, and to even earlier civilizations. The use of accounts for planning and control is likewise of great antiquity, but accounting is not built out of compound interest, ratios and percentages. That the two subjects were treated together by Luca Pacioli and others may have led to some confusion on this question.

It is suggested here that accounting was not the product of "the period of early capitalism" but was, in fact, introduced into the public sector much earlier in time, for planning and control purposes. The customs of the ancient Greek temples and Roman patricians are perhaps open to historical misinterpretation, but not so the practices of the Norman *curiae* in the eleventh and twelfth centuries or of the medieval manors of the same period. Lyon and Verhulst have described in detail how accounts were used by the Flemish, Norman and French royal courts in the task of mobilizing the countries of Northwest Europe and converting them from a subsistence to a money economy.[34] The records of the monastic manor of Norwich in England have informed us about the use of accounts in the management of the medieval religious manors.[35]

It is easy to understand, therefore, why, although double-entry bookkeeping is not observable before the beginning of the fourteenth century, when observed it displays the principal features recognizable in modern accounting practice. Music is another example of a conceptual framework which took several hundred years to develop, from a simple octave recorded by an eighth century monk to the polyphonic forms with which we are today familiar. It is important for our thesis, however, to see that the slow process of constructing complex systems of interlocking accounts began long before "the period of early capitalism," and is attributable to economic growth situations of many different kinds.

The march of events as we see it can be shortly stated: the decline of the Roman Empire was followed by several centuries of anarchy, from which Europe emerged only when feudal systems established a measure of political stability. This political stability permitted the exploitation of economic surpluses, which the Normans and others sought to mobilize, and it is perhaps not without significance here that the revival of commerce and industry which pre-

[33] Frank H. Knight, *Risk, Uncertainty and Profit* (Harper Torchbooks, 1955), p. 311.

[34] Bryce Lyon and A. E. Verhulst, *Mediaeval Finance* (Brown University Press, 1967).

[35] Kenneth S. Most, "New Light on Mediaeval Manorial Accounts," London, *The Accountant* (January 25, 1969), pp. 119–21.

ceded and accompanied the Renaissance was restricted to those lands which had once known the benefits of Roman administration. The Roman trading laws and customs appear to have been revived, for example, in the *Judgements ou Roles d'Oleron*, which are one of the principal sources of mercantile law, and these included the use of accounts, which were first applied to public administration and then taken up by private bankers, manufacturers and merchants.

Unlike Sombart, who attributes the primitive business records of the early Middle Ages to man's preoccupation with value in use rather than value in exchange,[36] we simply see in this evidence of the lack of educational facilities at that time, and point to other, earlier, periods when exact calculation and meticulous record-keeping were fairly common. As educational facilities expanded, through the efforts of the investment-minded rulers of the time, so the number of persons able to use accounts increased, and with them, the number of potential entrepreneurs. Combining this with a money economy, the important technical innovations of the time (arabic numerals; the clock; the printing press; the gun) and capital, however acquired, we arrive at a picture of conditions which were extremely favorable for the growth of capitalistic enterprises, to an extent previously unknown in human history.

Accounting, Planning and Control

The idea of accounting as a conceptual framework is clearly brought out in this statement by a German businessman:

The object of the businessman's work, of his worries, his pride and his aspirations, is just his undertaking, be it a commercial company, factory, bank, shipping concern, theatre or railway. The undertaking seems to take on form and substance, and to be ever with him, having, as it were, by virtue of his bookkeeping, his organization and his branches, an independent economic existence.[37]

Clearly, Rathenau could not have believed that his business was a real entity; he was describing a system which he had constructed. The use of accounts for this purpose is also hinted at in the following confession, from Rockefeller's *Memoirs*:

From my earliest childhood I had a little book in which I entered what I got and what I spent. I called it my account book, and have preserved it to this day.[38]

The modern entrepreneur may phrase it differently, but the idea has not changed:

What, then, do we chief executives expect nowadays from our information systems? First, continual and sensitive checks on our present progress. We need to know at once when we are off target. We need to identify where we have gone astray, so that we can take the necessary action quickly.... Isolating the relevant information and pruning away the irrelevant is an all-important accountancy function.

Second, we look for a really professional financial evaluation of the alternatives facing us in the major policy decisions we have to take. Decisions on such matters as capital expenditure projects, pricing policy and so on.[39]

Or this forthright statement:

You may take deferred cash flow, or any other method of comparing a business, but if those figures do not balance with the annual statement of accounts they are, in my view, folly and extremely dangerous.... I personally never use any figures that do not balance with the annual statement of accounts. . . . [40]

The separation between accounting and mathematics is very marked in these quotations.

When interpreting statements of businessmen, it is important to remember that they are primarily engaged in creating values, not in transacting. As Knight

---

[36] Sombart, *Quintessence*, p. 18.
[37] *Ibid.*, p. 173.
[38] *Ibid.*, p. 237.
[39] Sir Kenneth Keith, U. K. investment banker, reported in *The Accountant* (November 15, 1969), pp. 642–43.
[40] A. Chester Beattie, Chairman, Selection Trust, Ltd., reported in *The Accountant* (May 18, 1968), p. 668.

pointed out, productive arrangements are made on the basis of anticipations, and in an uncertain world these anticipations may vary from subsequently experienced reality.[41] The essential fact is that men are acting and competing on the basis of what they *think* of the future:

The whole calculation is in the future; past and even present conditions operate only as grounds of prediction as to what may be anticipated.[42]

Decision involves comparing a subjective judgment of the significance of a commodity to the decision-maker with an estimated future price, and it is in the elaboration of the subjective evaluation that accounting serves the planning function. Its use as a control mechanism follows from its planning function, since we define control as the systematic measurement of performance against predetermined standards, with the objects of evaluation and prediction linking it up again with planning.

The context within which this process takes place has been described by Mey, using the Limpergean formulation characteristic of the Amsterdam school of business economics.[43] We assume a flow of values—Quesnay's *produit social* seen in terms of Schumpeter's *Kreislauf*—which starts from gifts of nature and ends with final consumption. This flow requires the intervention of business firms, or producing entities, which are organized into branches, trades, industries and sectors; in the last we include organs of national and local government, without the cooperation of which production could not take place.

These subdivisions are connected by markets.

The entrepreneur contemplating participation in this process by contributing a product or service to a market must distinguish between the functions of: (1) The acquisition of means of production, resulting from investment, (2) the human tasks of utilizing these means of production, and (3) the marketing of the product or its distribution.

Each of these functions has financial implications, and where means of payment are involved in both acquisition and distribution, money measures can be imputed to investment and the work involved in production. The entrepreneur elaborates his business decisions using data derived from such an imputation, and represents them to himself and to his financiers in the form of accounts and financial statements. This is the planning function. Subsequently, he collects data, or measures performance, in the same way, and it is this control operation which we recognize as accounting. The planning operation, or "accounting for the future," is not different in kind. Our argument is that the control function of accounting presupposes a prior planning function, which is implicit in all accounting systems but only made explicit, in the form of business budgets, in a minority of cases.

[41] Knight, p. 272.
[42] *Ibid.*, p. 273–74.
[43] Abram Mey, "Le circuit économique et sa relation avec la théorie de la valeur et du calcul rationnel de l'économie industrielle," Paris, *Revue de l'Economie Politique* (1960), espec. pp. 8 and 12.

EARLY ACCOUNTING PROBLEMS
OF FOREIGN EXCHANGE

Raymond de Roover

EARLY ACCOUNTING PROBLEMS OF FOREIGN EXCHANGE[*]

Raymond de Roover

I

T would be a serious mistake to underestimate the importance of money substitutes in medieval and early modern times. The Italians especially were clever in replacing specie by other devices in the settlement of debts. Their ability in this respect much impressed foreign observers,

including the English mercantilist, Thomas Mun.[2] A French satirist, in the fifteenth century, marveled at the ability of the Italians to do business without money. In dealing with them, he said, one never sees or touches any money; all they need to do business is paper, pen, and ink.

This is doubtless an overstatement, but it contains an element of truth. Among

* For references, see end of article.

merchants, the "setting-over" of debts was a common practice despite the absence of negotiable instruments. Local payments were often made by transfer in bank (*ditta di banco*) or by transfer of credit (*ditta*) on the books of an ordinary merchant or a merchant-banker. Transfer orders were given not in writing, but by word of mouth.[3] This process is described by Luca Paciolo (or Pacioli) who tells us in his famous treatise on bookkeeping how one should deal with transfer banks and keep a record of such dealings.[4] In Paciolo's time, there existed transfer, or *giro* banks, either public or private, in Venice, Florence, Genoa, Barcelona, Bruges, and Constantinople (before 1453). The public banks of Amsterdam and Hamburg were established at a much later date. Where there were no transfer banks, as in London, for example, prominent merchant-bankers—always foreigners—sometimes accepted deposit accounts for clearing purposes.[5]

The use of oral commands to pay was rather satisfactory for the purpose of making local payments, but this method was not suitable for the purpose of making funds available in a distant place. In foreign trade, the use of written instruments was therefore an inescapable necessity. The bill of exchange became at an early date the principal instrument by which funds were transferred from place to place without shipping any specie.

As Paciolo explains, there were four kinds of exchange: manual exchange, exchange by bills, dry exchange, and fictitious exchange.[6] This study deals only with exchange by bills. Early bills of "exchange" always involved an exchange transaction, since they were payable at a future date, in a distant place, and in a foreign currency. As communications were slow, it took time for a bill to journey from the place of issue to the place of payment. Moreover, dealings in sight drafts were exceptional among

merchants; most bills were payable at usance. The usance was fixed by merchant custom and varied from one month between London and Bruges to three months between London and Venice or any other Italian city.[7] The purchase of a bill, therefore, always involved a credit, as well as an exchange, transaction. The business of foreign banking consisted in buying and selling bills. It is not surprising that the word "banker" had the connotation of "exchanger" or "exchange-dealer" in the English of Shakespeare's time.

Bills of exchange did not become negotiable until 1650 or thereabouts. The earliest endorsed bills date from 1610 and are exceedingly rare, which shows that the endorsing of bills was not yet a common practice.[8] Before the introduction of endorsement, a regular exchange transaction involved four parties and two payments: usually a banker, called "deliverer" (Ital. *datore*), bought a bill for ready cash from a taker (Ital. *prenditore*); at maturity the bill was then collected by the payee from the payor or drawee.[9] Normally the payee was the agent of the deliverer, and the payor the agent of the taker. But these relations could be reversed: it was not uncommon for an agent either to draw on his principal or to remit by sending him a bill for collection. As we shall see later, these details are important and should be kept clearly in mind.

In addition to the lack of negotiability, there was still another peculiarity about medieval or early modern bills of exchange. The Church condemned the taking of interest. It would be wrong to assume that the usury prohibition remained a dead letter. Quite the contrary. The canonist doctrine on usury had a profound influence on business practices, since interest could not be charged openly but had to be concealed under some form or other. As a result of the usury prohibition, bills were never discounted but were bought at a rate of exchange which fluctuated up and down according to the conditions prevailing in the money market. There is no doubt that interest was received by the banker who invested his money in the purchase of bills, for a hidden interest was included in the rate of exchange. Because of this subterfuge, the structure of the money market was such that exchange fluctuations were caused either by a change in the rate of interest or by a change in the terms of international trade.[10] Today the existence of a special rate for sight drafts or cable transfers permits the segregation, in accounting, of exchange profits (or losses) from interest income (or expense) and the separation, in economics, of the credit problem from the transfer-of-funds problem. But in the Middle Ages credit and exchange were welded together so far as foreign banking was concerned, and this fact cannot be emphasized too strongly.

Today a banker who "discounts" a bill knows his profit in advance, since the borrower receives credit only for the face value of the bill minus the discount. In the Middle Ages, however, a banker who "bought" a bill at a given rate of exchange did not know his profit in advance, but had to wait until his agent abroad returned the proceeds of the bill by way of re-exchange. To be complete, an exchange transaction necessarily involved two bills instead of one. In other words, a banker had to operate both "outward" and "inward."[11] Otherwise, he was unable to determine his profit on exchange, interest included.

In the normal course of events exchange dealings yielded a profit to the banker. But he could not tell how much of this profit was interest and how much of it was agio or disagio.[12] Medieval bankers, therefore, did not attempt to separate the different elements which made up their profits on exchange dealings or "banking," as it was called. For this reason the Italian merchant-bankers of the Middle Ages had

only one account, called *Pro e Danno di Cambio* or *Avanzi e Disavanzi di Cambio* ("Profit and Loss on Exchange"), in which were lumped together all profits and losses from exchange transactions. Profits from trade and miscellaneous income from other sources were kept separate, as we shall see.

The creation of this account *Pro e Danno di Cambio* did not solve all the accounting problems of the medieval banker. In order to engage successfully in foreign banking, he had to have correspondents abroad. Sometimes he acted as their principal, and sometimes as their agent. One of the banker's problems was that he had to keep his accounts straight with each of his foreign correspondents. Another problem was created by the fact that the profit of the banker, including interest, was determined by exchange differences. In order to take advantage of such differences, he had to operate in two markets and with different kinds of currency: two complicating factors.[13] Exchange dealings which involved three markets, instead of two, introduced additional complications. It would have been impracticable, if not impossible, to ascertain the profit or the loss on each single exchange transaction, since items relating to outward and inward exchange did not always match and offset each other. In view of these difficulties, how did a banker determine his profit? The main purpose of this study is to answer that question.

VOSTRO AND NOSTRO ACCOUNTS

Paciolo is of no help in this connection. He does not deal with this problem of profit-determination, either in his treatise on bookkeeping or in his treatise on exchange. It is therefore necessary to resort to the actual business records of medieval merchant-bankers. An examination of these records reveals that the bankers solved the problem under discussion by opening for their foreign correspondents two different accounts, a *Nostro* and a *Vostro* account. Such accounts are still kept today by firms doing business with foreign countries. There is little difference between the present and the past with regard to the external characteristics of these accounts. *Vostro* accounts are still kept only in domestic currency. In contrast, *Nostro* accounts have an additional memorandum column for foreign currencies. *Nostro* accounts also require adjustment for exchange differences in order to balance in foreign, as well as in domestic, currency. This was true in the fourteenth, fifteenth, sixteenth, and seventeenth centuries. Despite these analogies in form, *Vostro* and *Nostro* accounts were not used then for quite the same purpose as now, because business practices were so very different from those of the present day.

Nostro and *Vostro* accounts are found in the records of Francesco Datini, a successful Italian merchant-banker from Prato (Tuscany).[14] Sometimes he is called Francesco di Marco da Prato ("Francis, son of Mark, from· Prato"). He was born about 1335 and died in August, 1410. Datini had established his headquarters in Prato, but his firm had branches in Florence, Pisa, Genoa, Avignon, Barcelona, Valencia, and Majorca. A great number of Datini's account books and business papers have come down to us and form the most impressive and most complete collection of the kind.[16]

Datini's earlier account books were kept in single entry, but double entry was generally adopted in later years. This system is followed in the ledgers of the Barcelona branch which cover a period of five years, 1395 to 1400.

According to the ledgers and the correspondence, the Barcelona branch was engaged both in foreign trade and in foreign banking—a frequent combination. The branch extended credit to local merchants by buying their bills on places such as Florence, Genoa, or Bruges, where it had connections which might be other branches of the Datini firm or correspondents. The Barcelona branch would also accept and honor the bills of exchange issued by other branches or by its foreign correspondents.

There were in all, four possibilities open to a banker who operated in two markets, for example, Barcelona and Bruges: (1) Barcelona could remit to Bruges; (2) Bruges could remit to Barcelona; (3) Barcelona could draw on Bruges; and (4) Bruges could draw on Barcelona. If the banker operated in three markets, instead of two, a great number of combinations became possible. In order to build up a credit balance in Florence, a Barcelona banker could (1) remit directly to Florence, (2) instruct his correspondent in Florence to draw on Barcelona, (3) instruct his Genoese correspondent to remit to Florence, (4) instruct his Florentine correspondent to draw on Genoa, and so forth. Which of these alternatives a banker would choose depended not only upon the conditions prevailing in the money market at a given moment but also upon the state of his foreign balances and his expectations with regard to the rise or fall of the exchange rates. A banker was unlikely to draw on a place where he had no credit or to remit to a place where his balances were already piling up. Paciolo, Casanova, and other writers of commercial handbooks state that clever merchant-bankers always managed to be creditors where money was scarce and debtors where it was abundant.[16] Usually bankers were lenders, that is, buyers of bills, but they sometimes became borrowers, if they were in dire need of cash and were forced to draw because they could not wait for their correspondents to remit.

Any one of the four alternatives open to a banker operating in two markets could give rise to entries in either a *Vostro* or a

Nostro account. For example, a Barcelona banker remitting to Bruges would debit his correspondent's *Nostro* account if the remittance were sent at his own initiative. However, he would debit his correspondent's *Vostro* account if the remittance were sent upon instructions from Bruges. Upon receipt of the remittance, the Bruges correspondent would do the reverse, and credit the *Vostro* account of the Barcelona banker in the first case and the latter's *Nostro* account in the second case. When the Barcelona banker accepted a draft from Bruges on Barcelona, he would debit either the *Vostro* or the *Nostro* account of his Bruges correspondent. If the Barcelona banker was simply acting as agent, the correspondent being the principal, the draft would be charged to the *Vostro* account. If, however, the Barcelona banker was the principal and had given the order to draw, the draft would be charged to the *Nostro* account of the Bruges correspondent. According to this criterion, a *Nostro* account was the account of a foreign correspondent in his capacity of agent. A *Vostro* account, on the contrary, meant that the foreign correspondent was regarded as principal. A *Nostro* account in Barcelona, for instance, corresponded to a *Vostro* account in Bruges, and vice versa.

Nostro accounts usually had a debit balance representing money in the custody of an agent residing abroad. Most of the time *Vostro* accounts had a credit balance representing money held on deposit in behalf of a foreign principal. *Nostro* accounts, as already pointed out, had two extension columns, one for the foreign currency and one for the domestic currency, and were supposed to be balanced in both currencies. Any discrepancies were adjusted by transfer to the *Pro e Danno di Cambio* account described above. The foreign correspondent owed the debit balance, or was entitled to the credit balance, as stated in foreign currency. He was expected to send periodic statements of account, since accounts were rendered from agent to principal. *Vostro* accounts had only one extension column—for the domestic currency. They did not require adjustment for exchange differences but often included charges for commission and brokerage. The reason for such charges is that expenses for brokerage and the agent's commission were chargeable to the principal.[17] Periodic statements of a *Vostro* account were sent to the foreign correspondent instead of being received from him. *Nostro* and *Vostro* accounts were essential to the medieval merchant-banker as a tool of accounting and control, since the exchange business rested upon maintaining close contact with correspondents in distant commercial centers.

Let us now see how the bookkeeper of the Datini branch in Barcelona recorded each of the following transactions: (1) the purchase of a bill of exchange drawn on a foreign correspondent, (2) the issuance and sale of a draft on a foreign correspondent, (3) the acceptance and payment of a bill drawn by a foreign correspondent, and (4) the collection of a draft remitted by a foreign correspondent. Between two markets there were no possibilities other than these four. Exchange dealings involving three markets will not be considered for the present.

The purchase of a draft, as has been pointed out, involved the extension of credit, since the buyer or deliverer (*datore*) gave a certain sum of money to the seller or taker (*prenditore*) in order to be repaid at a future date, in a distant place, and in another kind of currency. The buyer of a bill could lend either his own money or money held in current account for a foreign principal. In either case the taker would receive credit for the amount of the draft which he had sold. If a firm lent its own money, the amount of the bill would be charged to the *Nostro* account of the correspondent, who was expected to collect the bill at maturity. The correspondent, being simply an agent, did not assume any risks for exchange differences. Nor was he entitled to any of the profits arising therefrom. If a firm lent funds belonging to someone else, the amount of the draft would be charged against this person's credit in the *Vostro* account (see Table I).

We remit(ted) to Albert & Bernard degli Alberti [payees] in Bruges in Diamante & Altobianco Alberti [payors] 550 écus [Ital. *scudi*, ▽] at usuance, at a rate of 9s. 6½d. per écu [▽], for the value given here to the Alesandri [takers or borrowers], broker Pagolo, for us.

The phrase "for us" means that the entry was to be charged to the *Nostro* account of Alberto and Bernardo degli Al-

TABLE I

LEDGER ENTRIES RELATING TO EXCHANGE BY BILLS BETWEEN TWO MARKETS

A. Firm in Barcelona

1. Remits to Bruges	2. Draws on Bruges	3. Accepts Bruges Bill	4. Presents Bruges Bill for Acceptance
Dr. a. If principal, the *Nostro* account of Bruges correspondent. b. If agent, the *Vostro* account of Bruges correspondent. *Cr.* Drawer or taker in Barcelona.	*Dr.* Deliver or lender in Barcelona. *Cr.* a. If principal, the *Nostro* account of drawee in Bruges. b. If agent, the *Vostro* account of drawee in Bruges.	*Dr.* a. If principal, the *Nostro* account of drawer in Bruges. b. If agent, the *Vostro* account of drawer in Bruges. *Cr.* Payee in Barcelona.	*Dr.* Drawee or payor in Barcelona. *Cr.* a. If principal, the *Nostro* account of Bruges agent. b. If agent, the *Vostro* account of Bruges principal.

B. Firm in Bruges

1. Presents Barcelona Bill for Acceptance	2. Accepts Barcelona Bill	3. Draws on Barcelona	4. Remits to Barcelona
Dr. Drawee in Bruges. *Cr.* a. If agent, the *Vostro* account of Barcelona principal. b. If principal, the *Nostro* account of Barcelona agent.	*Dr.* a. If agent, the *Vostro* account of drawer in Barcelona. b. If principal, the *Nostro* account of drawer in Barcelona. *Cr.* Payee in Bruges.	*Dr.* Deliverer or lender in Bruges. *Cr.* a. If agent, the *Vostro* account of drawee in Barcelona. b. If principal, the *Nostro* account of drawee in Barcelona.	*Dr.* a. If agent, the *Vostro* account of correspondent in Barcelona. b. If principal, the *Nostro* account of correspondent in Barcelona. *Cr.* Drawer or taker in Bruges.

In the memorandum book of the Datini branch in Barcelona, a typical entry relating to the purchase of a bill reads as follows:[18]

Rimettemo a Brugia ad Alberto e Bernardo degli Alberti in Diamante e Altobiancho Alberti ▽ 550 per uso a sol. 9 den. 6½ per ▽ qui agli Alesandri, sensale Pagolo, per noi.

This entry may be translated into English as follows:[19]

berti of Bruges. If the phrase *per loro* ("for them") had been used instead of *per noi* ("for us"), it would have indicated that the bill was chargeable to the *Vostro* account of the payee.[20] The entry in question was actually posted to Alberto and Bernardo degli Alberti's *Nostro* account in the ledger. This account was charged with £50 8s. 4d. Flemish or groat (550 écus at 22 groats) in the extension column for the foreign currency and with £265 7s. 11d.

Barcelonese (or ▽ 550 at the rate of 9s. 6½d. per écu) in the extension column for the local currency.[21]

A banker might take up money by selling a bill, if he needed cash on the spot but had money standing to his credit abroad. He might also sell foreign exchange if one of his correspondents, for instance, had overdrawn his account. In the first case, the money would be taken up in exchange for the banker's own account, but in the second case, it would be borrowed for the account of a foreign correspondent. Under such circumstances, the issuance of a bill usually gave rise to the following entry: *Dr.* the deliverer or buyer of the bill; *Cr.* the drawee's *Nostro* account, if the banker drew on his foreign balances, or the foreign correspondent's *Vostro* account, if the banker did not draw on his own balances abroad.

The memorandum book of the Datini branch in Barcelona contains the following example of an entry relating to a bill drawn on Bruges for the banker's own account:[22]

Traemo a Brugia ad Alberto e Bernardo [degli Alberti] per uso ▽ 419 e grossi 2 di grossi 22 lo ▽ in Diamante e Altobiancho degli Alberti e conpagni per la valuta a sol. 9 den. 11 [per] ▽ da Nicolaio Alberti, sensale Grasso, per noi ....£207 15s. 11d.

As the reader will notice by comparing this memorandum entry with the preceding one, the word *traemo* ("we draw") has been substituted for *rimettemo* ("we remit"). The entry mentions that the bill was drawn on Alberto and Bernardo degli Alberti of Bruges in favor of Diamante and Altobianco degli Alberti, another firm in Bruges, for the value received from Nicolaio Alberti in Barcelona. The words *per noi* indicate that the money was taken up "for us." The Datini ledger shows that the entry was duly posted to the drawees' *Nostro* account. The sum credited was £207 15s. 11d. in the local currency of Barcelona and £38 8s. 4d. in Flemish currency or groats.[23]

The usance for bills between Bruges and Barcelona was thirty days after sight in whichever direction the bill was traveling. Exchange rates were quoted in Barcelona currency on the basis of an imaginary écu (▽) of twenty-two Flemish groats. This method of quotation was used both in Bruges and in Barcelona. It is perfectly clear from the Datini records that the firm was in the habit of crediting the payee and debiting the drawer upon acceptance of a bill. The same custom is found in other medieval account books. Its prevalence proves that the acceptor of a bill considered himself primarily liable for its payment. When a bill was accepted, a banker would debit the *Nostro* account only if he had given orders to draw. If the correspondent had taken the initiative of drawing on his own balances, the *Vostro* account would be debited (see Table I). The text of the bill of exchange usually specified how it was to be entered in the books. An example is given in the following bill drawn by Giovanni Orlandini and Piero Benizi in Bruges on Francesco Datini and Partners in Barcelona:

Al nome di Dio, amen
dì 12 di dicembre 1399
Paghate per questa prima al usanza a Domenicho Sancio schudi seicento a s.10 d.5 per ▽ i quali ▽ 600 a s.10 d.5 per schudo sono per la valuta da Jachopo Ghoscho, e ponete a nostro chonto chosti. Idio vi guardi.
Giovanni Orlandini e Piero Benizi
e chonpagni in Bruggia
Acettata a dì 11 di gennaio 1399 [1400]

On the back is the address of the payor:

Francesco da Prato e chonpagni
in Barzalona
Prima[24]

As is evident from the text, this bill was made out in Bruges on December 12, 1399, and accepted in Barcelona on January 11, 1400. According to merchant custom it was payable thirty days later, on February 11. From our point of view, the important sentence is: *Ponete a nostro conto chosti* ("Charge [this] to our account here"),

which means that the drawer wanted the
bill to be charged to "his" account, meaning his *Vostro* account in the books of the
drawee or payor. In the ledger of the
drawer or maker of the bill, however, it
would be posted to the credit of the *Nostro*
account of the drawee or payor. In other
words, such a bill was one drawn by a
principal on his agent.

The entries in Datini's ledger reveal that
the instructions given in the text of the
bill of exchange were carried out. The
Orlandini *Vostro* account includes on the
debit side the following entry, dated January 11, 1400, relating to the acceptance
of the bill quoted above:

E deon dare a dì 11 di genaio ▽ 600 a *s*.10 *d*.5
per ▽ trasonci per uso in Domenicho Sancio in
questo a carta 293 debino avere, per altre n'ebono
da Giachopo Ghoscho........£312 *s*10 *d*.0²⁵

This entry, as the reader will notice,
contains the word *trasonci* ("they drew on
us") instead of *traemo* ("we draw") or
rimettemo ("we remit"). The rate of exchange and the face value of the bill
(▽600) are mentioned in the description
column, but there is no special extension
column for the foreign currency. The text
of the entry also gives the name of the
payee (Domenico Sancio) in Barcelona
and that of the deliverer (Giacopo Gosco)
in Bruges.

In some bills the words *Ponete a conto
per noi* or *Ponete a nostro conto costì* are replaced by the formula *Ponete a conto per
voi* ("Place [this] to your account") or
Ponete a conto qua per voi (Place [this] to
the account there for you").²⁶ The use of
this latter formula meant that the drawer
intended the bill to be charged to his
Nostro account in the books of the drawee.
In other words, such a bill was a bill
drawn by an agent on his principal.

The branch of the Datini firm in Barcelona frequently received remittances
from foreign correspondents. As soon as a
remittance had been accepted by the

drawee, the latter's account was debited
and the correspondent's *Vostro* or *Nostro*
account, as the case might be, was credited. The entries posted to the credit of
the foreign correspondent usually contained the phrase *rimisonci* ("they remitted to us").²⁷

Table I lists the different entries which
might be found in the ledgers of two correspondents, one in Barcelona and the
other in Bruges, who were dealing in foreign exchange with each other. There are
altogether eight possible combinations,
each involving two entries—one in the
books of the Barcelona firm and one in
those of the Bruges firm.

Bills in fourteenth-century Barcelona
were rarely paid in specie but generally
by transfer in bank.²⁸ There were in Barcelona several money-changers or bankers
—called in the Datini records *banchieri
in loggia*—who specialized in deposit
banking. The Barcelona branch of the
Datini firm dealt chiefly with three of
them: Pere Brunet (or Piero Brunetto),
Antonio Rabustiero, and the partnership
of Giame di Pue & Giovanetto Savasso.²⁹
The terminology used in the Datini
ledgers clearly suggests that transfers from
one deposit account to another were made
on the strength of an oral command to pay.
In the books of the depositor, credits in
bank were charged to the banker and
credited to the person who had ordered
the transfer. The formula used repeatedly
in the Datini ledgers is *diseci per* or *disonci
per* ("he told," or "they told us, that we
had received credit from so-and-so").³⁰
Payments in bank were posted by the
bookkeeper of the Datini firm to the credit
of the bank and to the debit of the person
to whose credit money was being transferred. In crediting the bank, the bookkeeper consistently used the same formula: *dison* (or *dise*) *per noi a* ("they told
so-and-so for us that his account had been
credited").

Exchange transactions involving three markets instead of two were fairly common and fulfilled a useful function in the adjustment of international balances. Owing to the existence of triangular exchange, it was possible for one country to pay for an excess of imports from another country with the balances accumulated in a third country through an excess of exports over imports. The Datini records contain numerous references to three-cornered exchange. The medieval merchant-bankers were certainly adroit in maneuvering on the money market. They were constantly on the lookout for opportunities to lend where money was dear and to borrow where it was cheap and abundant.

The balance of trade between Flanders and Spain was presumably in favor of Flanders, whereas the balance between Flanders and Italy was probably in favor of Italy. In any case, the credit balances of Italian merchant-bankers residing in Bruges tended to accumulate in Barcelona. They frequently drew on these balances in order to make payments in Italy. Here is an example of an entry posted to the debit of the *Nostro* account of Diamante e Altobianco degli Alberti e compagni, merchant-bankers in Bruges:[31]

E deono dare a dì detto [May 24, 1398] £260 s.13 d.4 barzalonesi ci trasono per loro da Genova [i] Ghalderotti in Giovanni Bonini e Domenicho de' Benedetti in questo c. 161, debino avere, per fl. 340 da Giovanni di Giovanni. . .£260 s.13 d.4

Apparently the Galderotti of Genoa drew on Datini in Barcelona in behalf of the Alberti of Bruges and in favor of Giovanni Bonini and Domenico de' Benedetti in Barcelona for the value received from one Giovanni di Giovanni in Genoa. The credit entry corresponding to the debit in the Alberti account is naturally found in the account of Giovanni Bonini & Domenico de' Benedetti. This entry contains the significant phrase *prometemo loro* ("we promised them").[32] As has been explained, bills were credited to the payee at the time of acceptance.

Correspondents in Bruges also paid debit balances in Majorca with the credits accumulated in Barcelona. To give an example, on October 21, 1395, the firm Luigi and Salvestro Mannini of Bruges was charged for the payment of a bill drawn on Datini in Barcelona by one Ambrogio di Messer Lorenzo residing on the island of Majorca. The face value of the bill was one hundred reals, worth £76 13s. 4d. Barcelonese, at 15s. 4d. Barc. per real, the current rate of exchange.[33]

As already stated, a regular exchange transaction involved four parties and two payments. There were many exceptions to this rule. In a number of instances, three parties instead of four were involved. The account books of the Datini branch in Barcelona contain many examples of exchange transactions in which either the payee and the payor or the deliverer and the taker were the same firm or individual. Usually such bills gave rise to a transfer of credit in the books of the payor who was also the payee, or in the books of the deliverer who was also the taker. Some bills drawn on the Datini firm by a merchant named Guiglielmo Barberi in Bruges were payable "to yourselves" (*a voi medesimi*). Those bills, consequently, involved only three parties instead of the customary four. From the Datini records, it is clear that bills of this kind were settled by a transfer from the account of Guiglielmo Barberi, the drawer and taker, to the credit of the deliverers, usually the Orlandini of Bruges, who had furnished the value in that city.[34] The occasion of three-party bills was often such that both the deliverer and the taker happened to have accounts with the same foreign correspondent. Three-party bills could also originate in dry exchange, which was in reality a local loan disguised under the form of an exchange transaction.[35]

Some bills of exchange involved only two parties instead of four and were payable "to yourselves" for the value received "from ourselves." The existence of such strange bills is discussed by writers on commercial law, but they seem to be uncertain whether such bills should be considered as genuine bills of exchange or not.[36] The Datini records throw much light on this controversial matter. Apparently real exchange transactions involving two parties only—let us say A in Bruges and B in Barcelona—could originate in a transfer from the *Vostro* account of A to his *Nostro* account in the books of B in Barcelona and in a transfer from the *Nostro* account of B to his *Vostro* account in the books of A in Bruges. Or the order might be reversed with *Nostro* substituted for *Vostro*, and vice versa. A clear-cut example of an exchange transaction of this sort is given in the Datini ledgers. It involves a transfer from the general account (*conto disteso*) of the Bruges firm Luigi and Salvestro Mannini to their special account, or *conto a parte*. The wording of the corresponding debit and credit entries is significant. In English the debit entry reads as follows:[37]

Luigi and Salvestro Mannini of Bruges must give on January 20, 1399, ▽ 171 *s*. 2 Barcelonese which we remit to them in themselves, at 9*s*. 9*d*. per ▽, value from ourselves and we draw on their special account in this ledger on fol. 250, they must have........................£83 *s*.9 *d*.3

The corresponding credit entry contains the significant formula "we draw on them in themselves, value given here to them in their general account" (*traemo loro in loro medesimi . . . qui a loro conto disteso*).[38] The reasons for making such transfers from the *Nostro* to the *Vostro* (or from the *Vostro* to the *Nostro*) account with the same correspondent are not stated in the ledger entries. The purpose may have been to make certain adjustments.

A *Nostro* and a *Vostro* account of the firm Luigi and Salvestro Mannini in Bruges are reproduced in Table II. As the reader will see, the *Nostro* account has one column for the Flemish, and another column for the Barcelonese, currency. The only entry on the credit side relates to a bill from Barcelona on Bruges. As the text in the description column indicates, the bill of exchange was drawn on the Mannini in favor of Piero Ulmone for the value received in Barcelona from Guiglielmo Invigles. The first two entries on the debit side refer to remittances, one for ▽400 and the other for ▽200, sent to Bruges for collection. In the first case, the value was received by Giovanni Bibero; in the second case, no value was given but the remittance originated in a transfer from the account of Diamante and Altobianco degli Alberti, who were also the drawees. The Mannini *Nostro* account is closed by a transfer of £6 3*s*. 4*d*. Barc. to the credit of *Pro e Danno di Cambio*, that is, the Profit and Loss account. The amount of £6 3*s*. 4*d*. Barc. represents a profit arising out of the fact that the Datini sold ▽600 short of exchange but were able to cover this transaction by purchasing two bills at a lower rate. This is consequently an example of speculation on a falling exchange.

The *Vostro* account of Luigi and Salvestro Mannini, as the reader will notice, has only one column—for the Barcelonese currency. The account, instead of being adjusted for exchange differences, includes a charge of 2*s*. 7*d*. Barc. for brokerage. The first entry on the debit side has already been examined in connection with the discussion of two-party bills. The second entry is another example of three-party, instead of four-party, exchange. On the credit side, the first and third entries refer to balances carried over from other Mannini accounts. The second entry relates to a bill remitted in behalf of the Mannini by the Datini *fondaco*, or branch, on the island of Majorca.

TABLE II

NOSTRO ACCOUNT OF LUIGI AND SALVESTRO MANNINI IN BRUGES

Dr. | | | | | | | Cr.

Explanation	Flemish Currency			Barcelonese Currency			Explanation	Flemish Currency			Barcelonese Currency		
	£	s	d	£	s	d		£	s	d	£	s	d
1398 Luigi e Salvestro Manini di Brugia deono dare a dì 28 di giugno ▽400 di Filipo di grossi 22 l'uno rimetemo in Perichone Salaverde a *s*.10 per ▽ qui da Giovanni Bibero in questo a carta 95 debe avere, vagliono di grossi............	36	13	4	200	0	0	1398 Luigi e Salvestro Manini deono avere a dì 28 gugno ▽600 di Filipo di grossi 22 l'uno traemo loro in Piero Ulmone a *s*.10 *d*.2 [per] ▽ da Ghugliemo Invigles in questo c. 182 debe [dare]............	55	0	0	305	0	0
E deono dare a dì 4 di luglio ▽200 rimetemo loro in Diamante e Altobiancho degli Alberti e conpagni a *s*.9 *d*.10 [per] ▽ qui da noi medesimi in questo a c. 160 debe.......	18	6	8	98	6	8							
E deono dare a dì deto £6 *s*.13 *d*.4 mesi a pro di canbi in questo a c. 357 debe avere....				6	13	4							
	55	0	0	305	0	0		55	0	0	305	0	0

VOSTRO ACCOUNT OF LUIGI AND SALVESTRO MANNINI IN BRUGES

Dr. | | | | | Cr.

Explanation	Barcelonese Currency			Explanation	Barcelonese Currency		
	£	s	d		£	s	d
1398 Luigi e Salvestro Manini di Brugia deono dare a dì 20 gienaio [1399] ▽171 *s*.2 barzallonesi rimetemo loro in loro medesimi a *s*.9 *d*.9 [per] ▽ da noi medesimi e traemo per loro conto a parte in questo a c. 250 debino avere..........	83	9	3	1398 Luigi e Salvestro Manini e compagni deono avere a di 29 dì diciembre per resto di loro ragione in questo c. 170 debino [dare].....................	20	10	4
E deono dare a dì detto ▽182 rimetemo loro in Alberto e Bernardo degli Alberti e conpagni a *s*.9 *d*.9 [per] ▽ qui a loro conto in questo c. 161 debino avere..........................	88	14	6	E deono avere a dì deto reali 200 a *s*.14 *d*.9 [per] reale ci rimesono da Mazo Biche per loro i nostri [di Maiolicha] in Andrea di Bancho e conpagni in una soma di reali 500 in questo c. 251 debino [dare].....................	147	10	0
£172 *s*.3 *d*.9 E deono dare a dì deto posto in questo c. 392 debe avere spese per sensaria....		2	7	E deono avere a dì deto £4 *s*.6 per resto d'una loro ragione in questo a c. 19 debino [dare]..................	4	6	0
	172	6	4		172	6	4

Source: Arch. Dat., No. 801, Fondaco di Barcellona, Libro verde C (July 11, 1397 to January 31, 1399), fols. 180ᵛ–181ʳ, 262ᵛ–263ʳ.

The Datini records, which end in 1410, probably contain the earliest known examples of *Nostro* and *Vostro* accounts. It is safe to assume that the practice of keeping such accounts with foreign correspondents became common during the fifteenth century. Examples are found in the account books of the firm Filippo Borromei & Co. of London (1436–39), the records of the Medici banking house (1395–1494), and the personal ledgers of Bernardo Cambi, a Florentine merchant-banker (1435–90).

The Borromei are a Milanese family who have given one saint to the Catholic Church and many bankers to the business world. In the fifteenth century, at least two branches of the family were engaged in banking, apparently with equal success. They had representatives in all the important commercial centers of medieval Europe. The London branch of the firm Filippo Borromei & Co. of Milan was established in 1436. The entire capital was provided by the Bruges branch of the same firm.[39] Business relations between the two branches were close, but they dealt with each other on the same basis as they did with independent concerns. Each branch was a separate legal entity, had a separate management, and kept separate accounts. The two branches charged a commission to each other as if there had been no common link. They sent remittances to each other and accepted each other's bills, as one would expect.

Some extremely valuable excerpts from the London ledgers have been published. According to this source, the London branch kept two different accounts with the sister organization in Bruges. One account was entitled *Filippo Borromei e compagni di Bruggia per nostro conto*. This is obviously the *Nostro* account. It has two extension columns, one for the Pound Sterling and the other for the Pound Groat.[40] The other account, called *per loro conto* instead of *per nostro conto*, has only one extension column and is certainly a *Vostro* account.[41] The balance of the *Nostro* account is in favor of London but that of the *Vostro* account is in favor of Bruges. The published excerpts also include samples of *Nostro* and *Vostro* accounts open to correspondents in places other than Bruges, as for instance the *Nostro* account of a Genoese named Oddo Rau, who later failed.[42]

There are in the Borromei ledgers several good examples of triangular exchange.

For instance, on March 17, 1436, the Bruges branch of the Borromei drew a bill of exchange, amounting to 150 ducats, on behalf of the London branch, on Arrighino Panigaruola in Venice. Value for the bill was given by Donato Pizamano in Bruges, and it was payable to Ghirardo Zigola in Venice. The rate of exchange at which the bill was sold in Bruges was 47¼ groats per Venetian ducat of twenty-four *grossi*. This transaction gave rise to the following entries in the ledger of the London house:[43]

Dr. Filippo Borromei e compagni of Bruges, *Nostro* account (*per nostro conto*), 150 ducats at 47¼ groats and 41⅙ sterlings per ducat, equals...
............£29 10s. 7d. gr. and £25 14s. 7d. st.
Cr. Arrighino Panigaruola of Venice, *Nostro* account (*per nostro conto*), 150 ducats at 41⅙ sterlings per ducat...£15 *di grossi* and £25 14s. 7d. st.

From the information given, it is easy to reconstruct the entry in the ledger of the Borromei in Bruges:

Dr. Donato Pizamano who had promised to give value for the bill.................£29 10s. 7d. gr.
Cr. Filippo Borromei e compagni of London, *Vostro* account (*per loro conto*)...£29 10s. 7d. gr.

When Arrighino Panigaruola accepted the bill drawn on him by the Borromei in Bruges on behalf of the Borromei in London, he probably entered the following item in his ledger:

Dr. Filippo Borromei e compagni of London, *Vostro* account, duc. 150 or........£15 *di grossi*
Cr. Ghirardo Zigola, the payee.....£15 *di grossi*

As appears from these entries, three different currencies were involved, the Flemish Pound Groat, the English Pound Sterling, and the Venetian Pound of ten ducats called *libra di grossi*. The bill of exchange itself is not extant. It probably was addressed to Arrighino Panigaruola and gave him the order to debit the Borromei of London instead of the Borromei of Bruges who wrote out the bill. The formula used was probably *ponete a conto dei nostri di Londra* ("charge this to the account of our people in London") or other words to the same effect.[44] Such phraseology is commonly found in drafts issued in connection with triangular exchange.

Since there existed no transfer banks in London, the Borromei branch there accepted deposits and transferred credit for local customers. This business was presumably important enough to justify the statement that the firm was also engaged in deposit banking.[45] In Bruges, in Barcelona, and probably in other centers, deposit banking was a separate business and was not combined with foreign banking as it was in London.

One of the local customers of the Borromei branch in London was the firm of Forese da Rabatta and Bernardo Cambi.[46] The latter resided in Bruges up to 1450 and then returned to Florence. He kept a personal ledger in which he recorded his private business transactions: purchases of real estate, insurance, foreign exchange, and investments in mercantile ventures.[47] Most of the accounts relating to exchange are *Nostro* accounts, as one would expect, since Bernardo Cambi was usually principal rather than agent.

According to the entries of another ledger begun in 1470, Cambi's London venture had by then been liquidated, but he still controlled a partnership styled "Antonio da Rabatta e Bernardo Cambi e compagni" in Bruges and a banking concern referred to as *La ragione del banco di Firenze* in Florence. Both of these establishments were probably *banchi grossi*, that is, banks dealing in exchange by bills. Bernardo Cambi had more than 5,600 florins invested in the Bruges partnership and only 2,800 florins in the Florentine bank.[48] The capital of medieval banks did not run into the millions and 5,000 florins was a large sum, for the purchasing power of money was high before the influx of gold and silver from the Americas in the sixteenth century.

Like Francesco Datini, the Medici were represented abroad either by branches or by correspondents. The firm maintained headquarters in Florence and had branches in Venice, Pisa, Rome, Milan, Geneva (later moved to Lyons), Avignon, London, and Bruges.[49] As in the case of the Datini *fondachi*, or establishments, each branch was a separate concern from both a legal and an administrative point of view. Ultimate control, however, was vested in the head of the Medici family, who owned at least fifty per cent of the capital of each subsidiary partnership. Each branch operated independently and opened current accounts for the main office in Florence and for other branches. Examples of *Nostro* and *Vostro* accounts are found as early as 1395, in a ledger kept in the main office in Florence during the lifetime of Averardo de' Medici.[50] Whether an account was a *Nostro* or a *Vostro* account was indicated by the words *per noi* or *per loro* written conspicuously at the top on both the debit and the credit sides. *Nostro* accounts as usual had two columns, one for the domestic currency and the other for the foreign currency. When an account balanced in foreign, but not in domestic, currency, the difference between debit and credit in the latter currency was adjusted by a transfer to Profit and Loss.[51] The different branches and a great number of foreign correspondents presumably had both *Nostro* and *Vostro* accounts in the books of the main office in Florence. For example, the surviving fragment of the Averardo de' Medici ledger contains both the *Nostro* and the *Vostro* account opened for the Rome branch, which was styled "Giovanni de' Medici e compagni di Roma."

Nostro and *Vostro* accounts appear not only in the books of the central office in Florence, but also in those of the various branches. Only a few scorched fragments of these branch account books have survived. According to a fragment of a Milanese ledger (1459), a *Nostro* account is designated by the words *per nostro conto corrente*, a *Vostro* account by *per loro conto corrente*.[52] In the ledger of the Bruges branch for the year 1441, there are two accounts with Cosimo de' Medici e compagni in Venice, the first a *Vostro* account (*per loro conto*) and the second a *Nostro* account (*per nostro conto là*), which is provided with the customary double column for the Venetian and the Flemish currencies.[53]

There is no essential difference in procedure between the Datini and the Medici (or Borromei) account books. The only significant change is that a set terminology seems to have gained general acceptance by 1450. In the Datini ledgers *Nostro* and *Vostro* accounts have no name (see Table II). In the Borromei and Medici ledgers of the fifteenth century the expressions *per nostro conto* and *per loro conto* are uniformly used with unimportant additions such as *corrente* or *di tempo*, in order to distinguish between current and time accounts. These expressions reappear without modification in the textbooks of the sixteenth and seventeenth centuries. The use of the third person (*loro*, "their") instead of the second person (*vostro*, "your") is a matter of convention. In French, *comptes "vostro"* and *comptes "loro"* are still synonymous today. Why the form *Vostro* instead of *Loro* triumphed in modern English usage is not clear.

STATEMENTS OF PROFITS

Most of the medieval banking firms were not specialized; they combined trade, banking, underwriting, and a great variety of other functions, including the recruiting of choir boys, the collection of annates, the hunt for lost classics, and the purchase of thoroughbred dogs.[54] Apparently they strove to take advantage of all opportunities that came along. As a rule, the profits

derived from banking were smaller than those derived from trade but larger than those derived from all other sources. Therefore, it is not surprising that merchant-bankers were primarily traders. Even the great banking house of the Medici followed the policy of emphasizing trade rather than banking. The Bruges manager wrote in one of his reports that commerce was no less profitable and more honorable than finance.[55] It is true that the latter was often tainted with usury. And this blot was not easily eradicated.

In medieval times, the distance between the import and the export specie points was rather large owing to the high cost of shipping bullion, to the insecurity of sea and land routes, and to the existence of seigniorage and other impediments to the to the free flow of specie. Exchange rates could thus fluctuate within a wide range without causing corrective specie flows. The amplitude of exchange fluctuations was undoubtedly a source of speculative profits for the banker, but he ran the risk of losing if he guessed wrong instead of right. Unless a banker had inside information (sometimes he was informed in advance of impending changes), his chances of gain were not any better than his chances of loss. Speculation, therefore, was not a secure foundation for exchange profits, especially not in the long run. Actually such profits were the result of the interest charges concealed in the exchange rates. Consequently, the structure of the money market was such that it favored the lender rather than the borrower and the buyer of bills rather than the seller [56] It is true that such a buyer could lose and sometimes did lose, if the swing of the exchange took a very unfavorable turn. In the majority of cases, however, adverse exchange fluctuations were not strong enough to overrule the counteracting influence of the rate of interest. Most of the time exchange transactions yielded a gross profit which was made up of interest plus a speculative profit, or minus a speculative loss.

Profits derived from banking (or exchange) transactions were an important source of income. This fact is not surprising, if one considers (1) that exchange transactions were largely based on time or usance bills; (2) that the resulting profits included interest; (3) that the interest

As the statement of profit and loss reveals, profits from trade, attaining a total of £689 11s. 5d. Barc., constitute the main source of income (Table III). Next comes an amount of £262 4s. Barc. representing the credit balance of the *Pro di Cambio* ("Profit on Exchange") account. With the exception of a few debit items, not exceeding £27 0s. 6d. Barc., this balance originates exclusively in transfers

TABLE III
FRANCESCO DI MARCO DA PRATO E COMPAGNI OF BARCELONA
STATEMENT OF PROFIT AND LOSS
JULY 11, 1397–JANUARY 10, 1399
(In Barcelonese Pounds)

Profits on Trade (*pro di mercatantie*)		£	689	11 5
Profits on Exchange (*pro di cambio*)			262	4 0
Credit Balance of Merchandise Expense (*Spese di mercatantie*)			133	13 7
Total of Gross Profits			£1,085	9 0
Deduct Expenses:				
Rent (*loghiere*) for eleven months	£ 36 13 4			
Irrecoverable account	3 8 0			
Convoy Expenses (*guidaggio*)	67 12 0			
Living Expenses (*spese fatte in mangiare e bere*) including seven months' rent	129 8 1			
Depreciation on Office Equipment (*danno di masserizie*)	16 17 0			
Reserve (*riserbo*) for Unpaid Taxes and Other Accrued Expenses	80 0 0			
Total Expenses			333	18 5
Net Income			£ 751	10 7

* Source: Arch. Dat., No. 801, Barcellona, Libro verde C.

rate was normally high (from eight to fifteen per cent) and rose even higher in times of monetary stringency.

Some idea concerning the importance of banking profits may be obtained from the Datini records. By using the data given in the ledger, it has been possible to reconstruct the statement of profit and loss of the Barcelona branch for a period of eighteen months beginning July 10, 1397, and ending January 31, 1399. During this period of time, the branch made a gross profit of £1,085 9s. 0d. Barc. and a net profit of £751 10s. 7d. Barc. after deducting all expenses. The latter figure agrees with that of the original balance sheet, a copy of which is still in the Datini archives.[57]

from *Nostro* accounts to the credit of *Pro di Cambio*.[58] This fact confirms what has been said before, namely, that exchange transactions were usually profitable to the banker. The inclusion of interest in the exchange rates was responsible for the existence of a margin between the exchange rate at home and abroad. For example, the écu of twenty-two Flemish groats was habitually rated higher in Bruges than in Barcelona. So long as this margin was unaffected by adverse exchange fluctuations, the *Nostro* account of the banker's agent abroad tended to have a credit surplus which required periodic adjustment. As the entries in the Datini account books clearly show, adjustments were the exclusive source of banking or exchange profits.

The statement of profit and loss of Datini's Barcelona branch reveals also that the credit balance of Merchandise Expense (*Spese di mercatantie*) was a third source of income. The anomaly of an expense account that has a credit balance can be explained by the fact that charges to customers for brokerage and other incidentals exceeded the sums of money which were actually spent. The merchandise expense account is also debited for a

exchange differences. The *Spese di mercatantie* account again has a credit balance, because more was collected from customers than was actually spent. A reserve for accrued taxes and other expenses "which remain to be paid" is also set up. Without such a reserve, profits would have been overstated. From the Datini records, it is clear that expenses incurred during one period were paid during the next period out of the reserve which was provided for

TABLE IV

Francesco di Marco da Prato e Compagni of Barcelona
Statement of Profit and Loss*

February 1, 1399–January 31, 1400
(In Barcelonese Pounds)

Profits on Trade (*pro di mercatantie*)		£249 17 10
Profits on Exchange (*pro di cambio*)		289 11 8
Credit Balance of Merchandise Expense (*spese di mercatantie*)		154 10 2
Total of Gross Profits		£693 19 8
Deduct Expenses:		
Bad Debts Written Off	£ 3 13 9	
Rent	40 0 0	
Depreciation (*danno di masserizie*)	20 0 0	
Living Expenses	85 11 7	
Reserve for Unpaid Taxes and Accrued Expenses	129 10 2	
Total Expenses		278 15 6
Net Income		£415 4 2

* Source: Arch. Dat., No. 809 (Nicastro No. 177), Barcellona, Libro di mercatantie D.

reserve of eighty pounds Barcelonese which was set aside in order to provide for the payment of unpaid taxes and other accrued expenses. So far as I know, this is one of the earliest examples of accrual accounting to avoid overstatement of profits.

It has been possible to reconstruct the statement of profit and loss for the succeeding period of one year, extending from February 1, 1399, to January 31, 1400 (Table IV). For this year, the profits from the purchase and sale of commodities were slightly less than those on foreign exchange or banking. They amounted to £289 11s. 8d. Barc. These profits were determined by the process, described above, of adjusting all *Nostro* accounts for

this purpose at the end of the former fiscal period. Incidentally, it is interesting to note that this statement of profit and loss includes an item of twenty pounds Barcelonese representing the estimated decline in the value of office equipment or furniture (*masserizie*).

The firm Filippo Borromei e compagni of London determined profits and losses according to a system somewhat different from that of the Datini branch in Barcelona. All operating results, whether they originated in trade, in banking, or in some other activity, were lumped together in one account called *Avanzi e Disavanzi* ("Profit and Loss"). With regard to commodities, the firm had a system of venture accounting: that is, a separate account was opened for each shipment and later closed to Profit and Loss after all the goods had been sold. Any balance left over represented either a profit or a loss. Profits arising out of banking were determined in the usual way by adjusting the *Nostro* accounts of foreign correspondents for exchange differences.

for instance, and resell these ducats, three months later, in Venice at the price of 45½ or 46 sterlings payable in London after another period of three months.[61] Thus a banker gained 2½ or 3 sterlings on each ducat over a period of six months.

While a banker usually made a profit, it could happen (and it did happen) that

TABLE V

FILIPPO BORROMEI E COMPAGNI OF LONDON
STATEMENTS OF PROFIT AND LOSS*
(In Pounds Sterling)

Explanation	1436	1437	1438	1439
Profits:				
On Merchandise	£ 46 0 0	£149 17 6	£136 8 7	£207 2 11
On Exchange	75 17 9	255 4 10	199 15 1	207 3 11
Commissions	3 8 10	105 1 6	144 13 2	155 1 2
Miscellaneous	2 12 6	... .	... .	... .
Total	£127 19 1	£510 3 10	£480 16 10	£569 8 0
Losses:				
On Merchandise	... .	£ 1 3 5	£ 53 3 0	£ 44 19 6
On Exchange	... .	136 2 11	103 14 1	14 2 7
Expenses:				
Organization	£ 22 5 2			
General	40 0 0	44 9 5	60 0 0	63 10 0
Mailing Charges	3 9 11	3 7 1	6 5 7	7 13 7
Rent	9 1 3	8 10 6	20 8 8	18 12 8
Salaries and Wages	7 6 11	9 16 1	12 6 11	12 17 8
Gifts and Charities	12 17 0	... .	2 6 8	2 1 4
Brokerage	7 16 2		... .	
Unclassified	5 0	3 10 0	1 13 6	11 6 7
Errors	... .	... .	5 16 9	6 12 0
Subtotal	£103 1 5	£206 19 5	£265 15 2	£181 15 11
Net Profits	24 17 8	303 4 5	215 1 8	387 12 1
Total	£127 19 1	£510 3 10	£480 16 10	£569 8 0

* Source: Gerolamo Biscaro, "Il banco Filippo Borromei e compagni di Londra," *Archivio storico lombardo*, XL (1913), pp. 381-85.

Under conditions of equilibrium, a lender was always bound to make a profit. For example, the Venetian ducat was usually worth from three to five sterlings more in Venice than in London. Similarly the Flemish écu of twenty-four groats was normally quoted one sterling higher in Bruges than in London.[60] This discrepancy automatically resulted in a profit for the banker, since he could buy Venetian ducats in London at 42 sterlings per ducat,

he lost on certain exchange transactions· The records of the Borromei firm in London show that there were losses, but that unprofitable transactions were much less frequent than profitable ones. According to those data, no losses on foreign exchange were incurred in 1436, the first year of operation (see Table V). In 1437, the Borromei made a profit on some accounts, but suffered a loss on others. Profits, however, exceeded losses by £119 1s. 11d. st.

The following year the firm lost a total of £103 14s. 1d. st. on several accounts, but this loss was made good by a profit of £199 15s. 1d. st. on other accounts, so that in the end there was still a net profit of £96 1s. 0d. st. In 1439, the Borromei had very few losses on exchange dealings. The emergence of losses on some accounts is attributable to the fact that exchange oscillations were sometimes violent enough to neutralize the influence of the rate of interest. The very fact that credit was tied up with foreign exchange made banking a speculative business.

The more familiar one becomes with the records of medieval merchants, the more clearly it appears that accounting had achieved a high level of perfection long before the middle of the fifteenth century. Francesco Datini died in 1410. His records contain examples not only of *Vostro* and *Nostro* accounts, but also of periodic financial statements, accruals, depreciation, cost accounting, and even of inventory valuation according to the rule "cost or market, whichever is the lower."[62] Not one of these topics is adequately discussed in Paciolo's famous treatise on bookkeeping. The explanation for this silence is not hard to find. In the opinion of competent scholars, Paciolo simply incorporated in his *Summa* a handbook on bookkeeping which was used by beginners in the Venetian schools. Such a work could hardly be expected to attempt complicated problems which beginners would be unable to grasp.

FOREIGN EXCHANGE IN EARLY TEXTS

Casanova (1558) was the first Venetian writer to touch upon the problem of foreign exchange. If his description of commercial practices is accurate and trustworthy, it seems that *Nostro* accounts were little used in Venice but were replaced by an impersonal account called "Exchange with Antwerp," (London, Lyons, or whatever the place might be).[63] The

exchange differences were eliminated from the current accounts with correspondents abroad by using a fixed exchange rate. As a result of this procedure, exchange differences appear in the Exchange accounts just mentioned.[64] This method has the serious defects of being cumbersome, of involving extra work, and of necessitating the arbitrary choice of a fixed exchange rate. I do not know why this method was preferred in Venice. It is certain that Venetian business practices frequently differed in important respects from those of other Italian cities.

One of the examples given by Casanova debits the account Exchange from Lyons to Venice (*Cambio di Lion a Venetia*) and credits the firm Antonio and Ludovico Bonvisi Brothers of Lyons. Casanova then debits the payor, a Flemish resident by the name of Daniel da Molin (van der Molen) and credits Exchange from Lyons to Venice.[65] This account does not balance, because the gold marks in the face value of the bill are converted into Venetian ducats at different rates in the first and the second entries. The resulting discrepancy between debit and credit is corrected by a transfer from the account Exchange from Lyons to Venice to credit of Profit and Loss. Incidentally, it appears from Casanova's examples that bills on Venice were paid by transfer in bank rather than in specie, which confirms what we know from other sources.[66]

In connection with foreign exchange, Casanova remarks that it would not pay to remit from Venice to Antwerp at any rate below seventy-one groats per Venetian ducat.[67] It is not clear from his explanations whether he means that this rate is the mint-par or the Venetian export specie point.[68] Casanova adds that, if the banker intends to return the money by re-exchange from Antwerp to Venice, it does not make any difference whether the exchange is above or below the rate of 71 groats per ducat. The banker, Casanova observes, is bound to gain so long as the price of the ducat is lower in Antwerp than in Venice.[69] There is much truth in this last remark of Casanova's. A banker who operated between two markets and was a deliverer in both always made a profit, if the rate of exchange was higher in the place whose currency was the fixed term of comparison than in the place whose currency was the variable term of the equation.[70] It did not matter whether the level of both rates was above or below the mint-par.

The illustrations in the work of Simon Grisogono, a Venetian author of the seventeenth century, are completely lacking in originality.[71] He copies Casanova's examples without any change.[72] Another Venetian author, Giovanantonio Moschetti, whose treatise on bookkeeping is far superior to that of Grisogono, gives two examples of dry exchange.[73] In one case, the borrower actually benefits from a loan and has to repay less than he originally borrowed. As has been pointed out, it sometimes happened that the borrower or taker gained at the expense of the lender or deliverer, if the exchange rates were thrown out of gear. Moschetti's second example deals with the more common case in which the borrower has to pay something in addition to repaying the principal. This "something" includes interest, but is not "pure" interest by any means. In Moschetti's case, a Venetian merchant raises 730 ducats by selling a bill of exchange on London at the rate of 54 sterlings per ducat. Since he has no credit in London with which he can honor the bill when it falls due, the agreement is that a correspondent in England will take care of this matter by drawing on Venice at the prevailing rate of exchange. In Moschetti's example this rate is 53 sterlings per ducat, with the result that the lender makes a profit of one sterling on each duc-

at, while the bills of exchange are traveling from Venice to London and back (see Table VI).

In this case the lender's profit (or the borrower's loss) arises out of the one sterling difference in the value of the ducat (54*d*. st. in Venice and 53*d*. st. in London). Any increase of this difference would naturally increase the lender's profit (or the borrower's loss). Any decrease of the difference would decrease that profit (or loss) up to the point where the ducat is rated as high in London as in Venice. At this point, the difference being zero, there would be neither a profit nor a loss. If the ducat were quoted higher in London than in Venice, there must needs be a loss to the lender and a profit to the borrower. Such a situation is not compatible with equilibrium and cannot be permanent, since lenders prefer to keep their money in strongboxes rather than to lend it at a loss. This attitude, by affecting the supply of loanable funds, would quickly lead to a restoration of equilibrium.

On the whole, the problem of foreign exchange did not receive adequate treatment in the early Italian works on double-entry bookkeeping. What little information they gave to beginners had to be supplemented by practical knowledge which could be acquired only in the counting house.

The early writers on bookkeeping in the Low Countries were strongly influenced by Paciolo and did not pay much attention to the problem of foreign exchange. Ympyn, however, has a chapter dealing with the four different kinds of exchange.[74] In connection with dry exchange, he observes that "it fortuneth sometyme that suche money is taken up to little losse, and sometyme to muche, like as the aventure requireth."[75] This statement is perfectly true, since the unpredictable swing of the exchange rates determined how much or how little a borrower would pay for a loan. In some cases, he might even have to repay

TABLE VI

JOURNAL ENTRIES RELATING TO DRY EXCHANGE BETWEEN VENICE AND LONDON
ACCORDING TO AN EXAMPLE GIVEN IN MOSCHETTI'S
TREATISE ON BOOKKEEPING*
(In Venetian Pounds)†

Description	Amount							
	Dr.				Cr.			
	£	s	d	p	£	s	d	p
(1) Alessandro Allegris (deliverer or lender)...................	73	0	0					
Exchange with London.............................					73	0	0	
For sale of a bill of exchange on London duc. 730 equal to 657 crowns or £164 5s. st. at the rate of 54d. st. per ducat.								
(2) Bondomier Bank (transfer bank)........................	73	0	0					
Alessandro Allegris.................................					73	0	0	
For receipt of the proceeds of the sale of a bill of exchange, written to our credit at the Bondomier Bank.								
(3) Exchange with London.................................		4	11	10				
Cash...						4	11	10
For payment in cash of the commission of the London correspondent, ¼% on 657 crowns of 5s. st. apiece equals 10s. 11d. st. at 53d. st. per ducat.								
(4) Exchange with London.................................	74	2	7	8				
Alessandro Allegris.................................					74	2	7	8
For acceptance of bill from London on Venice, face value duc. 741 grossi 7 piccioli 8 being the equivalent of £163 14s. 1d. st. at 53d. st. per ducat.								
(5) Alessandro Allegris....................................	74	2	7	8				
Bondomier Bank...................................					74	2	7	8
For payment of London bill of exchange, written to our debit and to his credit at the Bank.								
(6) Profit and Loss......................................	1	7	6	18				
Exchange with London.............................					1	7	6	18
To close the Exchange with London account.								

* Source: Giovanantonio Moschetti, *Dell'universal trattato di libri doppi* (Venice, 1610), pp. 170–171.
† The Venetian pound groat (*libra di grossi*) was divided into 20 shillings or *soldi* of 12 groats or *grossi* each. Each groat was subdivided into 32 *piccioli*. The Venetian currency system was based on the ducat of 24 *grossi*. One pound was worth ten ducats.

less than the principal, as in one of Moschetti's examples.

Aside from this chapter, Ympyn has little to offer. He is silent on the subject of *Vostro* and *Nostro* accounts and gives only one or two illustrations in order to show how exchange transactions should be recorded in the books.[76] Ympyn himself was an Antwerp mercer whose capital was certainly not large enough to engage successfully in banking. This circumstance may explain why banking does not receive more emphasis in his book.

Mennher, a Bavarian, and Savonne, a Frenchman, were both schoolmasters in Antwerp, where they taught arithmetic and their native languages besides bookkeeping.[77] Mennher scarcely mentions foreign exchange, but Savonne gives some details on the clearing of debts at the fairs of

Lyons.[78] The Dutch author, Claes Pieterszoon of Deventer, has two illustrations, one regarding the purchase, and the other regarding the payment, of a bill of exchange. He opens an Exchange account (*Rekening van Wissel*) for the foreign correspondent in order to record the acceptance of a bill of exchange. Upon payment of the bill, this account is closed by debiting the correspondent's current account (*Loopende Rekening*) and crediting *Rekening van Wissel*.[79] Why this useless complication is introduced is not clear to me. Perhaps the author did not know much about foreign banking himself. In the sixteenth century the art of banking was still considered a "mystery" whose secrets were closely guarded by the bankers.

The first Flemish authors who refer to *Nostro* and *Vostro* accounts are Barthélemy van Renterghem and his follower Zacharias van Hoorebeke.[80] The latter's book contains no text but only an illustration. *Nostro* and *Vostro* accounts called *mon* and *son compte courant* are opened for foreign correspondents. The purpose of having such accounts is not explained. Modern authors have criticized their predecessors for having no Notes Receivable or Notes Payable accounts.[81] I think that this criticism is unfair. One should not forget that there was little need for such accounts, since commerical paper was neither endorsable nor discountable as it is today.

The accounting problems of foreign exchange which received only scant attention from Paciolo and his imitators in Italy and in the Low Countries are dealt with at great length by the Dutch authors of the seventeenth century. Waningen van Kampen, for example, opens a special account for all bills payable or receivable at a certain fair.[82] These fairs grew up because the usury prohibition prevented the development of local credit institutions and because the *distantia loci* remained an essential feature of the exchange contract. The most important fairs were those of Lyons, Frankfort, Besançon, Genoa, and Piacenza.[83]

Waningen also takes up the problem of *Nostro* and *Vostro* accounts, which were designated by the words *mijne* (and *zijne*) *rekening* in the Dutch, and *mon* (and *son*) *compte courant* in the French, editions of his works.[84] He explains carefully that a *Vostro* account is opened for a foreign principal and a *Nostro* account for a foreign agent. Consequently, both accounts are needed, if a foreign correspondent is at times a principal and at other times an agent. Waningen's illustrations show that *Nostro* accounts are kept in two currencies and are adjusted for exchange differences. Waningen fails to stress the point that *Nostro* and *Vostro* accounts are of crucial importance in foreign banking.

The same approach to the problem is found in Antonio van Neulighem, in Abraham de Graaf, in the anonymous author of a textbook published in 1754, and in other Dutch authors.[85] M. de la Porte, whose book was the most popular treatise in eighteenth-century France, explains that a *Nostro* account (*mon compte courant*) has to have two extension columns because it is in foreign money that accounts are settled with agents abroad. "They always make," de la Porte explains to his reader, "all their collections and disbursements in the currency of their country."[86] The other explanations given by the author are good but contain nothing that is new.[87]

Among the early English writers on bookkeeping, John Carpenter was apparently the first to devote much space to the recording of exchange transactions. He explains in great detail what is to be done in a number of cases, for instance, when a bill is purchased, issued, accepted, or paid. He then makes the following remark, placed in italics in order to attract the attention of the reader: "But you must remember to make a difference betwixt his account and your account."[88] Carpenter goes on to explain what he means by "his account" and "your account."

As for example—All which another doth for you, you shall write it, Such are on *my* account.
And contrarily, that which you doe for him, you shall write it, such are on *his* account. [Italics mine]

Carpenter seems to think that it is possible to determine the profit or the loss on each single transaction. For example, he advises his reader to debit the acceptor and to credit the foreign correspondent's *Nostro* (or "my") account and Profit and Loss, whenever money is remitted by exchange "with gain."[89] For as much as foreign moneys are found "more for credits than for debts," such gains, according to Carpenter, should be carried at once to Profit and Loss. I do not believe that this is a practical suggestion. According to the records of medieval merchant-bankers, exchange differences were actually ascertained and transferred to Profit and Loss only periodically, usually when closing the books.

The definitions given by Carpenter suggest perhaps better than any others what the words *Nostro* and *Vostro* accounts really mean and how they came into use in the English language. A *Nostro* or "our" account is an account for recording those transactions in which "we" are principals. A *Vostro* or "your" account is an account for recording those transactions in which "you," the correspondents, are principals and "we" are agents. Since principals, and not agents, assume the responsibility for exchange differences, it follows that the foreign currency is the ruling currency in the case of *Nostro* accounts. In the case of *Vostro* accounts, on the contrary, the local currency sets the rule and determines who is debtor or creditor and for how much.

This survey of the early writings on

bookkeeping is rather disappointing. It reveals two striking facts: (1) the absence of any important innovations between the end of the fourteenth and that of the seventeenth centuries; (2) the lag of theoretical treatises behind actual business practices. This lag may be due to the fact that most early writers, including Paciolo, were schoolmasters with no practical business experience, or that didactic works necessarily give a simplified and distorted view of actual business practice. Whatever the truth may be, there is no doubt that by the end of the fourteenth century double-entry bookkeeping had reached maturity. With regard to banking, a satisfactory system had been worked out in order to keep a record of exchange transactions and to determine the profits accruing therefrom.

As our analysis of the Datini, Borromei, Cambi, and Medici records clearly shows, banking profits originated in exchange differences. Therefore, bankers were "extremely accurate in distinguishing My account from His account," as Postlethwayt remarks, and he knew very well what he was talking about.[90] The ledgers of medieval bankers do not contain any account called "Interest Income." Nor is there any account for Interest Expense. It is true that the Italian merchant-bankers often paid interest on time deposits, but it was called *deposito, discrezione, dono* ("gift"), *guadagno* ("gain"), or *provvedigione* ("commission").[91] The use of the word "interest" itself was avoided like the plague.

True, interest was concealed in the exchange rates, but the presence of the interest factor was boldly denied.[92] The merchants argued—and the canonists agreed—that exchange transactions did not involve a *mutuum* or a loan of money for certain gain. It is quite true that the profit on individual exchange transactions was uncertain. As the analysis of our data reveals, it did happen that occasionally the lender lost. Nevertheless, the reasoning of the canonists was fallacious: they overlooked an essential point, namely, that the presence of the time factor tipped the scales in favor of the banker. While he suffered a few losses, the banker was bound to gain on most transactions, if he was a clever and cautious manager. Losses occurred only when the exchange rates were not in a position of equilibrium. Such a condition could not persist over a long period of time, for the economic forces of the money market automatically tended toward the restoration of equilibrium. The profit-and-loss statements of the Datini and the Borromei firms and the illustrations in Moschetti's treatise afford conclusive evidence that the banking business was speculative but usually profitable.

The records of the merchant-bankers and the illustrations given by the writers on bookkeeping make it absolutely clear that bills of exchange were not discounted. The practice of discounting *domestic* bills did not develop until the middle of the seventeenth century. Prior to that time there were no domestic bills; all bills were foreign bills and nearly always involved a real exchange transaction. The writings of the early English mercantilists never mention the rate of discount, but are full of references to the rate of exchange. This fact in itself is significant.

In the Middle Ages, the word "discount" was not unknown but referred to what would be called today a "cash discount," that is, a refund to a customer for prompt payment.[93] "Discount" acquired another meaning in the seventeenth century when bankers, especially in England, began to deduct interest from the face value of domestic bills. The Frenchman de la Porte, whose *Science des Négociants* was first published in 1712, gives the two meanings of discount in the glossary of business terms included in his book.[94] The

Englishman Postlethwayt in his famous *Universal Dictionary of Trade and Commerce* (first edition, 1751) emphasizes that the word "discount" has different meanings among bankers and among traders or merchants.[95]

It is clear from the data examined here that "banking" in the Middle Ages meant "a traffic in bills of exchange." Even for the Frenchman de la Porte, early in the eighteenth century, *faire la banque* and *faire le commerce de lettres de change* are still one and the same thing.[96] There were also local transfer banks such as the Venetian *banchi di scritta* described by Paciolo, the famous Bank of St. George in Genoa, and later the *Wisselbank* of Amsterdam. (Such banks, according to Dafforne and others, did not exist in England.)[97] These are the two types of banking mentioned by de la Porte.[98] He knew no other. But he probably was not acquainted with conditions in England. By that time great changes had occurred across the Channel.

It is, of course, untrue that banking originated in the British Isles or that the medieval precedents can be dismissed as unimportant. The records of the Italian bankers testify to the contrary. But it is true that *modern* banking methods were first developed by the London goldsmiths and later by the Bank of England and the private bankers in Lombard Street. This "new fashioned mystery" of banking had no precedent either in England or elsewhere and consisted in the trade in bullion, the *discounting* of domestic bills, the issue of notes, and the acceptance of deposits payable on demand, or "keeping a running cash," as it was called in those days.

Postlethwayt, who was well informed, calls this type of business "domestic banking" and distinguishes it from "another species" which is properly known by the name of "foreign banking." This type of banking, Postlethwayt explains, consists largely in the "negotiation of foreign bills of exchange." This foreign banking is little practised in England as compared with the Continent where, however, little business is done in domestic bills.[99] Postlethwayt adds that "one motive to domestic banking" is the discounting of domestic bills, but that foreign banking requires "more sagacity," because of the "nicety" involved in the computation of the exchange rates. Foreign banking also requires extensive knowledge of "the ebbs and flows of the exchange" so that one knows "where to *purchase* bills cheapest and *dispose of* them dearest" [italics mine].[100] This last passage especially has a familiar ring. It is a repetition of similar observations made by Francesco Balducci Pegolotti, Giovanni da Uzzano, Luca Paciolo, Bernardo Davanzati, Alvise Casanova, and other Italian writers on the business of banking and foreign exchange.

REFERENCES

¹ This study is based largely on Italian material collected in 1938 during a trip made possible by a grant from the Belgian *Fonds National de la Recherche Scientifique.*

² Thomas Mun, *England's Treasure by Forraign Trade* (London, 1664; reprinted Oxford, 1933), p. 17.

³ Raymond de Roover, "The Lingering Influence of Medieval Practices," the ACCOUNTING REVIEW, XVIII (April, 1943), pp. 148–51.

⁴ Luca Paciolo, "Particularis de computis et scripturis," distinctio 9, tractatus 11, cap. 24, *Summa de Arithmetica, Geometria, Proportioni et Proportionalita* (Venice, 1494), fol. 206. English translations: John B. Geijsbeek, *Ancient Double-Entry Bookkeeping* (Denver, 1914), pp. 62–63; Pietro Crivelli, *An Original Translation of the Treatise on Double-Entry Book-Keeping by Frater Lucas Pacioli* (London, 1924), pp. 71–77.

⁵ The London house of the Borromei in the fifteenth century apparently accepted deposits from local merchants. See Gerolamo Biscaro, "Il banco Filippo Borromei e compagni di Londra (1436–1439)," *Archivio storico lombardo*, XL (1913), p. 283. Malynes (*A Treatise of the Canker of England's Commonwealth* [London, 1601], pp. 23–24) inveighs against the bankers because they accept deposits and make payments by "assignation." By these means, the bankers, according to Malynes, gather the wealth of London into their hands.

⁶ Paciolo, "De cambiis seu cambitionibus," distinctio 9, tractatus 4, *op. cit.*, fol. 167ᵛ.

⁷ For information on mercantile customs, see: Francesco Balducci Pegolotti, *La Pratica della Mercatura*,

ed. Allan Evans (Cambridge, Mass., 1936); Giovanni di Antonio da Uzzano, *Pratica della Mercatura*, Vol. IV of Gian-Francesco Pagnini, *Della Decima* (Lucca-Lisbon, 1766); *El libro di mercatantie et usanze de' paesi*, ed. Franco Borlandi (Turin, 1936).

⁸ Abbott Payson Usher, *The Early History of Deposit Banking in Mediterranean Europe* (Cambridge, Mass., 1943), pp. 103–105.

⁹ Raymond de Roover, "Money, Banking, and Credit in Medieval Bruges," *The Journal of Economic History*, II (1942), Suppl., p. 55. The terms *datore* and *prenditore* are apt to create great confusion because their meaning has changed in the course of centuries, both in Italian and in French. Today *datore di cambio* (Fr. *donneur de change*) means the person who gives the bill, consequently the drawer. The word *prenditore* (Fr. *preneur*) today refers to the payee or presenter of a bill. Up to the beginning of the seventeenth century the meaning of these terms was that indicated above, that is, the *datore* gave the money and received the bill; the *prenditore* took up the money and gave the bill.

¹⁰ On the theory of exchange in the medieval and mercantilist periods, see Raymond de Roover, "What is Dry Exchange? A Contribution to the Study of English Mercantilism," *The Journal of Political Economy*, Vol. LII, September, 1944.

¹¹ Clement Armstrong, in his *Treatise concerning the Staple*, inveighs against bankers who occupy their money by exchange, both inward and outward, and never bestow it on any merchandise of the Realm (*Tudor Economic Documents*, eds. R. H. Tawney and Eileen Power [New York, 1924], III, p. 107).

¹² As used here, the term "agio" refers to windfall profits originating in exchange differences. "Disagio" refers to windfall losses having the same origin. The terms "agio" and "disagio" come from the Italian words *vantaggio* and *disavvantaggio*. See Florence Edler, *Glossary of Mediaeval Terms of Business: Italian Series, 1200–1600* (Cambridge, Mass., 1934), pp. 107, 310.

¹³ Perhaps the reader may be tempted to compare medieval exchange dealings with modern arbitrage. There is indeed a certain degree of similarity. But, since the telegraph had not yet been invented, it was impossible in the Middle Ages for a banker to buy in one market and to sell simultaneously in another market.

¹⁴ Gaetano Corsani (*I fondaci e i banchi di un mercante pratese del Trecento: Contributo alla storia della ragioneria e del commercio* [Prato, 1922], pp. 86, 95) gives a few examples of *Nostro* accounts from the Datini records.

¹⁵ For the biography of Datini, see Enrico Bensa, *Francesco di Marco da Prato* (Milan, 1928). The only study available in English is an article by Robert Brun, "A Fourteenth-Century Merchant of Italy: Francesco Datini of Prato," *Journal of Economic and Business History*, II (1930), pp. 451–66.

¹⁶ Paciolo, "Dei cambiis seu cambitionibus," *op. cit.*, fol. 167ᵛ; Alvise Casanova, "Svegliamento agli insperti che per Anversa cambiano," *Specchio lucidissimo* (Venice, 1558), no pagination.

¹⁷ Bills of exchange were commonly bought and sold through brokers. The agent who paid the brokerage charges had the right to recover them from his principal. The entry was *Dr.* the principal's *Vostro* account, *Cr.* Brokerage (*Sensaria*).

¹⁸ Prato (Tuscany), Archivio Datini [henceforth Arch. Dat.], No. 841 (old No. 205 in Nicastro's published inventory), Fondaco di Barcellona [henceforth Barcellona], Libro di cambi e dette di banco, fol. 48ᵛ.

The date of the entry is November 4, 1399. The University of Illinois library has a duplicate set of the microfilms which the author made in the Datini archives.

[19] At that time the exchange rate between Bruges and Barcelona was quoted in both places at so many shillings and deniers of Barcelona per écu of 22 Flemish groats.

[20] There is an example of a *per loro* item on the same page of the memorandum book.

[21] Arch. Dat., No. 802 (Nicastro, No. 170), Barcellona, Libro nero D, fol. 239ʳ: Alberto e Bernardo degli Alberti e conpagni di Bruggia deon dare a dì 4 di novembre ▽ 550 di Filipo rimettemo loro per uso in Diamante degli Alberti e conpagni per la valuta a sol. 9 den 6½ per ▽ qui ad Antonio d'Alesandro e conpagni in questo carta 241 debe avere, sono di gr. 22 per ▽. £50 s.8 d.4 gr. £262 s.7 d.11 [Barc.].

[22] Arch. Dat., No. 841, fol. 55ʳ. The date is December 16, 1399.

[23] Arch. Dat., No. 802, fol. 240ʳ: E deon avere a dì 16 di dicenbre ▽ 429 1/11 di Filipo di gr. 22 per ▽ traemo loro per uso in Diamante e Altobianco degli Alberti e conpagni per la valuta a sol. 9. den. 11 per ▽ qui da Nicholaio degli Alberti e Filipozo Soldani in questo c. 244 debe dare, sono di grossi. . . . £38 s.8 d.4. £207 s.15 d.11 [Barc.].

[24] Arch. Dat., No. 1146, Cambiali. "In the name of God, Amen. 12 December, 1399. Pay by this first [of exchange] at usance to Domenico Sancio six hundred écus at 10s. 5d. per écu, which ▽ 600 at 10s. 5d. per écu are for the value [received] from Jacopo Gosco, and charge [this] to our account here. May God protect you Giovanni Orlandini and Piero Benizi & Partners in Bruges." On the back: "Francesco [Datini] from Prato & Partners in Barcelona. First [of exchange]."

[25] Arch. Dat., No. 802, Libro nero D, fol. 283ᵛ.

[26] Bensa, *op. cit.*, p. 333. There are other examples among the bills photographed by the author.

[27] Arch. Dat., No. 802, fol. 284ʳ: Giovanni Orlandini e Piero Benizi e conpagni di Brugia deon avere a dì 26 di dicenbre [1399] ▽ 200 a sol. 10 den. 6 per ▽ rimisonci per dì 20 di genaio in Giovanni Bibero ne la facia da lato debe dare, per altri ne diero a Piero Gilaberto . . . .
. . . .£105 s.0 d.0

[28] The same custom existed in Venice, Milan, Genoa, Bruges, and other European commercial centers. According to entries in the ledger of Jacopo Badoer, a Venetian merchant residing in Constantinople in the second quarter of the fifteenth century, Italian transfer banks were operating in that city. Fabio Besta (*La Regioneria* [3d ed.], Milan, 1922], III, p. 313) cites one entry. I have found numerous others in the original account book in Venice: Archivio di Stato; Archivio dei Cinque Savi alla Mercanzia; Busta, 958; Registro Badoer, 1436–1439.

[29] By a municipal ordinance of 1397 all money-changers were required to have their offices in the Exchange, called *Lonja* in Catalan and *loggia* in Italian. Pere Brunet is mentioned as a private banker in official records and in the account books (1377–82) of another Barcelona transfer bank, Pere des Caus & Andreu d'Olivella. See Usher, *op. cit.*, pp. 245, 258, 268.

[30] A typical example among many is the following: On December 26, 1399, the Datini branch in Barcelona received a remittance from the Orlandini in Bruges. This remittance was accepted on that date by Giovanni Bibero, the drawee, a draper of Barcelona. The entry in the Datini ledger to record the transaction is: *Dr* Giovanni Bibero, *Cr.* the Orlandini (see reference 27).

On January 24, 1400, when the bill fell due, it was paid by transfer in bank. The following entry was posted to the ledger: *Dr.* Piero Brunetto, banker, *Cr.* Giovanni Bibero. The debit to Brunetto's account reads:
E a dì detto disonci per Giovanni Bibero drapiere in questo carta 284 deb'avere £105.0.0
The credit to Bibero's account reads:
Giovanni Bibero dè avere a dì 24 di genaio £105 diseci per lui Piero Brunetto, in questo a c. 297 debe dare. £105.0.0
(Arch. Dat., No. 802, fols. 284ʳ, 297ᵛ)
Note the expression: *diseci per lui Piero Brunetto* ("Piero Brunetto told us for him" that we received credit for £105).

[31] Arch. Dat., No. 801, Barcellona, Libro Verde C, fol. 159ᵛ. The exchange rate was 15s. 4d. Barc. per florin of Genoa.

[32] *Ibid.*, fol. 161ʳ: Giovanni Bonini e Domenicho de' Benedetti deono avere a dì 24 di maggio [1398] £ dugiento sesanta s.13 d.4 bar. prometemo loro per lettera da Genova de' Ghalderotti per fl. 340 da Giovanni di Giovanni, sono per Diamante e Altobianco di Brugia in questo c. 159 debe [dare] £260 s.12 d.4

[33] Arch. Dat., No. 800 (Nicastro, No. 168), Barcellona, Libro rosso B, fols. 11ᵛ, 31ʳ.

[34] Arch. Dat., No. 802, Libro nero D, Fols. 283ᵛ, 284ʳ. The debit entry in Barberi's account reads as follows: E dè dare a dì 28 di dicenbre [1399] £520 s.16 d.8 traseci per uso in noi medesimi per ▽ 1000 di Filipo, n'ebe da Giovanni Orlandini e Piero Benizi per loro in questo c. 284 . . . .£520 s.16 d.8
The corresponding credit in the Orlandini account reads as follows: E deon avere detto dì £520 s.16 d.8 remisonci per uso in noi medesimi per ▽ mille ne die a Ghuigliemo Barberi per loro in questo a c. 238 debe [dare]. £520 s.26 d.8
The rate of exchange was 10s. 5d. Barc. per écu.

[35] de Roover, "What is Dry Exchange?" *loc. cit.*

[36] Jacques du Puys, *L'art des lettres de change* (Paris, 1693), pp. 34–36.

[37] Arch. Dat., No. 801, Libro verde C, fol. 262ᵛ. For the Italian text see Table II, the first entry on the debit side of the Mannini's *Vostro* account. Another example is found in No. 802, Libro nero D, fols. 39ᵛ and 114ʳ.

[38] Arch. Dat., No. 801, fol. 250 .

[39] Biscaro, "Il banco Filippo Borromei e compagni di Londra," *loc. cit.*, pp. 41–42.

[40] Excerpts from this account are given by Biscaro, *loc. cit.*, pp. 334–337.

[41] *Ibid.*, pp. 336–341.

[42] *Ibid.*, pp. 332–333.

[43] *Ibid.*, pp. 327, 334.

[44] Bensa, *op. cit.*, pp. 335, 349. There are several examples among the bills photographed by the author in 1938. One reads, *ponete a conto di nostri maggiori*, another, *por ete a conto di Deo Ambruogio di Parigi*, etc.

[45] Biscaro, *loc. cit.*, p. 283.

[46] *Ibid.*, p. 369.

[47] The author had the privilege of examining this ledger and other account books of the Cambi family in 1938. At that time these records were in the possession of Mr. Otto Lange of Florence. Later, they became the property of Prince Filippo Ginori Conti of Florence. The ledger covers a period from 1435 to 1459. The book was first kept in Bruges, where Bernardo Cambi resided from 1435 until 1450, when he returned to Florence, his native city.

[48] Ledger of Bernardo di Giovanni Cambi, 1470–1490, fol. 2.

[49] Heinrich Sieveking, *Die Handlungsbuecher der Medici* ("Sitzungsberichte der Kais. Akademie der Wissenschaften in Wien, Philosophisch-Historische Klasse," Vol. CLI, No. 5 [Vienna, 1905]), p. 9.

[50] Florence, Archivio di Stato, Mediceo avanti il Principato, Filza No. 133, No. 1.

[51] An excellent example is given by Alberto Ceccherelli, *I libri di mercatura della banca Medici e l'applicazione della partita doppia a Firenze nel secolo XIV* (Florence, 1913), pp. 28–29. The emergence of a profit or loss is due to the operation of the forces at work in the money market and not, as Professor Ceccherelli believes (p. 26), because the circulation of Pisan and other foreign coins was forbidden in Florence by the statutes of the *Arte di Cambio* or Bankers' Guild.

[52] *Ibid.*, p. 59.

[53] Florence, Archivio di Stato, Mediceo avanti il Principato, Filza No. 134, No. 2, fols. 240ᵛ–41ʳ, 249ᵛ–50ʳ.

[54] Armand Grunzweig, *Correspondance de la filiale de Bruges des Medici* (Brussels, 1931), I, xxiii; Biscaro, *loc. cit.*, pp. 96 f.

[55] Grunzweig, *op. cit.*, pp. 129, 131.

[56] This matter is fully explained in my article, "What Is Dry Exchange?" *Journal of Political Economy*, September, 1944.

[57] Arch. Dat., No. 1165 (Nicastro No. 1129), Quaderni del Saldo (Bilanci).

[58] Here are a few of those entries:

Per pro di cambi ▽ 600 rimisi a Brugia in questo c. 180 Luigi e Salvestro debino [dare] £6 *s*.13 *d*.4

Per pro di cambi a la ragione di Brugia di Diamante degli Alberti in questi c. 164 debe..........£3 *s*.0 *d*.0

Per pro di cambi al conto di Brugia di Giovanni Orlandini in questo c. 219 debino...........£7 *s*.10 *d*.0

Per pro de cambi al conto de' nostri magiori di Firenze in questo c. 241 debino...........£11 *s*.2 *d*.1 Arch. Dat., No. 801, Libro verde C, fol. 357ᵛ.

[59] *Ibid.*, fol. 391ᵛ. It appears from the ledger that the reserve was created by charging the account *Spese di Mercatantie*. The text of the entry posted to the debit of this account is as follows:... faciemo riserbo per lelde di Barzalona e Cholliveri e altre spese ci resto in questo conto [a] aconciare, in questo c. 295 riserbo debe avere.. ....£80 Barc.

Lelde were some kind of taxes or rather tolls levied on goods passing through Barcelona and Collioure (Cholliveri), a small port near the frontier between Catalonia and Roussillon. Other examples of reserve accounts are given by Corsani, *op. cit.*, p. 114.

[60] Biscaro, *loc. cit.*, p. 307.

[61] The usance for bills from London to Venice was three months either way.

[62] It should, however, be emphasized that the "cost or market" rule was applied only in isolated instances. In general, inventory valuation did not raise a problem, because of the prevalence of venture accounting. Medieval merchants expected to sell goods at whatever they would bring. See Balduin Penndorf, *Luca Pacioli, Abhandlung ueber die Buchhaltung* (Stuttgart, 1933), p. 37; *idem.*, "Inventar, Bilanz und Bewertung in der italienischen Buchhaltung des 14. Jahrhunderts," *Zeitschrift fuer handelswissenschaftliche Forschung*, XXIV (1930), pp. 489–95; A. C. Littleton, "A Genealogy for 'Cost or Market'," ACCOUNTING REVIEW, XVI (June, 1941), pp. 161–67; Laurence L. Vance, "The Authority of History in Inventory Valuation," ACCOUNTING REVIEW, XVIII (July, 1943), pp. 219–27.

[63] *Nostro* and *Vostro* accounts were certainly known to the Venetians, for Andrea Barbarigo kept such ac-

counts with foreign correspondents. Barbarigo's representative in Bruges was the firm Vettor Capello e compagni. In Barbarigo's ledger two accounts were opened for this firm: one called *Vettor Capello e fratelli per conto proprio* (the *Vostro* account) and the other called *Vettor Capello e fratelli per conto di Brugia* (the *Nostro* account). The latter has the customary two columns, the first for the Flemish currency and the second for the Venetian currency (*prima moneda da Bruzia, dopo moneda di Venixia*, as is explicitly stated in the narrative column). Some of these details are given by Besta (*Ragioneria* III, p. 307), and by Vittorio Alfieri (*La partita doppia applicata alle scritture delle antiche aziende mercantili veneziane* [Turin, 1891], pp. 78–79), but I have been able to complete them by going to the original manuscript in Venice, Archivio di Stato, Raccolta dei registri Barbarigo, Mastro di Andrea Barbarigo, 1430–1440, fol. 114.

[64] Casanova (*op. cit.*, no pag.) gives many examples, e.g., under the date of June 8, 1555, in his samples of a journal and on folios 14, 31, and 36 of his samples of a ledger. The influence of Venetian practices on southern Germany was very strong. It is, therefore, not surprising that the use of an Exchange Account for the purpose of absorbing exchange differences is also recommended by south German writers, especially by Gammersfelder. See Balduin Penndorf, *Geschichte der Buchhaltung in Deutschland* (Leipzig, 1913), p. 145.

[65] Casanova, *op. cit.*, fol. 36 of ledger samples. Apparently Casanova did not use fictitious names in his illustrations. This Daniel van der Molen was actually a Flemish merchant residing in Venice. See Florence Edler, "The van der Molen, Commission Merchants of Antwerp: Trade with Italy, 1538–44," *Medieval and Historiographical Essays in Honor of James Westfall Thompson* (Chicago, 1938), pp. 86–89. Casanova also mentions the famous Anton Fugger, the Lucchese bankers Antonio and Ludovico Bonvisi in Lyons, the Antwerp merchant Jean della Faille (Giovan dalla Faglia), etc.

[66] See his journal entries under the date of July 14, 1555.

[67] Casanova, "Svegliamento agli insperti che per An versa cambiano," *op. cit.*, no pag.

[68] If Casanova refers to the mint-par, his statement is wrong. In any case the English mercantilists deal more satisfactorily with this problem than do the Italians.

[69] See also an entry in the ledger of Andrea Barbarigo published by Alfieri, *op. cit.*, p. 79. Barbarigo states that he lost because he took up money by exchange at 44 st. to 45 st. in Venice and at 40 st. or thereabouts in London.

[70] This is a general rule. Equilibrium required, for example, that the ducat be rated higher in Venice than in Antwerp, that the French franc be rated higher in Paris than in Bruges, that the Flemish écu of twenty-two groats be rated higher in Bruges than in Barcelona, that the Pound Sterling be rated higher in London than in Antwerp, etc. A demonstration of the rule is given in my article, "What is Dry Exchange?" *loc. cit.*

[71] Besta, *op. cit.*, III, 400.

[72] Simon Grisogono, *Il mercante arricchito del perfetto quaderniere* (Venice, 1609), fol. 15 of ledger; a copy is in the Montgomery Library of Accountancy, Columbia University. Cf. Casanova, *op. cit.*, fol. 14 of ledger.

[73] Giovanantonio Moschetti, *Dell' universal trattato di libri doppi* (Venice, 1610), pp. 168–71. There is a copy in the Montgomery Library.

[74] His real name was Jan Ympens, Christoffelszoon

("Christopher's son"). See Raymond de Roover, "Something New about Jan Ympyn Christoffels," *The Accountant*, XCVII (1937), pp. 657–58.

[76] The quotation is from the English version of Ympyn's Treatise, published by P. G. A. de Waal, "De Engelsche Vertaling van Jan Ympyn's Nieuwe Instructie," *Economisch-Historisch Jaarboek*, XVIII (1934), 1–58. The French text is given in C. P. Kheil, *Ueber einige aeltere Bearbeitungen des Buchhaltungs-Tractates von Luca Pacioli* (Prague, 1896), p. 23.

[76] P. G. A. de Waal, *Van Paciolo tot Stevin. Een bijdrage tot de leer van het boekhouden in de Nederlanden* (Roermond, 1927), p. 114.

[77] de Waal states (*op. cit.*, p. 143) that Savonne was a merchant and that he never resided in Antwerp. The fact is Savonne lived in the rue des Israélites near the Bourse or Exchange. Both he and Mennher were members of the Schoolmasters' Guild. Mennher was admitted as a member in 1549 and died about 1569 or 1570 (Antwerp, Stadsarchief, Gilden en Ambachten, No. 4550, fols. 3, 36, 53, 56).

[78] de Waal, *op. cit.*, pp. 156 f.

[79] *Ibid.*, pp. 167–68.

[80] *Ibid.*, pp. 251–55.

[81] *Ibid.*, p. 255.

[82] Onko Ten Have, *De leer van het boekhouden in de Nederlanden tijdens de zeventiende en achtiende eeuw* (Delft, 1933), pp. 33–34.

[83] On this topic, consult Richard Ehrenberg, *Das Zeitalter der Fugger* (3d ed., Jena, 1922), II, pp. 69–146, 222–56.

[84] Henry Waningen, *Le thrésor de tenir livre de comptes à l'italienne* (Amsterdam, 1615), no pagination. Examples in wastebook from fols. 6–9; in journal, fols. 6–9; in ledger, fols. 6–8. There is a copy of this French edition in the Montgomery Library.

[85] Ten Have, *op. cit.*, pp. 47–53, 119, 175.

[86] M. de la Porte, *La science des négocians et teneurs de livres* (2d rev. ed., Paris, 1715), p. 38.

[87] *Ibid.*, pp. 112 f., 246, 252 f., 338 f.

[88] John Carpenter, *A Most Excellent Instruction for the Exact and Perfect Keeping Merchants Bookes of Accounts by Way of Debtor and Creditor after the Italian Manner* (London, 1632), pp. 57 f. Montgomery Library has a copy.

[89] *Ibid.*, p. 60.

[90] Malachy Postlethwayt, "Remittance," *The Universal Dictionary of Trade and Commerce* (2d ed., London, 1757), II, p. 579.

[91] Edler, *Glossary*, pp. 107, 110, 138, 227, 322; de la Porte, *op. cit.*, p. 543; Grunzweig, *op. cit.*, I, p. 131; Amintore Fanfani, *Le origini dello spirito capitalistico in Italia* (Milan, 1933), p. 41. Francesco Sassetti, general manager of the Medici banking house, uses both *discrezione* and *provvedigione* in his *libro segreto*, 1462–1472 (Florence, Archivio di Stato, Carte Strozziane, Series II, No. 20), fols. 11, 12, 13 and *passim*. Cf. Florence Edler de Roover, "Francesco Sassetti and the Downfall of the Medici Banking House," *Bulletin of the Business Historical Society*, XVII, No. 4 (October, 1943), pp. 65–80.

[92] The early English mercantilists (Malynes) and late canonists (Dr. Thomas Wilson) frankly admit the presence of the interest factor. See my article, "What is Dry Exchange?" *loc. cit.*

[93] Edler, *Glossary*, pp. 263, 405–6.

[94] de la Porte, *op. cit.*, p. 545.

[95] "Discount," Postlethwayt, *op. cit.*, I, 647.

[96] de la Porte, *op. cit.*, p. 533.

[97] Richard Dafforne, *The Merchant's Mirrour* (London, ed. of 1660), p. a3; Geijsbeek, *op. cit.*, p. 143.

[98] de la Porte, *op. cit.*, p. 533.

[99] No wonder that the continental de la Porte knew nothing about domestic banking which was a recent development in England.

[100] All these quotations are from the article, "Banking" in Postlethwayt's *Dictionary* (I, p. 197). It is surprising that the significance of this description of the different types of banking in England and on the continent has been missed.

THE HOLDING PERIOD TO 1800

CREDIT, BILLS, AND BOOKKEEPING IN A SIMPLE ECONOMY

W. T. Baxter

CREDIT, BILLS, AND BOOKKEEPING IN A SIMPLE ECONOMY

W. T. BAXTER

"FROM the point of view of the methods of exchange, there were three main stages of economic development: the prehistorical or early medieval stage of natural economy, where goods were exchanged against other goods; the later medieval stage of 'cash' (money) economy, where goods were bought for ready money; and the modern stage of credit economy, where commercial exchange was based on credit." Thus Professor Postan summarizes the views of nineteenth-century writers on the history of exchange.[1] He goes on to explain that these writers relied on abstract deduction when there were gaps in their knowledge of business history; and further, that their minds had been newly quickened by the doctrine of evolution. They not unnaturally reasoned that, if credit has now evolved to a high peak of importance, then credit was probably less and less significant at each earlier stage. To quote one such scholar: "It may even be doubted whether, in medieval trade, credit operations can be spoken of at all. Early exchange is based on ready payment. Nothing is given except where a tendered equivalent can be directly received." If loans were ever made, they were for consumption, not trade.[2]

Professor Postan goes on to shatter these deductions. Citing a mass of medieval debtors' obligations, he proves that credit was *not* a negligible force in the Middle Ages, but was indeed the essence of many bargains.

If credit has played its important rôle for so long, then surely the history of bookkeeping should supply further evidence on the point. Credit without written reckoning is almost impossible; the first and most fundamental reason for keeping accounts is to aid in remembering what we have trusted to our debtors.

Early bookkeeping records fall into two groups, namely, the accounts themselves, and textbooks on accounting. A few sets of accounts date back at least to the close of the Middle Ages. But the bulk of the available evidence (as well as the textbooks) is several centuries junior to these precocious survivors. Does such com-

paratively modern material shed any light on the issue?

My own experience has been chiefly with the accounts of American merchants of the period 1710–75. Some of the ledgers, journals, and statements of Thomas Hancock, his nephew John, his father-in-law Daniel Henchman, and their correspondents, have been preserved, doubtless because of John Hancock's prestige as one of the founders of the United States. Relatively youthful though these records are, they offer us a wealth of clues regarding trade practices in a primitive society. And, when we recall what sort of conditions the colonial traders had to work under, it seems fairly reasonable to suppose that their procedure may have been not unlike that of their medieval forebears. Their communications were still dead slow, their commerce was a mere trickle in volume, mass manufacture was unknown to them, and they had not yet set up transfer banks.[3] Their coinage was in great disorder, and presents a clear analogy with the money used by medieval traders.[4]

CONDITIONS IN COLONIAL NEW ENGLAND

The men who wrote the Hancock MSS all lived in Boston. And it so happens that eighteenth-century New England is a particularly good field for research into primitive conditions, because its money was much worse than that of many other places.[5] A bad monetary system was still no unusual thing—even England did not put her coinage onto a moderately sound

---

[1] M. Postan: "Credit in Medieval Trade," *Economic History Review*, I, 1927–28, p. 235. N. S. B. Gras has also summarized this interpretation of economic history, and pointed out its dubious features, in "Stages in Economic History," *Journal of Economic and Business History*, II (1930), p. 395.

[2] Karl Bücher: *Economic Evolution*, translated by Wickett (1901), p. 128 *et seq.*

[3] I have described these conditions fully in *The House of Hancock* (Cambridge, 1945), XVI. Chapter II details the accounting evidence, which is mostly housed in Harvard Business School, and from which I obtained all my following quotations unless the contrary is stated.

[4] A. Evans, "Some Coinage Systems of the Fourteenth Century," *Journal of Economic and Business History*, III, p. 481; A. P. Usher, *Early History of Deposit Banking in Mediterranean Europe* (Boston, 1943), p. 193.

[5] C. P. Nettels: *Money Supply in the American Colonies* (Madison, 1934), p. 163.

basis until 1696. But the plight of the New England colonies was exceptional. Nominally, their money consisted of pounds, shillings, and pence, each of these units being (in Massachusetts) worth about three-quarters of its British namesake. But I doubt very much whether the Hancocks ever saw any of these coins, which seem to have disappeared about 1700. For hard cash, the New Englanders relied on dollars and other foreign coins won in their West Indian shipping ventures.[6] If we turn to one of Henchman's accounts with a Pennsylvanian firm that had sold him flour, we find that he sent back this medley of coins in payment:

johannes (i.e. Portuguese gold piece)
moidores (i.e. Portuguese gold piece)
guineas (i.e. English gold piece)
French guineas
pistoles (French or Spanish gold coins)
doubloons (two pistoles)
"checkeens" (i.e. sequins, Italian gold coins)

Such moneys were valued by both giver and taker in the monetary units of their respective provinces before being entered in their accounts. In other words the local pounds shillings, and pence were still used as units of *value*, even when they were not the units of *exchange*.

This was by no means the end of the story. Perhaps one coin in a hundred was worth its face value. Most had been so sadly clipped and sweated that they would be taken only at a discount. "These guineas" writes Thomas Hancock "are very short of Weight and to pass them here would be a great Loss as they must weigh here 5 dwt. 9 grs." So householders kept scales for testing the coins that came their way. Journal entries were apt to treat coins like goods to be dealt in by weight, e.g., one entry tells of a debtor's payment in silver money "which I sold to —— 4 oz. 17 dwt. 13 gr. @ 12/-per oz."

But even these battered foreign coins were somewhat hard to get. The reason for the shortage is probably as follows. Although New England was a hungry buyer of British manufactures she could in return grow little that was pleasing to the mother-country. Consequently her merchants paid for part of their supplies by exporting all forms of coins and specie. A coin from the Indies might circulate for only a brief period before being shipped to London. As late as 1750 a visitor to Boston wrote "This is the first time . . . that Supplies of Silver Coin could be had from Boston, 'tis quite new to them—merchants that could supply 50,000 £ Value in stores cannot raise 5,000 £ St. in Cash."[7]

To fill this gap the New Englanders took what was then the bold and original step of making paper money (as early as 1690). And not only did each of the various provinces print official notes but groups of private individuals formed themselves into "banks" that experimented with large issues on the basis of silver, land, or merely personal credit. Soon both types of notes began to depreciate "owing to the idle suspicions of the ignorant." There followed a long and gentle inflation which rose sharply to a peak during the war of 1744–8. Conservatives sometimes accepted the private notes only at a discount which varied according to the issuer's status and they flatly declined to take the notes of the more exuberant bodies. Even the official notes were looked on with some misgiving; and as they had almost the status of legal tender they presumably helped to drive hard money from circulation.[8]

---

[6] For a description of the currency, see W. B. Weeden, *Economic and Social History of New England* (Boston, 1890), and J. M. Davis, *Currency and Banking in the Province of Massachusetts Bay* (New York, 1901), and articles in *Proceedings of the American Antiquarian Society* (February, 1898), and *New England Historic Genealogical Society Register*, LVII, p. 280.

[7] See the Canadian Archives' *Documents Relating to Currency, Exchange, and Finance in Nova Scotia* (Ottawa, 1933), p. 296.

[8] Davis, *op. cit.*, pp. 101–8.

The Hancock records leave little doubt about the scarcity of all forms of money, even in years when metal was being eked out by a considerable flow of paper. The shortage heightens the resemblance between Colonial conditions and those obtaining in medieval Europe. In both cases, it is worth noting, the standard of value and reckoning was often not the staple standard of exchange. This has led certain writers on medieval currency to talk of an "imaginary money of account." The phrase is apparently justified if it means that some of the units were not represented by coins, e.g., the "shilling" might not exist (and might indeed never have existed) but simply was a handy name for "a dozen pennies." Further, changes in the relative values of gold, silver, and copper might result, e.g., in the penny's (actual coin) ceasing to be the same thing as the penny (unit of account); the former was then rated at some such ungainly fraction as 20/29 of the latter. So the link between the two brands of money might well be slender. But I find great difficulty in conceiving of genuinely imaginary money. Surely price units must always have been anchored to real money or commodities by some rating system even if it was unofficial and based merely on the common consent of the market.[9] In the case of New England, prices and therefore money of account would seem to have been tied to the notes, though the links in the chain were elastic. Had money not been based on something less airy and illimitable than mental concepts the temptation to offer more of such cheap stuff would surely have been irresistible, and inflation swift.

In New England, the disappearance or scarcity of money did not result in a correspondingly low price level. True, any withdrawal of the official note issues produced a noisy outcry, checked trade somewhat and caused a downward pres-

sure on prices. But the drop was never so spectacular as might have been expected; and there was no bottomless depression. Instead of fettering themselves to the ordinary forms of money, the New Englanders turned to other and older means of exchange. The Hancock MSS show that trade was largely based on commodity money and barter. The accounts are richly seasoned with references to payment in grain, in rum, and in potash, etc. Many a debt is stated to be "received in molasses," or "settled this day in cordage," or "paid in pork."

This is not to say that commodity-money ranked on the same plane of acceptability as cash. Ordering 30 barrels of pork, a Halifax trader writes: "You were so kind to tell me when you found the difficulty of procuring Cash that you would let me have more pork should the people here be inclin'd to take it on Acco^t of payment."[10] As late as 1783, a Salem debtor is commanded to pay "in as much Cash as you can Obtain—and perhaps Some W. India Goods if the Price Suits." Goods, it should be noted, were never thought of as units of value. Like strange coins, they were weighed and valued in terms of Massachusetts money; thus a journal entry runs:

James Barrick Dr to Merchandise
Ballance due to him paid in Hemp this day, 130 cwt. 0.8 lbs. at 64   £416. 9. 2½
The goods were presumably appraised at the current market prices, or at the official values proclaimed by the legislature when taxes were collected in kind. This meant that a merchant might in theory have to "sell" commodity money to his creditors without making a profit; and the books contain traces of many such non-profit transfers. But doubtless the merchant would tend to glean some revenue. Barter lends itself to the exploitation of creditors.

---

[9] Usher, *op. cit.*, p. 217.

[10] Boston Public Library, Ch.M. 3.5, II, p. 221, July 30, 1767.

"He that bartereth hurteth hymself, for commonly the one partie ether for lacke of makyng his reconyng or for not hauyng knowledge of the wares or prises of the same, or dooth not consider the tyme whiche passeth and commeth, bee it long or short, (for as the prouerbe is: The Wolues eate not the daies, for thei passe bothe slepyng and wakyng) ie euer driuen to the worsse."[11] Abuses were particularly rife when servants were paid in kind. A New England pamphleteer explains how a carpenter loses by being paid his wages in depreciating notes, "and even this is further reduced, by obliging him to take one half in shop goods at 25 per cent or more advance above the money price."[12]

CREDIT IN A BARTER SYSTEM

The Hancock records suggest that credit was of greater rather than less importance under these conditions. Prompt payment in pigs, for instance, would often have been highly inconvenient alike to giver and taker. Commodity money was probably thought of more as "commodíty" than "money," i.e., its movement was bound up with considerations of harvesting, consumption, or resale. Delays in payment were therefore inevitable. Further, as the units were not always homogeneous or readily divisible (e.g., the hog) exact settlement was hard, and a balance of debt was often left over. Trade would scarcely have been possible without abundant credit.

Under such circumstances, bookkeeping was indispensable. Indeed, I feel that the system might well be named "bookkeeping barter." Account after account shows how, for instance, country shopkeepers would take manufactures from their Boston wholesaler, and would then pay by slow

and painful instalments—perhaps first some butter, then a bill of exchange, next a barrel of pickled beef, and so on. Between any two traders, goods normally flowed *both* ways; and the balance of debt might swing from side to side as the years went by. Per-contra payment was thus the rule, and any trim division of personal accounts into a debtors' and a creditors' ledger would have been out of the question; also, dealings were far too involved to permit of their grouping in specialized day books.

A certain amount of two-way trade would be natural enough in a small community; something similar is still found in rural South Africa, particularly in the trade of storekeepers in the native territories. But its volume in the Hancocks' time (and especially in the twenties, when monetary difficulties were unusually severe) can hardly be explained except by a great need for bookkeeping barter. Every Tom, Dick, and Harry was a credit manipulator. Thus Henchman kept a ledger account for his barber, who took corn as payment. The painter who decorated his house sent in an account-current, which shows that payment was extracted in driblets of cash, corn, and books. Henchman's ledger also shows his brother's being charged with board (in an account that runs on for eleven years, and is credited with various items such as oranges and oysters); even "Jean Whippo, our maid" has an account that is credited with her wages (at £5 per annum) and is debited with "1 suit of cloaths . . . £5," etc. The life and hopes of countless persons must have been sternly ruled by a ledger account.

Plainly, this type of trade does not fit into any neat historical analysis of barter, money, and credit stages. All three types of exchange exist side by side, and may indeed be met with in a single contract.

[11] Jan Impyn, *New Instruction* (1547), reprinted in *Economisch-Historisch Jaarboek*, 1934, p. 40.
[12] Douglas, quoted by Davis, *op. cit.*, p. 376.

For instance, credit may be allowed to a debtor who promises to pay later with one-third money and two-thirds goods (which are always valued and recorded in terms of money).

THE DEVELOPMENT OF
CREDIT TRANSFERS

Crude barter has two glaring defects: (1) if A and B are to exchange goods, their wants must be simultaneous; and (2) each must want what the other has.

Bookkeeping and credit enabled the New Englanders to surmount the first defect. To some extent, they contrived to overcome the second also. This was done by *triangular* barter. A sells goods to B; if B does not have what A wants, but is owed a debt by C, he may send A to look for acceptable things in C's store; a purchase there will mean that C has paid B, and B has paid A, although the goods in fact move only across the base of this triangle of traders. Such three-sided settlements were common as witness waste-book entries such as the following, in which Hancock fills the rôle of B:

Brown and Son Dr to Joseph Rhodes
for 15 boxes Tin plates

Were similar transfers made in the Middle Ages? Common sense suggests that the New Englanders probably inherited their technique of settlement from an earlier generation. And we know at least that transfers of goods took place when the goods had been deposited in a warehouse. Before the Christian era, the Egyptians could transfer rights to grain stored in granaries (with the help of a document corresponding to a cheque);[13] and transfers of hemp were made in the government rope factory of Venice in the fifteenth century.[14] Here are exact analogies to certain warehouse dealings that are mentioned in the Hancock MSS. For instance, Hancock had to hand over gunpowder for safekeeping to the official powder house; his account with this institution shows that he would then give orders to third persons entitling them to withdraw barrels. Much the same sort of thing happened when he had sent molasses to a distillery to be made into rum.

But if C is a warehouseman or a similar agent, perhaps we should be wary about speaking of triangular settlement. C is not here a fully fledged third party, but merely B in thin disguise. The goods still belong to B; thus Hancock did not always keep a money account with C (the powder house) but merely a stores account in terms of barrels. Happily for our theory, however, such warehouse transactions make up only one in a hundred of his triangular settlements. C was far more often an independent trader.

EARLY BILLS OF EXCHANGE

Should it prove that triangular settlements in kind were common in the Middle Ages, they may well explain the birth and popularization of double entry. What is more, they may perhaps throw light on the origins of bills of exchange.

Medieval scholars have shown us that recognizable ancestors of our bills had appeared by the fourteenth century. The very first evidence, we are told, consists of references to "letters of payment" in correspondence (dated 1291) from a Florentine company to its branch or agent in London. The bulk of the early evidence suggests that bills were used chiefly in foreign exchange; that they were somewhat complex in nature, often involving four parties; and that they became usual

---

[13] W. L. Westermann, "Warehousing and Trapezite Banking in Antiquity," in *Journal of Economic and Business History*, 1931, p. 49; A. T. Olmstead, "Materials for Economic History of Ancient Near East," *ibid.*, 1930, p. 224.

[14] F. C. Lane, "Rope Factory and Hemp Trade of Venice," in the same *Journal*, 1932, p. 836.

in home trade only at a much later date (in England, the seventeenth century).[15] In the Hancocks' own times, Acts of Parliament and Lord Mansfield's judgments were still reducing the law governing bills to order.[16]

This history does not seem altogether complete or convincing. It can say little with assurance about the *birth* of bills. It cannot yet be supported with any of the actual documents, which naturally are extremely scarce; and, as resounding legal deeds and important foreign letters are far more likely to be preserved than homely trade papers, there must surely be some risk of giving too much weight to the former types of evidence. One is left wondering whether the bill's origins should not be sought in something more simple and informal than letters to a foreign agent, and whether these early foreign bills had not some domestic parallel. On the face of the matter, evolution from foreign exchange to local payment, from the elaborate to the easy, does not appear likely. To my mind, the Hancocks' triangular transactions (especially those in goods), and the papers by which such transfers were engineered, suggest that our history of bills is one-sided. And it must be remembered that the Hancocks' legacy of MSS includes many papers of a type so informal that they would normally have been destroyed.

Yet I scarcely need to emphasize that what follows is intended as nothing more than a tentative line of research for the medieval scholar. It would indeed be absurd if, in an article that starts by taking to task theorists who prefer doctrines of evolution to facts, I were to make the same

blunder. In the field of biology, "evolution" is merely growth, not necessarily from inefficient to efficient, or from simple to complex; sometimes the growth may seem degeneration to us. The same may well hold of human institutions like exchange. At the beginning of the Middle Ages, the written, as contrasted with the verbal, contract was looked on with suspicion; so the first bills may well have been hedged around with formalities. Further, the medievalist can counter my suggestions by reminding me that the New Englanders had the very advanced English practices of the seventeenth century to build on; that foreign exchange loomed unnaturally large in the minds of the early merchants, because it was often a useful cloak for usury; and that the medieval merchant was at many points held back by conservatively minded jurists, whereas the new Colonies were relatively unhampered by legal aid. Let me describe the Hancock papers, and leave the reader to judge for himself.

The simplest group of "orders" to reach the Hancocks was part of their two-way flow of goods. A wants wares from B; instead of going for them himself, he sends a servant or agent. This was very usual in the case of a country customer, who would write to Hancock for goods, and add that these should be given to some carrier or to the captain of a coasting boat for delivery. Such transactions are no more than mail orders at a time when there was no parcel post. The Hancock MSS contain many examples; a slight variant, which I found on the other side of the Atlantic, may be seen in:

January the 25th 1763.
Loving Child,
please at your conveniency to allow to the poor wydow Bearer hereof and her Orphans one Bole of the Moulter of your Mill of Benbeculla, which Shall be Sustained at accounting with

[15] Usher, *op. cit.*, p. 73 *et seq.*; R. de Roover, "Early Accounting Problems of Foreign Exchange," ACCOUNTING REVIEW, 1944, p. 381; W. S. Holdsworth, *History of English Law*, VIII (London, 1923), p. 113.
[16] R. D. Richards, *Early History of Banking* (London, 1924), pp. 46–9; C. H. S. Fifoot, *Lord Mansfield* (Oxford, 1936), p. 91.

Dear Sir
Your affectionate father
Ronald McDonald Clanronald Senior[17]

Often the third person was a partner, since a great deal of trade consisted of joint-adventures by casual and short-lived partnerships.

The next group of orders was part of the triangular trade. Here the third person is no mere agent. When A asks B for goods, B gives him a written order on C. C then makes an entry such as:

T. Atkins Dr to Merchandize
for his note paid John More in Pork and
Flour   4. 12. 3.

B's entry will be like this:[18]

Andrew Symmes   Dr   to Capt John
Matchett
for my order on him for 6 Bushells of
Indian corn at 3/-   —18.—

An example of the note is:

Boston Decr 30 1769
John Hancock Esqr

Sir please to pay Mr. Joseph Moffat or order in goods One pound thirteen Shillings and 3d Lawful Money and charge your humble serv^t.

Thos Dawes

£1. 13. 3

A suitable receipt is often written on the back.

Great numbers of such notes have been bequeathed to us among the Hancock MSS. These survivors include forty-four from a single customer, for a period of only four months. Though there were many individual vagaries, most of the notes tend to use much the same word

formula, and even to be on paper of a standard size and shape, resembling our cheques. These facts, and the use of phrases such as "on demand" and "or order," emphasize the likeness of the notes to bills of exchange. And perhaps it is worth recording that the "bank" and provincial monetary notes, on the other hand, leaned towards the bills payable in kind, for their wording mentioned a *weight* of metal.[19]

Another, perhaps smaller, group of papers consists of bills payable in money. A lot of these, particularly the more formal documents, were for foreign trade, thus supporting the views of the writers mentioned above. On the other hand, many of the papers used at home were the same in effect as bills, although the informality with which they were sometimes drafted may disguise this fact. For instance, an order to pay one-third goods and two-thirds money would not now be classed as a bill by a lawyer; yet the results are the same.

EVERY MERCHANT A BANKER

The essence of our triangular settlements among A, B, and C is that C gives something of value to A on behalf of B. That something, as we have seen, was usually goods; it would have been idle to draw on C for cash if cash was not to be had. In the typical triangular settlement of to-day, C has blossomed into a banker, and the something is usually a credit in his books that is transferred from B's account to A's; settlement is made by the magic of a cross-entry. The question naturally arises: could the New Englanders also make settlements aithout moving goods or cash.

---

[17] Clanronald MSS, Register House, Edinburgh.
[18] A doubtful example is:
    Expence Dr to Joseph Scott
    for my note payable to Wm Warllan.
This may either be "two-way"—i.e., Warllan is an agent, or Warllan has rendered some service and is rewarded with the note, without any account being opened for him.

[19] Davis, *op. cit.*, p. 158, reproduces a note: "This bill of twenty shillings, due to the possessor thereof, from the province of Massachusetts Bay, shall be equal to three ounces of coined silver, Troy weight, of sterling alloy, or gold coin, at the rate of four pounds eighteen shillings per ounce and shall be so accepted in all payments, and in the treasury. Boston 1741."

The answer is that they could and did. This is proved by their odd use of the word "discount." Discount's original meaning was "abatement" or "deduction," e.g., by way of a counter-claim against a sum due. (Discount on a bill was one special type of abatement: "interest discounted.") Instead of taking goods from C, A might build up a credit with him (or lower an existing liability). So a variant to the notes runs:

> Pay into (or Discount with)
> Mr. James Dennie, or Order,
> Twenty Pounds.

Such "checks" might be endorsed and circulate from hand to hand.[20] I am not sure whether any "usance" was normal; probably, as in the above example, the drawer did not bother to specify when the payment or cross-entry was to be made. My impression is that a month here or there meant nothing in that easy-going society. Nobody seems to have fussed about "discount" in our sense. Perhaps the exchange rates tendered for foreign bills took the time factor into account, though the risk factor loomed a great deal larger in the mind of the buyer, who was willing to pay substantially more for bills drawn by merchants with first-class reputations.

Like the orders payable in kind, the notes may well have had their genesis in very simple requests, with the third person acting merely as agent or messenger. One possibility is shown by this letter:

> Boston Jan\ 10, 1769.
>
> Sir,
>
> Please to pay my Wife Mary Anderson Five doll\ per Month on Acco\

Wages due to me on board the Schooner Lucy & charge the same to

> Your humble Serv\
> Charles Anderson.

That the orders were widely understood is suggested by entries in Henchman's ledger for two carpenters, one his debtor and the other his creditor; he puts through "discount" entries to set off their balances. On occasion, a verbal order might be a good enough authority for such a cross-entry. Apparently anyone who kept a ledger might be called on to transfer credit; every bookkeeper thus performed one of the banker's functions, and clearance was not yet centralized.

Most merchants of standing probably performed several other of the banker's functions. In telling the story of the Hancocks, I have explained that any large firm of repute would naturally be called on to deal in bills, to finance military campaigns, to take charge of other people's funds, and to invest these in securities such as provincial loans or lottery tickets.[21] But much less important men also carried out many of the banker's tasks for their customers. Because there were no specialized bankers and little cash, trade and finance were perforce tightly intertwined. Henchman was mainly a bookseller, but an account for one of his country correspondents tells this tale. In four months, the correspondent makes eleven deposits (eight in the form of cash delivered by captains, or others, and three by notes). On the other side are shown a series of payments at the correspondent's order (e.g., for pasturing a horse); finally about £500 of cash is withdrawn, together with £950 made up of a wedge of gold and 25 double doubloons.

INTERNATIONAL CREDIT AND EXCHANGE

Importing provides another instance of the union between trade and banking. The

---

[20] Henchman's journal contains:
9 Sept 1732 Ebenezer Gennings Cr
By a note to disc\ with Mr. Beecham
 from Apthorp   £20
 David Mason   Dr
To Mr. Apthorp's Note to pay Beecham
 endorsed to me for   £20

[21] *The House of Hancock* (Boston,.1945), p. 204.

main financial burden of Anglo-American trade was shouldered by British exporting houses,. which might give the Boston importer a year's credit, free of interest, and extend the loan for a further period at 5 per cent. The Boston merchant distributed the goods to country shopkeepers and chapmen, noting in his journal "to pay in 4 [or 8, or 12] months." If the customer's account was not squared after a long time, the balance might be converted into a bond carrying 6 per cent interest. When the account was next reviewed, this bond might be replaced by a fresh one (including compound interest).[22] Like most other commercial documents, the bonds were informal. They might contain a clause stating that the debt was to be doubled if not paid when due. Probably they were not normally mortgages over land, etc., though on occasion even a share in a ship was conveyed as security; in some instances, a church pew was mortgaged.[23]

It will be seen that the Boston merchant was doing much work that has since been delegated to bankers, shippers, and other agents. He was the central link in a chain of credit that stretched from London to the frontier. A loan seems a great favor before we have obtained it; after, we are apt to regard it as an injury. The heavy load of debt of merchants to Britain was probably a major cause of the Revolution.

An account-current between a Boston merchant and his London creditor would provide an object lesson to those who believe in tariffs or exclusive trade agreements between two countries. It shows us the stark realities of international trade, unobscured by money or bankers. The British exporter had to be an importer too or go without payment. As in home dealings, the basis of trade was bookkeeping barter, often with triangular or more complex geometrical embellishments. If the Boston merchant had nothing that his London suppliers wanted, he would send provisions to Newfoundland, the West Indies, or Europe, and after one or more exchanges would get goods (or coins, or bills) that were acceptable in London.

Bookkeeping barter was by no means the only feature that was common to both local and international trade. Indeed, the New Englanders could probably see little distinction between the two trades. Foreign coins were everyday fare in Boston, and dealings with the next-door province involved currency exchange. Country trade must have shaded smoothly into interprovincial, interregional, and international trade.

As we have seen, country customers were forced by bad communications to appoint a Boston supplier as their general agent and banker. In overseas dealings, this dependence was the more complete; even the British government had to rely abjectly on Hancock for many supplies of credit, coin, and victuals, and for innumerable small services. Foreign exchange was not confined to specialists. Anybody might dabble in it; illiterate fishermen on the Newfoundland Banks provided Boston with many sterling instruments drawn on their Devonshire homeland. A merchant was always willing to deal in sterling bills on Boston 'Change, in general as a buyer,

---

[22] Thus on 22 June 1767, the journal shows a man being charged with:

Interest on his book debt after one year's credit on goods sold him	£ 4.11.9
Bond dated 27 September 1764 now given up	421. 8.6
Interest on this bond, 2 years, 8 months, 24 days	69. 2.2

After giving credit for some pork, a new bond was issued for the balance.

[23] Hancock wrote this letter to three men:

"The Pew [of the] late Capt John Bulkley in the meeting house whereof the Red Mr Saml Cooper is minister Being mortgaged to me the subscriber in 1754 which I have taken Possession of.

I am to Desire the favr of you Gentn to apprize the same that I may give the Estate Credit for it. Note there is an Incombrence of Two Grand Children of Mr. Bulkleys sitting in sd Pew which I can't well Refuse."!

but occasionally as a seller if he had some-how managed to build up credits abroad (e.g., by a lucky sale of whale oil). It is hardly surprising that bills, even those on the British Treasury,[24] were by no means certain to be honored; each depended on a circle of transactions, and a ship might be lost, or another bill might not be due, or a clerk might make an error in posting. A creditor was apt to get his dues only after exasperating delays, bickerings, and re-bates.

As in home trade, slight distinction was drawn between goods and money. Each was a "way of remittance." Money might be preferable, but the creditor could often be bullied into taking goods; thus Hancock, after telling a London firm that no gold or bills are to be had, asks in what form they would like a debt in local money to be re-mitted, "and the longer it lyes the worse it will be as our money is daily sinking." Among the bills sent to Jamaica was one "payable on demand in Molasses."

The Hancock MSS are worthy of study by monetary theorists on many grounds. They illustrate the working of an economy whose money, as we have seen, was largely made up of goods, private or external paper, and private paper based on goods. The quantitative importance of these seems to call for investigation. Perhaps a clue to the matter may be obtained from the effect of the great public note issue of 1741–9; the volume of Massachusetts notes jumped from some £220,000 to £2,200,000, but the price of silver, and exchange rates, merely doubled.[25]

EARLY TEXTBOOKS AS EVIDENCE

So much for eighteenth-century colonial accounts. To what extent were they typi-cal of other places and dates?

Europe was at that time producing a

fair number of accounting textbooks.[26] These were usually illustrated with full specimen accounts. There seems no reason to doubt that such specimens give an ade-quate bird's-eye view of contemporary trade methods, and provide us with fairly reliable standards of comparison.

A survey of eighteenth-century books swiftly dispels any theory that the Han-cock records were like those of western Europe. True, casual partnership, joint-ventures, and consignments are often met with, and some authors still talk of barter; but bookkeeping barter seems to become rare about the end of the seventeenth cen-tury (especially in home trade), and cash transactions abound throughout that cen-tury. The only triangular transfers spring from bills of exchange—and the latter are payable in money. In short, the textbooks are in some respects far more modern in flavor than the Colonial accounts. We may perhaps risk two generalizations:
(1) Textbooks and Colonial accounts are alike in their stress on joint-ventures, etc. (because companies had not yet replaced partnership as an outlet for the speculative), and on bills (because banks were not yet the staple agents for credit transfers). Incidentally, day books had nowhere won their complete victory over the journal, which sug-gests that the volume of straightfor-ward transactions was too small to call for grouping in specialized books of original entry.
(2) On the other hand, textbooks differ from Colonial accounts in assuming that money is always available, and payment in kind a rarity.

The further back we go, however, the less seems to be the gulf between the two sets of evidence. Textbooks dated 1718,

---

[24] Nettels, *op. cit.*, p. 201; Baxter, *op. cit.*, p. 104.
[25] Davis, *op. cit.*, p. 367; *Proc. of American Acad.*, p. 211.

[26] The library of the Society of Accountants in Edinburgh (where I made this survey) contains ten works of the eighteenth century, and four of the seventeenth.

1635, and 1610 show signs of bookkeeping barter. And Jan Impyn (1547) lists the following ways of buying and selling, whose kinship to Boston methods is patent:

"The first is with ready money. The second by tyme and daies of paimente. The third in geuyng wares for wares the whiche we call Bartery, and in Italien Barratto. The fourthe is with money, and part tyme. The fifth, with money and some wares, or other exchaunge. The sixt is by wares, and the rest for tyme. The seuenth by assignacion of one debtor to another. The eight one part by assignacion of redy money, and the other parte in wares, and tyme. And the nynth and last is by all condicions together, in geuyng money, wares assignacions, and for tyme."[27]

The researches of scholars lend color to the view that some of the Hancock methods had long been commonplace. "A general rule of Roman Law recognized transfer of obligation in books of account as a valid means of payment. Such operations were practiced by private persons as well as by the silversmiths (*argentarii*) who discharged many of the functions of the banker."[28] Professor Postan has mentioned medieval triangular transfers as substitutes for money.[29] And an able study of Italian accounts at the close of the Middle Ages confirms this; there was, we are told, a well-developed system of debt settlement based on substitutes for money—"the 'setting over' of debts was a common practice despite the absence of negotiable instruments. Local payments were often made by transfer in bank or by transfer of credit on the books of an ordinary merchant or a merchant-banker. Transfer orders were given not in writing, but by word of mouth."[30]

Let us now review our evidence. The Hancock MSS prove conclusively that, under Colonial conditions at least, any analysis of exchange into sequential phases of barter, money, and credit is indefensible; all three elements existed side by side, and were often interdependent. A comparison of the Hancock MSS with bookkeeping records of the Renaissance suggests that Europe was at that date emerging from a somewhat similar stage. We are thus not without justification if we regard Colonial accounts as clues to medieval practice; but conclusions based on the analogy must be very guarded until many more medieval records have been unearthed and studied. The last word obviously rests with the medieval scholars. I look forward in particular to further discoveries in the early story of bills. How is that story to be linked up with the innumerable notes that the Hancocks have left us? These seem to show that (a) orders in kind were an essential part of home trade; (b) bills could readily have developed out of the simple letters that shoppers would use daily when ordering goods; and (c) there was no marked gulf between home and foreign trade in the matter of payment methods.

If we discard the barter-money-credit theory of exchange phases, dare we hazard any alternative?

The phases suggested by accounting history are perhaps:

(1) *Pre-accounting age.* Presumably this is a time of crude barter, sometimes with credit.
(2) *Bookkeeping barter.* The "two-way flow" of goods allows traders to evade the worst drawbacks of crude barter. Some of the goods are commodity money. "Money of account" is the common denominator for reckoning, but the corresponding coins may not circulate much.
(3) *One-way flow.* Metallic and paper money are met with so freely that payment in kind is unnecessary. A merchant can divide his personal accounts into two groups, for suppliers and for customers. His transactions become so simple that he can segregate them in specialized day books.

[27] *Op. cit.,* p. 24.
[28] Usher, *op. cit.,* p. 4. Later pages mention many medieval analogies to the Hancocks' oral and written transfers of money.
[29] *Op. cit.,* p. 246.
[30] R. de Roover, "Early Accounting Problems of Foreign Exchange," ACCOUNTING REVIEW, 1944, p. 382.

(4) *Bank settlement.* Finally, the advantages of payment by cheque reduce cash settlements to a negligible scale. Clearance is centralized.

Such stages do not, of course, correspond crisply with successive periods of time. There must always have been some overlapping; probably all stages existed to some extent even in the Middle Ages. But each may well typify the procedure that was dominant in certain centuries.

Perhaps these accounting phases merely reflect steps in the evolution of the merchant. In the first, there are presumably few merchants, because craftsmen sell straight to customers without intervention by middlemen. In the second, the middleman has appeared, but he must be omnivorous, buying and selling almost everything, and so making his profits in a tediously roundabout way.[31] In the third, he can concentrate on one type of goods. In the fourth, he rids himself of the work of settlement, leaving it to professional bankers. If this analysis is correct, the key to exchange phases is *the merchant's degree of specialization.*

---

[31] A counterpart of the unspecialized Boston trader is suggested by E. F. Heckscher: "Natural and Money Economy as illustrated from Swedish History," *Journal of Economic and Business History*, III, p. 12.

A GENEALOGY FOR
"COST OR MARKET"

A. C. Littleton

A GENEALOGY FOR "COST OR MARKET"

A. C. LITTLETON

SEVERAL surveys of inventory practices have been made. The N.A.C.A Bulletin of March, 1937, showed that 87% of 197 companies used the rule of cost or market whichever is lower for raw materials in their balance sheets. A report of February 1938 by the National Industrial Conference Board analyzed 916 companies. The rule was applied to raw materials in 63% of the cases, to goods in process in 38% and to furnished goods in 40% of the cases. The research department of the American Institute of Accountants examined 500 annual reports for 1939. The figures tabulated in *The Journal of Accountancy* for October 1940 show that 56% followed this rule "or variations thereof."

These surveys as samples of practice show that the rule is in general use. But a rule may be widely useful in business without having the character necessary to make it a fundamental proposition of accounting. If we wish to search out the character of this rule, if we would like to determine whether it is a convenient and expedient rule of thumb or a basic accounting idea, we might begin by looking up its ancestry.

The information is not available to enable us to find the real origin or to trace step by step the way it came to receive the acclaim these surveys seem to show. But there is enough material at hand to indicate that it is a result of the mingling of two bloodlines: expediency and convenience. It is this mixed ancestry which accounts for the notion that taking an inventory is a process of evaluation rather than a process of cost-pricing.

I

Let us go back about five and a half centuries. If long established precedent is enough to justify a rule, the rule should stand, for cases are known as early as the beginning of the fifteenth century wherein goods in inventory were priced below their purchase cost.

A German scholar writing of the manuscript records of an Italian business man, Francesco di Marco,[1] pointed out that an estate costing 366 fl. in 1393 was valued in an inventory of 1412 at 240 fl. because the vineyard had been spoiled. He also showed that this man's furniture and utensils were valued by appraisers in 1408

at less than cost because the items had deteriorated. These cases we would now say reflected damage and depreciation. But there is more. A stock of almonds bought for trade in 1406 at a cost of 60 fl. appeared still unsold in a later inventory at 50 fl. Beneath the item was this notation: "We have entered the 10 fl. in the debit of goods profit account as damage [loss] because we no longer value them as above since they have fallen in price."

It is doubtful that these changes were made in the inventories merely for the satisfaction of producing an accurate profit calculation and a conservative statement of assets. It is very probable that there was present some compelling force other than a high resolve to record only the truth.

In another place we find a clue to the probable reason for the practice of taking up every possible loss. The same author[2] points out that the tax burden in Italian cities early in the fifteenth century was very heavy. Sometimes several levies of $\frac{1}{2}\%$ would be made in a single year besides several forced loans of 1%. These taxes were calculated on the amount of the citizen's property less certain deductions. In one example for the year 1427, the tax was assessed on a citizen's lands, investments and business capital, less an amount for debts payable, dwelling houses, etc. The author further points out that the amount of lands and investments could be determined by tax officials with considerable exactness and that therefore "endeavors to pay the lowest possible amount in taxes could be made only with reference to business capital."

Penndorf does not give the details of any method for stating business capital at a minimum. But recognizing every possible loss, even price changes, would have that

---

[1] Baulduin Penndorf, *Luca Pacioli*, introduction pp. 36, 37.

[2] Baulduin Penndorf, "The Relation of Taxation to the History of the Balance Sheet," THE ACCOUNTING REVIEW, Sept., 1930, p. 247.

effect. He does indicate, however, that some merchants kept two sets of records and that others retired from business rather than produce their accounts. In fact the tax burden was so heavy and tax evasion so widespread by 1458 that Italian taxation methods had to be revised.

There was therefore a good deal of incentive in the situation to bring men to seek plausible reasons for reducing the asset figures. Damage, deterioration, lower current prices, could furnish such plausible explanations.

"Cost or market" is often spoken of as a general rule of accounting. But it is to be noted that tax expediency was no more than a special condition. As such it could produce only a special rule covering special rule covering special circumstances. There is no basis in tax expediency for either a general rule of account-keeping or a general rule of reporting the results of double-entry bookkeeping.

II

Let us come a little farther down to date, down to about the time Columbus discovered America. Paciolo published the first printed text on bookkeeping in 1494. He begins his discussion with a long description of what we would now call an opening entry. He advises the merchant who desires to begin keeping systematic accounts to prepare a statement (*bilancio*) "of whatever he has in this world, personal property or real estate." Then he goes on to say that precious stones should be included "according to current prices"; for silver articles he mentions, "giving each thing its customary price." In addition to leaving us in doubt as to what prices he really means here he adds this disconcerting advice: "Make the prices rather higher than lower . . . so that you can make a larger profit."

Apparently "valuing" one's possessions at a high figure was thought to influence the price at which they could be sold. The idea sounds very modern. Some people, I fear, still believe that a high purchase cost is a basis for a high selling price. These people are as mistaken as Paciolo was. But it is more important for the present purpose to note that this discussion of inventory treatment was about an opening entry. Clearly the assumption was that the merchant had no prior records of original costs and must therefore give the items a price. In such a situation some kind of "valuing" was inescapable if a set of books was to be opened at all. Until adequate records could make possible some other way of finding the data from which to construct an opening entry, valuing was the only method available.

In the absence of dependable records this approach must still be used. Until systematic records came into use, *valuing* the inventory was no doubt the usual case and as such was a proper base for the inventory rules which Paciolo mentions. After records are in use, however, *costing* the inventory from the records should become the usual case and valuing the inventory the exception. The center of any rule should be the typical case, not the exceptional one. At the present time a complete lack of price records or purchase invoices is so infrequent that this situation can only be a basis for an exception to a rule. The rule itself should be that pricing an inventory is basically a costing problem.

Two other items are of interest here. One of Paciolo's followers, Pietra, writing in 1586 about bookkeeping for a monastery, offers the advice in his chapter 13 that a value should be given to things harvested and things manufactured, but this value should be lower than current prices "so that the proceeds will not fall below this value in case of sale." Does this not advise pricing the inventory so there will always be a profit upon sale?

About a hundred years later (1682,

1690) an English writer, Monteage, deals with livestock inventories. In one example, cows are priced in a later inventory at the same price as in the opening entry. In another example, cows are priced higher than the opening price apparently because of recent higher-priced purchases. Sheep are priced as in the opening entry; lambs unsold are priced at about 25% below the sales price received for their brothers. Both a bull and a ram are priced slightly below the opening figure. In another illustration is a Horses account bearing two credit entries, one an inventory priced at less than the opening figure—the other is a transfer to Loss and Gain, where the item is labeled "for their use and impairing."

In these situations, besides being mixed up with depreciation, the inventories again deal with special cases. Harvested crops and the natural increase in farm animals must be priced in some expedient way if they are to enter into statement calculations as they undoubtedly should. But it may be doubted if these today represent the typical situation under which inventories are used.

Since in these cases the use of the cost-or-market rule rests partly upon situations where actual prices are lacking, I believe it is a special rule of limited significance. Such conditions no longer provide the predominant occasions for taking inventory.

III

From France we get additional clues about early practices. Under an ordinance promulgated by Louis XIV in 1673, merchants and bankers were required to keep a journal of their transactions for reference in case of dispute. They were also to have the book authenticated by the signature of a public official. In addition, as Prof. Howard points out,[3] they were required to

[3] Stanley E. Howard, "Public Rules for Private Accounting in France, 1673 and 1807," THE ACCOUNTING REVIEW, June 1932.

make a statement (*inventaire*) of all their fixed and movable properties and their debts receivable and payable every two years. The French law at this point used words that are almost identical with those used by Paciolo in writing about the opening entry. That early writer's instructions about opening entries were thus reflected in European law regarding periodic financial reports. And our own courts seem to consider that the inventory, and the balance sheet, is still a valuation problem. They too are emphasizing the occasional situation, that is, the situation existing when solvency or the dividend base is in question. As a matter of fact, the usual situation is one involving the calculation of profits at the end of a fiscal period rather than solvency.

Jacques Savary, the principle author of the ordinance of 1673, published a book in 1675 entitled "Le Parfait Negociant" (*The Complete Tradesman*). In this he explained the statute and described current business practices. Among other things, he made some observations on the treatment of merchandise for inventory purposes. The reader is vaguely advised to take care not to estimate merchandise at more than it is worth. If the merchandise is newly purchased, he goes on to say, "and if one judges that it has not decreased in price at the factory . . . it should be put in at the current price."

The author's meaning here is not clear. He was speaking of newly purchased items and the phrase "current price" could mean the actual price recently paid. Did the phrase mean that the latest invoice price was to be applied to all units still unsold although some were bought at other prices? Is it possible that the author meant the words "current price" to mean merely "book price as already recorded," hence the actual cost price? If an item were not newly purchased, would its own cost price be used or the "current price" of similar items not yet bought? We begin to wish we could call up Savary's ghost and cross-question him. His answers might also throw some light on Paciolo's use of the phrase, "current price."

But Savary's next comments seem clear enough. If the merchandise has begun to deteriorate or go out of style, he says, reduce the price considerably. He adds that you should reduce the item in the inventory accordingly if you can now get similar units at the factory for 5% less.

Savary's advice to price the inventory was not aimed at tax avoidance. Nor was there any hint that the statement was prepared for credit purposes. And it is doubtful if a man of Savary's penetration would advocate these adjustments on the theory that current replacement prices were more nearly "true" than original purchase prices.

The explanation follows other lines. The French ordinance, it will be noted, was quite general in its phrasing. It seems intended as a means of preventing falsification. The records required were to be available for use in court as evidence, but only in cases where the issues concerned rights in succession, dissolution of partnership, business failure, or property held in common by parties to a marriage contract. In these situations cost of inventory items, even if known, would not be material to the issues involved. Perhaps such legal problems furnished the principal occasion in seventeenth century France for taking inventory. But I am sure they do not do so now in America.

Additional evidence is available to show that questions of business solvency were at the basis of the inventory practices fostered by the French law. The ordinance of 1673 was the basis for a part of the Napoleonic Code of 1807. In the section dealing with books of account, four items dealt with bookkeeping rules such as authentication, making an inventory of all property, etc., and six items dealt with the use of the records in case of litigation.

Professor Howard in the article previously mentioned has pointed out that French legal commentators have explained the relation of these rules to bankruptcy. Under the ordinance of 1673, the authenticated records would show the condition of the merchant's business at the time he became bankrupt and the antecedent conditions as well. The records would thus contribute a factual basis for a fair settlement with the creditors. If a merchant did not keep authenticated records, his bankruptcy was considered fraudulent and he was subject to the death penalty. This severity was altered in the code of 1807, but the essential use of the records in case of bankruptcy was kept. By this later code bankruptcy was fraudulent under several conditions, namely, if the merchant kept no records, if he concealed the records, or if the records did not correctly show his financial position. The penalty for fraudulent bankruptcy was at that time made a period at forced labor.

Legal regulations affecting inventories in France are thus seen to be related to frauds suffered by creditors at the hands of a bankrupt. Legal regulations affecting inventories appeared in Germany a little later, but here they were in connection with frauds suffered by stockholders at the hands of corporation promoters.

The German Commercial Code of 1897 provided, among other things, that securities and merchandise which have a price-quoting market should be valued in the balance sheet at the lower of cost or market, and that other property should be entered at cost of purchase or cost of production.[4] This law of 1897 was a revision of the Commercial Code of 1884. The latter was the outcome of an investigation into

---

[4] Joseph L. Weiner "Balance Sheet Valuation in German Law," *The Journal of Accountancy*, September, 1929.

the causes of a wave of promotion and stock speculation which began in 1870 and came to an abrupt and disastrous climax in 1873. Much of the blame was placed on prior laws. It was found that promoters and their attorneys had interpreted a phrase of the law of 1861 as permitting the use of probable sales price in stating balance-sheet assets. This enabled them to publish very attractive balance sheets and to sell vast quantities of stock on the surpluses shown.

Admittedly the code of 1861 was loosely phrased. The original draft of 1857 had proposed cost or market. But that wording was rejected as too specific and too restricting. "True value" was suggested but this was finally replaced by the phrase which went into the law: "The value which ought to be ascribed [to the item] at the date as of which the inventory and balance sheet are being drawn up." The vagueness thus deliberately written into the law was deliberately seized upon some years later to work a fraud upon security buyers.

It is easy to understand that the people would want such a law changed. It is easy to understand how a German court in 1873 was led to say that the figures in the balance sheet should not rest solely on willful individual judgment and pure surmise. It is understandable also how the law-makers, in going back over the earlier discussions, should turn again to the idea which had at first seemed too specific. Vagueness in 1861 had exacted its price; in 1884, it seemed desirable to be specific. The amended rule then written into the law was worded peculiarly but it was essentially the lower of cost or market. (Sec. 261 quoted in Weiner's article, p. 199.) As far as the effect of the law was concerned, it could as well have been cost alone. I do not know the reasons which prompted the Prussian representatives to make the original suggestion of cost or market to the conference in 1857. Prob-

ably they were merely following leads from the Napoleonic Code of 1807 and Savary's *Complete Tradesman* of 1675. Savary's book appeared in a German translation the next year.[5]

Both the French code and the German code were clearly designed to deal with inventory pricing. In both cases, however, it was with the intent of narrowing the opportunities for fraud. That is indeed a proper functioning of society's legal machinery; and lawmakers are justified in using such devices as appeal to them as appropriate. But it does not follow that accountants should give the resulting rule of law the status of a general rule of accounting. Unless accounting is considered to be a legal instrumentality, this use of inventory pricing could hardly be expected to produce an accounting rule. All that we have here is a special rule applicable to special circumstances.

In retrospect then we find convenience and expediency playing the major role in the early appearances of the cost-or-market rule. Sometimes, as in France and Germany, the rule was associated with the desire of lawmakers to narrow the opportunities for fraud. Sometimes, as in Italy, the rule seems associated with the hope of reducing the effect of a heavy tax. Surely fraudulent insolvency and tax expediency are not the predominant situations out of which a general accounting rule should grow. If these two cases represent infrequent and exceptional situations, they can only produce a special rule, that is, a rule which at best constitutes merely an exception to a general rule.

Agricultural inventories, opening entries and a few other situations also call for inventories on a noncost basis. But these situations no longer predominate. An inventory rule based upon them can no longer be called a general rule, even if once

[5] Jaeger, *Beiträge Zur Geschichte der Doppelbuchhaltung*, p. 171.

it could. It now would not cover a large enough portion of the cases calling for an inventory rule to make it a general rule.

If we must have a cost-or-market rule for special situations—and I do not concede that we need it even there—or if we must have a rule about valuing the inventory items when cost is unknowable, those rules should be made unmistakably secondary to the primary rule of inventories, and that rule should be that inventories should generally be priced at cost on a first-in, first-out basis. That rule has no mingled bloodlines to weaken its character; that rule does not come out of a single-entry conception of financial statements. That rule alone can show that the balance of a goods account has the same accounting characteristics as the balance of a cash account has.

THE AUTHORITY OF HISTORY IN INVENTORY VALUATION

Lawrence L. Vance

THE AUTHORITY OF HISTORY IN INVENTORY VALUATION

LAWRENCE L. VANCE

A WRITER who contends that the only proper principle of inventory valuation for general purposes is cost attempted, some months ago, to show that certain notable instances from the early periods of accounting development, which lend support to a cost-or-market rule, were explainable as the result of "expediency and convenience" and represented no true judgment upon accounting principles.[1] Since the article referred to seeks to support the proposition that the establishment of the cost-or-market method is the result of rather erratic and localized forces, and since this proposition is contrary to our knowledge of the way most institutions have grown which can be observed over long periods of time and over wide areas of the globe, the subject requires further examination. In the following paragraphs notice is taken of some of the references to valuations, other than cost, which the history of accounting up to the middle of the nineteenth century affords us (the list is not submitted as exhaustive), and then consideration is given to the question of whether the particular valuation basis at issue (cost-or-market) is the illegitimate offspring of unacceptable parents or the due (though imperfect) issue of commercial need.

For the sake of easy review of the chronology, the dates appropriate to each of the items are listed at the head of the paragraph in which the material is described.

1404–1406. The first records showing the use of cost-or-market are dated from this early period. They are found in the accounts of Francesco di Marco of Prato,

who was the head of extensive trading, banking, and cloth-making enterprises in the last half of the fourteenth century and the first decade of the fifteenth. Penndorf states in general terms that the method of inventory valuation in these accounts was cost except when market was lower, in which case market was used.[2] He gives two specific examples, one of which traces a lot of goods from an inventory of December 31, 1404, to the "next" inventory where it is written down and the difference carried to the account "loss of goods." The other notes that goods bought during the course of the fiscal year (Geschäftsjahr) 1406 were valued in the inventory at the end of that fiscal year at less than cost, with the explanation "we have put fl. 10. 16. 7 into the debit of the account 'profit on goods' on f. 264 as loss because we no longer value them as above since their price has gone down." The implication is clear that these examples are not isolated cases in the books in question.

The contention has been made that the policy of write-downs disclosed above was an effort at tax avoidance, made in a time when ad valorem levies upon personal as well as real property were heavy, and hence has no general significance for accounting principles. This supposition is open to many objections, the first of which is that it takes into consideration too little of the material available. Professor Littleton apparently relies on articles by Penndorf[3] in which some early fifteenth and

---

[1] A. C. Littleton, "A Genealogy for Cost or Market," THE ACCOUNTING REVIEW, XVI (June, 1941), pp. 161–167.

[2] Balduin Penndorf, *Luca Pacioli*, Abhandlung über die Buchhaltung 1494, . . . mit einer Einleitung über die italienische Buchhaltung im 14 und 15. Jahrhundert und Paciolis Leben und Werk (Stuttgart, 1933), pp. 36–37.

[3] "The Relation of Taxation to the History of the Balance Sheet," THE ACCOUNTING REVIEW, V (September, 1930), pp. 243–251, and "Inventur, Bilanz und

sixteenth century tax conditions and returns were described. Immediately following a discussion of some accounts of the Medici from the year 1440 to 1460, Penndorf notes that taxes at that time were very heavy, several levies of $\frac{1}{2}\%$ on property and several compulsory loans of 1% sometimes being made in one year, and further on that evasion had become so serious by 1458, being accomplished even by the keeping of two sets of books, that the system of returns by the taxpayer had to be replaced with an "apportionment" method. This is noted in the article which seeks to explain di Marco's accounts in terms of tax avoidance.

Penndorf also notes, however, that "according to the law of 1427, landed property, live stock, money, and business capital had to be assessed," and further on "As it is now with us, the property tax balance was not a true balance sheet, but a statement of property which had its foundation in the books and ledgers of the firm." Obviously we cannot apply the law of 1427 to di Marco's 1406 accounts, and although we concede that conditions were similar in 1406, the fact that the tax return then, as now, was entirely separate from the books of account leads us to conclude that there was no more necessity for identical valuation bases between them then than now. Hence, one who recorded inventories at the lower of cost or market in the accounts, referring to the "account for loss on goods," had no reason except a determination of profit and loss. In fact complete identity of valuation bases between the tax return and the books was not expected since, as Penndorf notes, real property was valued in the tax return at a capitalization at 7% "of the produce of the soil." Furthermore, there would be no

point in demanding a complete identity if the authorities reserved the right to revise the assessment submitted by the taxpayer. Again quoting Penndorf: "The officials wrote their remarks on the margin of the tax return and frequently increased the amounts."

The supposition that early evidence of the use of cost-or-market grew out of tax considerations is subject to other and more general objections. It might be expected that a method designed for tax purposes would include some reference to its purpose. But instead the explanation given is the kind which would appear if there was an accounting policy in effect that sought to recognize economic losses which were soon to be realized through sales—the statement that "their price has gone down." Furthermore, general conditions of what might somewhat inappropriately be called "public finance" in the fourteenth and fifteenth centuries were such as to make such a mild device as cost-or-market for the closing inventory insignificant as a tax-avoidance scheme. That period was replete with wars, abuses from a decaying feudalism, and much grasping clerical domination. Much revenue was raised by tolls and customs of every sort; tax farming was common (Italian financiers were active agents under this system); much of what amounted to taxation still depended upon feudal relationships, the exactions of which were often extremely heavy; and a favorite financing device which served as taxation was the forced loan, which was often disposed of by repudiation. With this background in mind, it is not hard to understand why men would keep two sets of books, or no books at all; why they kept their capital accounts personally, secret even from their employees; and why they would take pains to conceal physical wealth. There seems so little in common between these vigorous methods of tax evasion and the rule of cost-or-market that one may well be disinclined to classify them together.

A method of so little significance in tax policy and of such apparent appropriateness to an accounting policy which seeks to make the accounts more responsive to economic forces can not be explained away as a tax-avoidance scheme. In the case of Francisco this seems reasonable, since we note from Penndorf that he "was not an honest taxpayer" in that he represented himself as without means in response to an assessment in Avignon in 1375 when his balance sheet showed the contrary. Evidently this resourceful Italian had devices better designed for tax evasion than cost-or-market.

1494. In this year Paciolo[4] published the first work on accounting to appear in print in his *Summa de Arithmetica, Geometria, Proportione et Proportionalità*. Paciolo's references to valuation, which generally specify current prices,[5] are interpreted by opponents of cost-or-market as applicable only to an opening entry which Paciolo was describing. In view of the fact that the volume of trade was not so great than as now and the further fact that there was less diversity of merchandise, one might argue that a merchant could be called upon to remember cost prices for purposes of an

[4] The name is variously spelled. Penndorf, *ibid.*, uses "Pacioli."

[5] One exception is Paciolo's advice to "make the prices rather higher than lower; for instance, if it seems to you that they are worth 20 you put down 24, so that you can make a larger profit" (Geijsbeek translation, Ch. 12). Internal evidence suggests an interesting explanation for this: in Ch. 7 Paciolo says "Many keep their books in duplicate. They show one to the buyer and one to the seller, and this is very bad, because in this way they commit perjury." If we can attribute a considerable amount of moral inconsistency to Paciolo or follow the evidence of diversity of style in the book and conclude that there were two authors with different attitudes, we may interpret this valuation procedure as a means of furnishing the seller with evidence better calculated to convince the buyer of the value of the goods than the cost price would. One can easily imagine a seller, in those days of authoritarian price fixing in general and the *justum pretium* of the Church in particular, saying to the customer: "Look, here is my ledger and here is the entry for these goods. The price I'm offering you leaves me hardly any profit at all."

opening entry; and that specifying "current prices" for ginger and other items as Paciolo did (Chapters 12 and 16), indicated a preference for them. The author who is discussed in the next paragraph below, for example, supports this suggestion by indicating that he is using cost for certain items in an opening entry. In listing jewels he uses the phrases "que me coustent" (once), "que coustent" (twice), and "que couste" (once). Similar instances can be cited from Peele (1553) and Oldcastle (Mellis ed., 1588). Furthermore, it is at least apparent that Paciolo was not an adherent to cost valuation as applied to determine the figure at which receipts of bartered goods are entered. In Chapter 26 he states that the value of goods received in exchange shall be estimated and this amount used to debit the account with such goods and to credit the account which contained the goods given up.

1543. Jan Ympyn's *New Instruction* was published in Dutch and in French in this year. While it is for the most part a translation of Paciolo, it is most notable for Ympyn's own contributions: his thoroughgoing illustrative material and the fact that the book was an important vehicle for spreading a knowledge of the "Italian method" throughout Europe and in England. Ympyn specifically requires cost as the basis of inventory valuation, but he includes in his illustrative set an interesting transaction the accounting for which takes definite leave from the "cost principle." The transaction was an exchange of 44 pieces of English cloth for 110 pieces of Dutch cloth, the trade being considered an equal exchange according to Ympyn's statement in the journal entry recording it. To record the transaction he debited the other trader and credited a clearing account called "Goods in Exchange" for an amount which appears to be arbitrarily large (£320–16–8), then credited the trader and debited the clearing account with the same figure when the goods promised were received. The significant entry was made when Ympyn recorded his delivery of English cloth; here he credited the account for English cloth and debited "Goods in Exchange," explaining in the journal his computation of the amount as follows: "selling them ordinarily with a profit of ten per cent or thereabouts would amount to £229–18–0, which sum I have credited here." This figure is exactly 10% over cost on 44 pieces from the last lot of cloth charged to the English Cloth account. To conclude the record, Goods in Exchange was credited and Dutch Cloth debited for the £229–18–0. The only explanation for the use of the much higher figure in the memorandum entry to record the other trader's obligation to deliver seems to be that it would make a better case for the claimant in event of default by the party charged.

Evidently Ympyn had no scruples about

cates no allegiance to a "cost principle" as it has been enunciated in recent years, and suggests that cost may have been specified for the inventory without reflection upon the economic aspects of the method.

1550–1581. Valentin Mennher, a German who lived in Kempten, wrote books on arithmetic and bookkeeping which were published over this period. In his *Practiqve povr brievement apprendre à ciffrer, & tenir liure de comptes, auec la regle de coss, & geometrie* in the "Seconde partie . . . laquelle demonstre pour briefuement tenir liure de compte á deux liures, nouuellement composé" there is a clear use of current value for an inventory. On folio 5 of the ledger, illustrated in the 1564 edition, there is an account for French wine which may be transcribed, with the addition of the unit prices (expressed only in the journal entries in the original) and with rulings in modern form, as follows:

Laus Deo. Anno. 1564

French Wine

Debit	J.F.		Credit	J.F.	
15.Feb.64. from Ia.			12.Feb.64. sold to I.P.		
Lam 10 tuns at £ 6	3	60.-.-	10 tuns at £ 7	4	£ 70.-.-
3.Mr. bought of Lenart			12.Mr. sent to London		
Gall 10 tuns at £ 5	4	50.-.-	10 tuns at £ 5	5	50.-.-
15.Mr. bought of Iorge					
Boll 20 tuns at £ 6	6	120.-.-	15.June. to I.L.		
			3 tuns at £ 6	8	18.-.-
first of April. from Ian					
Pierre 5 tuns at £ 5	7	25.-.-	14.Sept. for the new		
28.April. bought of			books, 30 tuns at £ 5	10	150.-.-
Iacques Lam 8 tuns			9-14 for loss		15.-.-
at £ 6	8	48.-.-			
Total, 53 tuns.			Total, 53 tuns.		
		£ 303.-.-			£ 303.-.-

taking up a profit realized in goods as against realization in cash or accounts receivable. While the element of an exchange transaction distinguishes this entry from his precept on cost valuation of inventory, the procedure used clearly indi-

The date of the first debit entry wa[s] entered in error as Feb. 15; the journa[l] gives Feb. 12.

In the explanation for the entry to se[t] up the inventory on the "new books" entered on September 14, 1564, there i[s] included the following: "There remains to me for the new books 30 tuns of French wine which are worth at this time £5 per tun, which makes £150.–.–." It is noteworthy that when consigning goods to London (in the illustration) Mennher used cost, but when closing the accounts he used current value; this, with the diversity of purchase prices in the inventory, indicates a conscious and technically accurate use of a valuation procedure for closing purposes. That Mennher was consistent in using current value is shown in the brief *Livre de comptes a la mode d' Italie* contained in the *L'Arithmetiqve de Valentin Mennher, pour briefuement chiffrer, & tenir liures de compte* published at Lyon in 1558 by Gabriel Cotier. The last journal entry in this brief illustration (which consists of a journal, a book of "debts," and a book of merchandise accounts which is made to carry an inventory balance into a new ledger) values goods bought at £43 at the higher price of £44. Mennher gives a journal entry in the 1550 edition of his work in which a merchandise account is credited £14 on account of "dryness and dust," indicating a recognition of deterioration and obsolescence as a distinct problem. This lends more weight to the already clear fact that Mennher deliberately adopted a current market valuation for inventory, since he gave separate, explicit consideration to the distinct aspects of the problem.

1586. Pietra, a Benedictine monk, published at Mantua the *Indrizzo degli economi* dealing with bookkeeping for a monastery. He prescribes that goods be valued at a standard price, which price must be lower than the market price so that one may never have to sell at a "loss."[6]

1592. This year saw the publication of "Buchhalten mit zwey Büchern—" by the Danzig teacher Wolfgang Schneider, who signed his book Wolffgangum Sartorium, and whose work, due to the mediaeval preference for Latin, is known as that of "Sartorius." This curious work was done in rhymed couplets to facilitate the absorption of bookkeeping rules by the student. His instruction on inventory was that one should have the unsold goods "estimated," thus presumably suggesting market valuation.

1594. In this year there appeared in Hamburg, Passchier Goessens' *Buchhalten fein kurtz zusammen gefasst vnd begriffen nach arthvnd weise der Italianer—*. Goessens, according to Penndorf, was influenced by Dutch writers. His illustrative material includes no account with an inventory of unsold goods, but in his instructions he specifies that the value of goods unsold be estimated and the closing entry made accordingly. This evidently is to be interpreted as a market valuation, which interpretation is made by Penndorf[7] of this and of Sartorius' method as well.

1676. Savary, the author of the French Code of 1673, wrote a book called "The Perfect Merchant" (*Le Parfait Negociant*). In it he clearly expresses the cost-or-market rule for inventory valuation and expounds upon it at some length. He is credited with being the individual most responsible for the eventual wide establishment of the cost-or-market rule. Professor Littleton has sought to identify Savary's valuation method with the code of law he wrote and which bears his name. The argument runs as follows: Since the Code required a biennial inventory and the keeping of accounts by all merchants and bankers, and since it was directed at the

[6] See Hugo Renz, " 'Die Anleitung der Verwalter' v. Pietra Don Angelo, Genua, und der 'Tractat über die Weise das doppelte Hausbuch zu halten' von Lodovico Flori," *Zeitschrift für Buchhaltung*, V (July, 1896), p. 147.

[7] *Geschichte der Buchhaltung in Deutschland* (Leipzig, 1913), pp. 149 ff. and 186. See also Ernst Ludwig Jaeger, *Beiträge zur Geschichte der Doppelbuchhaltung* (Stuttgart, 1874), p. 257.

suppression of commercial frauds and to the needs of bankruptcy administration, and since it was written by Savary, and since Savary's manual was written at the request of the commissioners who served with him on the commission for the improvement of commerce which produced the Code, the cost-or-market rule was in this case the result of an effort to avoid fraudulent overvaluations.

This argument is defeated by one simple fact. If the lawmakers had considered the cost-or-market principle important in combating fraud, they could have prescribed it. They did not. They specified no valuation policy whatever. The evident conclusion is that the lawmakers were not so much interested in valuation as in seeing that records existed from which transactions could be proved. Savary, in *Le Parfait Negociant*, says of the merchant who uses the cost-or-market rule " . . . he has probably made a true statement of his property . . . ." In discussing the method, he points out that recognition of a decline in market value of goods will place the merchant in a position to bargain for their sale without being confused by the necessity of justifying to himself a sale at a loss on cost price; he specifies annual inventories, in contradistinction to the Code's two-year provision; and he also points out that revaluation of the goods on the books does not preclude a sale at a favorable price later if circumstances permit it. These remarks tend to show that Savary was dealing in his manual with what he considered principles of good management, and that the manual was intended to be an "improvement of commerce" over and above the requirements of the Code; as such, his valuation method must be looked upon as stating a conclusion about accounting principles. Furthermore, the commissioners could not have considered an inventory taken once in two years a satisfactory basis for determining values

for bankruptcy administration, since there would be no assurance in any specific case that it would be sufficiently current. As a means of periodically verifying the accounting record it was adequate.

1772. H. Magelsen, a German, wrote a book entitled "Die ersten Gründe des Buchhaltens samt anwendung derselben . . .," which was published in Altoma, near Hamburg, in this year. An average market price is suggested for inventory; in his illustration he uses cost price. It may be noted in passing that his discussion of the inventorying of furniture and other chattels –which involves depreciation concepts) also indicates a recourse to valuation as against "cost-pricing" procedure.[8]

1767, 1787. In each of these years there appeared editions of a business manual under the name M. De la Porte, called *La Science des Negocians et Teneurs des Livres*, in which the instruction on inventory valuation reads " . . . it is necessary to value the rest, it may be according to the purchase, or upon the basis of what this merchandise is then worth." Further on, in discussing the closing process, the author says "one values the rest" and gives an example in which only one lot of goods at a single price appears on the debit side and in which the balance is computed "on the basis of the purchase." In describing the general inventory required by the laws of that time he gives the instruction to "evaluate them according to their proper value." In the model of such an inventory which follows this last instruction, several kinds of goods are listed, the units in a number of lots under each type being listed and then added to be extended at a single price. This is a valuation procedure, as opposed to a "cost-pricing." In the author's model of a general ledger, cost is used as the inven-

---

[8] Penndorf, *Geschichte*, p. 241, and Max Lion, *Geschichtliche Betrachtungen Zur Bilanztheorie bis zum Allgemeinen deutschen Handelsgesetzbuch* (Berlin, 1928).

tory value, but the several merchandise accounts show no example of purchases of the same article at several prices to be accounted for as inventory, so the issue whether "identified cost-price" was intended by his use of cost cannot be settled. Earlier works under the name of this author appeared in 1685, 1699, and 1755 called *La Guide des Negocians et Teneurs de Livres* in which the instruction for inventory valuation requires one to take that proportion of the debit value in the merchandise account which the quantity of goods remaining bears to the total quantity bought, and so gives us an early statement of an average-cost method.

The books were published in Amsterdam and in Paris. There were two authors of the name De la Porte, father and son. While the circumstances which made possible the long career of this work—102 years—are not clear, Jaeger in his *Beiträge zur Geschichte der Doppelbuchhaltung* attributes the 1775 edition at least to the son.

1794–1873. The state of Prussia enacted the "Allgemeines Landrecht für die preuszischen Staaten" in 1794, which required that balance sheets be prepared using the lower of cost-or-market as a basis. When a conference met in 1857 to draft a uniform commercial code for the German states the Prussian delegation presented a draft specifying cost-or-market for goods. It was objected to as being too specific, and the statute as written required properties to be shown at the "value which ought to be ascribed" to them. A new corporation law, enacted after the panic of 1873, required cost-or-market for securities and merchandise having an exchange value, because investigation had shown that promoters had interpreted the old provision as allowing the use of an estimated sale price (which reflected much optimism), with the result of showing surpluses which were believed

by investors to represent earnings.[9] Professor Littleton cites this law as another instance of tampering with accounting principles for ulterior purposes. But here the concern was with the interpretation of statements by investors, and if this is not an appropriate determinant for accounting principles there is none. Some writers virtually disown the balance sheet in order to be consistent in advocating cost valuations, but it is none the less true that investors may be misled by surpluses which are allowed to exist in spite of evidence that normal turnover of current assets will soon result in their reduction. Furthermore, Weiner indicates that the German government was reacting in 1873 to valuations at estimated sales value, and it might therefore have selected cost instead of cost-or-market as the prescribed basis. The reform was intended particularly to make the prescribed valuation base more specific, and the government evidently selected the specific base it considered a proper accounting of surplus to investors. The judgment it expressed in adopting cost-or-market must be looked upon as an accounting judgment and, in view of the community of interest of managers and investors, the conclusion is of general significance.

1796. M.R.B. Gerhardt's *Der Buchhalter* was published in Berlin in this year, and is important, according to Penndorf, as the classical work on bookkeeping of the eighteenth century. In it the author specifies cost valuation for assets generally but says that where there has been a noticeable change in the value of similar articles one should adjust to such value, and makes the significant statement that this is proper where the items inventories are soon to be realized.[10]

[9] For a more complete discussion see Joseph L. Weiner, "Balance-sheet Valuation in German Law," *The Journal of Accountancy*, XLVIII (September, 1929), pp. 195-206.
[10] Penndorf, *Geschichte*, p. 241.

1804–1820. Johann Michael Leuchs wrote *System des Handels* (published in 1804), and *Theorie und Praxis des doppelten, des einfachen und des nürnberger Buchhaltens* (published in 1820). In his instructions for the inventory taking and entry at the end of a period he says, "We now weight the goods on hand and evaluate them at cost price, or if this should have decreased too notably, at the price we could buy them at now; for we should not deceive ourselves as possessing more than we can assume under the circumstances, and thus we should not evaluate the goods at a higher price than we can get for them." Apparently Leuchs' reference to what "we can get for them" is based on the usual presumption that cost and selling price are interrelated, since he specifies replacement cost for the actual computation of the inventory. He also suggests devaluations for deterioration of the goods.

This ends the list of instances. While, as stated above, exhaustive search has not been attempted, obviously the citations can not be explained away as reflecting wholly fortuitous events that have no common significance. It is to be noted, however, that of all the authors who wrote during the period here covered, but especially in the earlier part, those who specified cost valuation were considerably more numerous than the ones mentioned above as supporting another base. What little we know of actual practice indicates that cost was the usual basis. It is also to be observed that very early writers gave virtually no attention to theory, and such rules of valuation as can be found in their works are obtained by imputation; as we have noted, instances occur in which an author suggests a variant from cost valuation in his discussion and does not follow it up in his illustration. With these facts in mind, we are prepared to question the significance that the history of the cost-or-market rule may have for modern accounting theory, even though the cost-or-market rule gained ground during the last half of the nineteenth century and is still with us.

The first step in our interpretation of the facts is to note that we should not expect cost-or-market to appear on any extensive scale in early accounting literature and practice. In the very early stages transactions were not numerous by our standards, and were looked upon as individual deals rather than as parts of a continuous stream of operations. Parcels of goods were individual in character and were individually described in the accounts. A venture was one of the commonest modes of doing business: the purchase of an interest in a ship leaving for the East and the dispatching of an agent with goods to some outlying fair are transactions frequently met is the old records. Separate accounts were opened for the ventures; the profit or loss was computed and the account closed when the transaction was complete. In such circumstances the inventory problem as we know it did not exist. Inventories were likely to be relatively small. The closing of accounts was irregular; it was more apt to be done upon the liquidation of a partnership or when the ledger was filled than otherwise. Further, price-fixing was widespread and the doctrine of a "just price" was widely advocated (Paciolo says that all a merchant wants is a "reasonable profit"), hence price fluctuations may have been less then than later.

Under circumstances in which the venture point of view was appropriate, one cannot expect to see problems that are characteristics of the use of a fixed fiscal period, of the accumulation of large stocks, or of a mass-production type of manufacturing and selling operations. The cost-or-market rule is an effort to give effect in the profit computation of one period to the forces operating in that period which will not be reflected in the sales or cash accounts until a subsequent period, and this for the most part was no concern of the fathers of bookkeeping. It is obvious, however, that such problems must have presented themselves to the early merchants upon occasion. Now and then some organization, such as that of Francesco di Marco, would grow so large that its transactions would look like a continuous stream and its stocks would become relatively large. It is natural, furthermore, to attempt to assess one's financial progress in terms of periods of time. When faced with such situations or when in such a mood, the inventory problem as we know it undoubtedly suggested itself to our predecessors. We have such evidence as has been listed above that in some cases at least they reacted with a cost-or-market valuation. This also explains the occasional reference in a text to some other valuation than cost although the latter method is used as an illustration —the need for an alternative was not yet strongly felt though observed.

The clue to the significance of the history of this aspect of accounting theory lies in the fact that recourse to a cost-or-market rule becomes more frequent as the volume of trade grows and in the fact that it becomes common only after the Industrial Revolution has ushered in the modern era of production. What could appear necessary to businessmen of the late Middle Ages only rarely, and to the commercial world under mercantilism hardly more frequently, presents itself insistently under modern circumstances. Then there is need to take into account, as has been suggested above, the forces which have already cast the fate in one period of goods which will be sold in the next. While it must be made clear that the present effort is not an attempt to defend cost-or-market as such as a valuation principle,[11] it is of prime importance that the method be recognized as having grown, as did accounting itself, in response to the needs of businessmen. Such a view is in accord with the usual pattern of the historical development of human institutions, and, in addition to the specific refutations set down above, leads to the rejection of the contention that a cost-or-market rule is a result of "expediency and convenience," if those terms are given a deprecating connotation, and to the final conclusion that the direction of accounting development has been dictated by the refinement of method to serve better the need which has been described. Since this is clearly a logical direction, future developments may be expected to follow the same kind of pattern.

---

[11] The writer considers cost-or-market a very crude and inexact means of achieving the objective which his interpretation of the motivation behind it visualizes For the complete statement of his position see "Earning Power Valuation of Inventory," THE ACCOUNTING REVIEW, XVII: 376 (October, 1942).

ACCOUNTING TRIVIA

Henry Rand Hatfield

THE ACCOUNTING EXCHANGE

I

There are many fields in which useless survivals in custom continue for an almost indefinite period; perhaps the stock illustration is found in the buttons on a man's cuff, which once had a distinctly utilitarian purpose. But while this purpose has long since disappeared, the buttons are still found on the cuff. Bookkeeping is particularly subject to instances of atavistic survival. Some of them have disappeared. Paciolo devoted an entire, though short, chapter to the necessity of including in the journal entry the prepositions *per* and *a*. Much later, bookkeeping texts in England insisted on such a formula as "By Cash Debtor to Notes Payable Creditor." Through successive abbreviation "Debtor" and "Creditor" were dropped, still later "by" was omitted, so that the entry would read, "Cash to Notes Payable," and at the present time the custom is to give only the titles of the ledger accounts. While some of the earlier technical procedures have been dropped, these here mentioned still persist. How much longer will they continue?

II

One such universal custom which even today is occasionally found in textbooks is that of using the broad column in the conventional ledger to record the name of the contra account. Thus, a cash account in the ledger might conceivably show the following:

Dec. 25	Expenses	25
Dec. 27	Notes Payable	1,000
Dec. 30	Purchases	200
Dec. 31	Balance	1,200

In this case it is indicated that a debit of $25 is to be found in an account entitled Expenses, that a debit of $1,000 is to be found in an account entitled Notes Payable, etc.

In recent years the custom of thus recording the contra account has very generally been abandoned except in textbooks. This in part was due to the introduction in the early 17th century of compound journal entries with the consequent meaningless entry, "Sundries," as no single account represented the amount credited. The curious fact is that while the broad column is generally left vacant there still appears as a last item the word "Balance." This word, "Balance," similarly indicated the title of an account in which a contra debit —$1,200 in this case—had been entered. Such an account no longer exists in American ledgers. The curious fact is that the name of actual accounts in which debits have been made are omitted, but there still is retained the name of a non-existent account in which, of course, no debit can be made.

III

Closely connected with this is the entry as the first item in the account for the following period, "Balance, $1,200." Frequently this bears the longer title, "Balance Brought Down." The impression is therefore made that "Balance" as used in ledger accounts means the amount on hand instead of the name of an account in which the contra entry would appear. That this is incorrect is clearly shown by the fact that in early English texts the amount on hand is not called "Balance" but is called "Reste" or "Remayne." The same differentiation is made in other languages, as for instance in Italian, where the amount on hand is called "Saldo," while the name of the account in which the contra entry is made is titled "Bilancio." Furthermore, instead of the amount of cash on hand in the illustration above, $1,200, being brought down, historically it has made a long, roundabout journey, being debited to the Balance account, probably at the end of the ledger, while the debit in the Cash account for the following period is offset by a credit to a new account, the opening balance.

IV

The conventional form of balancing a ledger account is illustrated below:

Cash

2,425		1,225
	Balance	1,200
		2,425
Balance 1,200		

Some accountants have boldly stated that this is practically an essential of proper bookkeeping, that the account of the preceding period must show the debit footing equal to the credit footing. Why this idea has persisted it is difficult to understand. Such a method of showing the remainder is not used at all in the so-called Boston ledger, nor is it used in the three-column ledger which provides columns for debits, credits and balances. A much simpler procedure is shown as follows:

Cash

1,400	25
1,025	1,000
	200
2,425	1,225
Balance 1,200	

I can conceive of no reason why this is not satisfactory; it certainly is a labor-saving procedure, and any reasonably competent bookkeeper would have no difficulty in verifying the statement that $1,225+1,200=2,425$.

V

Another curious thing in accounting procedure is the listing in the balance sheet of an item called "Inventory." An inventory is a list, and while it is eminently desirable for the merchant to prepare a priced list of his merchandise it is not the list which is worth $20,000 but the merchandise. Why should not merchandise appear in the balance sheet as merchandise, just as the other items listed among the assets are presumably listed under their proper names, barring such intentional misrepresentation as the listing of discount on capital stock as goodwill?

VI

Not infrequently an item appears among the assets with the title "Cash on Hand." If this is intended to differentiate cash in the till from what is ordinarily called cash in bank, the term used is entirely proper. This is rarely the case, for the item "Cash on Hand" ordinarily includes bank deposits. Why do accountants think it necessary to say that the cash is "on hand" any more than to say the machinery is "on hand" or the office equipment is "on hand"? Even the merchandise is not ordinarily characterized as being "on hand," although some of it may be in the store and other portions in a distant storage warehouse.

VII

When by some sad mishap John Smith is debited $100 which should have been debited to Thomas Green, the recognized method of correcting the error in Smith's account is to credit his account with $100. This entry is ordinarily spoken of as a cross entry. The origin of that term is perhaps little known. It is not so called because it is written across the dividing line of the ledger account. The term originated when it was customary to indicate such a correcting entry by writing a small cross beside the entry in the margin of the ledger. This gave it the name of a cross entry. There is some likelihood that the cross was used in this case to offset any evil effect of having made a wrong entry. Thus the early devout accountants insisted that, in the words of Paciolo, a new ledger must be commenced with the "glorious sign of the cross, before which every enemy flees and the powers of Evil deservedly tremble."

HENRY RAND HATFIELD

ILLUSTRATIONS
OF THE EARLY TREATMENT
OF DEPRECIATION

Perry Mason

ILLUSTRATIONS OF THE EARLY TREATMENT OF DEPRECIATION

PERRY MASON

IT IS UNDOUBTEDLY true that the methods now in use for the systematic accounting for depreciation and many of the now generally accepted concepts of depreciation have a comparatively recent origin, and that much of the development of the subject has taken place since and as a result of the establishment of governmental regulation of public utilities and the enactment of income tax legislation. It would be difficult to believe, however, that the fundamental facts of depreciation—the exhaustion of capital investment due to the physical or functional exhaustion of service capacity and the necessity of recovering capital investment before any profit on a venture could be claimed—have not always been understood by those individuals who regularly engaged in business undertakings. If the records were available for inspection, one would expect to find evidence of some understanding of the phenomena of depreciation as far back in history as the origin of written records of business affairs.

The following items have been accumulated as an incidental part of another investigation, and are presented merely as interesting fragments of the entire picture of the evolution of depreciation accounting. The sources were found in the General Library and the Transportation Library of the University of Michigan and in the private library of Professor F. E. Ross of the University of Michigan.

1675

Debtor and Creditor Made Easie, by Stephen Monteage. Several entries are described which involve the valuation of animals and a lease.

"Ballance is Dr. to Account of Horses for 6 resting, valued at 7 *l*. apiece, £42. Loss and Gain is Debtor to the said, for their use and impairing, £6." The Horses account shows the following credit: "1676. Apr. 9. By Loss and Gain, lost by their use—£6." The result was to write down the horses from £8 to £7 each.

A lease is reduced at the rate of £20 per annum. "In the Account of Stock this Lease was valued at 300 *l*. but now a year being elaps'd, it is fit it should be valued at less, which will make no difference in the Account of Ballance; but only lessen the Gain."

Other entries include the valuation of cows at more than cost, and sheep at cost. A one-eighth interest in a ship is reduced from £250 to £225.

1744

The Gentleman and Lady's Accomptant (author not given). An entry is described to write down the value of household furniture.

In the journal: "Income and Expence Debtor: To House-Furniture for Ware and Tare . . . 10/10/0." In the ledger account: "March 25, 1742, By the Income & Expence charg'd for Wear and Tear . . ." The balance of the House-Furniture account is referred to as "the present value."

1757

Book-keeping Methodiz'd, by John Mair (5th Ed.). There is no illustration of depreciation in this book but the method described for handling the fixed asset accounts appears in most of the texts of that time and of the hundred or more years thereafter, and lends itself to the recording of depreciation by what might be called the inventory or revaluation method.

Accompts of ships, houses, or other possessions . . . contain, upon the Dr side, what they cost at first, or are valued at, with all charges, such as repairs, or other expenses laid out upon them. The Cr side contains, (if any thing be writ upon it), either what they are sold or exchanged for, or the profits arising from them; such as, freight, rent, etc. Here there are three cases. 1*st*, If nothing be written upon the Cr side, it is closed, by being credited by *Balance.* 2*dly,* If the Cr side be filled up, with the price of the ship, house, etc. sold, or otherwise disposed of, then the difference of the sides is the gain or loss made upon the sale; and the accompt is closed, by being debited or credited to or by *Profit and Loss.* 3*dly,* If the Cr side contain only the freight or rent; in this case first charge the ship, house, etc. Dr to *Profit and Loss,* for the freight or rent; and then close the accompt with *Balance.*

1764

Reports of the Late John Smeaton, F.R.S. 2nd Ed., vol. I, a report entitled "Of the Expense attending the maintaining and preserving of the Canal from Forth to Clyde, by way of Carron Water, and also for collecting the Tolls thereof." The following schedule is a part of the report:

	£	s.	d.
Common annual expenses	1,136	0	0
Supposed to be laid by every year, to answer the above, and for the purposes after mentioned	1,600	0	0
Then the annual overplus will be	464	0	0
This, in 20 years, will amount to	9,280	0	0

I suppose in 20 years' time many of the locks will want new gates, all of which will gradually fail in a few years after, I, therefore, suppose them all made at the end of 20 years, and, therefore, 72 locks at 60 *l.* per lock 4,320 0 0
The bridges, and other works of timber, will likewise want repair, which I suppose, upon the whole, to amount to one-sixth of the locks 720 0 0

Sum of these repairs 5,040 0 0

This, taken from the above accumulated sum of 9280 *l.,* leaves in hand at the end of 20 years 4,240 0 0
The interest of this sum for 20 years more, at 3 per cent 2,544 0 0
The accumulation of the overplus sum of 464 *l.,* will in the second 20 years, amount to, as before 9,280 0 0

Money in hand at the end of 40 years..16,064 0 0

The second set of lock gates will, at the end of 20 years more, want renewing as before, and as the thresholds will want renewing also, I estimate the re-

pairs at 70 *l.* per lock; this for 72 locks will be 5,040 0 0
And as the second repair of other work may be in the same proportion, that is, one-sixth of the locks, this will be 840 0 0

Repairs wanted at the end of 40 years, which deduct from the above sum on hand 5,880 0 0

Remains in hand at the end of 40 years 10,184 0 0

The interest of this sum, at 3 per cent, for 20 years 6,110 8 0
The accumulation of the overplus sum of 464 *l.,* will in the third 20 years, amount to, as before 9,280 0 0

Money in hand at the end of 60 years..25,574 8 0
At the end of 60 years I suppose the locks in general may need rebuilding, but as the greater part of the stone, and some other of the materials may be of service, and the excavation ready made, I suppose they may be as good as at first, for 300 *l.* each; at an average, therefore, will cost...21,600 0 0
And if we suppose the other works to follow in the same proportion as before, they will cost, to make all good as at first 3,600 0 0

To make all works as good as at first, at the end of 60 years, which deduct from the money in hand 25,200 0 0

There remains an overplus in hand, at the end of 60 years, after everything is made as good as at first 374 8 0
N.B. In the preceding estimate I have endeavored to shew what sum of money applied from the beginning, will preserve the work to perpetuity; but I apprehend this to be altogether a needless supposition; for, if the work will defray the common expenses and repairs for the first 20 years, viz., 1136 *l.* per annum, there is no doubt but that the increase of trade naturally following the use of these undertakings, will answer the greater repairs that must afterwards follow.

1765

The Young Book-keepers Assistant, by Thomas Dilworth. There is no specific illustration of depreciation, but the inventory method is described.

1768

Book-keeping Modernized, by John Mair. (2nd. Ed.) The same general procedure is described as in *Book-keeping Methodiz'd* and there are no illustrations of depreciation but the inference might be made that if the "value" of the property were less than cost, this decrease in value would be included in the charge to Profit and Loss.

. . . first give the account credit by *Balance*, for value of the ship or house, and then close the account with *Profit and Loss*.

1801

Book-keeping in the True Italian Form, by Wm. Jackson. In a "ship" account a credit is shown, "By Profit and Loss, for Wearing, Age, etc." and the balance forward is called "present value." The inventory method is prescribed, as follows:

1. Credit the account by balance for the value of the ship or the part you own thereof.
2. Close the account with profit and loss for the remaining difference.

1805

The Elements of Book-keeping, by P. Kelly. The inventory method of balancing the fixed asset accounts is illustrated without showing any deduction for depreciation, but in discussing the treatment of damage to ships while at sea, the author says:

In computing a General Average for Masts, Rigging, etc. cut away, a deduction is made of ⅓ from the Cost of replacing them, as the new articles are supposed to be so much better than the old. . . .

1830

A Connected View of the Whole Internal Navigation of the United States, by George Armroyd. The following schedule appears on page 290:

The daily expenses of a steam-boat of 10 horse power may be estimated as follows:

30 per cent. on the cost of the boat and engine, valued at $3,500, for interest, decrease of value, hazard, renewals and repairs, allowing only 300 working days, ...$ 3.50
For Captain 3.00
Engineer 2.00

Two hands 1.00
Fuel, 1½ cords of wood per day of 12½ hours, or from 15 to 20 bushels of coal, ... 3.00

Total for each working day $12.50

1833

Baltimore & Ohio Railroad, 7th Annual Report. One section was devoted to the presentation of estimates of the cost of construction and of repairs and renewals of rail way. The cost of replacing different parts was estimated in detail, the same unit costs being used as were incurred in the original construction. For instance, the total renewal cost per mile for oak sills and sleepers, and yellow pine string pieces was $3,342 and the estimated life was 12 years. The annual provision was expressed in terms of an annuity: "An annuity of equivalent value (to $3,342 due 12 years hence) to commence at the end of one year, to continue 12 years, reckoning compound interest at 5 per cent. is $209.97."

1838

Excerpt from a report of "a committee formed to shew the prospects of a company established in London for the conducting of the inland navigation of India by steam":

In Aug. 1835, the "Lord William Bentinck," after having been sixteen months in the water, was hauled up on the patent slip, and no marks of corrosion were visible. With this protection 20 years are confidently assumed for the duration of an iron vessel. The annual depreciation, therefore, on the vessels as well as on the engines, has been assumed at five per cent., and on the boilers at twenty per cent.

1839

American Railroad Journal, of September 1, 1839, a report by W. Edward on the Reading Railroad. In some analyses of costs, the computation of depreciation as a percentage of cost is indicated; for instance: "Repairs and depreciation of engine and tender estimated at 25 per cent on cost, $8,000. . . ."

1840

Nashua & Lowell Railroad, 5th Annual Report. Dividends are deducted from "total estimated profits" (total income less total expenses), "leaving a balance, including bad debts, etc., to be carried to general depreciation and contingency account of $3,955.87."

Report of the Select Committee Appointed to Investigate the Management of the Columbia & Philadelphia Railroad, James Nill, Chairman. The following schedule of estimated expenses of operating a section of the road appears in a report of the Engineer, J. Clements Stocker, to the Committee of Investigation:

Annuity to pay interest on first cost
of fifteen eight wheeled cars, at
$2,000 each, and replace principal
in 5 years, ... $6,934.50
Wear & tear of cars, 5 per cent. on
$6,934.50 .... 346.72
Annuity to pay interest on first cost
of ten baggage cars, at $500 each,
and replace principal in 5 years .. 1,115.00
Wear and tear, 17 per cent. on
$1,115.00 .... 189.00

1842

Norwich & Worcester Railroad Corporation, 7th Annual Report. The following item appears in a schedule of "expenditures . . . for running the road and repairs":

Contingent expenses. This amount being loss or depreciation of stock, which had, for the most part, been previously sustained, but had not been entered, $6,418.00.

1843

American Railroad Journal, of November, 1843. "Cost of Transportation on Railroads" by Charles Ellet, Jr. The following comments are made in regard to depreciation:

To those companies whose works are now new, and who *seem* to be making money, I would suggest the timely formation of a contingent fund, to prepare them for a contingency which will as surely reach them as the next new year. It is bad policy to divide the *annual expenses* [sic] as if they were real profits; the money that is earned at the expense of the rails, cars and machinery, should be hoarded to replace those things, and not distributed, as if they were to last forever. It can be shown that every company should annually store away, in times of prosperity, while their work is new, at least 6 cents for every mile travelled by their engines, 1 cent for every ton conveyed one mile, and 200 dollars for every mile of road, to replace decayed materials, and injured iron and machinery. If their profits will not permit that reservation, then the prudent man will avoid their stock. . . .

The above article is continued in the December, 1843 number of the *Journal,* and in speaking of the wear of iron rails the author says:

Great errors have been committed . . . by overlooking the fact that the progress of the wear is rarely ascertained, or, in the least, appreciated, until the rail is destroyed. The *annual* charge for iron is very small, because, in general, the track does not appear to give way until it is nearly unfit for use.... ... there is not now to be found in the country a single road which has renewed its iron out of the proceeds of transportation.

1844

Boston & Providence Railroad Corporation, 13th Annual Report. The report describes a tardy recognition of accumulated depreciation, the depreciation from January 1, 1834 to December 31, 1844 being recorded in 1844.

On the 31st ultimo we made a careful estimate of the present value of the cars, engines, and other personal property of the corporation, which had been charged to the account of construction, and have charged against such depreciation from the cost to income account, the sum of forty thousand dollars, and deducted the same from the cost of construction.

1845

Boston & Providence Railroad Corporation, 14th Annual Report. The continuation of the policy begun in 1844 is described. The construction cost accounts are carried forward at their depreciated amounts.

An appraisement of the stock of cars, engines, etc. was made by the Superintendent on the 31st ult., and their value being less than was charged to construction, or cost of road, etc. we have charged to income account the difference, say $36,004.84, and deducted this sum from the cost of road, etc.

Philadelphia & Columbia Railroad, report of Edward F. Gay for the year ending November 30, 1845. In a schedule of locomotives original cost is shown in one column and "present value" in another. Apparently each locomotive had been systematically written down.

James River & Kanawha Company, 11th Annual Report. In Appendix X a description is given of navigation on the Mississippi River in 1842, and in this description the following statement appears:

The estimated annual expense of the steam navigation, including . . . 20 per cent. for wear and tear, is $13,618,000.

1846

Boston & Providence Railroad Corporation, 15th Annual Report. The following comments upon the depreciation policy are found in this report.

No estimate has heretofore been made of the depreciation of the road, bridges and buildings. The road has been opened for use for nearly 12 years, and all the fixtures upon it have been kept in good repair. It is supposed that the whole depreciation may be justly estimated at about $20,000.

In 1844, the amount of $40,000 and in 1845, the amount of $36,004.84, was charged to income account for depreciation of cars and engines. The stock of cars and engines has not depreciated during the last year, the additions having much exceeded in value the deterioration of the old stock.

Eastern Railroad Corporation, 11th Annual Report. A contract for the lease of the Essex Railroad Company contained a provision in regard to depreciation of the leased line.

No claim other than the compensation already provided shall be made for interest on the cost or depreciation, further than provided in the current repairs. . . . When this contract shall terminate, the Essex Rail-road shall be delivered up to the party of the first part in fair running order; but the actual depreciation, if any, is to be borne by the party of the first, and not by the party of the second part.

1847

American Railroad Journal, March 25, 1848. The report of the Little Miami Railroad Company for 1847 was published in this number. It showed a deduction for depreciation from net income after deducting interest.

Less, also a charge to depreciation of machinery, 8 wheel cars, 4 wheel cars, and passenger cars, according to estimate of superintendent, $20,479.95.

1848

American Railroad Journal. April 1, 1848. "Depreciation of Railway Stock," part of a speech of a Mr. Glyn at a general meeting of the London & North Western shareholders. It tells how replacements have been charged against revenue, how new capital is required because of the capitalization of the cost of increased weight of rails, and asks for the creation of a replacement fund.

. . . your directors have thought fit, not only to take the usual course in regard to the relaying of the rails . . . but conceiving that, in the course of some fifteen or twenty years, the existing rails will, from the working upon them, require necessarily to be replaced by others, they have thought it their duty to call upon you to sanction the annual appropriation of £15,000 for the purpose of forming a fund to meet that contingency from time to time.

1849

Book-keeping, by D. Adams. A treatise on single entry bookkeeping. Statements of financial condition are set up by the inventory method which involves the revaluation of the fixed assets at the end of each period.

1850

Berkshire Railroad Company, 12th Annual Report. The omission of any depreciation is explained by the comment: "To be kept in perfect repair by lessees."

Boston & Lowell Railroad Corporation, 20th Annual Report. Prior to 1846 some replacements and improvements had been charged to repairs. From 1846 on, the new standard form for Massachusetts railroads is followed.

For repairs of locomotives $25,706.23
For new locomotives to cover de-
    preciation 1,911.62
For repairs of passenger cars 13,130.79
For new passenger cars, to cover
    depreciation 1,100.00
For repairs of merchandise cars . .   6,240.24
For new merchandise cars to cover
    depreciation 500.00
Estimated depreciation beyond the renewals—nothing.

1851

James River & Kanawha Company, 17th Annual Report. Report of the Chief Engineer on the cost of transportation.

The depreciation of boats and mules, assuming that they will last (taking into consideration the occasional loss of a mule) 10 years, will be per annum $136.40.

1853

A Practical System of Book-keeping by Single and Double Entry, by Ira Mayhew. The entire subject of depreciation is avoided by the omission of all discussion of fixed assets.

A Practical System of Book-keeping, by L. S. Fulton and G. W. Eastman. Depreciation is not specifically discussed, but the inventory method of balancing the accounts would take care of depreciation if the values had gone down.

Real Estate account is kept to show the gain or loss on real estate. It is made Debit for its cost—as purchase money, repairs, taxes, etc., and Credit for what it produces, either in rent or sales. If it is not all sold, the value of what remains unsold should be placed on the Credit side of the account. The difference between the Debit and Credit will be the gain or loss on real estate.

An Inductive and Practical Treatise on Book-keeping, by S. W. Crittenden. The inventory method is used to adjust and close fixed asset accounts. Appreciation is

taken in the revaluation of Real Estate. Depreciation is taken in the valuation of a ship but is not isolated from the other elements of expense; the income and expense items are credited and debited to the Ship account, the inventory is inserted, and the balance is carried to profit and loss.

1854

Colburn's Railroad Advocate, September 1, 1855. An excerpt from the 1854 report of the Cincinnati, Columbus & Cleveland road.

The annual depreciation of the superstructure of railroads, has not generally received the consideration it deserves; but experience has shown it to be very great, and it should therefore be provided for by setting apart from year to year, such sums as may be necessary to cover it.

The writer computes the depreciation per mile per annum of rails and says:

This sum then, or such sum as, with accruing interest, will amount to this at the end of eight years, should be set apart at the end of the first year to pay for renewals of iron.

1855

Colburn's Railroad Advocate, December 15, 1855. A rate of 8 1/3% per annum is suggested as the proper rate of depreciation for railroads.

1856

Colburn's Railroad Advocate, February 9, 1856. Excerpt from the report of the Nashville & Chattanooga road. Data are presented on the length of life of rails, locomotives, etc.

From the foregoing, you will be able to form a very correct idea of the rate our rails and machinery are wearing out; and in so doing, you cannot fail to see the propriety, and, indeed, absolute necessity of creating an adequate sinking fund to provide for this large item of depreciation.

To avoid doing so—passing it by, as something that can be provided for hereafter, is always attended with disastrous results. It is far better for the future prosperity of the company, to place it conspicuously in the items of the current expenses.

Another strong reason for appropriating, a sufficient sum to cover every description of loss by deterioration, is, to enable the officers and directors to know the *actual* cost of the moveage of tonnage, and thereby prevent them from falling into the popular error of railroad companies in fixing the tariff of charges *too* low. . . .

1856

Colburn's Railroad Advocate, March 22, 1856. A comment is made upon data relating to the wearing out of iron rails.

This fact shows that railroad directors should provide for the depreciation of iron from the first day of opening their roads. It is generally the case that any material depreciation is denied for the first few years of working the road, and after that it is underrated, until the time comes when an entire new track has to be laid down, and a dividend or so passed, and some portion if not the whole, charged to "construction."

1860

Agricultural Branch Railroad Corporation, annual report. The notations are made that the road has been "operated by the Boston & Worcester Railroad Company since December, 1855, under a lease . . ." and that depreciation is "to be assumed by Boston & Worcester Railroad Company." The lease (published in the 1855 report), however, only provides that the lessee will surrender the property at the expiration of the lease "in as good order and condition, reasonable use, wear, and decay thereof excepted, as was received by them . . ." and this will not cover real depreciation.

Boston & Maine Railroad, 13th Annual Report. The depreciation shown in the report is added to the dividends declared, and the total is deducted from "net earnings after deducting expenses."

1861

Common School Book-keeping, by H. B. Bryant, H. D. Stratton, and S. S. Packard. The inventory method is presented briefly. There is no specific discussion or illustration of depreciation.

Book-keeping, by W. Inglis. Under the discussion of "Taking Stock" of such accounts as buildings and machinery:

In such accounts, a yearly deduction of 5 or 10 per cent. requires to be made from the original cost, to allow for deterioration, or wear and tear.

In the illustration of a Furniture account, the following notation appears: "By Depreciation, 5% carried to Trade Expenses." The statement is made that a warehouse should be written down if it becomes "deteriorated in value from any cause," and that printing machinery undergoes "a yearly deterioration of 5 per cent. off the cost price . . . reducing the value of the machinery by this sum annually."

1863

Counting House Book-keeping by H. B. Bryant, H. D. Stratton, and S. S. Packard. No depreciation is specifically illustrated or discussed, but increases in value of fixed assets are demonstrated and the same method would apparently be used if values had declined.

In set II, Real Estate is inventoried at $2,000 more than cost and this difference is taken as gain for the period.

In set III, taxes are charged to Real Estate, and Rent is credited. There is no change in the inventory valuation.

In set IV, no change is shown in the Store and Fixtures account for the first month, but in the second month an appreciation of $2500 is recorded.

In the presentation of farm accounts, all assets are inventoried, no depreciation but some cases of appreciation being illustrated.

186–

The Handbook of Book-keeping, author not given. An entry is made debiting Profit and Loss and crediting Office Furniture without any explanation, but it looks like the recognition of regular depreciation.

1871

Book-keeping and Business Manual, by H. W. Ellsworth. The inventory method is used. There is no specific mention of depreciation.

Real Estate account is used to represent the outlay upon, and return from value invested in houses and lands, being debited for all outlay, and credited for all returns from the same. The balance of this account, after crediting it with the Inventory, shows the Loss or Gain on this species of property.

1872

Elements of Book-keeping, Irish National Board of Education, author not given. The inventory method of adjusting and closing accounts with ships, houses, etc. is described but there is no specific illustration of depreciation. Part of the instructions is a literal copy from "The Young Book-keepers Assistant," by Thomas Dilworth, published in 1765, without any reference being given as to its source.

1873

Practical Book-keeping, by W. A. Drew. No mention is made of depreciation, but apparently the inventory method would be used.

The Logic of Accounts, by E. G. Folsom. There is very little material on fixed assets. The inventory method of adjusting the accounts is described.

The Boston & Worcester Railroad Annual Reports 1838-1867

The annual reports of the Boston & Worcester Railroad Corporation to the State of Massachusetts contain a number of references to depreciation.

1838—7th Annual Report

Before declaring the last dividend, the directors reserved for deterioration of perishable materials in the road, and depreciation of engines and cars, beyond the repairs, the sum of $15,000.

1839—8th Annual Report

The amount expended during the last two years, and charged to the account of construction, was ....$ 137,791.43

The amount previously expended and charged to the same account, as by annual report of 1838, was $1,710,294.39

Making a total of $1,848,085.82
From which deduct amount reserved from income and carried to reserved fund on account of decay and wear of road, engines, etc. beyond what is replaced by repairs and new work, ...$ 48,830.00

Present valuation of road, depot, buildings, engines, cars, etc..$1,799,255.82

1840—9th Annual Report

The same arrangement of data is used as in the 1839 report, but the wording of the depreciation deduction is somewhat different:
Deduct: reserved fund for decay of sleepers, and wear of road engines and cars, etc., beyond repairs, ...$60,000.00

1841—10th Annual Report

The "reserved fund, for decay and wear, beyond repairs" is not deducted from the total construction cost as before, but is simply shown as a special item in the report. In a group of "expenditures ... exclusive of the amount charged to construction," appears the following item:

For repairs of engines and cars, of which, taken from reserved fund for new cars, $9,900, ...$25,286.46

1842—11th Annual Report

The "amount of reserved fund" is shown as $38,293.28, and under "expenditures during the same period":

For repairs of road and bridges $51,457.22
Deduct, charged to reserved fund 10,000.00 $41,457.22

1843—12th Annual Report

The amount expended for construction ... after deducting the amount credited to this account from the profits, for deterioration, is $2,836,168.58.

The expenditures during the same period, were . . . including $16,092, allowed for deterioration of cars, $133,579.99.

1844—13th Annual Report

At this time a definite policy seems to have been worked out for handling depreciation. The following excerpt is an unusually clear and complete statement of directorial policy:

Great care has been taken, by the directors and superintendent of the road, to obtain accurate accounts and estimates of the actual cost of the operations of each year, including the proper average current charges of maintaining the road, bridges, buildings and machinery, without depreciation in value . . . . . . it is obvious that the actual expenditure in any single year is no criterion of the actual decay. The only mode of arriving at a satisfactory result, is to be guided by the experience of successive years, and to apportion upon each year an amount equal to the average cost of making good the value of each description of value at the expiration of each year, before making the dividend of the year. In conformity with this principle, it was the early practice of the directors to make an annual allowance for the deterioration when the expenditures for repairs were not deemed equivalent to the waste from wear and decay; whereby a fund was created to meet expenditures of succeeding years, whenever they should exceed the average cost of the necessary repairs. This fund is now exhausted, and it is the intention of the directors, in lieu of such a fund hereafter, to make an annual expenditure in repairs, and in the supply of new machinery in place of old, or new rails in place of those which are broken or injured, to an amount which will keep the property as nearly equal, as is practicable, to the original cost, and in this manner to avoid the error of confounding with net profits, such portion of the income as is required for preserving the capital entire . . . . . . in estimating the net annual income of the road, a proper caution has been used, before declaring dividends or profits, to allow an amount which shall be sufficient, and no more than sufficient, to preserve the capital stock entire.

1845—14th Annual Report

In this report the application of the policy set forth in the report of 1844 is described, and the policy again explained and defended.

The expenditure of $69,443.65 . . . for road repairs, includes, in addition to the ordinary repairs of road, bridges, and buildings, a large charge for the renewal of rails on a part of the old track, by the substitution of a heavier rail, and some extra charges for the enlargement of depot buildings. . . . It was deemed proper to make the whole amount a charge on the income of the year, as a part of the current expenses, instead of charging it to the construction account, representing capital; inasmuch as the expenditure charged within the year to the account of repairs of engines and cars is inadequate to meet the heavy depreciation from wear and damage, to the very large number of engines, tenders and passenger and freight cars, required for the business of the road. It would be difficult were it desirable, so to apportion the current expenditures of every year in each separate branch of account, as to preserve an exact equilibrium between the wear and the renewal, on each division of property, but the object of determining the net divisible income of the year, is sufficiently attained, if the aggregate of the expenditures for repairs is sufficient to maintain the value of the whole property against wear, decay, damage and depreciation from every cause. Such a charge in some form, either of expenditure or reserve, must evidently be made, and deducted from the income of the year, before the proper divisible profits can be ascertained. On a valuation of the present stock of passenger and freight cars, it is estimated that an amount equal to that stated ($25,000—the excess charged to repairs of road, bridges and buildings over estimated amount of ordinary repairs), is required to be credited to that account, to make good the deficiency of appropriations to it, in the last and several preceding years.

1846—15th Annual Report

In 1846 the State of Massachusetts prescribed a new form for annual reports of its railroads. A section of the form was headed "Motive Power and Cars" and provided for the following information:

For repairs of locomotives xxxx
For new locomotives, to cover depreciation xxxx
For repairs of passenger cars ...xxxx

For new passenger cars to cover
depreciation xxxx
For repairs of merchandise cars ..xxxx
For new merchandise cars to cover
depreciation xxxx
For repairs of gravel and other
cars xxxx

Total for maintenance of motive
power and cars ....　　xxxx

Another section which followed the showing of dividends and surplus asked for the following information:

Estimated Depreciation beyond the Renewals, vis:
Road and Bridges xxxx
Buildings xxxx
Engines and cars xxxx

In the report of the railroad the following comments were made on the new form and the depreciation policy of the company was restated:

In the returns . . . of current expenses, a slight departure from the form prescribed in the printed schedule has been rendered necessary from the manner in which these expenditures are charged in the books. Under the several heads of *repairs,* . . . are entered all expenditures not only for repairs strictly speaking, but for new constructions, improvements, or additions; unless the additions so made exceed in value the deterioration of the property . . . , beyond the amount which represents it in the general stock; in which case, the excess is charged to the appropriate head of the general account, and the residue to repairs. For this purpose, an estimate is made, as nearly as is practicable, before the closing of each year's accounts, of the property under each head of account, and of the amount of depreciation beyond the repairs in comparison with the additions. . . .

At another place in the report the statement is made: "Original cost of road and equipment, with that of additions, when the amount exceeds in value that of depreciation . . . $3,485,242.43." In the section of the report headed "Estimated Depreciation beyond the Renewals" the word "none" appeared.

1847—16th Annual Report

There are no comments in regard to depreciation in this report, but in the "Motive Power and Cars" schedule appear both repairs and purchases of locomotives and passenger cars. The company had apparently changed its bookkeeping procedure so as to accumulate the information required in the standard form.

1848—17th Annual Report

In this report an explanation is made in connection with the statement that the considerable increase in capital stock represented actual increases in property and was not used for repairs, which included the following comments upon the depreciation policy:

On making up the periodical statements of income and expenses, for the purpose of determining the amount of net profits properly subject to dividend, it has been the practice of the directors to ascertain, as nearly as is practicable, whether the amount of repairs, or of new works furnished at the charge of income, is equivalent to the depreciation from wear, decay, unfitness for further use, or damage; and, in such case, to credit an amount, adequate to meet the depreciation, to the appropriate head of the construction account, and to add the same to the amount of current expenses, charged in the income account. . . .

1849 to 1867

During this period a considerable amount of experimentation with methods of presenting depreciation data is evident, for the figures are seldom presented in exactly the same way for more than two or three years in succession, but there is no indication of a change in depreciation policy. In the report of 1853, figures were inserted in the section headed "Estimated Depreciation beyond the Renewals" and deducted from surplus. In 1867 there was no indication of a charge for depreciation, and in this year the company was consolidated with the Western Railroad Company to form the Boston & Albany Railroad Company.

REVIVAL IN THE 19TH CENTURY

7

THE BACKGROUND OF ACCOUNTING

Elmer Hartzell

THE BACKGROUND OF ACCOUNTING

Elmer Hartzell

Accounting is usually regarded as an adjunct of commerce or industry which has at the most a tenuous relationship to the structure and theory of science and slight discernible similarity to forms of political organization. An inspection of a few of the fundamental outlines of the subject indicates, however, that science, political organizations and accounting are interrelated and that a change in one of them presumes an alteration of the others. It is intended in what follows herein to sketch several of the organic similarities.

It was no accident that the double entry system of accounts was introduced in Italy in the territory and prior to the period in which Galileo performed experiments to prove conclusions concerning the action of gravity and the phenomena which modify its effects. Experimentation involves controlled observation of a series of events and in the case of the experiments there was an observation of their action against a background of natural forces, the results of which were put into summary expression or formula known as a law. Accounting has the same general background in that the effects of a selected group of activities in its reaction with its environment are recorded; it is one of the tools for the control of a business.

Accounting centers around two classes of records, the balance sheet and the profit-and-loss statement. Taken together they exemplify the mechanical theory of physics as well as the physiological or organic theory which is associated with evolutionary processes in which time is cardinal. An initial and fundamental point of contact and the basis for both the physical sciences and accounting is present, to begin with, in the number system which is common to both. The number one (1) is primary in that every other number is divisible by it, thus presuming the homogeneity and divisibility of those things to which the numbers are assigned. Their homogeneous and divisible character is further amplified by the operations of addition and subtraction. In physics the action of the forces of nature are measured by assigning numerical values of the number system to carefully defined units and their combinations; in accounting things are, likewise, brought together into a complex whole by the assignment to things of values which have been worked out through the action of many buyers and sellers. The positive sums of these values are, on a balance sheet, called assets and the negative ones are referred to as liabilities. The principle of the equation is utilized by the insistence that the two sides must balance. This is accomplished by offsetting the assets by the true liabilities and, in addition, by a sum, which remains over and above these, which is designated "proprietorship."[1] It represents what belongs to certain individuals as the result of the interplay of economic forces and thus points to the oncoming of a régime of private property and individualism. The fact that numerical values may be assigned to property is indicative of a drawing apart of the ownership and use of wealth inasmuch as it may now be regarded with the impersonality requisite for putting the possessions within the framework of numbers; and the operations carried on arithmetically with the values of the balance sheet, involving as they do a shifting about from one place to another, imply a society so organized as to make possible a considerable mobility of capital and the legal transfer of the same through a market from one person to another.

The conceptual foundations of accounting were essentially the same as those of the physical sciences. Double entry bookkeeping rests on the basic principle, logically carried out, of "comprehending all

---

[1] Under modern conditions proprietorship has become a liability to stockholders.

phenomena purely as quantities,"[2] and "it was the supremacy of book values, whose abstract system was quickly detached from personality by double-entry bookkeeping and worked forward by virtue of its own inward dynamism, that produced the modern capital that spans the whole earth with its field of force."[3] The action and reaction of Newtonian mechanics is duplicated in accounting by the offsetting of every debit by a credit; the law of the conservation of energy is paralleled in the maintenance of capital and by the requirement that receipts and expenditures shall balance;[4] and the co-ordinate geometry of Descartes has its locus in the business world in the balance sheet. The assignment of numerical values to goods and services was, moreover, evidence of the appearance of that impersonal attitude presumed to be an important characteristic of the scientific method. In the handicraft stage the efforts of men were not mediated to the extent now prevalent by a host of accessories which separate them from the rhythm and action of the forces of nature. The personal relationships thus established were not susceptible except implicitly to definitive quantitative determination and the scale of values was thus of a qualitative rather than a quantitative character. The leading principle mathematically was one of "order" rather than numerical equivalence. Ethically the shift was one with wide ramifications. The greater use of a quantitative form of expression implied a cleavage between an inner and an outer, that is, between the spiritual and the material. As the separation widened mind was set in opposition to nature and with the growing independence of it the separation between means and ends became wider and the spiritual hierarchy centering in the Kingdom of God and represented by the Church gradually gave way to agnosticism or materialism and the predominance of temporal power.

It is apparent that the sharp distinction made by Thorstein Veblen[5] between the ethical conduct of the engineer, the applied scientist, and that of the business man is not a fundamental one. The pecuniary system of which he speaks and the ethical standards governing it have the same root as the science which he eulogizes. Science is concerned with means rather than ends and thinking in terms of money is essentially comparable to that of the scientist. In both instances the simplicity of direct contact has been mediated by abstractions which enable the relations of impersonal forces to be co-ordinated. It is in the field of technology that practical use is made of the laws thus obtained and it is within the setting of the technical apparatus of the machine civilization that the business man carries on his work. The measure of the results obtained is money. It is one of the mediums, the essences, through which the interplay of men with their environment is expressed. As such it is abstract and subject to the impersonal characteristics, as to its effects on others, of a calculation in theoretical physics. Money and credit expressed in terms of money are, in fact, focuses of power and are analogous conceptually to electrical energy—an invisible, homogeneous, indefinitely divisible source of power. The transition from metallic coins as a medium of exchange to credit has taken place coincidentally with the investigation of physical phenomena which, as an electric current, may not be seen or felt as a material object.

The first treatise on double-entry bookkeeping had its origin fittingly enough in the country and the period which produced Machiavelli's "The Prince." The State at that time had fallen into a number of warring principalities and political aims were to be realized according to Machiavelli by methods which were coldly calculating, ruthless, and selfish. The goal of action was

---

[2] Sombart, *Der Modern Kapitalismus*, II, 119.
[3] Spengler, *Decline of the West*, II, 493.
[4] In practise this becomes a "moving equilbrium" of money values or of "inputs and outputs" of energy.

---

[5] Among other places, in his book, *The Engineers and the Price System.*

to be referred to the conspirator himself, thereby subordinating or relegating to the background the norms of the Church. A portent of the new order was contained in the new system of bookkeeping. In it may be seen the forerunner of the disintegration of the old hierarchies of feudalism. The locus of a group of worldly values now passes over to business firms within which is the center of reference and the measure of value is to become an impersonal medium —money. The conquest of nature and the organization of the means for that purpose which were on the way were also eventually to be expressed in the classifications or categories of the balance sheet. In it, fixed capital was to be distinguished from circulating capital and the interplay of mechanical operations and business transactions was to be summarized in a proprietorship account which rose or fell according to the varying fortunes of the business. A régime of private property was in the making, indispensable to which was the separation of one person's wealth from that of others and a way by which increases or decreases in value might be registered. In a later day the impetus to a separation of control and ownership was accentuated by the use of borrowed capital and in the modern corporation the changed structure of society is apparent in the control of vast resources through holding companies, as well as the diffusion of ownership through shares of stock.

The correlation between the form of business ownership and the form of political government is no less direct, evidence for which may be obtained by observing the successive changes in the "proprietorship" account. As the simplest units we have, originally, numerous small firms in whom ownership as well as management centered in a single individual. This form then gave way to the partnership in which liability for debts was absolute yet participation in the activities might or might not be active. The next stage in the transition was reached in the joint stock company in which neither activity in the management or unlimited liability was de-

manded, and in the corporation of today the functions of a management elected through the stockholders may be as completely separated from ownership as are those of the political representatives of the people.

The problems to be dealt with by the accountant are carefully limited as in any scientific procedure by confining attention to only a section of the field of business, that is, to some particular firm. This is made possible without losing contact with the world at large through the system of values which is worked out on a personal basis in all parts of the exchange organization, the generalized results of which may be transferred impersonally to accounting records. The chief problem of the accountant is to represent adequately the fundamental categories of space and time in conformity with the requirements of business and to bring them into a harmonious relationship. This he accomplishes through the balance sheet and the income statement. The details of the give and take of business are not entered, however, directly into these records. In connection with them are kept a series of books which classify in more or less detail the raw data under the various headings found in the income statement and balance sheet. It is an important principle that every entry must be offset by a contrary one of equal amount or, in other words, for every debit there must be a credit. The mass of raw data is by this systematic classification and the opposition of one item by another converged through a process of cumulative change toward the broad divisions of the income statement and the balance sheet of which the focus in the one is net profit and in the other proprietorship (or capital stock and surplus). This procedure is broadly analogous to the solution in economic theory of a problem of the price of a commodity, in which the total quantity of the article that is desired at each particular price is compressed into a table. The manipulation of such data has as part of its background the idea of a supply which is co-ordinate with a demand. The next step forward from this simplicity is the enrichment of the meaning of the concept supply and demand by splitting it into parts expressed as terms of the right and left hand members of an algebraic equation. The equation is then elaborated by extending it into a series whose central unifying fact is brought out as in the solution of simultaneous equations. This way of treating prices as part of a process or moving equilibrium is explicitly that of Gustav Cassel in his *Theory of the National Economy*[6] and it has been exemplified more recently with greater mathematical completeness by H. L. Moore.[7]

The procedure of accounting in which a mass of data is converged and resolved into a group of representative accounts is also broadly analogous to that of dynamics in which by the use of "fluxions" or the calculus and a vector analysis the action of a body is followed under the pull of opposing forces. In the same way, in the doctrine of natural selection a struggle for existence takes place which, through a series of successive changes, determines the make-up of an organism and, likewise, in the political arena of a liberal or democratic state the conflict of political parties, composed as they are of voters who express their choice by the ballot, has as its resultant the emergence of a victorious candidate. The succession of office holders is, moreover, not fixed as with a hereditary succession of monarchs or a dictatorship but is subject to review at frequent intervals by a repetition of the same competitive process.

The balance sheet characterizes essentially the category of space in that the assets within it are largely of a material nature; the income account on the other hand represents a process and its category is time. The two are fundamentally similar, yet the exigencies of the situation require that they be separated inasmuch as a frame of reference, the classifications of the balance sheet, is necessary as a background against which to trace the results accomplished as recorded in the income accounts. The difficulty is overcome by viewing the one, the balance sheet, as referring to a succession of events in a period of time, say one year. By thus regarding the same situation from the standpoint of a particular point in time the sense impression of a totality is obtained thereby giving rise to the static and material objects of the balance sheet, whereas in the income account the material aspect is subordinated by diffusing the impression of the situation in a process which extends over a period.

The character of this procedure is in accord with the modern view that objects do not possess the materiality which is usually attributed to them. Implicit in such a doctrine is the acceptance of a space-time rather than a space and a time, that is, space and time are not distinct. The relevance of such a conception to accounting consists in the recognition that the balance sheet and income account are inseparable, the former of which views the set of factors at a point of time whereas the other views it in its temporal aspects. The income account, in other words, is merely a statement of what takes place with the assets in a succession of instances, and theoretically therefore the one could be reduced to the other. This conclusion has an important bearing on the question of capital and income, concerning which the prevailing opinion appears to be that income is a conception more fundamental than capital[8] and that capital value is derived by capitalizing income. The fact is, however, that the emphasis placed on income is an arbitrary one which is derived from the peculiar vantage point of the expositor. In accordance with recent physical science it may be stated as an emphasis arising from an observer who is in motion rather than at rest with respect to some frame of reference. In a society such as our own, for instance, in which violent or even convulsive

[6] See in particular Chapter IV on "The Mechanism of Pricing."

[7] See his book on *Synthetic Economics*.

[8] See J. B. Canning, *The Economics of Accountancy*, p. 175.

disturbances are as typical as slow progress, the tendency would be present to emphasize processes or the temporal character of events and thus in theory to obtain capital values by the capitalization of income. On the other hand, in a society in which change is slow the emphasis could just as reasonably swing over to the other extreme. The difference in a practical way is brought out by the care exercised to conserve the principle of an investment, as is customary in France, as compared with the more speculative attitude towards his funds which is characteristic of the American.

Accounting as it is now conducted is concerned with the effect of a policy on the individual firm or business, only incidental consideration being given to the larger social setting. It is presumed in theory that the economically proper thing will be worked out through the action of the price system. As corporations grow to great size, however, their own policies have a perceptible effect on events and an imperceptible shift is begun toward a view which envisages the total situation. The management of the American Telephone and Telegraph Corporation, for example, limits the return on its invested capital to a moderate amount, and the actions of the U. S. Steel Corporation in raising or lowering wages are regarded as having an important influence on other firms. The opinion may be hazarded therefore that there will be a movement toward a resolution of costs which may be called Social Accounting, the objective of which will be the harmonization of the viewpoints of the business firms and human interests at large by tracing the effects of particular policies on groups other than those directly concerned. The work of Pigou in *Wealth and Welfare* points the way by the application of a calculus which treats economic quantities as variable magnitudes so related to one another that for every value of one there is a corresponding value for the other. John Maurice Clark has, likewise, gone at the problem by using the accounting concept of overhead costs, an essential fact of which

is that an increase or decrease in output does not involve a proportionate change in costs. Such a functional analysis aims to show, for instance, how the burden of unemployed workers is passed on from the individual concern to society and how such unemployment may be minimized by smoothing out seasonal and other business cycles. It involves essentially a type of enlightened control which is carried on within the price mechanism by a large number of separate entrepreneurs, thereby accomplishing within a capitalistic framework that which would be aimed at by a central board with dictatorial powers.

It is plain that here has been a shift in ideas from those of bookkeeping to accounting and from the latter to a broader field of social accounting, a part of the significance of which is that a transference of ideas may take place between it and the social sciences with reasonable ease and without confusion of the subject matter. Accounting itself has been acquiring the characteristics of a science in that (1) a number of basic principles for governing accounting procedure have been established concerning which there is a general agreement, (2) a technique has been developed for a detailed reporting of facts which have a precise meaning with respect to a given objective and (3) the measurement of the results of business operations in terms of the objective, vis., profits, enables a control to be exercised over industrial processes. As an offshoot of these developments the technical subject of cost accounting has become prominent, the newness of which has obscured the manner in which its technique may be given broader application. It is sometimes said, for instance, that cost accounting is really a separate subject, the inference being that the development of its major outlines is having an independent growth. It is likely, however, that the familiarity of the accountant with the conceptual apparatus of cost accounting will be conducive to the origination of a social accounting with the requisite breadth, flexibility and precision. The cost accountant is, in brief, concerned with problems of value in that he has the task of bringing a host of factors without mathematical equivalence and with differing degrees of commensurability into a functional unity or coherent pattern. Expressed mathematically he obtains concrete evidence of the fact that a cost is a "function of many valuables" and his work thus may pass over into economics and become concerned with problems of social cost in that a technique is being worked out which will be useful in equating such imponderables as the relative values of a quantity of labor and of capital, and the indirect costs of unemployment.

Other evidence which points to an enlargement of the scope of accounting is indicated by the stages of the following outline wherein a line of development is suggested which appears to be definitely towards a national outlook:

1. Bookkeeping of small firms and partnerships.
2. Accounting of corporations.
3. Accounting from the standpoint of an industry.
4. Accounting from the standpoint of a group of industries.
5. National accounting, under conditions which vary from a minimum of governmental control to a "planned economy" or socialism.

(a) Application of accounting principles to the measurement of the balance of foreign trade.[9]
(b) Application of accounting principles to the measurement of the national wealth and income.

The trend which is pointed to should occasion no surprise inasmuch as it has been exemplified in the shift from small, privately owned business of fifty years ago to the large corporation of today with widely dispersed groups of stockholders. Consolidated balance sheets and income statements, which co-ordinate the reports of the several units of a corporation, have in the meantime become commonplace and it is but a step from that point to a consideration of an industry, and from there to industry as a whole. It may be anticipated as a result that the meaning of such fundamental ideas as costs and profits will be transformed as the means become available for bringing a national perspective into a quantitative relationship with the affairs of individual corporate units.

---

[9] The book by Cleona Lewis on *The International Accounts* is a good example of the way in which the principles of accounting have been utilized for the measurement of the volume of foreign trade; also the recent annual bulletins of the United States Department of Commerce which summarize the balance of trade of the United States.

THE GENESIS OF COST CONTROL

Paul Crossman

THE GENESIS OF COST CONTROL

Paul Crossman

Associate Professor, University of Omaha

THE PRESENT EMPHASIS upon cost control may tend to indicate that this is a comparatively new function of accounting and management. This is not the case, however, inasmuch as two or more centuries ago a few writers expressed the idea that the accounting records should supply data useful to management in controlling costs. In fact, Garner states:

... Certain modern cost techniques and practices had their origin in the period 1400-1600. Even the purposes of the early systems appear modern, in that they were set up (1) to establish accounting control over the steps of production and (2) to curb wastes in the use of material and labor.[1]

However, he also points out that literature on cost accounting was conspicuous by its rarity before the beginning of the Industrial Revolution.[2]

Accordingly, the available literature of the eighteenth and nineteenth centuries has been examined to discover when the idea of controlling costs was first rather clearly expressed and to trace the steps which were subsequently taken in developing the function of cost control.

Hamilton, in a discussion of "Tradesmens Accompts," was one of the early authors who included material related to cost control in his writings. For example he proposed that cost data should be recorded in more detail than was customary in the usual journal or ledger and he recommended keeping departmental records to determine the resulting gain or loss on each principal activity.[3]

Hamilton apparently recognized the value of comparison as a technique of cost control because this statement appeared in his explanation of "A Book of Wages," "In some trades, it may be convenient to keep the book of wages in the form of a ledger, and allot an accompt for each journeyman, where the quantity and the value of the work he performs is entered."[4] In subsequent paragraphs he used the word "value" in the sense of selling price, therefore, this book probably was used for custom work (in which the material was furnished by others), with each account being debited for wages paid and credited for income received. Thus, this record provided a comparison between cost of wages and the related selling price which was valuable information for control purposes.

It is of interest to note that Hamilton covered the subject of "Tradesmens Accompts" (an early discussion of cost accounting) in approximately two pages.

Some fifty years later, another author pointed out the need for keeping and analyzing manufacturing costs by stating:

The great contribution introduced by machinery, and the application of the principle of the sub-division of labour, render it necessary for each producer to be continually on the watch, to discover improved methods by which the cost of the article which he manufactures may be reduced; and, with this view, it is of great importance to know the precise expense of every process, as well as the wear and tear of machinery which is due to it.

One of the first advantages which suggests itself as likely to arise from a correct analysis of the expense of the several processes of manufacturer, is the indication which it would furnish of the course in which improvement should be directed.[5]

---

[1] S. Paul Garner, "Historical Development of Cost Accounting," THE ACCOUNTING REVIEW, October, 1947, pp. 386-87.

[2] *Loc. cit.*

[3] Robert Hamilton, *An Introduction to Merchandise*, 2nd ed., Edinburgh, 1788, pp. 486-88.

[4] *Ibid.*, p. 487.

[5] Charles Babbage, *On the Economy of Machinery and Manufacturers*, London: Charles Knight, 1832, pp. 203-04.

In addition to emphasizing the need for detailed cost information classified by departments, Babbage also stressed the fact that cost analysis is a basic part of cost control. Furthermore, he set forth the close relationship which exists between controlling costs and reducing costs— activities which are uppermost in the minds of progressive managers today.

Toward the close of the nineteenth century, even though much of the accounting literature described specific forms and records, more of the writings stressed the importance of keeping adequate cost records and of analyzing these records for the enlightenment of management. Also, there was some indication that at least a small number of manufacturers were attempting to keep satisfactory cost records. It was likewise apparent, however, that the attempts to establish a separate cost department were accompanied by a number of difficulties. In addition to the technical obstacles involved, it seemed that financial accountants were not particularly interested in learning the methods of "Costing." For example, Gibson stated that some companies established a separate department, "the prime cost department . . . with which the accountant had no concern,"[6] in an attempt to obtain more cost data. He then went on to explain that, as a rule, the records of the prime cost department were not controlled by the general books, which immediately created a new problem because the cost records often showed a profit whereas the statement prepared by the financial accountant disclosed a loss. To correct this difficulty, the author recommended keeping a subsidiary prime cost ledger for each contract or job. Apparently the selling price was credited to each subsidiary account because Gibson explained that the profit or loss on each job was closed to the

trading and profit and loss account in the general ledger. Here, "General Charges," consisting of indirect wages, salaries, depreciation, and other indirect costs were listed individually as debits. Likewise, the profit or loss on each contract, including the name of the job, was listed separately in this account. The balance of the trading and profit and loss account represented the operating profit or loss for the year.[7]

The advantage of closing the trading and profit and loss account in this manner was stated to be:

Now this is something which is both intelligible and useful to the practical manager of the business. It follows the operation of his mind in the control of his trade; it shows definitely how far his estimates have been proved by results; . . . in particular it directs his attention to the figures of wages and expenses which are not allotable to each contract, which are unproductive and must be allowed for as a percentage in making his estimates.[8]

In this article, Gibson introduced "control" as a function of management and pointed out the need for separately reporting indirect expenses in order that they might be analyzed and controlled. He also indicated that cost information could be used as a basis for determining bid prices on contract or custom jobs; a new use at that time. In connection with this, he stressed the importance of comparing the estimate with the final cost, and the final cost with the selling price. However, there was nothing to indicate that this comparison was made other than on an historical basis.

A few years later another writer, G. P. Norton, suggested keeping a "Manufacturing Account" for each department of the factory. Norton explained this account and the procedures involved in keeping the related records, substantially as follows. The total manufacturing cost of each department or of each process was deter-

[6] Arthur H. Gibson, "Trading and Profit and Loss Accounts," *The Accountant*, June 18, 1887, p. 360.

[7] *Ibid.*, p. 361.
[8] *Loc. cit.*

mined by means of a distribution schedule or "Analysis Sheet." Here, all manufacturing costs, both indirect and direct, were allocated to each department or process. Indirect costs included items such as supplies, salaries of mill manager, rent, taxes, insurance, repairs, and depreciation. The total cost for each department was debited to Section II of the Manufacturing Account. This section was then credited with the work done by each department at trade prices, i.e., prices which would be paid if this same work were done by outsiders who performed similar processes on a custom basis. The difference was a profit on manufacturing departments.[9]

The value of the Manufacturing Account was explained by this statement:

> With this Manufacturing Account before him, the proprietor may satisfy himself at once as to the precise cause of any change in the amount of profits arising out of his business. . . . Section II will show him whether his departments of manufacture have been carried on profitably, and will point out to him the particular department where any leakage has taken place. This is precisely what the manufacturer wants to know. Are my prices right? And, if so, am I making my goods economically? And further, what department, if any, requires to be overhauled if it is not paying?[10]

Norton also indicated that other items such as warehouse, office, and financial expense were deducted from the manufacturing profit to determine the "Net Profit as Per Trading Account." Thus the Manufacturing Account segregated production costs and showed the gross profit on manufacturing, which was a step forward in the development of the cost control function.

Although there were indications that progress in the art of keeping cost records was being made, the general status of cost-finding systems was indicated by the title of an article, "Notes on Cost Records: A Neglected Branch of Accountancy,"[11]

which also appeared in 1891. This article is noteworthy because it presented two new ideas relating to the purpose of keeping cost records. These objects were:

> "1. *To examine and explain past results.*
> 2. *To form a guide for future trading.*"[12]

The first object was definitely based upon historical cost analysis which is of minor importance in controlling costs, but the second object indicated a forward-looking purpose for keeping cost records which is of primary importance today in planning and controlling business activities.

Furthermore, Mann emphasized the importance of preparing statements which contained useful data and also attempted to explain a remedy for the justifiable lack of interest on the part of management in accounting reports as they were usually prepared. In this connection, the following passages should be especially interesting to the accountant who has difficulty in explaining statements to his client, or to the cost accountant who thinks that his reports are not properly received by management. Mann first discussed the:

> . . . Slight attention paid by a manufacturer or a trader to the details of his Profit and Loss Account prepared from his books with so much trouble. . . .
> These details [of the Profit and Loss Account] seem meaningless to him; they do not interest him, they are of no value to him. . . .
> You say to yourself 'My labour is thrown away in ascertaining accurately all these details, in discriminating between wages and salaries, between works expenses and office expenses—a Balance Sheet or even a state of affairs is good enough for such a man.' But perhaps the fault is your own. You have not succeeded in making your elaborate reports interesting enough. Can you not make them more interesting?[13]

Mann then recounted a situation in which the profit and loss account showed a loss but the manufacturer thought he had

---

[9] G. P. Norton, "A Manufacturer's Trading Account," *The Accountant*, October 31, 1891, pp. 762–64.
[10] *Ibid.*, p. 764.
[11] John Mann, *The Accountant*, August 25 and September 5, 1891, pp. 619–21, 631–37.
[12] *Ibid.*, p. 619.
[13] *Ibid.*, p. 620.

made a profit. He described the resulting predicament in the following manner:

How can you convince him that you are right and that he is wrong? You may treat him to some well worn platitudes of the infallibility of double entry, but in many cases that client has a lingering feeling that your bookkeeping or auditing has been of no practical help to him in his daily work, has not cleared up the fog that he is in, and when it comes to paying your fee, it may be grudged, and perhaps the audit is given up.

We can in turn mentally dub our client a blockhead with no grasp of bookkeeping—that will not mend matters. But are we not in fault in refusing to give the man what he wants? He wants *not only* to know whether he has made a profit or loss, and how much, but *why, where,* and *when* he has made it.[14]

In the same article, Mann also indicated that he was aware of the value of comparing actual cost with estimated cost, as the work progressed, which would permit the manufacturer to take corrective action, if necessary, before the job was completed. This was an important step closer to the present-day function of cost control. Furthermore, he brought out the importance of promptly determining costs as the jobs were completed instead of waiting until the end of the year to find out what total cost had been.

During the last decade of the nineteenth century, writers on subjects related to cost finding and to factory management continued to stress the need for cost data which might be used as the basis for cost control systems. In this connection, they introduced a number of new concepts which were, perhaps, the forerunners of present-day cost control procedures. The following were among the significant factors discussed during this period:

1. In order that costs might be controlled and reduced, cost records should be kept not only for each job but also for each part or process entering into the complete job. The following passage emphasized this point:

[14] *Loc. cit.*

... It would be difficult [if only one order was issued] to determine the cost of any one piece. ... It is not only important to know the cost of each individual article produced, but equally so to ascertain the cost of any particular part, or of any particular process of manufacture. Localization of cost should be carried as far as possible so that the varying rates of realizable profits on parts may be known, and the pressure to minimize cost of production be applied in the right direction. The tendency to the specialization of labour has grown ... and the economy thereby induced can only be rendered thoroughly effective by a complete analysis of cost.[15]

2. Statements should be issued more often than once a year. This is significantly pointed out in these passages:

It is essential that a manufacturer should know periodically what the costs of his productions are, without waiting until the financial year terminates, and then be informed generally of the total result of the year's trading, for verily it is then like telling him to close his stable door after his steed is gone.[16]

Employers should not ... be entirely dependent upon the periodical profit and loss accounts for their knowledge as to the financial result of their transactions, but should at any time, and at any stage of manufacture, be able to ascertain ... rapidly and reliably, the actual, and not merely the estimated cost of production of any given article of their manufacture.[17]

3. Current actual costs should be compared with estimated figures, or prior actual costs, for control purposes. Plumpton indicated this by writing:

By looking in the Abstract [cost] Book monthly, a manufacturer can closely watch the cost and progress of the work in the shops, and comparing same with the estimates and contracts, he can soon discover when any miscalculation in the estimate has occurred, or he can closely watch the margin between cost and sales price so as to economise. ...[18]

4. Cost accounts should be included in

[15] Emile Garcke and J. M. Fells, *Factory Accounts,* 4th ed., London: Crosby Lockwood and Son, 1893 (earlier editions not available), p. 61.
[16] Thomas Plumpton, "Manufacturing Costs," *The Accountant,* March 26, 1892, p. 269.
[17] Garcke and Fells, *op. cit.,* p. 5.
[18] Thomas Plumpton, "Manufacturing Costs as Applied to Engineering," *The Accountant,* November 19, 1892, p. 888.

the general accounting records. Garcke and Fells clearly stated this point as follows:

Factory books must not, however, be considered, as is generally the case, to be memoranda books, which are not necessarily required to balance. They should assimilate to the books of the countinghouse that the obvious advantage of having a balance-sheet made up from the General Ledger, which includes the balances of the ledgers and books kept in the stores and warehouses, is not sacrificed.[19]

5. The use of a Stores Ledger and a stock Ledger was recommended. The following passages indicate the several uses of these records:

It is claimed for the system of accounts we have explained in these pages, that one of its chief advantages lies in the fact that it obviates the necessity of taking stock simply for the purpose of drawing up a balance-sheet. The economic advantage . . . can scarcely be overrated, for it removes one of the most powerful obstacles to the frequent closing of the books. . . . There is no doubt that save for a survey being a troublesome and expensive matter, balance-sheets would be made up much more frequently than is usually the case, and that proprietors would be kept more fully *au courant* with the tendency of their business than can be the case when the books are closed only at one time. . . .

. . . Articles should not be issued without the issuer receiving a formal requisition for them from some authorized persons. . . . Should either the storekeeper or warehouseman feel that he has not a sufficient control over articles in his charge, owing to their not being in the magazine or warehouse . . . the articles may be chained, padlocked, sealed, or otherwise distinguished in such a manner to show that they are still either "stores" or "stock."[20]

The latter part of this quotation indicates some rather heroic methods which might currently be of interest to the harassed storekeeper. Any plan which will

control the entry of materials-outlay into the cost stream is surely an important step toward over-all cost control.

One other characteristic of the nineteenth century which warrants reemphasizing was the tendency of accountants to ignore the cost-keeping function. A review of the first edition of Garcke and Fells' *Factory Accounts* made this point clear:

We have read this book with much interest, though, owing to the peculiar style in which it is written, not without difficulty. . . . It does not purport to deal with the ordinary factory books. It is rather concerned with the wages and time books, stock books, and matters of a similar nature, which, as a rule, do not come within the scope of an accountant's duties.[21]

Furthermore, it is interesting to note that the practice of treating cost data as secret or forbidden information acted as a hindrance to the development of cost control. This was clearly indicated by Plumpton when he said:

This is now the leading point of my paper tonight, for I am about to explain to you what [The Cost Office] has been for years, and is to a fair extent now, a "secret closed chamber," where no other members of the staff are allowed to assist . . . only the principals or managing directors are permitted access to its secrets.[22]

The following quotation effectively summarizes the advanced thinking with reference to the need for and the use value of cost records at the close of the nineteenth century:

When we come to the conversion of raw material and labour into saleable products, there is in addition to the complicated transactions of an extensive trader, a series of operations to be watched, the supervision of which demands a rigorous method of accurately and swiftly realising the progress made. The active forces of production if not guided and controlled with intelligence . . . have an inherent tendency towards the annihilation of profit, and even to disastrous loss. It is this inherent tendency of production forces to go astray, and of organisation to decrease in efficiency, wherein lies the immense importance of

[19.] Garcke and Fells, *op. cit.*, p. 7.
See also George Pepler Norton, *Textile Manufacturer's Bookkeeping*, 4th ed., London: Simpkin, Marshall, Hamilton, Kent & Co., Limited, 1900 (earlier editions not available), p. 4, and J. Slater Lewis, *The Commercial Organisation of Factories*, London: E. & F. N. Spon, 1896, p. vi.
[20] Garcke and Fells, *op. cit.*, pp. 115–20.

[21] *The Accountant*, May 5, 1888, p. 278.
[22] Plumpton, *op. cit.*, p. 884.

periodical balance sheets [which included the profit and loss account] made up at short intervals, accurately reflecting the complex operations of the interior of a large manufacturing establishment. These will enable the principles to rigorously compare period with period and item with item. . . . Any symptoms of deterioration in efficiency are then immediately brought to light, and can be investigated and dealt with accordingly.

It is frequently assumed . . . that it is sufficient merely to deal at wide intervals with the results of trading as a whole. No mistake is more fatal, as will be realised when manufacturing accounts are considered . . . in the light of aids to the proper government and control of organisation. . . .

In manufacturing accounts we examine not so much the ultimate figures . . . as [we examine] the means and methods which have led up to these results. It is manifestly most injudicious to deal with lump sums and to leave unrecorded for purposes of comparison the intricate details of daily work: those 'little things' which, by reason of being repeated day by day, form so large a proportion of the total expenditure, and the neglect of which too often neutralises all the advantages of careful organisation in other directions. Briefly

speaking, the only road to success in modern industrial competition is an inflexible determination to adopt and carry out a system of accounts . . . which shall, for purposes of frequent comparison, register all classes of expenditure to the last penny.[23]

Thus, at the close of the nineteenth century, it seems rather clear that the genesis of cost control is to be found in the works of certain forward-looking authors who wrote on the subject of factory accounts during that century or prior thereto. However, it remained for a few outstanding pioneers in the fields of cost accounting and industrial engineering to develop and refine these basic concepts into well-defined and accepted techniques of cost control. And so, cost control, an outstanding management tool, has gone through a long period of growth and refinement before arriving at its present state of usefulness to management.

---

[23] Lewis, *op. cit.*, pp. xxxv–xxxvi.

EDWARD JONES'S "ENGLISH SYSTEM OF BOOKKEEPING"

Basil S. Yamey

EDWARD JONES'S "ENGLISH SYSTEM OF BOOKKEEPING"

BASIL S. YAMEY

"Jones, in fact, occupies in Book-keeping the place which Macpherson with his "Ossian" fills in literature. Both prove that success can be achieved by unblushing impudence." (J. Row Fogo)

IN 1796 Edward Jones's *The English System of Book-keeping* was published in Bristol. The first edition contains a list of over 4,000 subscribers resident in all parts of England. The Bank of England and the Honourable East India Company each subscribed for five copies. The author is said to have profited to the extent of £25,000 from his "invention,"[1] a large portion of which amount, it seems clear, must have accrued from the patent fee of one guinea, "first had and received," payment of which authorized the practical

---

[1] Jäger: *Die Berechtigung der Einfachen Buchhaltung*, 1868, p. 13.

application of the *system*[2] His *system* is stated to have been widely used in both England and America.[3] His book is prefaced by a handsome testimony, signed among others by the Governor of the Bank of England, D. Giles, Esq., and by Robert Peel, M.P. His work ran into at least sixteen editions in England, one as recent as 1882, had several American editions as well, and was translated into German, French, Italian, and Russian. It gained an international reputation in a short while, and is probably the only English work on accounting, leaving out of account the more recent works of Pixley, Dicksee, and their successors, which has had considerable influence, if only for a brief time, upon the development of accounting on the Continent.

Yet it is the author of this book whom Row Fogo has seen fit to compare with Macpherson; and another sober historian, Dr. Jäger, has made it clear that Jones's significance lies solely in the advertising campaign, novel in its blatancy, which introduced his *system* into commerical circles during the Napoleonic wars.[4]

The 150th anniversary of the publication of the *English System* is not far off, and perhaps it is fitting to review the memorable work and the circumstances surrounding its launching into the world. It may be stated at once that the historian writing today should not revise the opinions of his predecessors (though some have tried to do so) and adopt a more generous attitude towards his subject. Jones was almost certainly a rogue or, what is scarcely a more generous verdict, the guileless victim of his own powers of persuasion. But his success is his partial vindication, and the traditions of English accounting literature in bygone days, rich as they are with the extravagant eloquence and mercantile hyperbole of men like Deighan, Robert Colinson, and Stephen Monteage, are enriched and enlivened by his career.

About Jones himself little can be said. His memory, unlike that of his literary counterpart, Macpherson, is not perpetuated in the *Dictionary of National Biography*. In his book he is reticent about his career, if not about his capabilities. But it is evident that he had an extensive experience of accounting in practice. His book ends with a restrained advertisement: "Mr. Jones presents his Respects to the Bankers, Merchants, Tradesmen, etc., of Great Britain, and offers his Services to them as an Accomptant, in the Settlement of Partnership Accounts, or in the Affairs of Bankrupts, in the Balancing or Examination of Books, or in the Settlement of any Disputed Accounts by Arbitration or otherwise." The "otherwise" suggests possibilities of powers not directly associated with the mystery of accounting, but both Jones and history remain silent about them.

The publication of the *English System* was preceded in 1795 by *An Address to Bankers, Merchants, Tradesmen, etc., intended as an introduction to a New System of Book-keeping*. This *Address*, which is in substance reproduced as an Introductory Address in the main work, sets out in the author's compelling style the faults, demerits, and positive dangers of the existing bookkeeping methods, both by single and double entry, without so much as giving a foretaste (other than of its promised excellence) of the magnificent new system about to be made known to the long-suffering commercial world.

The two Addresses are of great interest, as they must be held largely responsible

---

[2] Jones was apparently worried about the unauthorized use of his system. In the first edition a reward of 100 guineas was offered "payable on conviction, to any person who shall give me information of any one using this system without my permission." In a later edition there is this appeal: "May I, without offence, request of the Subscribers not to lend this Volume to Non-Subscribers?"

[3] Jäger: *op. cit.*, p. 13.

[4] Jäger: *Altes und Neues aus der Buchhaltung*, 1889.

for the material success of the system. And just as Jones was wise to withhold his invention until he had elaborated upon the evils of existing practices, it may be advisable to reproduce parts of his Addresses before describing the new system in any detail.

He begins by justifying the need for his new system. He is aware that it is generally the fate ". . . of new inventions to meet with disapprobation and opposition, until their utility has been proved by experience." "Antiquity and general use are deemed sufficient reasons for rejecting even the *consideration* of improvement." He deplores this inertia of the human mind, but he reasonably agrees that an invention must be substantiated before ". . . the public attention should even be asked." "But though, I confess, it has received *unprecedented sanction* from men of candour and liberality, I shall feel obliged to take notice of the *uncandid* opposition it has met with, from a few unthinking and illiberal men." He asks those who oppose him to reflect upon his work." "Then will the English System of Book-keeping rise to its proper level and the men who continue to oppose it be left in a *sullen minority—dark* as the *principles* on which they have grounded their opposition." And he adroitly uses his testimonies from "Gentlemen of the first respectability" to refute any suggestion that he is "indulging in a 'take-in'."

Having established his good faith and having hurled imprecations against his adversaries, he declares boldly that ". . . an invention more *extensively useful*, more *advantageous* to the commercial and trading interests of these kingdoms, by its preventing fraud and imposition in accounts, or more *respectably recommended*, perhaps, never yet made its appearance." And a parting shot is delivered at his detractors: "The intention, therefore, of the man who opposes it *ought* to be *suspected*."

His wide experience of accounts brought him up against the evils that abounded. But a comparatively trivial incident, such as often marks the turning point in a man's career, determined him to end these evils, "A set of Books came under my notice, which had been used, in the same trade, through *four different Partnerships,* and never *balanced,* or the accounts with either Partnership regularly settled! In fact the men were not Accomptants, and the person in whom they had placed confidence deceived them. . . . The consequence was the fourth Partnership was dissolved; the Books were then balanced, and the concern unexpectedly *proved insolvent!* It was this that made me determine never to give up the matter, till I had compleated such a System as would, to a certainty, counteract these alarming Evils." It took him "the leisure moments of more than five years" spent "in wearisome and fruitless endeavours" before he succeeded beyond his "most sanguine expectations." Shrewdly he disclaims that he alone noticed the evils of contemporary practice, ". . . for I do not mean to arrogate to myself any exclusive or superior intelligence to other men." But he cannot entirely resist the pleasure of self-praise. "But it is not every man who reflects upon an Evil, that chooses to set about providing a remedy."

He then proceeds to inveigh against single and double entry book-keeping. In brief, his criticisms are that their complexity makes fraud and deception easy, that the process of balancing is difficult and wearisome, and that frauds and errors remain undetected. Concerning fraud, he is less vehemently disposed towards single entry: "Of the two Systems, the method by Single Entry claims, in a certain sense, a preference; as that by Double Entry, being more complex and obscure, admits of greater secrecy in case of fraud, and is more capable of being converted into a cloak, for the vilest statements that designing ingenuity can fabricate." The arithmetic balance provided by double entry lulls the readers of accounts into a false sense of security. "If a Bankrupt should be a dishonest instead of an unfortunate man, and had had his Books kept by Double Entry, what a cloak for *deception* is the *apparent* regularity of them; especially if they be produced in a balanced state at the Creditors' meeting." "Surely there never was a more *infamous* and *cunningly devised* System ever formed, though not intended to be so originally," he says elsewhere.

Each point he makes is tellingly illustrated by tales culled either from his experience, or, one suspects, from his ample imagination. The danger of undetected errors in accounts is brought home to the reader by the story of the gentleman who committed suicide in his counting-house. The only reason that could account for his unnatural behavior that his Balance Sheet, "which lay open on his desk, showed a very large deficiency: but it is very painful to add, that this supposed deficiency was afterwards discovered to be an error."

Having listed the defects of contemporary accounting practice, he enumerates the virtues of his own system with a not unexpected liberality. His system requires less labour and is easier to check. When balanced the accounts are "correct to an absolute certainty." "It is impossible to produce a false Statement from Books kept after this plan, that will not be immediately detected." His system is so simple ". . . that it is suited to the capacity of a school-boy." "And it is worthy remark, that the plain and simple manner in which the profit and loss in any concern may be ascertained, *precludes* the *possibility* of the most ingenious man deceiving his partner, if possessed only of common understanding."

The reader may be impatient to come to grips with the heaven-sent system. But Jones has to allay one more fear." I cannot conclude without taking notice of a remark, which has been made upon the injury my System is likely to occasion to persons employed as Book-keepers, etc., in the compting-houses of Merchants, etc., with whom it is supposed it will materially interfere, and that many will lose their employments." It is the spectre of what today we call technological unemployment, and which Jones must have vividly appreciated in the age when machine-wrecking by the irate employees displaced by newly-introduced machinery was not uncommon. In answer to this fear Jones is at first highminded: "Were such the Truth, perhaps I might, in favour of a general good, justify a partial evil." But he is spared this unpleasant, if noble, task since ". . . the office of the Book-keeper is still the same; its duties are relieved only from that which renders it an irksome task." Forever gone will be the disappointment and "painful sensations" which book-keepers suffer when they cannot balance the accounts, and when in hunting the elusive error ". . . a fancied confusion appears on every leaf, and their minds are racked."

The main books required by Jones are two in number, the day-book and the ledger. The ledger is the book ". . . in which the Man of Business can open an account with every person of whom he buys Goods or receives Money; sells Goods or pays Money to, etc., selecting from the diary [day-book], and posting to its relative account in the Ledger, the date and amount of each transaction." This statement is not strictly correct, since there is also a Capital account in the ledger which Jones nowhere explains. The cash account also appears in the ledger: "The cash account, being a personal account, on which much depends, the name of the Cashier, and the cash account, should always be entered in the Ledger." The same reasoning presumably applies to the inclusion of a bills payable account in the ledger. In short, the

ledger is a personal ledger of debtors and
creditors, together with capital, cash, and
bills accounts, and one other account to be
met with later.

The day-book is the book of original
entry, drawn up as follows (inessential
details being omitted):

Dr. Sundry Accounts		Drs. & Crs.	Cr. Sundry Accounts
	Cr. Notes and Bills Payable, accepted Andrews draft	£1,000	£1,000
£1,000	Dr. John Antonio for my acceptance of his draft	1,000	

The rules for debiting and crediting the
ledger accounts are the same as in double
entry, with the very important exception
that there will be only one entry, in debit
or in credit as the case may be, for those
occurrences in which a nominal account
would otherwise be affected; for, as has
been explained, the ledger does not contain the usual nominal accounts.

In the day-book the amount of every
entry, regardless of whether it is a debit
or a credit entry, is entered in the center
column entitled "Drs. & Crs."; while the
other two columns contain, respectively,
the debit and the credit entries. The
columns are balanced monthly, quarterly,
and annually,—in the latter case to show
the profit for the year, as will be described
below.

Jones explains the procedure of making
the entries in the day-book, and its merits,
as follows; "But as a hurry of business
will sometimes take place in almost every
compting-house, which may cause the
entries to be made to the debit instead of
the credit of an account in the day-book,
and to the credit instead of the debit, I
have endeavoured as much as possible to
counteract the evil, by having only one
column for receiving the amount of every
transaction, whether debits or credits, at

the instant of making the entry. And for
the convenience of separating the debits
from the credits, previous to posting, which
is necessary to prevent confusion and per-
plexity, I have two other columns on the
same page."

The ledger which Jones advocates appears at first glance to be a mass of columns. Closer examination shows, however,
that it contains the customary ledger
rulings, with an additional set of four
money columns on both the debit and
credit sides. Each of these four columns is
allocated to one of the four quarters of the
year. Every entry in the ledger is entered
first in one of the ordinary columns, and
is then repeated on the same side of the
account in the appropriate quarterly
column. Thus the ledger reveals not only
the state of the account in the usual way,
but it also shows, by reference to the
quarterly columns, the transactions relating to each of the four quarters.

Jones makes much of the fact that by
totalling the debits and the credits in the
day-book and in the quarterly columns of
the ledger, the business man can ascertain
the "amount of all his transactions" and
whether "the whole of those amounts were
correctly posted into the Ledger," since
the day-book and ledger totals for each
quarter must agree to be correct. He points
out that no other system provides a similar
check. "And yet any thing short of this
information, is placing dependence on a
broken reed." He also attacks the facile
acceptance of the trial balance as a "proof"
of double entry records: "How is it that
Men of Common understanding can believe that the Debits and Credits of a Ledger balancing or agreeing in amount, is a
proof of it being a fair and correct repre-
sentation of the Day-book, which, surely,
is the most material point in Book-keeping! Would two pictures being exactly
alike, prove that they were a correct copy
of the original: or would my putting two

guineas of equal weight into a balance, prove that they were weight by the standard?"

He goes on to point out that even if the day-book totals agreed with the ledger totals, this would not be absolute proof that individual items had been posted to the correct ledger accounts. This proof he obtains by giving a letter to each ledger account. "These letters being used as marks of posting, and affixed to each amount in the Day-book, as it is posted, it is only necessary, therefore, to compare, and see that the letter affixed to each entry in the Day-book, is the same as is prefixed to the same name in the alphabet [index]; a difference here shows, of course, an error; or else it must be right."

As a final example of Jones's ingenuity one must mention his prescription for "taking off the balances of the Ledger." In brief it is that the total of all the debit entries in all the accounts less the total of all the credit entries in all the accounts must be equal to the total of all the balances on all the accounts! "By this means," Jones claims in prominent capital letters, "every page will be proved as you proceed, and the balances of ten thousand ledgers on this plan, could not unobservedly be taken off wrong."

The final merit claimed by Jones for his system is the "plain and simple" manner of discovering the profit of the business. In the day-book a single-entry debit for the "Stock of goods unsold" is passed, there being a Stock account in the ledger. The total debits and credits for the year are cast, the latter total subtracted from the former, and the difference is the profit, which is credited in equal shares, in his example, to the capital accounts of the partners, Abraham Bold and Charles Wise. A similar calculation is made in the ledger, the one reckoning being used as a check on the other.

The basis of the profit calculation may be simply stated, though Jones attempts no elucidation of the procedure. Occurrences requiring two equal but opposite entries (i.e. the passing of cash or bills to or from creditors or debtors) can be left out of account since they cannot affect the calculation in any way. The remaining entries (the single ones) reflect sales for cash or on credit on the debit side; and purchases for cash or on credit, and expenses, on the credit side. The unsold stock being introduced as a debit, the difference between debits and credits must reflect the profit for the year in the simple circumstances postulated in Jones's example. For there are no stock, debtors, creditors, or cash at the commencement of trade. And a few adjustments could take account of the existence of opening assets, if any, though assuredly at the risk of depriving the system of its much-vaunted simplicity and plainness.

The above is an outline of the system based on single entry. But his plan is also adaptable to double entry, "on the same principle of correctness." A separate sales book, containing goods accounts for the various types of merchandise, is necessary. But plainly Jones is not enthusiastic about double entry, even when it is wedded to his own invention. Among other objections he dislikes the confusing notion of nominal accounts, or, as they were more commonly known as in his day, of "fictitious" or "imaginary" accounts. He takes the instance of "A.B. Dr. to Wine." "Now if A.B. owes Wine money, why not let Wine call for payment? But if A.B. do not owe Wine money, why make the entry in such a way as only tends to confuse the mind of a person who is not a good Accomptant?"[5]

[5] This verbal quibbling is reminiscent of Mathew Quin in his *Rudiments of Book-Keeping* (1796), in which he objected to the classification of the profit-and-loss account as an imaginary account: "If I have the misfortune of having my House and Goods burnt to ashes, no

Jones's panacea has been described, and it would be of little purpose to emphasize and catalogue in what respects it is completely unworthy of the introduction which precedes it, particularly as some of his contemporary critics will be quoted below. Except for the elaborate arithmetical checks which his multi-columnar books make possible, his system is distinctly inferior to ordinary double entry. The multiplicity of columns itself may as likely as not have caused as much confusion and error as it was designed to eliminate. The method of profit determination, though formally sound, would give an uninformative profit and loss calculation and the whole scheme would admirably suit the nefarious purposes of the host of commercial crooks portrayed by Jones as preying upon the ignorant and gullible.

The profitable reception which was accorded Jones's System has already been sketched. Yet from an early date he had his critics, as his *Addresses* testify. In England, according to Woolf,[6] several publications appeared defending double entry against Jones's onslaughts, and in their turn exposing the defects of his system. Even James Mill, the illustrious father of John Stuart Mill, participated in the controversy. A tract from his pen published in 1796 (entitled "An Examination of Jones' English System of Book-keeping, in which the insufficiency of that mode of keeping accounts is clearly demonstrated and the superiority of the Italian method fully established") pointed out that " . . . of the amount of goods bought and sold during the year Mr. Jones remains altogether ignorant until the time of stock-taking, and then he can only ascertain the quantity in hand. Hence there is no check against

embezzlement; and, strange to tell, in this little concern, fabricated purposely to show the excellence of this system, he lost ten pieces of calico!" This acute comment is well-founded; for in Jones's example 1,300 pieces of calico are purchased, 1,045 are sold, and the stock-taking reveals a balance of 245 pieces. A similar loss of half a pipe of Red Wine remains unaccounted for, though stocks of liquor are notoriously subject to "shrinkage."

In Germany, Andreas Wagner, author of a commendable textbook on accounting, gave the English System a welcome in which friendliness was tempered with envy, and praise with helpful criticism. He annotated a translation into German entitled "Edward T. Jones's newly discovered single and double entry English Bookkeeping, in which it is impossible that a mistake, be it ever so small, can remain undetected," published in 1801. He remarked that Jones was unfairly prejudiced against single entry; that his criticism of double entry went too far; and that his comments on its terminology were weak. "It remains an invention which is a tribute to the human intellect." His more fundamental criticisms were that the system did not show the profits on individual ventures; that transactions in foreign currencies were not mentioned; that Jones did not require detailed invoice books; and that his "dead accounts" (for cash and bills) would puzzle the uninitiated. He generously ascribed these shortcomings to the brevity of Jones's exposition and believed that could easily be remedied. His general opinion was that "because of its unusual brevity, certainty, its prevention of errors and the ease with which it could be mastered, the System is so far ahead of other systems that it deserves, with suitable modifications, to be widely adopted."

But Wagner held that the system was not entirely new. Earlier writers had rejected double entry as being circuitous

---

Casuist or Logician would ever attempt to persuade me that my *loss* is not *real* but *imaginary;* yet a *learned* Book-keeper will immediately insist upon its being put down as *profit* and *loss*."

[6] A. H. Woolf: *A Short History of Accountants and Accountancy*, 1913, p. 141.

and uncertain, and had suggested easier and shorter alternatives. In particular, a German, Johann Christian Ferber, had published in Hamburg in 1712 his *Wohlunterrichteten Kaufmann*, in which he proposed the use of a three-columnar day-book, similar in essentials to Jones's. "Any impartial expert may decide whether Ferber's method is not the same as Jones's English System; save that in form it is slightly different, in that the debit, credit, and total columns are next to one another. It is a pity that Ferber did not develop this system, so that the total of German inventions would have been increased by yet another which is now claimed by a foreigner."[7]

J. G. Meisner, a fellow-countryman and contemporary of Wagner, published his *Newly discovered German Book-keeping— a counterstroke (Gegenstück) against Jones's English Book-keeping* in Breslau in 1803. Though Meisner explained that his work was intended not so much as an attack on Jones, as a significant improvement upon its English relative, he nevertheless criticised the English system as being impractical where foreign currency was concerned. He also pointed out the obvious fact that the system could not prevent fraud, since fraudulent entries in the day-book would naturally remain undetected however elaborate and numerous the arithmetical checks on postings might be. He instanced the receipt of cash from debtors, which even if only credited to the personal accounts of the debtors and not debited to the cash account, would not have upset the agreement between the ledger and the day-book. Meisner's German system, it may be noted, had as its main feature the separation of the book of original entry into a cash book for the cash

entries, and a memorial for the other entries. This newly discovered technique can be found in earlier practice as well as in published texts.

The most significant proof of the inadequacy of Jones's system is not the criticisms of his contemporaries, but the fact that he himself gradually abandoned his own invention. Though the title was retained in all his later editions, the innovations were dropped one by one, in some cases to be replaced by new inventions of his fertile imagination. In 1831 the ledger no longer contained the array of columns, and the three columns had disappeared from the day-book. In 1837 there is a reference to the "important improvements" since the 1796 edition. He was still critical of double entry though time had moderated the expression of his strictures, and though in fact he was describing double entry in his books. The two main improvements were the Balance Book, in essence a quarterly trial balance in columnar form with countless checks on the arithmetic; and the Abstract Book, which served to localize errors in posting to the ledger from the day-book, in that any entry would be revealed if it were inadvertently or intentionally posted to a nominal account instead of a personal account, or vice versa.[8] Jones's capacity for devising checks on the arithmetic seems to have been endless, and in some respects he even anticipated later developments; for instance, his Abstract Book contains the germ of a system of total or control accounts.

Must we dismiss Edward Jones as either an impudent trickster or else an artless crank, a colourful but completely unimportant figure in the development

[7] Jones himself with pride claimed his invention for England: "And surely it should be the boast of an Englishman, that he can change his system of bookkeeping [the Italian] for a better."

[8] Jones explained that such mis-postings would seldom occur unintentionally, where trade (personal) accounts are segregated from the private (nominal) accounts in the ledger. "In the absence of integrity, perhaps the best prevention to fraud is fear, arising from the certainty of detection; therefore we deem it our duty to introduce the Abstract-book."

of accounting? His direct contribution towards the development of the art is insignificant; so much is clear. But his system and its striking success were symptomatic of serious defects in the practice of book-keeping at the time he published his work. Granted that much of his success was due to the boldness of his methods, his salesmanship, and—at least in England—the happy choice of title, it remains that he would not have obtained such glowing testimonies and impressive sales figures unless there had been a pressing need for improvements in the art of bookkeeping.

The slavish adherence to established conventions and stylized practices, the failure to adapt the system of record-keeping to more complicated requirements, the air of mystery which surrounded the teaching and practice of double entry since its earliest days, the neglect of quantitative controls in accounting—all contributed to a low standard of commercial (and public accounting, which seriously incommoded the work of tradesmen and which provided plentiful opportunities for swindlers and impostors of all types.

Others besides Jones advocated reforms in the practice of accounting, particularly by double entry, aimed at increasing the speed and accuracy with which the ledger could be written up. Thus John Lambert in his *Perpetual Balance* (1812) stated: "Some additional aid is required by which this generally-approved system may be rendered more perfect, by which its various parts may be quickened into maturity, and arrive, by a more early and easy process, at that desirable ultimatum of the whole, the General Balance, the access to which is at present attainable only at distant periods, and by a very tedious and wearisome operation." And Michael Power in his *Book-keeping no Bugbear* (1815) complained that the ledger was not entered " . . . till after such a process as it is tire-some to read, and a most irksome task indeed to accomplish."

The difficulties attached to posting and balancing the ledger are as old as the art of book-keeping itself. We are told that the Bank of St. George, which was so powerful that in 1453 the Republic of Genoa ceded to it the island of Corsica, closed its doors for two months each year in order to check and balance its books.[9] And Cotrugli, the Italian whose work on accounting was written before that of Pacioli though not published until 1573, recommended that a merchant should close his business every seventh year, so that he could close off his books.[10]

The problem of fraud exercised the minds of many writers on accounting. Invariably their volumes are introduced by an account of some incident of embezzlement or deceit. And there is little reason to doubt that an unthinking reliance upon the arithmetical check provided by double entry was often the rogue's unwitting accomplice. Even Ympyn, the Flemish translator of an early Italian text which contributed considerably to the spread of double entry through Europe, was guilty of this uncritical attitude. He wrote that, as experts were well aware, it would be impossible for anyone to commit irregularities in a set of books kept by double entry without being detected.

The efforts of reformers to remove the possibility of fraud in accounts or to facilitate the speedy detection of the culprit were naturally doomed to failure, since improvements in accounting methods alone are insufficient to insure commercial

---

[9] F. W. Krassel: "Zur Inventur der Firma Fugger aus dem Jahre 1527," in *Österreichse Zeitschrift für das kaufmännische Unterrichtswesen*, 1906, p. 98.

[10] Krassel: *op. cit.*, p. 98; H. Sieveking: *Aus Venetianischen Handlungsbüchern*, p. 323.

K. P. Kheil, *Benedetto Cotrugli Raugeo*, 1906, states: "Because such a rest-year could scarcely have been the practice of the merchants in those days, one must assume that Cotrugli, in making this recommendation, analagous to the seventh day of rest, was expressing his extreme piety."

probity. Double entry was still subject to attacks as being the guilty weapon of the dishonest partner or servant. Thus towards the end of the nineteenth century Franz Boucken, a disciple of Theodor Ezersky, author of the Russian Book-keeping System, described double entry as a device " . . . with the help of which one partner can deceive his associate, and a servant his master, by posting thousands from one account to another, and so finally into his own pocket"; and .that " . . . maintaining the wretched precision of the balance sheet, he could continue to let a substantial portion of the assets fall through the meshes of an Italian bookkeeping net into his pocket."[11] To prevent fraud, as was becoming increasingly clear, a comprehensive system of audit was necessary. As Alexander Pulling wrote in *A practical Compendium of the law and usage of mercantile accounts* (1850), " . . . without some more stringent regulations as to the mode of auditing the accounts of Joint Stock Companies than the law now provides, the accounts themselves rather

facilitate than prevent mismanagement and fraud."

We may conclude by again quoting J. Row Fogo, to the effect that Jones "indirectly exerted a great influence on the development of the art." The publication of his system aroused a widespread and unprecedented interest in the subject. The practice of double entry was minutely studied by his critics, and the scope for "alterations in detail which may be introduced in the matter of tabulating and posting accounts" was explored and found to be almost without limit. The practice, though not the fundamentals, of double entry was substantially modified, so that "the very words 'after the Italian manner' fell out of the terminology of the trade."[12]

[11] T. Drapala: *Die Buchhaltungskunde in ihrer wissenschaftlichen Pflege*, 1889, p. 77.

[12] J. Row Fogo: in Brown *A History of Accounting and Accountants*, p. 168. It is doubtful, however, whether Row Fogo's explanation of the disappearance of the term "Italian bookkeeping" is correct. In so far as the use of the term disappeared, it is more probable that this was due to the accounting "nationalism" of which the English and German "Systems" are symptoms. Wagner, for instance, deprecated the use in Germany of the Italian terms "scrittura doppia," "conto mio," "conto pro diversi," etc., and welcomed their gradual elimination and replacement by German equivalents. "The time is past, thank God, when the merchant was ashamed of his mother tongue."

CHARGE AND DISCHARGE

Stanley E. Howard

CHARGE AND DISCHARGE

Stanley E. Howard

ISTRICT of Massachusetts . . . to wit:

"BE IT REMEMBERED, that on the tenth day of February, in the eighteen hundred and fourth year of our Lord, and in the twenty-eighth year of the Independence of the United States of America— THOMAS TURNER, of the said district, hath deposited in this office the title of a book, the right whereof he claims as author, in the words following, to wit:

"'AN EPITOME OF BOOK-KEEPING BY DOUBLE ENTRY, delineated on a scale suited to the faculties and comprehension of Senior School Boys and Youth designed for the Mercantile line. Comprising systematic and unerring Rules for the forming Monthly Statements of books, as well as those for opening, conducting, adjusting and closing them; with explanations of Theory, and exhibitions of Practice, rendered easy to the smallest capacity, and calculated to initiate them in the true Principles, and to make them perfect in the Rules, by a little practice. . . . To which are added, Rules for keeping Retail Books by Double Entry, without altering the process of Single Entry in the Day-Book or Journal, for all sales of merchandise; by which one-half the writing is saved, and the Ledger exonerated from items, and rendered a prompt and sure proof of Monthly Balances and Annual Profits. . . . Also, The most easy, concise and safe way of calculating any Rate per Cent and especially that of Six per Cent per Annum. . . . By THOMAS TURNER, Professor and Teacher of Book-keeping, at Portland.'"

"In conformity to the Act of Congress of the United States, intitled, 'An act for the encouragement of learning, by securing the copies of maps, charts and books, to the authors and proprietors of such copies, during the times therein mentioned;' and also to an act . . .' etc., etc. . . .'"

Thus reads in part the unpromising copyright notice of a little old textbook, a leather bound volume of 148 pages, each measuring 4" x 6¾". The book was printed by Jenks and Shirley "for Thomas Clark (proprietor) and [was] for sale at his Bookstore, *Fish Street* [in Portland], and by the principal Booksellers in the *United States*." It is a curious little work, fascinating to students of accounting and of value to those interested in historical and descriptive economics. Its pages contain not infrequent sparks of wit or humor and evidences of a humanness of business relations which in present day popular thought are often considered no longer to exist. Interest attaches to the book also because it contains a contribution to the history, if not to the theory, of pedagogy; it is one of the earliest American specimens of textbook production in the field of commercial subjects. It has its place in the literature of education.

Whether this little volume was ever formally reviewed is doubtful. It is not the intention of the present writer, however, to "review" the book. Rather this memorandum is intended to translate or interpret the spirit of Professor Turner's treatise.

It is clear that Professor Turner had a fairly definite conception of his educational objectives and a high opinion of the social usefulness of his profession. He says (pp. 7-8):

The increase of the commerce of this country, and the unbounded field open to it for speculation and commercial prospects, will exceed all common calculations; and most likely those of the most sanguine friends of prosperity. In this view, it is an object of the first consequence to that part of the rising generation designed for mercantile pursuits, to become early acquainted with the principles of book-keeping; and the most judicious rules that can be devised to obviate error in the process, and embarrassment in the adjustment and closure of books.

Again (p. 7):

> Experience has proved to the author, that youth may be initiated in the principles and made perfect in the rules, by a little practice, when arrived at the last stage of schooling; and when they are capable of associating and connecting their ideas, and of drawing conclusions from premises laid down and delineated in a manner suited to their faculties and comprehension.

And again also (p. 144):

> The object of this work is to initiate youth, when at the last stage of schooling, and to insure their having a right conception of book-keeping by double entry, and the rules appertaining, thereto; so that on their entrance into the merchant's employ, or engagements in business, they may be able to perfect themselves, without the smallest difficulty.

The author also had a clear conception of what he considered to be sound and effective pedagogical methods to be employed. His method of instruction was this. After the reading of the pertinent explanations and instructions (which were very brief), and the study of a miniature set of books designed to present a conspectus of double entry procedure, the student was given a laboratory problem, or rather two such problems. The first of these dealt with the affairs of an enterprise of the sole proprietor type; the second with the affairs of two brothers, John and Thomas Mercator, who were partners. In each case there was presented a series of transactions journalized in good form (with all the usual informal explanations), posted in good form, and accompanied by all the necessary or recommended subsidiary records, papers and statements. Thus instruction was by the use of models rather than by the long discussion of principles and rules. The procedure of the student in the performance of the two laboratory exercises was, first, to copy in his own journal verbatim and with exact imitation of the technical forms prescribed,

all that he found in the "copy book." Then, after studying the model ledger, he was to put aside his text, post his journal entries, close the ledger and prepare the statements. In brief, the laboratory instruction employed was chiefly of the copy-book type. Incidentally, the student must copy, either in a note book or in his journal all the principal rules and explanations presented in the text. Apparently Professor Turner had great confidence in a system of study and work which required of the student writing as well as hearing and seeing. At any rate he says (p. 148):

> After the [second] exercise, a scholar of common capacity will know how to proceed with any set of books, and will gain a sufficient knowledge to be able to form a small set of books from his own ideas, by the rules he has gone through, and from the knowledge he then must have acquired of the regular process, from commencement to the closure of books.
> The rules for commencement, progression, adjustment, and closure, should be gotten by heart by every scholar. . . .

There is in this little text nothing which approximates a theory or thoroughgoing explanation of debit and credit entries, such as is found in modern college texts in accounting. It can hardly be said that the author's rules of debit and credit are comprehensive. He says (pp. 9-10):

> Book-keeping by Double Entry is a system of charge and discharge.
> A Charge is a single entry, exhibiting the debtor side only, and does not form a complete account without the discharge.
> A Charge and Discharge, exhibits a complete account of debtor and creditor, with the balance due on either side.
> One or sundry accounts made debtor, is the charge.
> One or sundry accounts made credit is the discharge.
>
> The amount of charge and that of discharge, must be always equal—consequently the total amount of the additions on the debtor side of all the accounts open in the ledger,

when posted up, must be equal to the total amount of the additions on the credit side, or otherwise there must exist an error either in the wrong addition of the sundries in the journal, or a wrong posting therefrom in the ledger.

And again (p. 143):

> That there is nothing abstruse or difficult in charge and discharge by double entry, is evidenced both from its nature and proof.— If a person knows how to make a charge, common sense dictates the discharge, and tells him it must be given to that head of account standing charged therewith on the books; . . . and the exercise of common reason will at all times, with as much facility, dictate the account to be charged and that to be discharged, by only considering what accounts are affected by the transaction.

If there was any "philosophy" underlying such instruction, it was one which was expressed in terms of responsibility and one which employed or implied a personification of the ledger accounts.

The miniature set of books already referred to illustrates this point. The proprietor of this miniature enterprise is represented as having commenced business in Portland on Jan. 1, 1803 with a capital or "stock" of one hogshead of rum valued at $100. Rum account is debited and Stock account (our modern Capital account) is credited. Or, in the language of "Professor" Turner (p. 14):

> Rum account takes up the charge and becomes accountable to Stock account, the representative of the person and his sole concern.

Next, on Jan. 2, the rum is sold to one John Toper for $110.

> John Toper takes up the charge, discharges Rum, and becomes accountable.

But John Toper is not, apparently, a satisfactory open account debtor, and immediately gives his non-interest-bearing note for $110 payable in sixty days.

Notes Receivable takes up the charge, discharges John Toper, and becomes accountable.

Subsequently, 41 days before maturity, the note is discounted at the bank at "½ per cent."—apparently for 30 days. Cash and Notes Receivable are respectively charged and discharged in the amount of $110. Cash is at once discharged in the same amount, and Interest and Bank are charged in the amounts of $0.76 and $109.24 respectively.

"Closure" follows. Rum transfers to Profit and Loss a credit item of $10; Interest a debit item of $0.76. Profit and Loss closes to Stock a credit item of $9.24. Bank is closed to show a debit balance of $109.24; Stock to show a credit balance of the same amount.

Which [as the author says, p. 15] proves the charge to be equal to the discharge, and the books to be right; and business commences with a new and augmented capital.

It is interesting and from a historical point of view instructive to follow through the "stories" of the two laboratory exercises. In the first of these the proprietor is represented as being one of the sons of James Mercator; whether John or Thomas, the partners of the second exercise, is not specifically indicated. This young man of small affairs, perhaps intentionally regarded as in many respects similar to the students "at the last stage of schooling," commenced business on Jan. 1, 1802, with a net capital investment of $29.25, of which $25.00 was in cash and the remainder the excess of certain accounts receivable balances over the balances of accounts payable. Parental encouragement, of truly Yankee characteristics, appeared on Jan. 20 in the form of a loan of $50.00 in cash, explained in the journal thus (p. 24):

> For my Note given this day to my honored Father, payable in 6 months, for a Loan of this sum granted me on the commencement of my business, and which he promises to relinquish on proof of my good conduct.

Whether this "good conduct" was to be interpreted in terms of economics or of ethics is not clear from the context. At any rate on June 20 Notes Payable was charged and Stock discharged in the amount of $50.00, with this explanation (p. 30):

For this sum, due on my Note to my honored Father, dated 20th January last, now cancelled by a gift thereof to me, for assistance in my future business, . . .

When the books were closed ten days later. Stock showed a new credit balance of $101.84. Profits, exclusive of the gift were thus $22.59, or over 70 per cent on the initial capital.

Apparently "Professor" Turner with all his regard for the copy-book method of laboratory procedure assigned no special importance to frequent repetitions of routine entries. Rather he seems to have attempted to "sample out" the types of transactions in which a young merchant in a seaport town of approximately 7,000 population, trading under the conditions of the first decade of the nineteenth century, would be likely to engage. And so we find entries which not only serve to instruct in the procedure of account keeping but also render more vivid the mercantile life of the period. It is in this part of the text that there is a real contribution to the materials, if not to the literature, of American economic history.

For example, it is represented in the first exercise that on Feb. 15, 1802 young Mercator "adventured" certain merchandise to "the Havanna." The goods, 5 quintals of fish purchased on credit (by a note given) of John Cod, and 10 pieces of Nankeen similarly purchased on credit of Samuel Draper, were charged, at $27.00 invoice costs plus certain accessory charges (the cost of an empty hogshead for the fish and costs of "package and truckage") to Adventure to the Havanna. They were shipped on "the brig Speedwell, Captain John Goodluck, on my own account and

risk" (p. 25). Sundry appropriate accounts were "discharged." At Havanna, Captain Goodluck sold the fish and cloth for $55.00, deducted duties, freight charges and commissions amounting to $8.75, and reported net proceeds of $46.25. Captain John Goodluck was charged and Adventure to Havanna discharged in this amount. But this was not the end. The good captain bought with the proceeds of the consignment sales of fish and cloth two barrels of sugar, 6 cwt., at $7.00 per cwt., added a commission of 5 per cent, $2.10, and a freight charge of $2.00. Sugar account was charged $46.10 and Captain John Goodluck correspondingly "discharged." This left the captain owing 15 cents; which debt was in due time discharged by cash payment. As a sequel, young Mercator bartered one of the barrels of sugar for ten pieces of India cotton. The sugar was valued for the exchange at $12.00.

Apparently Professor Turner considered ability to handle consignments important under the contemporary trading conditions. He had his young merchant sell to Peter Paywell silk cloth ("Lustrings") shipped on consignment by John Trader of Boston. From the selling price of one piece of such cloth, $12.00, there were deductions of freight, $0.25, and Mercator's commission, $0.60, leaving proceeds of $11.15. This was on March 8. Apparently John Trader in Boston gave liberal terms for prompt settlements. Under date of April 5 Mercator charged Trader and "discharged" Interest $0.06—"For Interest on $11.75 [$11.15?], being on my anticipated remittance to him this day, as per Account Current, per post, at 12 [½?] per cent" (p. 28). The remittance appears to have been truly "anticipated", for not until April 30 did Mercator actually remit "to [John Trader's] order in John Sharp's bill on Paul Punctual, at sight, for nett proceeds of Lustring." The amount was $11.09.

In this first laboratory exercise, in a

series of journal entries covering only nine small pages, transactions which sample an amazing variety of business events are set down for intensive study and transcription. In addition to those events which have been already indicated, goods were bought and sold in simple transactions notes were received and given, business was done with the bank, and expenses were incurred and paid. Samuel Neverpay, a trade debtor, became bankrupt and his creditors received 90 cents on the dollar. The hat was passed in the street for "the relief of Mr. Timothy Worthy, an unfortunate trader" (p. 31). Mercator subscribed and paid one dollar, charging the item to "Expence Account." This may be doubtful accounting. Likewise it may today be regarded as of doubtful propriety to charge "Expence" for "a new Surtout," for a "pair of Pantaloons," for a hat, and for miscellaneous petty sums taken for "Pocket Expences." But Mercator was by the conditions assumed a sole entrepreneur. The law recognized no distinction between his business and his personal affairs. Perhaps there was none.

As one might expect, the second laboratory exercise was somewhat longer and more complicated than the first. John and Thomas Mercator were equal partners, each contributing $100.00 of original investment, partly in cash and partly in sugar, India cottons, coffee and molasses. Each partner had his own Stock account; likewise his own "particular" account, to which were charged withdrawals of merchandise and of cash. Also, it appears that on April 8 (the books are represented as opened on Jan. 1, 1803) James Mercator, the father of the partners, purchased "1 piece [of India cotton] delivered to our mother," $8.00; and on the 15th of the month one piece [of silk or "Lustrings"] similarly delivered, $20.00 (p. 69). On Dec. 2 the charge to father Mercator was canceled, the journal explanation being (p. 82):

For Balance of his Account, being for 1

piece Lustring and 1 piece India Cotton delivered to our honored mother, and which we mutually agree to cancel in this manner, as a small token of gratitude to our honored parents for their parental solicitude for our welfare, and their unremitted attention to our education.

The charge was equally divided between the "particular" accounts of the two partners.

These partnership books, too, contain some interestng stories of "adventures," one "to the West Indies," another "to Havanna," and a third "of Rum to Baltimore." Since it clearly appears that Professor Turner in his preparation of good "copy" was trying to simulate on a miniature scale the conditions of contemporary commerce, it may be well to trace the outline of these adventures.

On Feb. 5, 1803, Adventure to the West Indies was charged $69.30 for fish and butter at invoice prices plus truckage, package and insurance. The goods were laden in the "ship Success, Captain Wm. Fearnot, bound to the West-Indies and a market" on consignment to the captain (p. 66). The Fish and butter were sold at destination; sugar and molasses were purchased and brought to Portland; customs duties were paid, as likewise a small balance due to Captain Fearnot. Subsequently the molasses was distilled into rum and became the basis for the "Adventure of Rum to Baltimore." The rum was sent thither in the schooner Jane, consigned to Simon Steady, apparently a Baltimore merchant, who sold the rum, bought "30 barrels of superfine flour" and shipped the same to Portland on the brig Nymph.

The account Adventure to the West Indies shows a gross profit of $60.70 on a recorded investment of $69.39. Adventure of Rum to Baltimore shows a profit of $43.00 on a recorded investment of $212.50. The "Adventure to Havanna" was less fortunate. Flour and fish at a total cost of $213.00 were shipped on the brig Flora on consignment to the captain,

James Smart, "on our account and risk." But John Risk carried the insurance to the amount of $200.00 in consideration of a premium of $10.00. This was on July 20. The vessel and cargo were "burnt in Hispaniola by the Blacks when in a state of insurrection" (p. 83), and John Risk on Dec. 3 made good the insurance. Apparently others in Portland lost in similar adventures in the brig Flora, for John and Thomas Mercator paid $2.00 as their share of the cost of translating the papers "covering loss of our Adventure to Havan-

na." Profit and Loss was also charged and Adventure to Havanna discharged for $13.00 "short insurance."

Such is, or was, the romance of enterprise as recorded by the "charges and discharges" of these laboratory exercises in bookkeeping. In one year these two young men increased their combined proprietary equities from $200.00 to $667.95, by a series of transactions arranged by the instructor to introduce, if not render intimately familiar, a wide variety of business relationships and events.

EMERGING SPECIALIZATION

THE BEGINNINGS OF
BUSINESS BUDGETING

Edwin L. Theiss

THE BEGINNINGS OF BUSINESS BUDGETING

Edwin L. Theiss

B UDGETING now occupies a prominent and permanent place in the field of business administration. Anyone, therefore, who undertakes the study of modern budgetary technique and principles will do well first to observe the major stages of development through which budgeting has passed in its evolution. A brief account of its origin and growth will provide a desirable perspective and introduction to the study of modern budgetary principles and procedures.

Although budgeting, in the modern sense, was a postwar development in business management and had extensive application first in the United States, we must go elsewhere to find the beginnings of budgetary procedure. It was first used in England during the eighteenth century, not in business, however, but in government.

EARLY DEVELOPMENT OF BUDGETARY PROCEDURE IN ENGLAND

The budget was originally used in England as a means of controlling governmental expenditures. As early as 1760, the Chancellor of the Exchequer presented the national budget to Parliament at the beginning of each fiscal year. This budget was the chancellor's report on national finances. It included:

1. An accounting report of governmental expenditures of the past fiscal year.
2. An estimate of the expenditures for the coming year, in the form of an accounting statement.
3. A recommendation as to methods of levying taxes that would be needed to provide funds for the estimated expenditures.

After the chancellor had presented his budget speech, Parliament considered his list of estimated expenditures and after discussion and debate acted upon the proposal. Tax levies were then enacted and the budgeted appropriations served as fixed limitations for the succeeding year.

Two-fold Purpose of the English Budget: Why did England adopt budgetary procedure in the management of its national finances? There may have been several reasons, but at least two of these are readily discernible. Apparently budgetary procedure was adopted:

1. To check the king's power to levy burdensome taxes upon his subjects.
2. To control more effectively the spending of money by public officials.

The English Budget—A Tax-control Measure: During the eighteenth century taxes had become burdensome. The king had had up to this time unlimited power to tax his subjects. The representatives of the people in Parliament observed with concern the injustice and hardships imposed by the Crown in taxing citizens heavily for revenue, and finally placed a curb upon the king's powers, by requiring him to present to Parliament, through the chancellor of the exchequer, a budget of his expenditures in advance, along with the estimates of expenditures for all other government departments. The new plan centralized the taxing powers of the government in the hands of Parliament. To this extent the budget was a means of protecting the taxpayers against excessive taxation, and thus provided a forward step in the development of democratic government. The budget thus served as a means of controlling "the power of the Crown to impose taxation."[1]

---

[1] *Financial Administration of Great Britain*, by Willoughby, Willoughby and Lindsay, p. 266:
"The formal statement of the chancellor of the Exchequer thus forecasts the nature of the revenue or finance act rather than that of the appropriation act.

"This has been so almost from time immemorial. The struggle of the House to control the public purse has been one to control the power of the Crown to impose taxation rather than the power to expend money. All of its efforts were directed to the establishment of the principle that no new burden could be imposed upon the people without its consent. It was not until comparatively recent times that Parliament concerned itself with the matter of the expenditure of the funds, the raising of which it had authorized."

English Budget—A Means of Controlling Public Expenditures: A second reason for adopting budgetary procedure in England was to control public expenditures more effectively, not expenditures of the king, but those of public officers. It was the custom for a long time to have the national accounts inspected by "Auditors of the Imprest." This however proved to be inadequate and ineffective.[2] The "Auditors of the Imprest," whose duty it was to make an annual audit of all departmental accounts, assigned this work to clerks, who merely checked the records for mathematical errors and failed to check "the fees, pre-requisites and gratuities given to persons in official situations."[3] As a result fraud became common.

This condition was corrected somewhat by William Pitt's abolishment of the office of "Auditors of Imprest" and the subsequent appointment of a board of five commissioners "with the largest and most stringent powers of auditing the public accounts of every department."

Such were the conditions that existed in England at the time when governmental budgeting was first used. It is not unlikely, therefore, that budgetary procedure was adopted in the hope that it might aid in holding public officials more "strictly accountable" in their administration of public funds. But the budget failed to accomplish its maximum purpose immediately upon its adoption. In 1800, however, its effectiveness was materially increased when the responsibility for the enforcement of the budget was placed in the hands of the Cabinet, and finally in 1837 it was made fully effective by the Reform Acts, which provided for the enforcement of the budget by a truly representative Parliament.[4] Thus the English

people slowly but eventually perfected budgetary procedure with the result that early in the nineteenth century it became an effective means for holding public officials strictly accountable. Their disbursements were limited to budgeted appropriations, and all their incomes were properly accounted for by the annual audit.

Accounting Environment of Early Budgeting: Thus it seems the early English budget came into existence in an environment that was distinctively of an accounting nature. Its purpose was primarily to aid in the control of national finances, not only in restricting the king's power of taxation which provided the revenues, but also in limiting the disbursements of public officials by fixed appropriations. Thus the English budget was intended to provide a more effective accounting for incomes and outgoes. In other words, budgetary procedure was adopted with the idea of making accounting control more effective.

Moreover, two of the three parts of the English budget took the form of an accounting statement, namely the formal report of past expenditures—and the estimated expenditures of the future. Incidentally, the budget was prepared by the financial officer in charge of the national accounts, the chancellor of the Exchequer. Recognition of this early connection of budgeting with accounting will help the reader to understand the relation that exists between modern business budgeting and accounting.

The English Budget Provided a "Supply": The English word "budget" is derived from the Latin word bulga,[5] meaning a leather bag or knapsack, used for carrying supplies of food. Later the use of the word budget

---

[2] *History of Accounting and Accountants*, by Richard Brown, p. 90.

[3] Brown quotes from Lecky's, *England in the Eighteenth Century*, v, 30.

[4] *Evolution of the Budget Idea in the United States*, by F. A. Cleveland, p. 4. (Reprint from "The Annals of the American Academy of Political and Social Science," Philadelphia, November, 1915, Publication No. 942): "The one who submits the financial proposal should be responsible to all—he should be accountable for the management of the affairs of the whole government. . . . It was for this reason that Great Britain did not

succeed in establishing a true budget system till after 1800 when the principle of solidarity of responsibility was forced on the cabinet. Even then the budget could not be made effective until a means was provided for enforcing this responsibility through a truly representative Parliament—until the Reform Acts of 1837, which made Parliament in effect the people in session."

[5] Apparently the word bulga is of Gallic origin; that is, it was probably first used in Romanized France. The derived form in old French was "boge" or "bouge." Modern French created the diminutive "bougette" (little bag) from which came the Middle English "bogett" or "bougett" and later the English word budget.

was extended to mean not merely the container, but also the thing contained. Thus the term was applied to the budget speech itself, which was carried in the leather portfolio of the Chancellor of the Exchequer, when he appeared before Parliament at the beginning of a new fiscal period. His budget speech included not only a formal report, accounting for the past expenditures of the government, but also an estimate of future expenditures, together with a recommendation for a tax levy—in other words, ways and means of providing the "supply of funds" needed for future expenditures.

The word "budget," therefore, connotes primarily the idea of supply, or provision for a supply, and not the idea of restriction of expenditures. The basic concept of budgeting, therefore, is positive and not negative, a fact which is ignored by many American government officials,[6] when they prepare estimates of government expenditures, and also ignored by many business men when they set up their operating budgets. Unfortunately the negative idea of restricting expenditures is often stressed to the point of minimizing, and in some cases of ignoring, the positive idea of "supply," basically inherent in budgeting.

GOVERNMENTAL BUDGETS IN THE UNITED STATES

Municipal Budgets: The idea of govern-

mental budgeting was brought into the United States by English immigrants. It was applied early in some of the towns and cities. The earliest municipal budgets, however, were imperfect and experimental. It was not until 1895 that municipalities began in large numbers to take budgeting seriously. This increase of interest in budgeting in municipalities during the 90's was probably due to the fact that during that decade administrations of the larger cities were compelled by a strong public opinion to adopt greater economy in city finances. By 1920 practically all American cities and towns had adopted budgeting as a part of better city administration.

The larger cities led the way; for example, New York, Chicago, Boston, Philadelphia and Cleveland set up budgetary systems that were copied by smaller cities and towns. The public press generally supported the idea of municipal budgets and the public was advised to adopt budgetary measures in the interest of the municipal economy. The whole question of improving city administrations[7] was made a matter of general interest, and when budgets were once adopted by the larger cities, it was not long before they were adopted also by smaller municipalities, as well as by townships and counties.

EARLY PROPOSAL OF A NATIONAL BUDGET—DEFEATED

During these three decades, 1890–1920, the public was so thoroughly aroused to the need for governmental economy that the budget idea was suggested for adoption also in the machinery of the national government. It was especially during the administrations of President Cleveland, President Theodore Roosevelt, and President Taft that the public conscience was aroused on such matters as the stewardship of public officers, the need for destruction of special interests, represented by political bosses, and the prevention of extravagance and

---

[6] The essential difference between the nature of governmental budgeting in the United States at present, and that in England, is well summarized thus, by Willoughby and Lindsay, *Financial Administration of Great Britain*, pp. 265 and 266:
"In the United States and in Europe one thinks of the budget primarily as a document through which a program of expenditures is laid before the appropriating authority. So much is this the case that the term "budget" more often than not, is employed as a synonym for estimates of expenditures. Just the contrary is the case in England. There the budget is the document or speech through which the finance minister outlines the policy of the government in respect to revenues—the estimates of expenditures having already been laid before Parliament and considered in Committee of the whole. One cannot possibly understand the significance of the English budgetary procedure until he appreciates the fact that the interest of Parliament and the people centers on the receipts and not on the expenditure side of the budget. . . . The formal statement of the chancellor of the Exchequer thus forecasts the nature of the revenue or finance act rather than that of the appropriation act."

[7] During the period, 1890–1920, much interest was created in other methods of city administration, problems of city taxes, municipal ownership of utilities, control of school funds and the creation of park boards.

waste. It was the leadership of these three presidents that disclosed to the American public the need for efficiency and economy in national finances. Thus was built the substructure for our national budget.

President Taft made a special effort to introduce budgetary measures. Even before he was elected he stressed the desirability of managing public affairs in a businesslike manner. After his election in 1909, he was soon charged with having "surrendered to the interests," a charge that was made against him mainly because of his tariff revision policy. While political opponents were hurling their charges, President Taft asked Congress for an appropriation of $100,000, "to enable the President to inquire into the methods of transacting the public business— and to recommend to Congress such legislation as may be necessary to carry into effect changes found to be desirable, that cannot be accomplished by executive action alone." Later President Taft asked for and received an appropriation of $75,000 for the continuation of the survey.

This survey revealed the need for a national budget, the reorganization of governmental functions, introduction of better business practices and the preparation of improved accounting reports. These matters were reported to the President. As a direct result of these reports, departmental committees prepared detailed statements of expenditures for the purpose of studying and analyzing each class of expenditure. In July, 1911, budget forms were prepared and soon approved by the President. These forms were sent to department heads, to be filled in by them and returned by November 1, but they were not returned until early in 1912.

The commission submitted its final report on "The Need of a National Budget" and this was transferred by the President to Congress in June, 1912. He endorsed the report and urged its adoption by Congress, but delay followed. President Taft sensed the opposition but nevertheless proceeded to prepare the 1913 budget, which he finally submitted to Congress on February 26, 1913. This budget was referred to the Committee on Appropriations and was never revived.

Public interest, however, did not subside. Although party opposition in Congress defeated the adoption of a national budget, and the proposal was laid aside in Congress for political reasons, the public press carried on with the idea and public interest continued to increase, with two definite results:

1. Many municipalities adopted budgetary procedure, through the activity of civic organizations.
2. State commissions were appointed to inquire into the problems of state financial control, and most of the states passed budget acts.

State Budgets: From 1911 to 1919 forty-four states enacted budget laws. California and Wisconsin were the first to pass such a law, in 1911. Arkansas, Ohio and Oregon followed. Then in 1915 seven more states passed budget laws, in 1916 four, in 1917 seven, in 1918 six, and in 1919 fifteen states adopted budgetary control.

State budgets were of three kinds: executive, commission, and legislative.[8] In the executive type the governor was made the budget director, in the commission type a board was given the ultimate authority, and in the legislative type the State legislature was entrusted with the work of preparing the budget and enforcing it.

Quite a number of states have modified their original laws since 1915, in favor of the executive type. At present all states in the Union are on a budgetary basis. This accomplishment, however, was the result of at least twenty years of awakening and educating public opinion. The adoption of budgets by states was merely the last step in its evolutionary development, and although most of the states adopted budgetary procedure from 1911 to 1919, it must be remembered that public opinion first had to be created for the adoption of such measures, and this necessitated considerable open controversy in the public press and much political debating in the state legislatures, and in most states the creation of state commissions for

---

[8] For this classification see Cleveland, F. A. and Buck, A. E., *The Budget and Responsible Government*, pp. 124–125.

the purpose of studying the reorganization of state governments in the interest of efficiency and economy.

Budgeting in Public and Private Institutions: Budgetary procedure was also adopted for institutions owned by cities and states. All government schools, hospitals, penal institutions and park boards were placed on a budgetary basis. Likewise privately owned institutions adopted budgets, as did all clubs and societies of a social, athletic or educational nature. The budget idea was thus accepted quite universally and very rapidly, with the idea of controlling expenditures of funds entrusted to public and private officials and thus requiring of them a complete accounting periodically or at the expiration of their term of office.

Budgeting in institutions and social groups followed closely the governmental type of budgeting by making specific appropriations, primarily for the purpose of controlling expenditures.

Adoption of the National Budget in the United States: On June 10, 1921, Congress passed the national "Budget and Accounting Act," by which the President is authorized to present to Congress at the beginning of each fiscal year a complete budget of Federal expenditures and incomes. This estimate is discussed by Congress and when finally approved, the appropriations become authorizations by law and to this extent must remain unchanged for the coming year. There was much debate in Congress as to the type of budget to be adopted, and the opposition made strong protests against placing central authority in the hands of the chief executive. Political bossism struggled for the retention of the old system, whereby appropriations had been asked for by departmental heads. But public opinion had grown sufficiently strong to overpower the interests of politicians and the budget act was finally adopted.

Since its adoption the national budget has been praised and criticized, and recently its effectiveness has been seriously questioned, especially because of the creation of two separate budgets. Extravagance and waste have not been eliminated from government finance. It is not enough to consider the national budget merely as a means of balancing expenditures and incomes; still another objective must be attained, namely the national budget must be prepared and enforced on the basis of standardized operations and thus it will become an effective means of measuring efficiency of governmental services. In other words, the governmental budget must be operated more like a business budget if economy and efficiency are to be a reality.

THE BUDGET IN BUSINESS

The object of all business enterprises from earliest times has been the making of profit and the acquisition of more wealth. Tillers of the soil have kept their eyes upon the market so that they could realize a profit by disposing of their surplus crops. Merchants and traders have always bought those commodities which they had reason to believe they could sell at a profit. Manufacturers also have from earliest times attempted to hold their purchases of raw materials within their production requirements and have planned to make only those products for which there would likely be a market. Thus in all branches of business enterprise, the primary motive has always been to plan for profits. This planning, of course, was not scientific. It required, however, an estimating of future conditions, both possible and probable. Man's desire to forecast has always characterized business enterprise, even in those early days when Joseph, the Prime Minister of Egypt, was bold enough and wise enough to forecast the seven lean years in his interpretation of a mere dream. Much progress has, of course, been made since the days of Joseph. We are still engaged in the solution of the same old problem of planning for what may and will happen in our economic and business life. We have progressed from dreaming to guessing, and in some cases from guessing to more scientific forecasting.

This basic concept of profit planning, old as it may be in business, is still the primary motivating idea of modern business enterprise, and because of this fact, budgeting has, to a great extent, appropriated this same profit motive as its primary objective. The basic idea in budgeting is to conserve and increase the capital of a business. This fundamental idea of profit making and wealth conservation has motivated practically all experiments in business budgeting. Budgeting has merely aided business management to realize its profit objective by providing a scientific technique for forecasting business operations and establishing standards. We shall now consider the early stages of development of business budgeting.

While budgeting was being adopted by governmental units, the budget idea was also being applied by some of the larger businesses in the United States, but for the most part these business budgets were of the governmental type and fragmentary in nature.

Fragmentary Budgets of the Governmental Type: For example business first undertook to limit only those expenses which were thought of more as luxuries, rather than costs, as advertising, welfare, research, personnel and plant extensions. It was not the intention in these early attempts to budget those expenses with the idea of measuring their effectiveness. The purpose was merely to restrict them, and to keep them within fixed limits. Thus business budgeting at first followed the governmental idea of limiting appropriations. It was applied only to a few expenses and therefore fragmentary. A few businesses also attempted quite early to fix quotas for their salesmen, not primarily to measure the efficiency of salesmen, however, but to stimulate their production. Little or no attention was given to the problem of standardizing the salesman's potential income, nor was any scientific standardization made at his expenses or other marketing costs.

Standardization in Production: Production costs were for a long time not computable, except in a general way. It was not until Taylor attempted to standardize production operations, by time studies and test runs, that production costs could be accurately computed. His effort to create standards for efficiency provided the basic groundwork for later experimentations in the control of production processes. Principles and procedures of standardization took on definite form. Measuring precisely every production operation by means of time studies for labor and standard specifications for material provided an effective means of cutting costs in production, which was imperative as industrial competition increased. Taylor and his immediate followers thus supplied measuring a technique that is being applied with equal effectiveness to all other operations of a business, as well as production, by means of budgetary procedure. Sound methods of standardization are an essential prerequisite for budgetary control. Unless standards are first created, a business budget is little more than a guess. Obviously therefore one important phase of the early history of business budgeting reaches back to the pioneer work of Taylor in the application of the scientific method to the establishment of production standards.

Cost Finding and Cost Reduction: Another major phase of the history of budgeting reaches back into the early development of cost accounting. Especially the earliest stages of cost finding and cost reduction. The effort of industrial engineers to reduce costs made cost finding a matter of prime importance. Cost accountants, therefore, first of all had to provide adequate cost records. Secondly they attempted to summarize these records currently for management. This led to a great amount of experimentation among cost accountants in designing cost systems from which the current reports for management could be most quickly and accurately prepared. The resulting multiplicity of cost systems and the effort expended in their development, as well as the reasons for their abandonment in many cases, would provide a large amount of material for a history of early cost accounting. Another major portion of such a history would trace the evolution of cost accounting theories. For example, the question, what is true cost, has been under consideration since approximately 1910, and in an attempt to answer that question, cost accountants proposed the use of predetermined burden rates. This early experiment to apply burden to production on the basis of activity, by predetermined normal burden rates, was extended to material and labor costs. Thus ultimately standard costs were evolved, and this in turn has led naturally to the more recent idea of estimating expected costs in the form of a budget.

Cost finding in itself was not enough; and costs were necessary, to be sure, but the need for current cost control was more important. Thus in the development of standard production costs, cost accountants provided one of the most valuable and essential prerequisites of modern business budgeting. Later all operations of a business, not merely production costs, were standardized. Thus with standards set for the manufacturing, selling and financing functions, budgets could be scientifically prepared.

Summary of the Early Development of Budgeting: The early development of business budgeting may be summarized briefly thus:

1. A few of the larger business budgeted certain luxury expenses. The methods used were taken over from governmental budgeting.
2. Industrial engineers provided the scientific methodology both for standardizing operations and measuring the efficiency of actual performance by comparing actual performance with the standards.
3. Cost accountants developed cost records, and attempted not only to find costs, but also to control them by developing standard costs in production.

Thus the earliest beginnings of business budgeting may be said to have been grounded deeply in the early evolution both of industrial engineering and cost accounting. Budgeting grew like a plant grows from a seed. The years 1895–1920 were the germination period, for during that time budgeting grew steadily below the surface. Its two major roots reached down into the fields of industrial engineering and accounting. Finally after the close of the World War the plant made its appearance above the surface. We shall now consider the

major factors that contributed to the more recent development of business budgeting.

RECENT DEVELOPMENT OF BUSINESS BUDGETING IN THE UNITED STATES

Since 1920 budgeting has grown rapidly and substantially in the United States. This rapid growth can be accounted for by the fact that during this recent period a number of influential factors have been at work to produce conditions that were favorable for budgetary development. Some of these factors came from within individual businesses, while others arose from sources separate and apart from individual business enterprises. The most important factors included the following:

1. Industrial expansion and competion.
2. Open-mindedness of business executives.
3. Production standardization by industrial engineers.
4. Coordination of all business functions by management engineers.
5. Emphasis on internal trends and cyclical movements by statisticians.
6. Establishment of financial accounting control and development of standard costs, by accountants.
7. Endorsement of business budgeting by banks, credit men, and insurance companies.
8. Exchange of ideas through trade associations.
9. Training in educational institutions.
10. Production of budgetary literature.

Industrial Expansion and Competition: Since Taylor's time, industrial enterprises have increased greatly in number and size, while business management and research have been improved to such an extent that they may now be properly considered a science. All of this recent expansion in American industry, stimulated by increasing competition, has provided a most excellent clinic for the testing of various budgetary methods and procedures. Many businesses of all kinds and sizes have experimented with budgetary procedures, and thus a large variety of systems have been tested and tried.

Open-mindedness of Business Executives:
Business executives have been for the most
part open minded and charitable in the
adoption of budgetary procedures. Neither
have they considered their methods as
secrets. They have exchanged ideas freely.
American business men have learned that it
is profitable to share their experimentations
with each other. Workable ideas are passed
on to others. This open minded attitude of
business leaders has aided materially in the
rapid growth of business budgeting in
America.

*Production Standardization by Industrial
Engineers:* Industrial engineers have made
a two-fold contribution. In the first place
they have perfected methods of standardizing factory operations. They have applied the general principles of all science,
such as accuracy, orderly procedure, complete collection and precise analysis of data,
testing and interpretation of facts, to the
problems of factory management. The result
has been the establishment of scientific
standards, without which budgeting could
not have made much progress. Their second
contribution lay in their personal efforts.
They either assisted plant managers or
themselves supervised the preparation of
factory budgets. For this task they were
already well fitted by experience. Their
own problems of factory management required careful planning and schooling of
operations. Making estimates scientifically
was a part of their regular work. Thus they
were able to transfer, without difficulty,
their experience and knowledge acquired in
the performance of their regular engineering
duties to the somewhat similar work of preparing manufacturing budgets.

*Coordination of Business Functions by
Management Engineers:* Management engineers also have performed a constructive
service in the development of business budgeting. They have aided mostly in problems
of business organization. Management engineers are business doctors. They diagnose
the organization ills of a business and pre-
scribe remedies, so that maladjustments can
be removed. Their special work is to co-
ordinate all the functions of a business into
a unified whole. This they have accomplished for many businesses and in so far as
their services have helped businesses to co-
ordinate all their functions, to that extent
they produced conditions in individual businesses that were favorable to the introduction of budgetary procedure. Management
engineers also have given due recognition to
the primary functions of the comptroller, in
respect of standards and records, and in the
interpretation of accounting data for management.

*Emphasis on Trends and Cyclical Move-
ments by Statisticians:* Statisticians, employed by businesses have applied statistical
methods to the problems of management.
They have collected facts on production and
sales and then analyzed and summarized
them for management.

They have designed methods for making
fairly reliable market analyses and determined the potential sales of a business. They
have applied standard statistical procedures
to the problems of measuring seasonal variations and secular trend. In brief, they have
gathered necessary data on any special
problems that confront management,
whether it be a question of costs and expenses, or of profitability of departments and
products, or a question as to the efficiency
of salesmen in various territories. Their
major contribution, therefore, to the development of business budgeting has been in
the efficient methods they have provided for
finding the facts of a business, discovering
the trends, and summarizing them for management. Without the statisticians' machinery for fact-finding and trend observations,
management would not be able to predetermine incomes and costs accurately; in other
words, budgeting would be nothing more
than guessing. So much for the services of
statisticians within a business.

Mention should also be made of the contributions of economic statisticians and
professional statistical service organizations.
Within the past fifteen years general business forecasting has made substantial progress mainly because statisticians have
studied the general movements of business

and have succeeded in discovering some of the laws of the business cycle. Some statistical services attempt to forecast recurring changes in the general economic cycle, while others specialize in reporting probable trends in certain sales or production fields. These reports, when scientifically prepared, have aided individual businesses in budgeting to the business cycle.[9] These statistical organizations have made it possible for management to observe the correlation that exists between the cycle of an individual business and the general business cycle. This emphasis by statisticians outside a business upon the necessity of knowing the movements of the economic cycle has been their substantial contribution to the development of business budgeting.

Contributions by Accountants: Accountants, both public and private, have been leaders and pioneers in budgeting. Public accountants have taken over budget installations as one of their services. Private accountants in industries have designed and installed budget systems and also supervised the preparation of current budget reports. A more basic contribution by accountants, however, was made in that they provided adequate books for the recording of business transactions. From the very beginning accountants have considered the recording of business transactions to be their major function. Thus they have provided managements with a history of their past performance, which is an indispensable source for information that must be considered when budgetary estimates are prepared. Without accurate and complete information on what has happened in a business it would be quite impossible to predetermine to any appreciable degree of reliability what can and should happen in the future.

Accountants have also assumed, as their second function, the interpretation of accounting records for management. This work of interpretation has grown steadily from the preparation of current financial statements to the preparation of compara-

[9] *Budgeting to the Business Cycle,* by J. Barber.

tive statements, the use of percentages and graphs, and the adoption of ratio studies and comparisons of ratios for a number of fiscal periods. Most of this interpretation, however, has been merely of the post-mortem type and was considered finished when management was informed of what had happened and the causes explained. Much has been said by accountants recently about the possible necessity of extending their interpretation functions into the field of prediction and budgeting. Management engineers also have criticized accountants for not keeping pace with management. For example, Mr. Monarch V. Hayes, in the preface of his recent book, *Accounting for Executive Control*, says, "The science of management has made much progress during the past decade, but the science of accounting has not kept pace with it. The development in the science of management has made necessary a restatement of the purposes of accounting. If accounting is to serve management best, it must accomplish the purpose of all science—that of prediction." What Hayes wishes to say is this: Accountants have been interpreting the past merely as historians. Now they ought to provide interpretations that will be of specific and direct help to management in preparing budgetary estimates. In other words, he suggests that accountants enlarge their function of interpretation to include the preparation of future balance sheets and income statements, together with a comparison of ratios on future statements with those on the actual statements at the beginning of the budget period. Some accountants refuse to accept this new challenge, while others believe that budgeting should be taken over as a regular accounting service. The latter have given much time and effort to budgeting and have insisted that, when budgets are prepared, accounting principles should not be violated.

Cost accountants also have had a major part in the recent development of business budgeting. During the past fifteen years substantial progress has been made in the development of standard and differential costs. Standard costs, based on accurate cost standards have facilitated budgeting. Cost accountants have cooperated closely with industrial engineers in the control of production costs by recording all variances from standards.

Endorsement of Business Budgeting by Banks: Financial institutions have recently recommended to their depositors the adoption of budgetary procedure. Some banks give a higher credit rating to businesses that operate a budget than to those who fail to plan ahead. Although some banks claim that businesses having a budget are not given a higher credit rating, bankers generally endorse the idea strongly, even though some of them do not have a budget for their own banks.

Credit men, throughout the country, also have endorsed budgetary procedures as a means of strengthening the financial position of their customers. In their national association meetings budgeting has been discussed at various times, and numerous articles on the subject have appeared in their national publication.

Some of the larger insurance companies have given wide publicity to the advantages of business budgeting, primarily to create goodwill among their policy holders, but also to aid policy holders to improve their financial position. About 1920 the Metropolitan Insurance Company began to make surveys on budgetary procedures in various lines of business and published its findings through its Policy Holders' Service Department. Finally in 1926 these pamphlets were assembled and published in book form.[10] This publication was widely read and thus much information on budget forms and routines was brought to business men throughout the country. The Metropolitan Insurance still maintains an active interest in business budgeting, as is evidenced by the recent publication of several additional pamphlets.[11]

Exchange of Ideas Through Trade Associations: Many trade associations have discussed budgeting in their meetings and trade

journals have carried many articles on various phases of budgetary procedure. In this way, members of the association benefited generally by learning of the experience of others; but especially the interest and enthusiasm of smaller business units for budgeting were stimulated and maintained even to the point of experimenting with budgetary procedures.

Trade associations have thus given impetus to the development of budgeting by distributing widely among their members reports of actual budgetary experimentations. Many of these accounts tell about methods and ideas that were in process of development. Some of the results thus published may have been unscientific. Most of it, however, was valuable as laboratory material, and, to the extent that trade associations have served as clearing houses for ideas on budgetary procedures and principles, to that extent they have made a most valuable contribution to the development of business budgeting.

ACADEMIC TRAINING

During the past decade, business budgeting has progressed far enough in its development so that the best methods and procedures can be selected, and a beginning can be made in the codification of budgetary principles. Whenever a science arrives at this stage in its development, the professional educator begins to study the field and subject whatever knowledge is available to further classification. Thus it is in the field of budgeting. The field has now become a subject of academic study.

Business budgeting is now being taught in most of the larger colleges and universities and in most schools of business administration. Class room training has, however, been handicapped by a lack of suitable texts and standardized problems. These are now in the making and undoubtedly during the next decade better texts will be published. Teachers of budgeting have been compelled to develop their own instruction material out of surveys made by themselves and by assembling problems from a few scattered sources in budgeting literature.

[10] *Applied Budgeting*, by Henry Bruère and Arthur Lazarus, published by A. W. Shaw Company, 1926.
[11] *Budgeting Control in the Manufacturing Industry.*

Budgeting Literature: Up until 1920 most of the literature on budgeting covered only the field of governmental budgets. The literature of business budgeting did not begin to take form until after the close of the World War. It appeared first only in the form of periodical articles, and much that was published in the early 20's was ephemeral and, therefore, cannot properly be included as a part of budgetary literature. Although it was a crude beginning, it was soon followed by more scientific contributions both in periodical and textual treatises.

During the past ten years a considerable number of books have been produced on the subject of business budgeting. Moreover most texts on accounting and financial administration published during this period include one or more chapters on budgetary control.

Periodical literature on the subject also increased substantially. Many articles on business budgeting can now be found in publications of trade associations, accountants, both public and cost accountants, industrial and management engineers, statisticians, economists, financial executives, credit men, bankers, and teachers of accounting. Teachers of budgetary control courses have made substantial contributions. Likewise bureaus of business research, affiliated with colleges of commerce and schools of business administration, have published valuable studies on various phases of budgeting. Since 1933 several texts have also appeared in Germany, France and England.

Business budgeting has also been a popular subject for discussion in many groups of business executives, accountants and teachers of business administration. These discussions have usually followed the presentation of some scientific treatise dealing with budgetary technique and principles. Consideration has been frequently given to the objectives of a business budget and the relation of business budgeting to such fields as statistics, engineering and accounting. Out of such discussions has come a greater clarity of thinking and a better understanding of budgetary terminology. Many of these technical papers are published and thus become a valuable addition to budgetary literature.

Mention should also be made of the papers presented at the first International Discussion Conference of Budgetary Control held at Geneva, Switzerland, from July 10 to July 12, 1930, under the auspices of the International Management Institute. These papers were presented by various executives from the United States, Canada, Great Britain, Belgium, Germany, Switzerland and France, and covered the following subjects:

The Budget as an Aid to the Determination of Policy.
The Budget as an Aid to the Control of Performance.
The Preparation of the Sales Budget.
The Preparation of the Expense Budget.
Budgeting for Stock and Working Capital Requirements.
Budgeting for Equipment and Fixed Capital Requirements.
How to Overcome Opposition when Introducing a Budget Control System.
Common Mistakes and Misunderstandings in the Use of Budgets.
The Management of Industrial Concerns and the Budget.
Budget Principles and Procedures in their Broader Aspect.
The State Budget as Compared with the Business Budget.
National and International Economic Planning.

Two hundred delegates were present from twenty-seven countries. This conference recommended the formation of research groups that would study the application of budget control in individual cases, and that the findings of each group be made available to all the others. Furthermore, in different branches of industry there should be formed national and international groups for the study of the application of budget control.

As a result of this conference, seven international groups have been organized to study the application of the principles of budgetary control in the following industries:

    Iron and Steel
    Mechanical Engineering
    Electrical Engineering
    Motor-Car Manufacture
    Textiles
    Public Utilities
    Food Industries

The papers of this first International Conference were published in the proceedings of the Conference and are now available in French, German and English. No doubt much more valuable material will be added to the literature of budgeting when the results of study by the seven international groups have been completed and published.

A recent contribution to our knowledge of budgetary practices was made by the National Industrial Conference Board of New York by means of a survey of 294 representative manufacturing companies, the results of which were summarized in a book entitled *Budgetary Control in the Manufacturing Industry*. The purpose of the survey was to discover to what extent budgetary control has been adopted by manufacturing concerns, what methods are being used and what the results have been. The report of the Board gives an accurate summary of the progress that business budgeting has made in the United States. It is especially valuable because it presents both the favorable and unfavorable features of present day budgetary practices and reveals the reasons why some budgetary experiments have failed. Eighteen causes for failures are cited. These have, in themselves, well justified the publication of the report. It is advantageous to be able to observe at times what progress has been made and discover the causes of opposition or defects in methods. Any science developed under such circumstances is assured of a permanent and more rapid growth. The United States is the only country in which such a summary has been made possible. In other countries business budgeting has not yet been adopted to such a degree that a comprehensive summary is possible.

Business Budgeting in Other Countries: Some of the European countries have recently been adopting budgetary procedures in their industries. Germany seems to be taking the lead. The Germans have taken the post-war rationalization of business seriously. The Reichkuratorium (National Industrial Committee) was frequently referred to in the International Conference as a model plan for adoption by industries of other nations. Dr. Ludwig has published a fairly complete treatise on budgetary procedure,[12] primarily to stimulate German business leaders to adopt American budgetary procedures. German journals of business have been carrying numerous articles on various phases of budgeting. Max H. Schmid and Heinz Pulvermann have contributed freely to German budgetary literature.

In France also some alteration has recently been given to business budgeting. French business journals have contained reports of successful budgetary developments in the United States and some accounts of experiments carried on in French industries. Thus far, however, no substantial text on business budgeting has appeared in France.

The situation in England is well described[13] by A. W. Willsmore, in his recent book on *Business Budgets*, which incidentally was the first complete text on Business Budgeting to appear in England, as follows: "Although budget control has not yet been adopted on a sufficiently wide basis in this country to enable a comprehensive summary to be given of the practical advantages that have been realized, there is sufficient evidence to indicate quite clearly that budget control is a logical development that can be expected to take a permanent place in the technique of business management in Great Britain. It is significant to note the wide range of industrial activity represented at the International Conference." Then Mr. Willsmore mentions eleven British industries that were represented in

---

[12] *Der Budget Control*, by Heinz Ludwig.
[13] *Business Budgets*, by A. W. Willsmore, published in 1932 by Sir Isaac Ritman and Sons, Ltd., London. See especially pp. 220–221.

the Conference, which may be considered evidence that business budgeting has already taken a permanent hold on British industry.

In Russia the famous five year plan for economic production has centralized business budgeting in the machinery of the National Soviet government, while in Italy the national government also directs and controls to a large degree industrial operations.

Belgium and Switzerland are also making some progress in the application of budgetary procedures. Both countries were represented by business leaders, two of whom presented formal papers on the program of the International Conference at Geneva, Switzerland, in 1930.

Other countries represented in the conference were: Algeria, Argentina, Austria, Bulgaria, Canada, China, Hungary, Ireland, Italy, Japan, Lithuania, Netherlands, Poland, Roumania, Czecho-Slovakia, Sweden, Spain, which is an indication that business budgeting has spread widely. This development has emanated mainly from the United States, and has spread to other countries through the medium of budgetary literature, produced in the United States.

It is interesting to note for example that budgeting which originally came from England to the United States, and primarily of the governmental type, has the past fifteen years been transformed to the business field, and is now being carried back to England to be applied there also in the industrial field. Most writers on business budgeting in foreign countries make frequent references to the success of business budgeting in this country, and recommend to business leaders of their own countries the adoption of similar methods.

EVOLUTION OF THE INTEGRATION OF THE COST AND FINANCIAL RECORDS

[S. Paul Garner]

CHAPTER VI

EVOLUTION OF THE INTEGRATION
OF THE
COST AND FINANCIAL RECORDS

THE COST DEVELOPMENT DISCUSSED IN THIS CHAPTER HAS PROVED OVER the past decades to be one of the more dramatic phases of the evolution of modern costing techniques. The transition from the accounting for merchandising concerns to that for factories was slow in taking place; and when it did come, the records devised for costing in manufactories were, for the most part, extramural to the financial or commercial books. Even then they were often crude and unsatisfactory, mainly because few factory managers would trust them implicitly, since (1) they were not coördinated in any way with the general accounts, and (2) only the roughest sort of internal check was possible. In addition, many plants used modified trading concern books, with the addition of an account for "manufacturing." The various reasons for this slow development were considered in detail in Chapters II and V, and need not be reiterated here. It is sufficient at this point to state that even after 1885, when modern costing really began, numerous authorities who delved into the subject often succeeded in leaving it more confused than before they had attempted their exposition. Gradually, however, over a fairly long period of time, there emerged more and more specific techniques until at the present time the ideas are considerably more uniform, often differing only in particulars.

Up until the early 1880's very little had been done in regard to the consolidation of the factory and general accounts. Wherever a factory opened up two or three accounts on its financial or trading ledger—one of which was usually "manufacturing"—such a scheme within itself had some of the features of a merger of the cost and general records. In the true sense of the word, however, one should not call such a technique actual costing of the product; it was rather a record of expenditures, and only a very crude estimate could be derived as to the cost of the manufactured articles. Even to obtain these guesses, inventories had to be taken at periodic intervals, the intervals often covering a year or more in time. More than likely, however, when later cost authorities began to consider methods for tying in cost accounts with the financial ledger, they drew heavily upon the earlier attempts at ascertaining costs along these lines.

By 1885, the idea that ordinary commercial records were not satisfactory for factory account keeping was fairly well established, even though no one had presented a thorough description of an improved system. In that year an American Army officer, Henry Metcalfe, published his *Cost of Manufactures,* which, while not pertaining directly to industrial plants, was devoted in part to the present subject. His system of costing involved the use of cost sheets on which would be accumulated all the elements going into the product. The cost sheets, labor records, and stores ledgers were not tied in with his "cash accounts," which were separate and distinct; but a partial reconciliation of the two could be made at the end of each month. For instance, the labor element of cost as shown on the cost sheets was supposed to reconcile with the aggregate disbursements for services on the abstract of disbursements, as he called it. The material element was checked "by two necessities: First, of accounting for all material received, whether paid for or not; and, second, of charging to some shop order all material expended or subject to expenditure, whether by accident or design."[1] The third element of cost, overhead, was almost impossible to reconcile, according to Metcalfe; at any rate, the technique which would be required would be so comprehensive and difficult to carry out that the results would not be worth the extra trouble. In connection with this problem, Metcalfe admitted that he had tried in vain "to find some simple current method" of making the reconciliation, but was convinced that, not only was that

impossible, but that "substantial truth" would be "neglected for the
sake of striking a balance."[2]   His reasons for the failure to reconcile
the items were: (1) that the shop was always paying out in one month
for material which was used in another; (2) that the shop did not
necessarily use at once all that was paid for; and (3) one could not
always ascertain whether "what we are expending has been paid for
or not, still less whether it has been for the time covered jointly by the
two sets of accounts or previously."[3]   These reasons are interesting
as indicating the state of cost thinking during the period under
consideration.   Metcalfe concluded that even if the reconcilement
could be carried out completely it would more than likely "paralyze
the manufacturing." He seemed to think, also, that the three elements
could never be proved independently, but only in aggregate, which,
obviously, would be of small benefit so far as their control was concerned.   All in all, he made a rather hopeless case out of the proposition of consolidating the cost with the financial records and of
showing the flow of costs through the accounts.   It was not long,
however, before other cost experts began to inquire into the nature of
the problem.

In fact, just two years later, the English practicing cost authorities, Emile Garcke and J. M. Fells, wrote into their *Factory Accounts*
the, at that time, extremely novel suggestion that the factory books
should never be considered as mere "memoranda, which are not
necessarily required to balance."[4]   There was not the slightest hint that
the factory accounts should ever be outside of the regular double entry
framework.   Their scheme provided for a number of modern features.
A goods in process account (they called it a "manufacturing account,"
but the context implies the other concept) was to be set up on the
commercial ledger, to which would be charged (1) all the material
consumed from the raw materials account, and (2) the labor from
the wages account.   In addition, although they were not very specific
on the point, the overhead element of cost was also to be charged to
that account.   As goods were completed, they were to be taken out
of the "manufacturing" (goods in process) account and transferred
to finished stock account.   Except for their hazy details as to the
handling of the establishment charges (burden), this procedure was
the same as that often used today.   A major hurdle had been taken,
therefore, when this treatment appeared; furthermore, the internal
transactions, showing the flow of costs through the ledger, had been
partially developed.   As was common, however, among the English

cost authorities of the time, Garcke and Fells continued to refer to
the prime cost books and all the paraphernalia connected therewith.
It is probable that their technique represented the more advanced
ideas of the period, even though the system described was evidently
in current use, especially since these two practical cost experts were
not given to theorizing or philosophizing to any great extent.[5] According to Garcke and Fells, the tie-in was not to be sacrificed or
neglected just because the plant happened to have a large number of
departments, or a number of subsidiary ledgers; these factors only
made the coördination more imperative. As a matter of fact, one of
the important advantages would lie in the close check which could
be maintained, to give one example, over the stores ledger and the
storekeeper. For instance, the physical inventory would prove the
stores sheets, while the total of the stores sheets would check with
the stores account on the commercial ledger. Incidentally, Garcke and
Fells referred to the "commercial ledger"; their system did not con-
template the use of what is at present called a "factory ledger," which
is, in turn, tied in with the "general ledger" by means of a reciprocal
account. This technique did not appear until somewhat later, as will
be explained on subsequent pages.

It should be emphasized, however, that the procedure advocated
by the preceding English authorities was not adopted immediately
by other English factory cost accountants. In fact, it was around
1910 before the English began to use the type of coördination provided by the Garcke and Fells arrangement. As will be developed in
later pages of this chapter, the American writers on the topic soon
took up the idea, but the English insisted on independent "cost accounts" until well into the twentieth century. Even in the same year
that Garcke and Fells wrote, another English accountant made the
statement that the "cost books, being supplemental to, and outside of,
the commercial books, cannot be used for the purpose of embezzling."[6]
This viewpoint of the advantage of distinct cost books permeated
the arguments of several later authorities, especially those outside of
this country. Two years later, the immediately preceding theory
of non-adunation was again expounded by G. P. Norton, a practicing
accountant in northern England. Norton referred to the idea of
merging the cost records and the financial or counting house records
as being entirely unfeasible and undesirable, stating that the intention of such a plan was "perfectly right, but the method is altogether
injudicious."[7] Norton went on to provide a rather complicated, al-

though workable, system of costing in the departments and processes of a textile mill, claiming, however, that the accounts required therefor should be separate and distinct from the trading account and the ordinary accounting transactions and records.   His concluding statement left no doubt as to his position on the matter: "Much unnecessary complication is introduced into a comparatively simple operation when the details of the departmental accounts are mixed up with the books of the counting house."[8]   Even though Norton thus dismissed the idea of consolidating the cost accounts with the general accounts, he showed, nevertheless, on his commercial ledger some accounts which contained the germ of later developments.   For example, the stable account collected all the charges pertaining to the hauling and drayage expense of the mill; and was credited for (1) any balance which might be carried forward as an asset to the next period, (2) the amount that was transferred to the mill account for services rendered thereto, and (3) an amount that was transferred to the warehouse account for the expenses of delivering the finished product.   This procedure is carried out today through the medium of a burden distribution sheet.   Incidentally, this description was quite advanced for that period, which makes his ideas on the "merging" all the more surprising; it is not definitely known why he was so utterly opposed to the tie-in.   It may be surmised, however, that he felt that the necessary details were better handled, and a more adequate control provided, if the two ledgers were kept distinct.   An integral part of Norton's costing presupposed that the results of operations would be contrasted and compared with what it would have cost to obtain the products from some outside firm—the basic advantage of imputed costing arrangements— and this procedure may have been one of the contributing causes of his preference for separate cost books, unconnected with the counting house accounts.

A few years later, in an unsigned article in *The Accountant,* an English publication, a statement was made that formerly the cost accounts of a factory "were invariably quite distinct from the books of account proper."[9]   This unknown authority continued by pointing out that in view of this, professional auditors rarely, if ever, investigated the nature of those records, the reason being that they (the auditors) were disinclined to "embark upon a line of action that necessitated a more or less intimate acquaintance with the technique of each different class of business whose accounts they were called upon to verify."[10]   After a further discussion of the relation of auditors to the cost accounting of a firm, this expert specifically recommended that the cost accounts be kept entirely separate from the financial books, just as Norton had suggested. His reason for adopting such a procedure was the later familiar argument that if the two were separate, any errors or fraudulent items would show up at the end of the period, especially in the inventories. In other words, the two sets of accounts would give a mutual check on each other. He did not discuss, however, just how a reconcilement was to be made; it is evident that he had some sort of checking scheme in mind or else he would not have been so definite in his insistence that the accounts be uncoördinated. It should be remembered, though, that Garcke and Fells had given the same reasoning in support of the adunation arrangement. Obviously, the latter was preferable, at least in the light of later developments; but at that time this unknown writer concluded that "those who prefer that the two sets of accounts shall form a complete and scientifically constructed whole may readily modify our system to this end by means of adjustment accounts."[11] Nothing was said, however, as to how the adjusting was to be carried out; that was something outside the bounds of practicality. Incidentally, the books required under his system of cost accounts were: wages book, stock book, cost book, summary of cost accounts, and a reference index. Such was the force of precedence, and the power of the status quo, that even though this authority admitted that the integrated scheme was the one that was "complete and scientifically constructed, and theoretically preferable," he chose the other possibility as the one which should be ordinarily adopted.

Even though the English cost authorities around the turn of the century were thus almost unanimously agreed that the cost accounts as such should be separate from the general financial records, they continued to search for some simple method of reconciling the two. For example, although he was quite specific in holding that the factory records should not be coördinated with the others,[12] F. G. Burton thought it desirable to have some means of checking the special cost accounts. His scheme was rather naïve; a monthly "approximate" profit and loss statement was to be compiled from the shop accounts, somewhat like the accompanying illustration on page 261.

The figures for the statement were to be derived for the most part from the regular commercial ledger, and Burton pointed out that the stock accounts would have to agree or check with "the total stock of the cost sheets"—this last being a rather hazy description

Approximate Profit and Loss Account for Month of March, 1895[13]

Debit		Credit	
To Stock March 1	xxx	By Sales	xxx
Purchases	xxx	Additions to Plant:	
Salaries	xxx	Material	xxx
Etc.	xxx	Wages	xxx
Estimated Charges, viz:		Estimated Charges:	
Rents, Rates, Taxes	xxx	Work in Progress	xxx
Interest, Gross	xxx	Stock March 31, viz.	xxx
Depreciation, Gross	xxx		
By Profit	xxx		
	xxx		xxx

of the method of proving that important item of cost. He continued by suggesting that the costs of an establishment be collected by the use of three groups of "sheets," namely, sheet "A" for departmental accounts; sheet "B" for process accounts; and sheet "C" for contract or job accounts. The method of operating these "sheets" was discussed in the previous chapter. It is sufficient to state at this point that a summary of the balances of the three groups of sheets was to be drawn up each month, and, as he described it, "we shall find that we obtain exactly the same profit or loss"[14] as shown by the approximate profit and loss account illustrated. The reason why this agreement could be effected was that the cost accounts were a complete duplication of the financial records; the sales were even recorded in both sets. This idea of a duplicate set of independent accounts was elaborated upon at length by later English cost experts, culminating in the extraordinarily complex system devised by E. T. Elbourne in 1921, which will be described at the end of this chapter.

The partially integrated technique employed by J. S. Lewis, 1896, should be treated at this point. Lewis' costing contemplated the use of a "manufacturing" account on the ledger (he recommended just one ledger) to which would be posted the "prime costs" (his term) of a period. The stores used, for example, would be debited to the manufacturing account and credited to stores, while the wages incurred would be debited to manufacturing and credited to wages account. The products completed at prime cost would be taken out of the manufacturing account and debited to finished stock account. Thus, as can be easily seen, the manufacturing account was really a work in progress account except that prime costs only were recorded in it. At a balance sheet date, however, this British accountant advocated the addition of the factory overhead items, properly allocable to both the work in process and the finished goods, to the prime costs of those still on hand.   This was to be done through a rather cumbersome suspense account arrangement, and was the principal defect in his otherwise admirable system.   Lewis was not willing, or perhaps did not know how, to show not only the flow of prime costs through the ledger, but also the burden element of cost.   He discussed the handling of "establishment and shop charges," as he called them, at length, but did not present a procedure for carrying them along with the prime costs; the prime cost precedent seemed too strong for him to entirely overcome.   He at least did not advocate separate and distinct factory ledgers and accounts uncoördinated and not tied in with the general or commercial accounts in any way.   Incidentally, he was one of the first, after Garcke and Fells, to advocate the integration of the accounts; his place in the history of the subject would have been much more secure, however, if he had not refused, or failed, to provide for the flow of total costs through the accounts.   His work was unusually thorough and complete in other respects; charts of accounts and illustrations were given in profusion to help the reader in understanding his preferred procedures.[15]

One of the earliest American authorities to consider this topic, after Metcalfe, was President Frank Broaker of the American Association of Public Accountants (later The American Institute of Accountants).   In an address which he gave before the Association in 1897,[16] he chose as his subject the organization of cost accounts.   While his remarks were not very detailed, he did describe a procedure for coördinating the cost and the financial records.   The tie-in was to be handled through what he called a "consumption journal," the exact purpose of which he did not make clear.   It was, however, a book which connected the various costing sheets and other detailed labor and material data with the financial ledger.   In addition, it served as a check upon the manufactured articles "as received and the raw material and labor as consumed, proving not only the labor charges upon the costing slips and other dockets, but controlling the labor pay rolls in aggregate and bringing the entire factory working . . . under the crucial test of double entry in every particular."[17]   Here was indeed the semblance of a new idea and it is unfortunate that he did not dwell more upon the uses of the consumption journal.   Beyond some

generalized remarks, which are given in the reference notes, he gave
no further information about the nature of his integration scheme.[18]
Evidently, however, he had in mind a type of double entry technique
which would serve to bring together the costing and the commercial
ledgers.

H. L. Arnold, a few years later, while discussing the cost records
maintained by some fifteen prominent American firms of that period,
mentioned that the common practice of the time was to keep invio-
late the distinction between the financial and the cost books. One
firm,[19] for instance, had adopted an accounting arrangement in which
the two had no relation or connection or modifying influence whatever on each other. A few concerns, however, according to Arnold,
did attempt to carry some of the factory accounts on the commercial
books; this idea, though, in his opinion served no real need. Absolutely no advantages, it seemed, would be obtained thereby which
could not be gained by the complete independence of the cost accounting. Arnold concluded by stating emphatically that the factory accounting should be as separate as though the manufacturing
division and the sales division were in wholly different hands, that is,
independent corporations.

The most prevalent doctrine around the turn of the century,
therefore, did not provide for the integration of the cost and general
records. There were a few dissenters among the authorities, but their
views did not carry much weight. The consensus among the manufacturing firms, as well as among those who wrote on the topic, was
that there should be a distinction made between cost accounts as
such and the financial record keeping. Some authorities, however,
saw the necessity for their reconcilement; yet their methods, on the
whole, for carrying it out were crude and generally unsatisfactory.

One of the first authorities to suggest the use of a separate factory ledger tied in with the general ledger by means of reciprocal
accounts was E. Andrade, an English Chartered Accountant, who
wrote in 1899.[20] This was almost an entirely new idea, although
various experts had been hunting for such a scheme for some time.
In fact, his discussion probably grew out of the work which had
been done by his predecessors, such as Broaker in this country. In
essence his scheme was rather simple. A "connecting account" was
to be opened in each ledger (cost and general), to which, at closing
date, all the accounts in each ledger which pertained to the other,
were to be closed. The balances of the two accounts would then

agree, according to Andrade, thus affording a definite proof of the accuracy of the respective accounts and the postings therein. The scheme would also allow the cost accounts, so-called, to be balanced independently on the double entry principle. Except for the fact that his procedure contemplated the delaying of the postings to the connecting accounts until the end of a fiscal period, the system described would still be standard. Andrade did not give any illustrations of how it would be handled in actual practice, nor did he mention just what accounts would appear on each ledger. The big hurdle, though, had been taken; later authorities did not have too much difficulty in filling in the details of the technique.

Since Andrade had brought the issue to a critical point, the controversy between the integrationists and the nonintegrationists soon began to wax warm. In 1900, the editor of *The Accountant*, an influential English publication, took cognizance of the problem and devoted several editorials to a discussion of the matter. It was his conclusion that only in quite rare, exceptional cases, would it be practicable to incorporate the cost accounts with the financial books; in most instances it would be better to leave them entirely independent. He at least admitted, though, that their consolidation was not an impossibility. Incidentally, his rationalization on this point was somewhat unusual. The two sets of accounts should not be coördinated because, in his own words, "costing clerks belong to a somewhat different category to ordinary bookkeepers; and it is desirable that the two . . . should be kept separate, for this reason if for no other."[21] He did not state wherein this difference was to be found, nor whether his remarks were designed as dyslogistic to the cost group or to the other accountants. During the next several years, four or five additional articles were published in the same magazine, arguing the question at length. The main point involved seems to have been the proposition that if the cost books were kept entirely separate, there could be exercised over the factory superintendent and foremen a modicum of internal control which would be lost if the integration plan were adopted. As a matter of fact, later developments proved that the consolidation scheme gave more audit assistance along these lines than any noncoördinated system ever devised.

Around this time, also, the matter of reconciling the results of operations as shown by the cost books and the general accounts came back into prominence. Sir John Mann, for example, in his article contributed to the *Encyclopaedia of Accounting* in 1903, while recommending that the nonintegration plan be adopted, did stress the importance of comparing the results. In fact, he made the specific point that the cost system should be framed in such a way as to allow for the comparison. The reasons for such a necessity were, in his opinion, quite obvious. One was that any erroneous "guess work" in connection with the allocation of factory overhead might be corrected; or, again, if any omissions of sales data, or other errors, had crept into the commercial records, they could be found by the reconciliation. His procedure for making the contrast, however, was rather hazy as to details. Summaries were to be prepared from time to time; the wages charged in the cost books were to be reconciled with the wages paid out; the materials consumed, "after adjustment of increase or decrease in stocks, will disclose either a surplus or a deficiency when compared with the actual inventory"; and the overhead was to be examined, and adjustments made, if necessary, in the future rates.[22]

Cost accountants in England during the next two decades followed, for the most part, Mann's treatment of the subject; that is to say, they recommended that the factory records remain uncoördinated with the general accounts, with perhaps a partial reconciliation being made at intervals. As a matter of fact, the very names of their published works gave an indication of their feeling on the matter. Practically all of their important contributions included the words "cost accounts" in their titles, implying to some extent at least that the factory records were more or less a separate entity. Some examples are given in the reference notes.[23] The philosophy underlying the English viewpoint was very well expressed by Stanley Pedder in 1905, when, after indicating that he preferred the extramural costing arrangements, he pointed out that, in his opinion, the essential difference between the financial or commercial accounts and the cost accounts proper lay in the fact that the latter were analytic, while the former were mostly synthetic. As he stated it:

> Cost accounts endeavor to arrive at the net result of manufacturing by an analysis—a separating of all details and particulars of costs—showing in the end, as it were, a *series of small trading or profit and loss accounts.* Commercial accounts aim at grouping together the results, not of each item of work, but each class of expenditure.[24]

It might be noted, in connection with the "small" profit and loss accounts mentioned by Pedder, that the entering of sales and returns in the cost records was almost invariably a feature of those English cost systems which were being described during the decade under discussion. In essence, then, those authorities really recommended the use of two sets of books, each containing somewhat the same information, except as to details. This last conclusion is borne out by Pedder's remarks that both systems (cost and general records) should arrive at the same results, except for such minor inaccuracies as the difference between overhead allocated and incurred.

While the preceding statements and conclusions hold true so far as the English techniques in general are concerned, one other development in that country should not be overlooked. This was the gradual evolution of a distinction between costing arrangements based on the job cost principle and those based on process cost systems. (See Chapter XI.) Several English authorities in the period under review began to treat rather extensively process cost accounting, and wherever that distinction was made there was more tendency to merge the cost and the financial records and accounts. Following this trend, there were, during the first decade of this century, several references to the use of a "manufacturing" account on the general books, which served for all essential purposes the same function as a work in process account.[25] The conclusion is that it seemed easier for the English cost experts to recognize the advantages and techniques of coördinating the accounts under process cost conditions than under other circumstances.

The Canadian viewpoint around the turn of the century was given by Eddis and Tindall in 1902. It was their opinion that although the cost accounts themselves should be kept apart, they should, nevertheless, form an integral division of the ordinary commercial books. In addition, they should be so designed as to permit their balancing in conjunction with the commercial accounts. Following the English practice of the period, they divided the general costing systems into what are now called job costs and process costs arrangements. In order to obtain the tie-in, they recommended the use of a cost ledger account on the general ledger; the general ledger was merely a summary record of all the details which had previously been entered on the cost ledger itself. As each job was finished a separate record was kept for it in the cost ledger, and at periodic intervals, say a week or month, all the completed jobs were summarized on a schedule, and manufactured stock was debited while the cost ledger account was credited. The cost ledger account was thus a sort of work in process account. On the debit side it had columns for date, particulars, folio, factory wages, material, direct expenses, factory expenses, and total; while on the credit side were to be found columns for date, particulars, wages, material, direct expenses, estimated factory expenses, and total. The use of this scheme permitted, then, the subdivision of the jobs into their cost components.[26] The debit side was posted from the purchases journal and the cash payments book, in total, each six months. The uncompleted work was carried forward in this cost ledger account, by elements of cost; these two authorities, however, were indefinite as to how the amount of goods in process was to be determined. Supposedly, though, the totals of the job accounts in the cost ledger itself would give the desired information. Incidentally, the difference between the amount of the factory expenses column of the cost ledger (which showed the total overhead incurred) and the estimated expenses (credit) column (which showed the amount allocated to jobs) was closed out to the "trading"[27] account at the close of the fiscal period of six months. In general, therefore, the conclusion must be drawn that the Canadian authorities dismissed as being entirely inadequate the nonintegrated systems which had been advocated so strenuously by the English.

Attention should be turned now to developments in the United States. The various American authorities were somewhat divided as to the procedures to be employed; that is to say, some advocated the coördination and some opposed it and there was less uniformity of opinion than in England. A few experts soon began to break away from the two-sets-of-accounts idea, but the trend took place comparatively slowly. The views of J. E. Sterritt might be cited as an illustration of the non-integrationists group. In an address before the Pennsylvania Institute of Certified Public Accountants in 1903, he argued along practically the same lines as Stanley Pedder.[28] Sterritt, however, preceded Pedder by two years, and recommended the maintenance of two entirely distinct systems of books. He did mention that in a few instances ("almost unworthy of consideration")[29] the cost books could be coördinated with the financial ledger. The financial ledger accounts were to be arranged, however, so as to facilitate the collection of data which would be needed by the cost clerks; the two were to work along together "as a harmonious whole." In summary, it was Sterritt's opinion that the ideal system of cost accounts, even though separate, should "use the checks and balances of double entry, and reassemble the totals shown by the financial books in such a plan as will show the cost of the article produced, not only in total, but in its constituent elements."[30] Unfortunately, he did not give any other details about the topic under discussion.

H. L. C. Hall was even more certain that the cost system should be extramural to the commercial ledger or accounts. In fact, according to him, the functions of the former usually ended where those of the latter started. To quote: "The cost accounts are in no wise a part of general accounts,"[31] and no complex set of books was usually required to ascertain costs.

At about that same period, the integration ideas of the Canadians, Eddis and Tindall, began to filter into this country. H. C. M. Vedder, for instance, described a coördination system similar to theirs. On the main ledger an account called "manufacturing" was to be established which controlled the cost ledger; it was thus a work in process account, and was handled in exactly the same way as that account is handled at the present time. Vedder's discussion was rather general in scope, but a person with some prior knowledge of what he was attempting to do would not have had much difficulty in understanding his exact procedure.[32]

Other American authorities soon began to build on, or to adopt in toto, the ideas of Vedder. John Whitmore, who elaborated upon and explained in considerable detail the costing system advanced by A. Hamilton Church, adopted the manufacturing account (work in process) arrangement for controlling the factory cost sheets.[33] Church had neglected to discuss this important subject when he wrote his earlier series of articles in 1901.[34] Since there was little that was new in Whitmore's contribution it may be passed over briefly at this time. It is sufficient to point out that he emphasized the importance of synthesizing the cost and the general accounts, as well as providing for the flow of costs through the ledger, through a series of journal entries and the maintenance of the necessary detailed subsidiary ledgers.

By 1908 cost experts in this country were referring to the "production ledger" and the "general ledger," not definitely tied in, however, with each other, even though the germ of the idea was present. One authority, C. M. Day, for example, in discussing the nature of the production ledger, listed the following accounts which might be maintained on it: general ledger account, work in process account, material account, labor account, and production expenses. The general ledger account was to have whatever balance was necessary to establish a self-balancing "production ledger."[35] So far as the general ledger itself was concerned, no details were supplied as to the nature of the offsetting accounts, if any, which might be opened. While there was thus much that was vague and obscure about this accountant's explanations, he did add a further notion in connection with the development of the coördination technique.

By the end of the first decade of this century, therefore, cost accountants in this country were generally recommending for factories the adoption of an integrated system of accounts in which the flow of costs would be shown on the ledger.[36] In spite of this advanced procedure, however, the various authorities who treated the subject had considerable difficulty in devising a system of interlocking ledgers for use in case, for some reason or another, the factory ledger was to be kept in a separate place or in different hands. C. M. Day had hinted at the matter but his technique was defective in several respects. One of the best statements made before World War I regarding the advantages of integration was given by F. S. Small in 1914: "The system herein described and illustrated does not separate the regular bookkeeping from the cost work, but inaugurates the cost work as a part of the general accounting. The reason for so doing is that the profit and loss figures shown in reports of costs and the balance sheet of the same date must correspond, whereas in other systems not so combined, the accuracy of the cost accounting reports cannot be proved, there being no balance sheets made at corresponding dates."[37]

The viewpoint of the English authorities in the period immediately before the First World War was somewhat the same as that described for the years around the turn of the century, except that there was more emphasis on the reconciliation of the cost accounts as such and the financial books. Moreover, a deflective note began to appear in some of their discussions. W. Strachan, for instance, although recommending the avoidance of the procedures which intermingled cost accounts with the general financial records, emphasized the "blending and the proving" of the results, as well as the comparison of the total costs as shown by each system.[38] L. W. Hawkins, on the other hand, frankly recognized the advantages to be derived from the integration technique; but he overstated the difficulties involved, and as a result, in the end, concluded that a dual system was the best.[39] He seemed to think, too, that the coördination would require a triple entry procedure. As a matter of fact, his own suggested accounting involved more entries than the later popular, fully-articulated method; but he would not recommend the use of the latter, preferring rather to devote several pages to a discussion of reconciliation schedules and all the elucidation necessary in connection therewith. Historically speaking, the comparison-and-reconciliation-technique of costing reached perhaps its finest development in the hands of Hawkins; he made provision for the determination and investigation of all the possible reasons why the costs accounts (separate) did not show the same details, totals, and results as the financial, or "general books," as he called them.[40] No stone was left unturned; his discussion of this topic alone covered some forty pages.

It should not be assumed that all English accountants during this period recommended the use of entirely separate factory accounts. L. R. Dicksee, for example, while concluding that a reciprocal account arrangement should not be adopted, did suggest that a tabulated adjustment account be set up on the cost ledger, ruled with distinctive columns for each separate class of items dealt with in the cost ledger. The advantage of such a scheme, according to Dicksee, was that the cost ledger could be very simply balanced, independently of the financial books, and the totals of the columns in the adjustment account reconciled with the general ledger. In addition, on the general ledger books, there was to be a work in process account, which would be used, however, only as an inventory account for balance sheet and profit and loss purposes; that is, at the end of a fiscal period, it would be closed to "trading" account, and the new inventory of unfinished goods debited to it, while the credit for the final inventory would go to "trading" account. Entries would be made in the work in progress account, therefore, only at the close of each fiscal period, and not continuously during the period, as is often done today, and as had been recommended by the integrationists. Dicksee's deflection, in the last analysis then, was more nominal than real; his views were not very different from those of Hawkins and other Englishmen of the period, especially in view of his statement that "the cost records are, as a rule, best kept quite separate from the financial books."[41] A few years later M. W. Jenkinson, a Chartered Accountant, made an effort to describe two types of work in progress accounts, which could be used, he insisted, for proving the clerical accuracy of the entries in the cost books. One of these was for the direct labor in process, and the other was for materials in process; both were to be handled somewhat as they would be handled today. This authority neglected to mention the third account of that sort which is sometimes used at the present time, that is, the burden in process; the nearest he came to it was in advocating the valuation of manufactured goods on hand at a balance sheet date at the total cost of manufacture. He was consistent, however, with his accounting procedure, when he suggested that partially completed goods should be valued at prime costs only, omitting the burden charge which might have been incurred. His system, then, contemplated the integration of the cost and the commercial records so far as prime costs were concerned, which step, in general, went much farther than most of the English cost authorities of the period. He deserves credit, therefore, for that development if for no other.[42]

American authorities, by the time the First World War started, were for the most part adopting the theory and practice of articulated costing arrangement along the same lines as are in general use today.[43] Statements were being made such as the following: "It must be borne in mind that, generally speaking, a system of factory accounting does not reach its highest efficiency unless there is this control exercised by the general ledger over the balances of the subsidiary ledgers."[44]

At about the same time, J. Lee Nicholson, in his *Cost Accounting* (1913), described a procedure for coördinating the cost and financial ledgers, allowing the two to be separate in a physical sense, yet tied together by means of reciprocal accounts, one on each ledger. The reciprocal accounts were the now familiar "factory ledger" and "general ledger" accounts. The use of these two accounts permitted each ledger to be independently balanced without destroying in any way the integration of the accounts involved. Nicholson recommended that the following accounts be established on the factory ledger: raw materials and supplies, labor, indirect expense, work in process, partfinished stock, finished stock, and general ledger. The flow of costs from the materials, labor, and indirect expense accounts was accurately described and illustrative journal entries were given. Costs allocated to goods finished were transferred from work in process to finished stock, and, finally, the cost-of-goods-sold entry was made. When he came to the description of the financial or general ledger, Nicholson mentioned that either of two techniques might be employed for articulating the accounts of a factory. One was along the line of the recommendations which had previously been made, that is, the use of just one ledger containing accounts with material, labor, indirect expenses, work in process, and finished stock. The second method, on the other hand, was the reciprocal account arrangement, which called for a factory ledger account on the general ledger. If the second procedure were adopted the details of the costs would be found in the factory ledger, but the factory ledger was fully controlled by the general accounting office.[45] This last point, then, was the essential difference (although there were others) between the technique recommended by this American authority and that which had been almost continuously proposed by the English cost experts.

It was not very long, after Nicholson's exposition, before other writers began to consider various refinements in his technique. Stephen Gilman, for example, recommended the use of three work in process accounts instead of the usual one. Jenkinson, the Englishman, had suggested this some two years before; but Gilman decided that if three were used—one for each element of cost—more data would be currently available regarding the profits and financial condition of a firm. Each one of them, too, would act somewhat as a control, and mistakes or errors could be found with greater ease.[46] Other than these last advantages, Gilman's technique was similar to that of Nicholson.[47]

William Kent, in 1918, proposed a rather novel control account arrangement which might be considered at this point, although it is not of any great historical importance. It was his suggestion that not one, but two control accounts be opened on the "general books." The first was to be called "factory plant," and was to be used to record the company's investment in the permanent equipment of the factory, such as the land, buildings, and machinery. In reality, this appeared to be merely a control account for the factory fixed assets, the details of which would be kept at the factory itself. The second of the control accounts on the general books was given the name "factory operations," and it would be charged with all the cash sent to the factory for pay rolls, incidental costs, and other charges which the factory had to bear. The factory operations account would be credited (and here is where Kent differed to some extent from Nicholson) with the "value" of the products shipped from the plant. According to Kent, there were several sorts of "values" which might be adopted;[48] either the so-called "factory cost or the cost of sales"[49] might be used, depending upon the desire of the management. There were, he stated, three types of factory costs, namely, actual, recorded, and normal; he did not explain, however, just exactly what he meant by the terms. As for the cost of sales, there were also several possibilities. For example, the catalogue list price could be used, less an estimated percentage to cover trade discounts and selling and administrative expenses. A second possibility was the use of actual selling prices less a fixed percentage, or a percentage varying with business conditions (prosperity and depression); while still a third "value" might be the total of the charges against the factory operations account "during a month, or other fiscal period, plus the decrease, or minus the increase, of the inventory during that period."[50] Although Kent did not discuss the matter of "values" further, it was not so easy a problem as he implied. In fact, the use of any of the "values" except factory cost would have caused a considerable number of complications which he slighted entirely. Evidently what he had in mind in this connection was to charge the factory operations account with all the costs incurred at the factory, and to credit it for the output on one of the several bases listed above. But what was to happen to the account at the end of a period? Where were the factory inventory accounts to be located? Kent did not answer either of these two questions, even though they were vital to the problem.

The English cost authorities after the First World War still recommended the disadunation of the cost and general books. Their ideas reached perhaps their finest development in E. T. Elbourne's *Factory Administration and Cost Accounts.* His system not only contemplated the separation of the factory records, but also was so independent and self-contained that balance sheets, profit and loss statements and financial accounts could be compiled from them. In a word, he advocated the use of a dual set of accounts. He was aware that such a procedure would take more work and be more expensive, but he thought that the overlapping and duplication was well worth any additional trouble. His reasoning was interesting, even though partially fallacious:

> Such duplication or overlapping that may seem to exist is justified on the two grounds of (1) independence of each set of accounts—cost and financial; (2) the summarizing effected by the manufacturing ledger involves practically no more work than if the cost ledger were developed to provide the condensed information required for the financial accounts.[51]

He did not think it possible, it appears, to maintain an integrated system of accounts; his cost records, moreover, were so complete that he did not bother very much about reconciling any differences between the two sets of books. In fact, the financial or commercial records would be quite incidental under his scheme; he did not even discuss them at any length. In summary, it was his opinion that the interlocking technique was too difficult to carry out in practice, even though perhaps the more desirable procedure in theory, and, as he stated it: "The difficulties are all dissolved by having a self-contained cost accounting system."[52] Interestingly enough, however, his discussion was strikingly more complex than that of his American contemporaries.

By 1924, so much progress had been made that one American authority, James L. Dohr, was able to state:[53] ". . . some cases will be met in which the cost accounts are not only kept in a separate ledger from the general accounts, but in addition are not in any way connected with, or controlled by, the general accounts. . . . This scheme has very little to commend it, in that the costs so determined do not have the advantage of being verified by the general accounts and are consequently less apt to be accurate."

The mechanisms and the techniques for the adunation of the cost and financial books were now complete, at least in so far as this country was concerned; few important developments have taken place since the early 1920's. Various statistical costing devices have been perfected, especially in connection with the use of tabulating machines, but these involved no new principles. In addition, certain supplementary accounting arrangements have been advocated from time to time, such as the handling of the imputed interest on investment charge, external to the main cost books, and not integrated with them.[54] All of these more recent trends are interesting developments, but are not of any great importance in connection with the subject matter of the present chapter.[55]

Before concluding this chapter it might be appropriate to quote from the works of one of the modern observers of the integration problem, Katsuji Yamashita; he called his technique the "Third Form of the Profit and Loss System":

> Through this last form of bookkeeping system, that is, by the complete whole incorporation of cost accounting to the financial accounting of the manufacturing enterprise, it became possible for us to calculate industrial income accurately, which method is no

other than the individualized accounting of industrial accounting. It is neither the system of simple periodic profit and loss accounting nor the system of individual profit and loss accounting. It rejects both systems, but it is a new system of profit and loss accounting incorporating both systems into one organic whole. This we may characterize as the third form of the profit and loss accounting system. The periodic profit and loss accounting system that first developed as the calculation of commercial income is now assuming, from the necessity of meeting the demands of calculating the industrial income, a form commensurate with the calculation of modern industrial income, and the over-all periodic profit and loss accounting system is assuming an individualized acounting method. This is the present tendency of development of the profit and loss accounting system.[56]

EXECUTORSHIP REPORTING SOME HISTORICAL NOTES

Leon E. Hay

EXECUTORSHIP REPORTING—SOME
HISTORICAL NOTES

Leon E. Hay

Associate Professor, Indiana University

THE earliest example of an executorship accounting report of which we have record is one prepared by the executors of the estate of Eleanor, consort of Edward I of England, who died in 1290 A.D. The concept of executorship is, of course, much older than that. Reppy and Tompkins report that:

Documents resembling a will were in existence in Egypt five thousand years ago. The Code of Hammaurabi, King of Babylon 2285–2242 B.C., provided for both testate and intestate succession, and instruments classed as wills seem to have been recognized in Assyria, Hebrew countries, Greece, and Rome. By the time of Justinian's Code, 534 A.D., the Romans had evolved a will which in many ways, resembled the will which is recognized in modern American and English law.[1]

Legal Background

The Roman law of wills allowed the testator to name a *fiduciarius haeres* to act as his personal representative after death. The *haeres* discharged his duties under the supervision of a magistrate. It is known that the *haeres* was required to submit an inventory of the assets of the estate if he wished to limit his liability for the debts of the decedent to the value of the assets; whether any other accounting reports were required does not seem to be known.

Roman legal concepts were disseminated over the world as known at that time. In common with other institutions they were all but lost sight of for several hundred years. Legal historians say that in England, in Anglo-Saxon times and for two hundred fifty years after the Conquest, there was no such thing as a general representative of a decedent.[2] Executors were known, but their duties were restricted, until the thirteenth century, to the dis-

tribution of the personal property bequeathed by the decedent. The distribution of personal property was under the jurisdiction of the ecclesiastical courts, and if the decedent did not leave a valid testament (as the instrument in which a person directed the disposition of his personal property was called), or if the executor named in the testament could not serve, the estate was administered by the bishop of the diocese in which the property was located. In this period, the family of the decedent was liable for his debts whether or not he left sufficient assets to pay them. This rule worked a hardship on the heirs in many cases, especially since the officers of the ecclesiastical courts, if not the bishops themselves, were often overzealous in attempting to aggrandize the holdings of the Church (or their own personal fortunes) by retaining the assets of the decedent and leaving the liabilities for the heirs.[3]

In the thirteenth century executors were given the right by the second Statute of Westminster (13 Edw. I, c. 23) to sue debtors of the estate to collect the amount owing. The office of administrator was created in 1357 by the Statute of 31 Edw. III in an effort to alleviate the previously described abuses in the administration of intestate estates. In this period neither administrators nor executors were required by statute to submit inventories and accounts for all estates probated; however, collections of wills written in the fourteenth and following centuries indicate

---

[1] Alison Reppy and Leslie J. Tompkins, *Historical and Statutory Background of The Law of Wills, Descent and Distribution*, Probate and Administration (Chicago: Callaghan and Company, 1928) p. 14.
[2] *Ibid.*, p. 130.
[3] *Ibid.*, p. 116.

that inventories were frequently filed and accounts occasionally filed, apparently in compliance with court orders. It was not until 1670 that administrators were required by statute (22 & 23 Cor. II, c. 10) to prepare inventories and accounts, and 1705 (4 Anne, c. 16) that the same was required of executors. The ecclesiastical courts retained jurisdiction over the transfer of personal property until 1857 when the Court of Probate Act established a Court of Probate and gave it jurisdiction over decedents' property both real and personal.

For almost eight centuries before 1857 the distribution of real property of a decedent had been under the jurisdiction of civil courts. The decedent's wishes as to the disposition of his real property were expressed in a document called a "will." (The term today includes the former meanings of both "will" and "testament.") The influence of the feudal system was such that, before the passage of the Statute of Wills (32 Henry VIII, 1540), civil courts in many sections of England disregarded the will and distributed the real property according to local laws and customs. Both before and after the passage of the Statute of Wills, executors or administrators did not take title to real estate. The same is generally true today in the United States.

Early English Executorship Reports

Executors in England during most of the eight-century period under discussion seem, in general, to have prepared their accounts in narrative form. The report of the executors of the estate of Eleanor of England, referred to in the opening sentence of this article, was prepared on a parchment roll. It is not illustrated in any books locally available, but it is said to show the payments for each day in narrative form, ". . . each day, week, and month being totaled up at the end, and the gross amount of each section being carried out

into the margin, in a sort of elementary money column."[4] Brown indicates that this form of report was typical of the accounting reports prepared in thirteenth century England.[5] Clearly differentiated money columns did not come into general use in English executorship reporting for several centuries, judging from executors' statements included in collections of English wills of the fourteenth through nineteenth centuries.[6]

Two fifteenth century executors' statements are particularly interesting as examples of the evolution of reporting technique. The first, that of the estate of Bishop Skirlaw, who died in 1406, presents the inventory and report in narrative form with no clear separation between the two documents. No money columns are used, nor is there much grouping of like items, although the late bishop had been immensely wealthy and left a long will full of detailed directions as to the duties of the executors. The account apparently satisfied the court, for at the end of it is the inscription, "Compotus redditus et Executores dismissi 1 Feb 1407."[7]

In contrast with the report of Bishop Skirlaw's executors is that of the executors of Canon Duffield of York, who died in 1452. The executors of this estate evidently had access to better accounting advice than the ones of Bishop Skirlaw's estate because like items are listed in paragraph form, one after another within each paragraph, with the amounts of each shown. The "summa" of the amounts listed in each paragraph is entered at the end of the

[4] Arthur H. Woolf, *A Short History of Accountants and Accountancy* (London: Gee and Company, 1912), p. 94.
[5] Richard Brown, *A History of Accounting and Accountants* (Edinburgh: T. C. and E. C. Jack, 1905), p. 54.
[6] Various volumes of publications of the Surtees Society, the Selden Society, the Chetnam Society, and other English historical societies are devoted to wills and inventories of this period.
[7] These documents are reproduced in *Testamenta Eboracensia, Part I* (London: Surtees Society, 1836), pp. 306–325.

paragraph. The grand total is shown at the end of the statement. Money columns were not used in this statement either, however.[8]

The form of accounting report known as the "charge and discharge statement", which many writers have erroneously said was the form customarily used by English executors, was developed in Scotland in the fifteenth century by government accountants.[9] It was used in succeeding centuries by Scottish executors [10] and, even in the twentieth century, is said to be the form customarily used there. It was adopted by stewards of English manors and by accountants for various English governmental bodies, but does not appear to have been adopted on any large scale by English executors. The latter seem to have clung to the narrative form of statement until the methodology of double entry bookkeeping and the practice of drawing statements from ledger accounts became generally accepted.

Accounting histories say that double entry bookkeeping was introduced into England in the sixteenth century and the preparation of statements from ledger accounts was introduced in the seventeenth century.[11] Generally, histories discuss only commercial accounting and do not mention the adoption of such ideas in the area of executorship accounting. An examination of eighteenth and nineteenth century English accounting texts and collections of wills of that era indicates that executors' accounts were kept in double entry form in the eighteenth century, but that narrative statements were customarily used until the nineteenth century.[12] From that time until the present, English executors have apparently generally submitted their statements in the form of ledger accounts.[13]

Early Executorship Reporting in the United States

English usages in both law and accounting were transplanted to the colonies in North America in the seventeenth and eighteenth centuries. English influence continued to be felt strongly in the nineteenth century and even in the early part of the twentieth, particularly in accounting. It is not surprising then that much of the discussion in preceding pages as to English executorship accounting holds true for American executorship accounting.

Historical societies in the United States have published many volumes of probate records. The earliest are those of Essex County, Massachusetts, for the period of 1635 to 1681.[14] The Essex County records consist of wills and inventories, but no executors' accounts can be found—apparently the court of that colony did not require them. The Provincial Court of Maryland did, however. In the records of that tribunal, under the date of "11 Octobr 1650" there is the following entry:

John Thumbleby Admr of Peter Mackarell ac-

---

[8] This report is reproduced in *Testamenta Eboracensia, Part III* (London: Surtees Society, 1864), pp. 125–152. The documents are in Latin, of course, but an English translation of the column headings of this statement is given by W. S. Holdsworth, *A History of English Law* (London: Methuen & Co., 1909), III, pp. 466–467.

[9] The terms "charge" and "discharge" are found in reports of an earlier date, but Brown, *op. cit.*, p. 58, states that the earliest example of a statement in the form called "charge and discharge" was that of the Lord High Treasurer of Scotland for the period 4 August 1473 to 1 December 1474.

[10] George Lisle, editor, *Encyclopedia of Accounting* (Edinburgh and London: William Green and Sons, 1903), II, p. 54.

[11] A. C. Littleton, *Accounting Evolution to 1900* (New York: American Institute Publishing Co., Inc., 1933), pp. 98, 130–140. Also Brown, *op. cit.*, pp. 126, 152–154.

[12] Two of the more interesting accounting texts are William Weston's *The Complete Merchant's Clerk* (London: R. Griffiths, 1754), and Thomas Dilworth's *The Young Bookkeeper's Assistant*, 12th ed. (London: A. Miller, 1792), or "new edition" (London: Thomas Wilson & Sons, 1822). Good references for late nineteenth century and early twentieth century practices are the various editions of Lawrence R. Dicksee's *Advanced Accounting* (London: Gee and Co.), Roger N. Carter's *The Student's Guide to Executorship Accounts* (London: Gee and Co., 1899), and Oswald Holt Caldicott's *Executorship Accounts*, 3rd ed. (London: Gee and Company, 1906).

[13] Lisle, *op. cit.*, p. 54, and F. Sewell Bray and Thomas Kenny, "Executorship Accounting Reconsidered," *Accounting Research*, I (1950), pp. 403–442.

[14] *Probate Records of Essex County, Massachusetts*, (Salem: Essex Institute, 1917) Vol. I, 1635–1664; Vol. II, 1665–1674; Vol. III, 1675–1681.

cording to a former order this day pduced his Accompt concerning the sayd estate to the court and prayed for his Quiet est. And the said Accompt being pvsed by the Court and found to ballance the totall of the Inventory and publique Proclamacon being made thereof in open court and noe obieccon made to the contrary The Court allowes of the Accompt and doth order that the Admr may have his Quietus est and the Bond taken for his true Administracon to bee voide and Cancelled.[15]

The "Accompt" is reproduced below the court order. It is merely a listing of items such as "by pd Willm Assiter by Bill 255" and "By pd for funerall charges 400." The items are not classified in any discernible manner, but are simply totaled.

The duties of Administrators in the colony of New York were set forth by "An Act for the superviseing Intestates Estates and Regulateing the Probate of Wills and granting of Letter of Administracon" dated November 11, 1692. It does not require the administrator or executor to submit either an inventory or an account. Courts evidently required an inventory in some cases, however, for inventories are found in conjunction with some wills.[16]

Judging from available records, the courts of Connecticut were comparatively strict about requiring inventories and accounts. An entry in the probate records of "4 January 1713–14" says:

John Humphrey and Samuel Pettebone of Simsbury, Adms. on the estate of John Mills, late of Simsbury Decd, exhibited an Account of their Adms:

	£ s d
Inventory	120-15-06
The Real part whereof is	75-10-00
The Debts and Charges	30-15-00
There remains to be distributed	92-06-00
Account Allowed. Order to Dist:[17]	

The arrangement of the above account is quite neat, particularly for that time, but it seems to be lacking in clarity of explanation and accuracy of arithmetic.

The examples of eighteenth century American executors' accounting reports reproduced or described above seem to be typical of the ones which are published in compilations of colonial wills. If these compilations contain statements representative of the ones prepared in that century, and there is no reason to believe that they do not, it may be said that the level of accounting skill displayed by executors in America was no higher than that displayed by their contemporaries in England. In both countries executors' reports were generally little more than narratives. In neither country was the Charge and Discharge statement or the ledger account form of statement in general use.

The earliest American accounting text examined which contained a discussion of executorship accounting was a copy of *North American Accountant* by P. Duff, published in 1848.[18] Duff's treatment of estate accounting is similar to that of English authors of the time. He described the entries to be made for many different types of transactions and gave reasons for the entries he described, reasons which are still generally considered sound. Duff did not, however, present any suggestions as to the form of report to be rendered to the probate court, nor even mention that such a report was required.

Eighteen years after Duff's text appeared, Bryant, Stratton, and Packard published a book, *Bryant and Stratton's Counting House Bookkeeping*,[19] which appears to be the earliest American text to mention executorship reporting. The mention is brief, indeed, and the authors do not illustrate or describe any particular form

---

[15] William H. Browne, editor, *Archives of Maryland: Judicial and Testamentary Business of the Provincial Court 1649/50–1657* (Baltimore: Maryland Historical Society, 1891), p. 35.

[16] *Early Records of Albany: Mortgages, 1658–60, and Wills, 1681–1765* (Albany: The University of the State of New York, 1919).

[17] Charles W. Manwaring, *Early Connecticut Probate Records* (Hartford: Charles W. Manwaring, 1904), p. 573.

[18] P. Duff, *North American Accountant: Single and Double Entry Bookkeeping* (New York: Harper & Brothers, 1848).

[19] H. B. Bryant, H. D. Stratton, and S. S. Packard, *Bryant and Stratton's Counting House Bookkeeping* (New York: Ivison, Phinney, Blakeman & Company, 1866).

of report to the court of jurisdiction or to the heirs.

In the early years of the twentieth century the subjects of executorship accounting and reporting enjoyed a wide popularity in American accounting literature. In 1902 the Accountants' Guide for *Executors, Administrators, Assignees, Receivers* and *Trustees*, by Francis Gottsberger, was published.[20] Joseph Hardcastle's lectures before the New York University School of Commerce, Accounts, and Finance on "Accounts of Executors and Testamentary Trusts," were published in book form in 1903.[21] John R. Loomis contributed a comprehensive article on "Contents and Mode of Stating Executors' Accounts" to *The Journal of Accountancy* in 1907.[22] The efforts of these three men furnished a basis for Charles E. Sprague's chapter on "Fiduciary Accounts" in his text, *The Philosophy of Accounts*, published in 1908.[23] Gottsberger, Hardcastle, Loomis, and Sprague set the pattern used by most authors down to the present time.

[20] New York: George S. Peck, 1902.
[21] New York: New York University, 1903.
[22] Vol. III, pp. 219–232.
[23] New York: C. E. Sprague, 1908.

THE AUDITOR AND THE
BRITISH COMPANIES ACTS

Leonard W. Hein

THE AUDITOR AND THE BRITISH COMPANIES ACTS

Leonard W. Hein*

I. INTRODUCTION

THE leaders of the accounting profession in the United States have frequently expressed the fear that the profession may some day be subjected to onerous statutory control. The profession in Great Britain at the present time does practice under a more detailed statutory control than that imposed upon accountants in the United States. This situation provides a clinical case worthy of study.

The controls under consideration are those imposed by the British Companies Act. This Act imposes controls on several phases of the practice of the accountant, *e.g.*, (1) the auditor, (2) the balance sheet, (3) the income statement, (4) consolidations, (5) prospectuses, and (6) dissolutions. This paper is confined to those concerning the auditor. The controls affecting the auditor may be subdivided into: (1) qualifications; (2) appointment, tenure, and remuneration; and (3) duties and reports.

The time period selected for study is that beginning in 1844 and ending with the present time. The year 1844 was selected as the beginning date because in that year the modern era of business incorporation methods came into existence, *i.e.*, a business could be incorporated merely by a formal process of registration.

II. THE QUALIFICATIONS OF THE AUDITOR

That the quality of an audit of a complex set of transactions is likely to be no better than the qualifications of the auditor performing the audit would appear to be a self-evident truism. Yet this is a quite modern concept that has emerged in comparatively recent times. Prior to 1844, the general body of proprietors tended to elect two groups of representatives. The one, designated as the managers, operated the enterprise; the other, called the auditors, ascertained that the results of the managerial activities were properly reported back to the main body of proprietors Both groups were ordinarily selected from the members of the company. The managers were likely to be selected from those who were prominent in organizing the company, and hence presumably possessed some managerial ability. There is little to indicate that the auditors were selected on the basis of their aptitude for the position.

The first statute to be considered in the period 1844 to the present is the Act of 1844 entitled "An Act for the Registration, Incorporation, and Regulation of Joint Stock Companies."[1] Section 38 of this Act provided for the appointment of "One or more Auditors of the Accounts of the Company," but the Act was completely silent as to who could serve in the position(s) or what his (their) qualifications should be.

When the Gladstone Committee considered the question of joint stock company legislation from 1841 to 1843, none of the witnesses recommended that the auditors should have any special qualifications. In fact, the only mention of such qualifications was a denial that the company employed a public accountant in the capacity of auditor.[2]

In 1855, the important privilege of limited liability was granted to all companies

---

* Leonard W. Hein is Associate Professor of Accounting at Los Angeles State College.
[1] 7 & 8 Victoria, c. 110 (1844).
[2] "Report of the Select Committee on Joint Stock Companies," House of Commons, *Sessional Papers* 1844 (119) VII, 1, q. 1908.

willing to register under the Act of 1855.[3] The framers of this Act attached increased importance to the position of auditor, in the hope of protecting third parties from being harmed by their inability to go beyond the assets of the company to the personal assets of the proprietors in the event of insolvency. Section 14 of the Act required that at least one of the auditors be approved by the Board of Trade, but set no necessary qualifications to receive such approval.

The Act of 1855 was repealed in 1856, and a new, liberal concept of company law was embodied in the Act of 1856.[4] The precept set forth by Robert Lowe, then Vice President of the Board of Trade, that "having given them a pattern the State leaves them to manage their own affairs and has no desire to force on these little republics any particular constitution,"[5] applied especially to accounting and auditing regulations. All compulsory controls of this nature were eliminated, and only model regulations supplied. The original bill was amended and rewritten four times, but this part remained unchanged.[6] The model regulations, even though not compulsory, did introduce the novel concept that "the Auditors need not be Shareholders in the Company."[7] This appears to be a significant departure from the idea that the position of auditor should consist of one segment of the company checking on another segment, and it appears to open the way for the position of auditor to be filled by professional accountants. The concept of independence was also introduced in this same article by stating that: "No Person is eligible as an Auditor who is interested otherwise than as a Shareholder in any Transaction of the Company; and no Director or other Officer of the Company is eligible during his Continuance in Office."

Audits did not become compulsory again until 1900.[8] Nevertheless, a number of attempts were made in the intervening years to reestablish, as compulsory, requirements similar to those contained in the Joint Stock Companies Act of 1844.[9] Probably induced by the failure of the City of Glasgow Bank in 1878, in which fraud was covered by falsification of its accounts, Parliament imposed such provisions on all banking companies registered with limited liability under the Companies Acts in 1879.[10] Some banks, incorporated under charter or by special act of Parliament, had operated under compulsory audit requirements prior to that date. It is interesting to note that the general manager of the National Bank of Liverpool, Ltd., when he gave testimony before the Select Committee on Limited Liability Acts, recommended that the compulsory audit be abolished.[11] Finally, in 1895, the Davey Committee recommended that the audit once again be made compulsory for all companies registered under the Companies Acts,[12] and this recommendation was accepted by Parliament in 1900.

During the period 1844 to 1906 little attention was given to the qualifications which an individual should possess in order to hold the position of auditor. In fact, for 44 years of this period (1856 to 1900) the appointment of an auditor was not compulsory for ordinary registered companies.

---

[3] 18 & 19 Victoria, c. 133 (1855).
[4] 19 & 20 Victoria, c. 47 (1856).
[5] Hansard, *Parliamentary Debates*, Third Series, Vol. CXL, col. 134 (1856).
[6] House of Commons, *Sessional Papers*, 1856 (2) IV, 181; 1856 (87) IV, 289; 1856 (152) IV, 347; 1856 (232) IV, 399.
[7] 19 & 20 Victoria, c. 47, Table B, art. 75.
[8] By the Companies Act, 1900, 63 & 64 Victoria, c. 48, sec. 23.
[9] *E.g.*, the Companies Amendment Bill, House of Commons, *Sessional Papers*, 1877 (45) I, 299 and the Companies Bill of 1884, *ibid.*, 1884 (38), II, 133.
[10] By the Companies Act, 1879, 42 & 43 Victoria, c. 76, sec. 7.
[11] "Report of the Select Committee on the Companies Acts," House of Commons, *Sessional Papers*, 1867 (329) X, 393, q. 1826.
[12] "Report of the Departmental Committee on Amendments to the Companies Acts, 1862 to 1890," *ibid.*, 1895 (c. 7779) LXXXVIII, 151.

As early as 1856, however, the possible usefulness of the professional accountant was officially recognized. The model articles included the clause that the auditors "may, at the Expense of the Company, employ Accountants or other Persons to assist him in investigating such Accounts.[13]

In 1906, another committee investigated needed changes in the Companies Acts. Twenty-three chambers of commerce from England, Scotland, and Wales submitted memoranda concerning auditors. Of these, six recommended that one or more of the auditors should be professional accountants.[14] Only one organization of professional accountants submitted a memorandum to this committee. It made a similar recommendation.[15] The Committee, however, did not include this recommendation in its report. Nevertheless, the bill introduced into Parliament, which in its preface stated that it represented the Committee's recommendations, contained the clause that "the auditors, one at least of whom, in the case of every company whose authorized capital amounts to fifty thousand pounds, shall be a person who publicly carries on the business of an accountant."[16] Standing Committee C of the House of Commons deleted this clause.[17]

The Wrenbury Committee, reporting in 1918, also failed to report favorably on this subject. It said, "We have made enquiry into the question whether the law should be amended by requiring that the auditors must have some and what professional qualification. We do not make any recommendation to that effect. We have not traced any mischief which requires remedy in the matter."[18] No legislation concerning auditors resulted from the Wrenbury report.

Seven years later another committee, the Greene Committee, took evidence preparatory to the enactment of new company legislation. One point of inquiry concerned the desirability of changing the clauses in the Companies Act which pertained to auditors. The majority of memoranda submitted by the witnesses either omitted comment on this point or stated that the existing requirements were satisfactory. Five memoranda did recommend that the auditors should possess professional qualifications. Three of these were memoranda submitted by organizations of professional accountants.[19] Only two non-accountant groups joined in the demand for increased statutory control over the qualifications of auditors appointed pursuant to the Companies Act.[20] Apparently this testimony was insufficient to convince the Committee, for it said in its report that, "Cases in which auditors fall below the level of their duty are few and far between."[21] Parliament apparently agreed with the Committee, for the Companies Act, 1928,[22] contained no clause requiring that auditors appointed pursuant to the Act have professional qualifications, nor did the Companies Act of 1929, into which the Companies Act of 1928 was consolidated prior to taking effect. The latter Act did prohibit three classes of persons from appointment as an auditor, viz., (1) a director or officer of the company, (2) a partner or an employee of an officer (except in the

---

[13] 19 & 20 Victoria, c. 47, Table B, art. 83.
[14] "Appendix to the Report of the Company Law Amendment Committee," House of Commons, *Sessional Papers*, 1906 (Cd. 3053) XCVII, 249.
[15] *Ibid.*, memorandum submitted by the Society of Accountants and Auditors.
[16] House of Commons, *Sessional Papers*, 1907 (208) I, 407. sec. 21(1).
[17] *Ibid.*, 1907 (321) I, 441, sec. 19(1)
[18] "Report of the Company Law Amendment Committee," *ibid.*, 1918 (Cd. 9138) VII, 727, par. 58.
[19] Departmental Committee on Amendments to the Companies Acts, *Minutes of Evidence* (London: H.M.S.O., 1925), the Joint Committee of Councils of Chartered Accountants of Scotland (app. U, par. 8), the Institute of Chartered Accountants in England and Wales (app. AA, par. 8b), and the Society of Incorporated Accountants and Auditors (app. FF, par. 8d).
[20] *Ibid.*, the Trust Companies (app. G, par. 6) and the Federation of British Industries (app. X, par. 8).
[21] "Report of Company Law Amendment Committee," House of Commons, *Sessional Papers*, 1926 (Cmd. 2657) IX, 477, par. 73.
[22] 18 & 19 George V, c. 45.

case of a private company), and (3) a body corporate.[23]

The Cohen Committee was appointed in 1942 to once again make recommendations for amending the Companies Act. It circulated a questionnaire to various organizations and individuals, requesting comments and suggestions on certain particulars, including "Appointment and functions of Auditors."[24] Not all respondents included this item in their memoranda. Some, of course, merely said that the existing clauses were satisfactory. Four accounting groups submitted memoranda. Of these, two made no recommendations concerning professional qualifications,[25] one recommended that future consideration be given to the problem,[26] and the fourth recommended that provision immediately be made to limit the position of auditor to professional accountants.[27] There is an explanation for this apparent lack of interest on the part of the societies of professional accountants. They were once again attempting to settle the problem of professional registration. However, the various parties were unable to agree on terms for registration, so no accounting regulatory bill was ever submitted to Parliament.

By this time other organizations and individuals were convinced of the desirability of restricting the position of auditor to professional accountants. Memoranda to this effect were submitted by legal societies,[28] by various industrial and business organizations,[29] and by governmental officials dealing directly with businesses.[30]

This time the Committee did concur, and included in its report the recommendation that to those persons ineligible for appointment as auditor of a company be added "a person who is not a member of any body membership of which has been designated by the Board of Trade as qualifying its members to audit the accounts of companies or who has not been designated

by the Board of Trade as qualified to audit the accounts of companies."[31] A clause to this effect was included in the Companies Act, 1947,[32] and then consolidated into the Companies Act, 1948,[33] which is the current statute. The societies recognized by the Board of Trade at this writing are: the Institute of Chartered Accountants in England and Wales, the Institute of Chartered Accountants in Ireland, the Institute of Chartered Accountants of Scotland, and the Association of Certified and Corporate Accountants.

The Companies Act has again been reconsidered, and the Jenkins Committee was appointed for this purpose.[34] The Committee, at this writing, had not completed its investigation and therefore had not yet published its report. It had, however, published some of the minutes of the evidence taken before it. The non-accounting organizations which have so far submitted evidence appear to be satisfied with the present clauses respecting the qualifications of auditors. The accounting societies have submitted several suggestions for change. Those which have been recognized by the

[23] 19 & 20 George V, c. 23, sec. 133.
[24] "Report of the Committee on Company Law Amendment," House of Commons, *Sessional Papers*, 1945 (Cmd. 6659), IV, 793.
[25] Committee on Company Law Amendment, *Minutes of Evidence* (London: H.M.S.O., 1941-43), the Association of Certified and Corporate Accountants (app. JJ, par. 46, p. 532) and the Joint Committee of Chartered Accountants of Scotland (app. OO, par. 12, p. 619).
[26] *Ibid.*, the Institute of Chartered Accountants in England and Wales, app. Z, par. 9(B), p. 390.
[27] *Ibid.*, the Society of Incorporated Accountants and Auditors, app. II, par. 58, p. 503.
[28] *Ibid.*, the Council of the Law Society (app. Q, par. 9; p. 240) and the General Council of Solicitors in Scotland (app. S, par. 7, p. 246).
[29] *Ibid.*, e.g., the Institute of Industrial Administration (app. K, par. 10, p. 135), the British Insurance Association (app. LL, par. 8A, p. 565), the Federation of British Industries (app. NN, par. 8, p. 597), etc.
[30] *Ibid.*, the Chief Registrar of Friendly Societies (app. E, par. 19, p. 45) and the Chief Registrar of Companies (Winding-Up) (app. K, par. 7, p. 120).
[31] "Reports," *op. cit.*, p. 67.
[32] 10 & 11 George VI, c. 47, sec. 23.
[33] 11 & 12 George VI, c. 38, sec. 161.
[34] Minute of the President of the Board of Trade dated January 5, 1960.

Board of Trade under section 161(1) of the Act of 1948 wish to have their names specifically mentioned in the Act.[35]

The Companies Act, 1948, section 161(1) (pertaining to qualifications of auditors) does not apply to certain companies known as "exempt private companies." These are mainly small, family corporations. The major accountancy bodies wish to have exempt private companies subject to the same auditing requirements as are public companies.[36] The Association of British Chambers of Commerce agrees with this position.[37] One "unrecognized" (*i.e.*, by the Board of Trade pursuant to the Companies Act) accounting society has taken exception to both positions. It would define qualified accountant as any member of an incorporated society;[38] or failing this, it suggests the setting up of two classes of recognized societies—one permitted to audit exempt private companies and one permitted to audit all others.[39]

III. THE AUDITORS' APPOINTMENT, TENURE, AND REMUNERATION

Appointment. The Joint Stock Companies Act of 1844 provided that one or more auditors be appointed at the annual meeting, and that at least one of these auditors were to be appointed by the shareholders. Should the auditor not be appointed on behalf of the shareholders, then, on the application of any shareholder, the Board of Trade was directed to appoint such an auditor.[40] This essentially sets forth in statutory form the method of appointment of auditors described by witnesses before the Gladstone Committee.[41]

The Joint Stock Companies Act, 1856 deleted all compulsory auditing requirements, but did include in its model articles provisions for electing one or more auditors at "their First Ordinary Meeting in each Year."[42] The specific provision that at least

one of the auditors would be selected by the shareholders was omitted, presumably because the term "elect" implied that all auditors would be so selected.

As a result of the Davey Committee Report of 1895, the Companies Act, 1900, provided for the compulsory election of auditors, in effect making a portion of the model articles of the Act of 1856 mandatory. Section 23 provided for such election at each annual general meeting, and for the appointment of an auditor by the Board of Trade if no auditor were appointed by the Company. In addition, the directors were granted the authority to appoint the first auditors, who would serve up to the first annual general meeting.

The Company Law Amendment Committee of 1906 recommended that a fourteen day notice of intention to change the present auditors be required and that the auditors and shareholders be sent such a notice.[43] Parliament agreed, and the Companies Act, 1907,[44] and the resulting consolidation act in 1908,[45] contained the clause:

A person, other than the retiring auditor, shall not be capable of being appointed auditor at an annual general meeting unless notice of an intention to nominate that person to the office of auditor has been given by a shareholder to the company not less than fourteen days before the annual general meeting, and the company shall

[35] Company Law Committee, Minutes of Evidence (London: H.M.S.O., 1961), the Association of Certified and Corporate Accountants (app. XXXIV, par. 71, p. 893), the Institute of Chartered Accountants of Scotland (app. XLVII, par. 22, p. 1340), and the Institute of Chartered Accountants in England and Wales (app. XLVIII, par. 183, p. 1424).
[36] *Ibid.*, app. XXXIV, par. 76, p. 894; app. XLVII, par. 22, p. 1341; and app. XLVIII, par. 201, p. 1427.
[37] *Ibid.*, app. XX, par. 22, p. 483.
[38] *Ibid.*, the Association of International Accountants Limited, app. XIX, p. 425.
[39] *Ibid.*, qq. 1999–2007, pp. 389–391.
[40] 7 & 8 Victoria, c. 110, sec. 38.
[41] "Report," *op. cit.*, qq. 1902–1913.
[42] 19 & 20 Victoria, c. 47, Table B, art. 77.
[43] "Report," *op. cit.*, par. 44.
[44] 7 Edward VII, c. 50, sec. 21(4).
[45] 8 Edward VII, c. 69, sec. 112(4).

send a copy of any such notice to the retiring auditor, and shall give notice thereof to the shareholders . . . not less than seven days before the annual general meeting.

A point noted by the witnesses before the Cohen Committee was that the clause of the 1908 Act cited above required that the auditor was to be given notice of intention to nominate someone in his place, but no notice was required if the intention was merely to drop an auditor, *e.g.*, if there were several auditors and one or more were to be dropped. The accounting profession considered this point quite important.[46] It was further recommended that in the absence of a substantive resolution to replace or drop an auditor that he should be deemed to be reelected.[47]

The legal authority to appoint the auditor(s) has thus resided in the shareholders. In actual practice, however, the directors would select the auditors and the shareholders in general meeting would ratify, or, perhaps more truly, "rubber stamp," this selection. A number of witnesses before the Cohen Committee noted that this situation constituted a non-functioning of the law as written. One such witness, Charles Norton a veteran of thirty years of practice in company law, suggested the selection of the auditor be taken completely away from the directors and placed in the hands of a shareholders' committee "of say the 50 largest shareholders."[48]

This particular suggestion was not adopted, but the Cohen Committee did recommend that the seven day notice of intention to change auditors be increased to twenty-one days, and that a retiring auditor be deemed reelected unless notice of intention to not reappoint him is given not less than twenty-eight days before the annual general meeting.[49] Parliament adopted the principle of requiring notice to drop an auditor,[50] but reduced the notice period to fourteen days in both cases.[51]

The evidence recently taken before the Jenkins Committee tends to indicate general satisfaction with the methods for appointing auditors contained in the Companies Act, 1948. One dissident opinion is worthy of note. The Institute of Chartered Accountants in England and Wales reversed its position concerning the automatic reappointment of auditors saying, "There is no necessity for the automatic reappointment procedure and its removal would facilitate the clarification of the position of partnership firms."[52]

Tenure. The Joint Stock Companies Act of 1844 provided that the auditor(s) be appointed annually at a general meeting,[53] hence implying that the tenure of office was to be from one annual meeting to the next. This concept of one year's tenure in office has, in general, prevailed to this day.[54] The Act of 1844 was silent concerning the eligibility of the auditor for reappointment, but the model articles of the Act of 1856, although not compulsory, did specifically provide for such eligibility.[55] This clause was not expressly included in the body of a companies act until the Act of 1907.[56] Nevertheless, reappointment of the existing auditors, as long as their performance was satisfactory, became fairly customary.

Testimony taken before the 1906 Amendment Committee indicated, however, that failure to reappoint the auditors could point to unsatisfactory performance on the part of the directors as well as on

---

[46] "Report," *op. cit.*, the Institute of Chartered Accountants in England & Wales (app. Z, par. 9, p. 390).
[47] *Ibid.*
[48] *Ibid.*, app. N, par. 10, p. 174.
[49] "Report," *op. cit.*, p. 67.
[50] Companies Act, 1947, 10 & 11 George VI, c. 47, sec. 24(3).
[51] *Ibid.*, sec. 2(4)(c).
[52] *Minutes, op. cit.*, app. XLVIII, par. 186, p. 1427.
[53] 7 & 8 Victoria, c. 110, sec. 38.
[54] Companies Act, 1948, 11 & 12 George VI, c. 38, sec. 159(1).
[55] 19 & 20 Victoria, c. 47, Table B, art. 79.
[56] 7 Edward VII, c. 50, sec. 21(4).

the part of the auditors. The Chamber of Commerce of Manchester stated:

> The Board are of the opinion that the auditor should be entitled to have notice of and attend and take part in every general meeting in the same manner as if he were a shareholder, but not so as to have any vote by virtue of his office. This would tend to prevent an auditor being removed from his office because of his refusal to act in the manner desired by a board of directors, at any rate without its being made known to the shareholders generally why his removal is contemplated.[57]

A somewhat similar opinion was expressed by the Chamber of Commerce of Newport[58] and by the Society of Accountants and Auditors.[59] No action on this point was taken either by the Committee or by Parliament at this time, nor did the Greene Committee Report of 1926 recommend action. Nevertheless, the Act of 1929 included the clause:

> The auditors of a company shall be entitled to attend any general meeting of the company at which any accounts which have been examined or reported on by them are to be laid before the company and to make any statement or explanation they desire with respect to the accounts.[60]

This, of course, fell somewhat short of that which the witnesses in 1906 had deemed necessary. The witnesses before the Cohen Committee, 1943, again took up the need to protect the auditors in those cases where their reappointment was jeopardized because of adverse criticism of the managers or directors. The Chief Registrar of Friendly Societies, for example, recommended that auditors be given a "right of appeal against dismissal to the Board of Trade or other appropriate authority."[61] A similar recommendation was made by the Association of Certified and Corporate Accountants.[62] Several witnesses recommended that the auditors be given the right to receive notices of and attend all meetings of the company.[63] The Cohen Committee reported:

> We think the auditors should be given the right to receive notices of and attend all general meet-

ings of the company, and the right, if other auditors have been nominated, or if there is a proposal that they should not be reappointed, to put their views before the shareholders orally at the meeting and in writing prior to the meeting.[64]

Parliament approved this recommendation in the Companies Act, 1947.[65]

Current law, then, provides for the auditor to have tenure from annual general meeting to annual general meeting, to be eligible for reappointment, and to have an opportunity to defend himself before the members in the event that he receives notice of intention that he will not be reappointed. Lacking is a method by which an auditor may be removed should reasonable causes exist which indicate that his removal would be desirable. This point has recently received attention by the Jenkins Committee. The Law Society has recommended that "auditors shall be removed automatically at any time on specified grounds, that is to say, bankruptcy, conviction for fraud, unsoundness of mind, or disqualification as a member of an approved professional organization."[66] Also lacking under current law is a provision for the resignation of an auditor. The Law Society believes that this, too, should be specifically incorporated into the statute.[67]

Remuneration. The Joint Stock Companies Act of 1844, while it provided for the compulsory appointment of auditors, was silent as to the remuneration of such auditors; salary for an auditor appointed by the Board of Trade upon failure of the

---

[57] "Appendix to the Report," *op. cit.*, p. 52.
[58] *Ibid.*
[59] *Ibid.*, p. 85.
[60] 19 & 20 George V, c. 23, sec. 134(3).
[61] *Minutes, op. cit.*, app. E, par. 27, p. 46.
[62] *Ibid.*, app. JJ, par. 43, p. 532.
[63] *E.g.*, the Institute of Chartered Accountants in England and Wales (*ibid.*, app. Z, par. 9, p. 390) and the London Chamber of Commerce (*ibid.*, app. KK, p. 535).
[64] "Report," *op. cit.*, par. 112, p. 66.
[65] 10 & 11 George VI, c. 47, sec. 22(2)(c).
[66] *Minutes, op. cit.*, app. XLIV, par. 158, p. 1204. A similar recommendation was made by the Board of Trade (*ibid.*, app. LI, par. 177, p. 1590).
[67] *Loc. cit.*

company to appoint an auditor on behalf of the shareholders was to be set by the Commissioners of the Treasury and paid by the company.[68] The Act of 1856 in its model articles provided that the remuneration should be "fixed by the Company at the Time of the Auditors Election,"[69] but this article was not compulsory. The Act of 1862 contained an article in Table A (similarly permissive in nature) stating that the remuneration of the first auditors be fixed by the directors and for subsequent auditors by the company in general meeting.[70] This requirement was incorporated into the body of the Companies Act, 1900.[71]

Little further discussion concerning the statutory control over the auditors' remuneration occurred until the Cohen investigation. A number of witnesses before the Committee stated that the remuneration was in fact frequently set by the directors and ratified by the company in general meeting, and that this custom and the fact that the remuneration should more appropriately be arranged after than prior to the audit required changes in the law to legalize present practice.[72] The Cohen Committee recommended that the remuneration either be fixed by the company in general meeting or as directed by the company in general meeting, but if the fee be fixed by the directors, it should be separately stated in the accounts.[73] This recommendation was adopted in the Companies Act, 1947.[74] At this writing, no recommendations for changes in this aspect of the Companies Act had been placed before the Jenkins Committee.

IV. THE AUDITORS' RIGHTS, DUTIES, AND REPORTS

Rights and Duties. The auditor's report may be said to be his *raison d'être*. To adequately prepare his report he must perform certain duties and he must be in a position to perform these duties by right rather than by permission. The Joint Stock Companies Act of 1844 provided for all these functions. The auditors' duties were to examine the accounts of the company and the balance sheet.[75] They were granted the right and power to examine the books of account and of registry at all reasonable times throughout the year and to "demand and have the Assistance of such Officers and Servants of the Company and such documents as they shall require for the full Performance of their Duty in auditing the Accounts."[76] They were required to report on the accounts and the balance sheet.

The Act of 1856 repealed the compulsory nature of these requirements. In its model articles, however, it strengthened the position of the auditor by permitting him to hire, at the expense of the company, "Accountants or other Persons to assist him in investigating such Accounts."[77]

The Companies Act, 1879, contained compulsory auditing provisions for banking companies only. It added an item to the auditors' duties by requiring him to sign every balance sheet submitted to the annual or other meeting of the members of the company.[78] The Davey Committee, reporting in 1895, made the interesting recommendation that the auditors and directors prepare and sign a detailed "private" balance sheet. This was to be far more detailed than that supplied to the shareholders, and was to be preserved as a part of the records of the company.[79] Par-

[68] 7 & 8 Victoria, c. 110, sec. 38.
[69] 19 & 20 Victoria, c. 47, Table B, art. 78.
[70] 25 & 26 Victoria, c. 89, Table A, art. 88.
[71] 63 & 64 Victoria, c. 48, sec. 22.
[72] *Minutes, op. cit.*, the Institute of Chartered Accountants in England and Wales (app. Z, par. 8, p. 391), the Federation of British Industries (app. NN, par. 8, p. 597), the Joint Committee of Councils of Chartered Accountants of Scotland (app. OO, par. 12, p. 619, and the Imperial Chemical Industries, Ltd. (app. XX, p. 59, p. 743).
[73] "Report," *op. cit.*, par. 113, p. 66.
[74] 10 & 11 George VI, c. 47, sec. 24(8).
[75] 7 & 8 Victoria, c. 110, sec. 39.
[76] *Ibid.*, sec. 40.
[77] 19 & 20 Victoria, c. 47, Table B, art. 83.
[78] 42 & 43 Victoria, c. 76, sec. 8.
[79] "Report," *op. cit.*, par. 54.

liament did not adopt the recommendation. It did, however, adopt other recommendations of the Committee in the
Companies Act, 1900, which turned the
basic rights and duties specified in the
model articles of the Act of 1856 into bind-
ing statutory clauses.[80] Thus the statutory
rights and duties of the auditor as specified in the Joint Stock Companies Act of
1844 were restored after an interim of
forty-four years.

The Greene Committee paid some attention to the question as to whether the
auditor should have the statutory duty to
verify the securities owned by the company. The two major accountants' societies took opposing views. The Society of
Incorporated Accountants and Auditors
stated that it should be compulsory for the
auditors to inspect the securities, except
that certificates from banks would be
acceptable in the case of securities held for
the company by the banks, or from agents
appointed by the auditor in the case of
securities held abroad.[81] The Institute of
Chartered Accountants in England and
Wales took the position that "to make it
obligatory for Auditors to inspect all the
Securities would be imposing a duty upon
them which it would in many cases be
impossible for them to perform."[82] The
Committee agreed with the position of the
Institute.[83]

There has been almost no further agita-
tion to make additional changes to the
statutory clauses pertaining to the rights
and duties of the auditors except those
pertaining to the auditors' reports.

The Auditors' Report. The Joint Stock
Companies Act of 1844 provided that the
auditor should confirm the accounts and
the balance sheet and report generally
thereon, or, if they did not see fit to confirm them, report specially thereon.[84] Although all compulsory aspects with respect
to the auditor were repealed by the Act of
1856, that Act, in its model articles, spec-

ified in more detail what the report should
contain:

> The auditors . . . in every such Report . . .
> shall state whether, in their Opinion, the Balance
> Sheet is a full and fair Balance Sheet, containing
> the particulars required by these Regulations, and
> properly drawn up so as to exhibit a true and cor-
> rect View of the State of the Company's Affairs,
> and in case they have called for Explanations or
> Information from the Directors, whether such
> Explanations or Information have been given by
> the Directors, and whether they have been satis-
> factory.[85]

In 1877, a Select Committee of Parliament met to consider possible amendments
to the Companies Acts, 1862 and 1867.
They submitted a draft bill to Parliament
which contained the following auditors'
report:

> We have examined the above Balance Sheet
> and Profit and Loss Account, and compared the
> same with the books and vouchers of the com-
> pany, and with the certified stock accounts, and
> bankers and other balances, and have examined
> the schedules of assets and liabilities, and certify
> that to the best of our knowledge and belief, they
> are correct.[86]

This form was drafted by David Chad-
wick, M.P., a former president of the Manchester Institute of Accountants.[87] The bill
was withdrawn without being acted upon.

The Davey Committee, reporting in
1895, made no attempt to set forth a recommended wording of the report. Its
recommendation was enacted into law in
the Companies Act, 1900. The Act, however, did specify that the auditors "sign a
certificate at the foot of the balance sheet
stating whether or not all their requisitions
as auditors have been complied with."[88]
The auditors were also required to report

[80] 63 & 64 Victoria, c. 48, sec. 23.
[81] *Minutes, op. cit.,* app. FF, par. 8.
[82] *Ibid.,* app. AA, par. 8.
[83] "Report," *op. cit.,* par. 74.
[84] 7 & 8 Victoria, c. 110, sec. 41.
[85] 19 & 20 Victoria, c. 47, Table B, art. 84.
[86] House of Commons, *Sessional Papers,* 1897 (45)
I, 299, Form B.
[87] "Report of Select Committee on the Companies
Acts of 1862 and 1867," *ibid.,* 1897 (365) I, 419, q. 1947.
[88] 63 & 64 Victoria, c. 48, sec. 23.

to the shareholders in general meeting as to "whether, in their opinion, the balance sheet referred to in the report is properly drawn up so as to exhibit a true and correct view of the state of the company's affairs as shown by the books of the company."[89]

The Amendment Committee reporting in 1906 recommended that these two items, the certificate and the report, should form one document. It further recommended that the words "according to the best of their information, and the explanations given them and," should be inserted between the words "affairs" and "as" in the above report.[90] This was a somewhat watered-down version of the recommendation of the Chamber of Commerce of Nottingham, which wanted the report to be confined to a statement by the auditor "that all his requirements to enable him to conduct this audit have been complied with."[91] The Committee's recommendation was adopted in the Companies Act, 1907.[92]

The Companies Act, 1900, provided that the auditor was to report "on the accounts examined by them, and on every balance sheet laid before the company in general meeting."[93] No specific reference was made to the statement of profit and loss. In fact, the general feeling was that profits, and particularly components of profits such as sales, etc., were secrets not to be disclosed even to the shareholders. Illustrative of this feeling is the report of the Amendment Committee in 1906:

Such balance sheet should be examined and reported upon by the company's auditors. We do not intend that such balance sheet should include a statement of profit and loss. Although it has been objected that filing such a balance sheet would be detrimental to companies by giving some information as to their profits, and so stimulating competition, we consider that such a balance sheet should be filed annually.[94]

It was not until the investigation of the Cohen Committee that pressures appeared

demanding that the auditors' report also cover the statement of profit and loss. This in spite of the fact that the Companies Act, 1928, provided that the directors shall "once at least in every calendar year lay before the company in general meeting a profit and loss account."[95] Recommendations on this point came from the accountants' societies,[96] the British Insurance Association,[97] and a number of important individuals.[98] The Committee concurred,[99] as did Parliament.[100]

There also was considerable discussion by the witnesses as to the wording and contents of the report. The words "true and correct" were challenged, with the words "full and fair" recommended as a substitute.[101] This was also accepted by the Committee,[102] and incorporated into the Companies Act, 1947.[103] Other recommendations did not receive such favorable treatment. F. R. M. de Paula, well-known industrialist and accountant, recommended that the auditors' report state that the balance sheet and statement of profit and loss are "properly drawn up in accordance with accepted accounting principles

---

[89] *Ibid.*
[90] "Report," *op. cit.*, par. 44.
[91] "Appendix to the Report," *op. cit.*, p. 53. A somewhat similar opinion was expressed by the London Chamber of Commerce (*ibid.*, p. 79).
[92] 7 Edward VII, c. 50, sec. 19(2)(b).
[93] 63 & 64 Victoria, c. 48, sec. 23.
[94] "Report," *op. cit.*, par. 33.
[95] 18 & 19 George V, c. 45, sec. 39(3).
[96] *Minutes, op. cit.*, the Society of Incorporated Accountants and Auditors (app. II, par. 60, p. 503) and the Institute of Chartered Accountants in England and Wales (app. Z, par. 9, p. 391).
[97] *Ibid.*, app. LL, par. 8, p. 564.
[98] *Ibid.*, Arthur Whitworth, financier (app. H., par. 8, p. 126); Charles Nordon, solicitor (app. N, par. 11, p. 174); and F. R. M. de Paula, industrialist and Chartered Accountant (app. MM, par. 24, p. 568).
[99] "Report," *op. cit.*, par. 114, p. 66.
[100] Companies Act, 1947, 10 & 11 George VI, c. 47, sec. 22(1)(a).
[101] *Minutes, op. cit.*, Horace B. Samuel, financial consultant and barrister-at-law (app. TT, par. 15, p. 679).
[102] "Report," p. 68, the words decided upon were "true and fair."
[103] 10 & 11 George VI, c. 47, Second Schedule, art. 3(2).

consistently maintained so as to exhibit a true, correct, and complete view of the company's affairs and of its revenue transactions."[104] Arthur Whitworth, financier, suggested that a statutory set of uniform accounts be required. He made the following pointed criticism:

There must be something wrong when some companies' accounts disclose a great deal of information and secure an Auditor's certificate, and another company's accounts disclose no such detailed information and yet secures the same form of certificate.[105]

The Cohen Committee further recommended,[106] and the Companies Act, 1947, provided,[107] that the auditors' report should expressly state whether, in their opinion: (1) They have obtained all information and explanations necessary for the purposes of their audit. (2) The Company has kept proper books of account. (3) The balance sheet and profit and loss account are in agreement with the books of accounts and returns. (4) The balance sheet gives a true and fair view of the company's affairs as at the end of its financial year. (5) The profit and loss account gives a true and fair view of the profit or loss for its financial year. This represents the current law.

The Jenkins Committee, on the other hand, received recommendations to simplify the auditors' report. One such was to shorten the report to: "Audited in accordance with section 'X' of the Companies Act, 196–." Additional statements would be made only when the audit reveals failure to comply with standards specified in the act.[108]

One other type of recommendation has been received, *viz.*, to hold the auditor responsible that his report contain neither over- nor under-valuations of the assets of the company. This recommendation was made by the Faculty of Advocates with the full awareness that the auditor may not be a qualified assessor or appraiser. The importance here lies in the prevalence of take-over bids.[109] Shareholders may be hurt by receiving false information as to the value of assets owned by the company.[110]

Use of the Auditors' Report. The Joint Stock Companies Act of 1844 provided that the auditors' report be sent to every shareholder and that it be read at the general meeting of the company.[111] It further required that the report be filed with the Registrar of Joint Stock Companies.[112] These requirements were abolished by the Joint Stock Companies Act of 1856. The auditing provisions of the Companies Act, 1879, although pertaining only to banking companies, merely required that the auditors' report "be read before the company in general meeting.[113] The Companies Act, 1900, extended this requirement to all companies registered under the Act.[114] The Amendment Committee, reporting in 1906, recommended that a copy of the report be open to the inspection of any shareholder requesting it.[115] Of the twenty-three chambers of commerce which submitted memoranda to the Committee, ten stated that the report should be published, four that it should not, and the remainder were some-

---

[104] *Loc. cit.*
[105] *Loc. cit.*
[106] "Report," p. 68.
[107] 10 & 11 George VI, c. 47, Second Schedule.
[108] *Minutes, op. cit.*, the Association of Investment Trusts (app. XXIX, par. 21, p. 733). Similar recommendations were made by the Board of Trade (app. LI, par. 183, p. 1591), the Association of Certified and Corporate Accountants (app. XXXIV, par. 73, p. 894), and the Institute of Chartered Accountants in England and Wales (app. XLVIII, par. 196, p. 1426).
[109] A take-over bid has been defined by the Institute of Chartered Accountants in England and Wales as "a general offer to acquire shares or other securities of a particular class or classes, usually with a view to obtaining a controlling interest in the equity capital of the company and involving both a time-limit for acceptance of the offer and a minimum volume of acceptances." (*Ibid.*, app. XLVIII, par. 78, p. 1409.)
[110] *Ibid.*, app. XLV, par. 22, p. 1302.
[111] 7 & 8 Victoria, c. 110, sec. 42.
[112] *Ibid.*, sec. 43.
[113] 42 & 43 Victoria, c. 76, sec. 7(6).
[114] 63 & 64 Victoria, c. 48, sec. 23.
[115] "Report," *op. cit.*, par. 44.

what noncommittal on the subject. The Committee's recommendation fell short of actual publication of the auditors' report. It did recommend, however, that the right to inspect the reports be granted to preference shareholders and debenture holders to the same extent as enjoyed by the holders of ordinary shares.[116] These recommendations were accepted by Parliament in the Companies Act, 1907, which granted companies the right to charge for reports at the rate of sixpence per hundred words.[117]

The concept of charging for company reports was challenged before the Greene Committee,[118] which reported to Parliament that the facilities for obtaining copies of reports were insufficient.[119] As a result, the Companies Act, 1928, provided that any member of a company or any holder of debentures of a company would be entitled to receive copies of company reports gratis.[120]

There has been little further demand for changes in the clauses pertaining to the uses of the auditors' report. The current law, the Companies Act, 1948, provides that a copy of the report shall be annexed to the return filed with the Registrar of Companies,[121] it shall be annexed to any copies of the balance sheet and profit and loss account which are circulated or published,[122] it must be sent to every member and every holder of debentures of the company,[123] and it must be read before the company in general meeting.[124]

V. CONCLUSION

In evaluating the causes of provisions in the Companies Acts and their effects upon the auditor, it appears to be significant to consider the sources of the pressures which generated the controls and the stated reasons for their need. Demands for controls and suggestions as to their form came from many major segments of the business world, from government, from the legal profession, and from the accounting profession itself. It is interesting to note that demands would usually come from several but not all the segments of society which submitted memoranda to or gave testimony before the various investigating committees. Rarely, however, would the witnesses state definite opposition to proposals. The more usual negative position would be a somewhat neutral statement of belief that "present provisions in the act are adequate for the purpose." In the case of provisions affecting auditors, the reason most often stated was that the control was needed "to strengthen the position of the auditor." This reason was advanced not only by other segments of the witnesses but by those representing the accounting profession as well.

The question arises as to whether these controls were needed because of the failure of the accounting profession to set up and enforce its own controls. In the early period of the Companies Acts there was, of course, no organized accounting profession. As the profession developed, practices within the profession were gradually improved, but the profession apparently was not effectively able to enforce these practices on the business community. One piece of evidence on this point is a statement by the Greene Committee in 1926:

Certain of the alterations in the law which we have recommended on the subject of accounts will strengthen the position of auditors by giving statutory sanction to what is already the best professional practice.[125]

That, from the viewpoint of the professional accountant, the general trend of

116 *Ibid.*, par. 82.
117 7 Edward VII, c. 50, sec. 19(3) and sec. 23.
118 *E.g.*, by the Society of Incorporated Accountants and Auditors, *Minutes, op. cit.*, app. FF, par. 8.
119 "Report," *op. cit.*, par. 68.
120 18 & 19 George V, c. 45, sec. 41.
121 11 & 12 George VI, c. 38, sec. 127(b).
122 *Ibid.*, sec. 156.
123 *Ibid.*, sec. 158.
124 *Ibid.*, sec. 162(2).
125 "Report," *op. cit.*, par. 73, p. 37.

auditing controls of the Companies Acts has had a salutory effect upon his practice can hardly be doubted. The filling of the role of auditor has changed from utilizing any member of the company whether qualified or not to being restricted to a highly qualified member of selected organizations of accountants. The auditor is backed by both legal sanctions and those imposed by his professional societies, which strengthen his position of independence.

The question further arises as to whether the controls exercised by the statutes have had a stultifying effect upon the development of auditing theory and practice. These controls without a doubt set a lower level below which the practice cannot legally sink. Some have argued that this also sets a ceiling above which the profession cannot rise. That this is not true is fairly well shown by the fact that the quite common reason given for changing the law is "to give statutory sanction to what is already the best practice." Others claim that such statutory controls tend toward stagnation because amendments to existing statutes are difficult to achieve. In the case of the British, this charge does not appear to be substantiated by the foregoing review. The British have developed the custom of periodically investigating the companies legislation with a view to amending and updating the act then in force. In the past, both the investigating committees and Parliament have been prone to accept revision where the need for such has been adequately demonstrated. That this tradition still lives is evidenced by the appointment of the Jenkins Committee and its report recommending further amendments to the current act.

EARLY DEVELOPMENTS
IN AMERICAN AUDITING

C. A. Moyer

The Accounting Review

VOL. XXVI JANUARY, 1951 NO. 1

EARLY DEVELOPMENTS IN AMERICAN AUDITING

C. A. MOYER

Professor, University of Illinois

IT IS NATURAL that recent developments in auditing receive considerable attention from accountants. However, early developments and an examination of the influences which brought about these early changes, in addition to being interesting in themselves, may lead to a better understanding of what is happening in the present and may offer clues to what future trends may be. The literature and other information available which relates to auditing in America up to about the beginning of the twentieth century seem to indicate that auditing was then completing its first major phase of development.

The first audits in America were of course patterned after the British general audit. In fact, much of the auditing work was done by visiting British auditors retained by British investors in American corporations. It is generally recognized that auditing in Great Britain had been instituted to a great extent by specific statutory requirements. The principal function of an audit was considered to be an examination of the report of stewardship of corporation directors, and the most important duty of the auditor was to detect fraud. The search for defalcations resulted in a minute, painstaking check of the bookkeeping work done by the employees of the client. Almost all of the time of the auditor's staff was devoted to checking footings and postings in detail, in looking for bookkeeping errors, and in comparing the balances in the ledger with the trial balance and with the statements.

This detailed type of audit was no doubt well-suited to British needs at the time. No attempt will be made in this discussion to trace the influences which led to the extensive general audit required by statute in Great Britain. It is probably sufficient to point out that the early industrial history and the practices of early corporations in Great Britain were primarily responsible for the establishment of required audits in connection with reports to stockholders.

Inasmuch as statutory audits were not present in America, and British auditors were available to do much of the work, the accounting profession grew slowly in this country in the nineteenth century until near the turn of the century. A study of occupational directories[1] shows that in New York City, 31 local practitioners were listed as public accountants in 1880, 66 in 1890, and 183 in 1899. In the city of Chicago only 3 were listed in 1880, 24 in 1890, and 71 in 1899. Display advertisements published in the same directories

---

[1] "Directory of Early American Public Accountants," Bulletin No. 62, Bureau of Economic and Business Research, University of Illinois, 1942.

give some idea of the type of service offered to the public.

> "Complicated, disputed and confused accounts, also accounts of executors, trustees and estates in assignment investigated and stated. Books opened and closed. Suspected accounts confidently examined. Partnership settlements made" (1881).
> "Books opened and closed, commercial branches taught. Highly recommended by banks, business houses. Proving arithmetic, detecting errors in trial balance, computing interest and discount, averaging accounts" (1886).
> "Railroad, industrial, banking, commercial, corporation, syndicate, and general accounting. Books designed, opened, kept, examined, adjusted, audited and balanced" (1894).

Announcements of this nature indicate to some extent the nature of American auditing during this early period and also reflect the influence of British auditing upon early American practice. In the first edition of his text,[2] Robert H. Montgomery, a contemporary observer, called the early audits "bookkeeper audits." The program of examination usually consisted of vouching all cash disbursements, checking all footings and postings, checking the ledger to the trial balance and the trial balance to the financial statements (pp. 80–81). He estimated that three-fourths of the audit time was spent on footings and postings, whereas experience had shown that three-fourths of the defalcations were hidden by failures to account for income or cash receipts (p. 258).

In a backward look over his career[3] the same author later repeated the opinion: "Much of our time in those days was consumed in the endless checking of postings from one book to another" (p. 14). "Frequently books had been out of balance for months or years, and the finding of the errors was a terrific task. . . . In some audits, and not only small ones, we verified

² *Auditing Theory and Practice*, Ronald Press, New York, 1912.
³ *Fifty Years of Accountancy*, privately printed, 1939.

every footing and every posting" (p. 19). The auditor fifty years ago . . . "was little recognized because the matters which were referred to him were relatively unimportant and this unimportance tended to reduce him to the level of a clerk" (p. 316).

Little auditing literature appeared in America during the nineteenth century, but the small amount available does throw some light upon the changes taking place.

H. J. Mettenheim's *Auditor's Guide* appeared in 1869. Its sixteen pages hardly furnish a guide to auditing. Suggestions are given for preventing fraud: require all entries to be clear, full, explicit; rule in money columns to prevent slovenly work; make it the duty of the cashier to have a voucher for every payment; require a record of the detailed composition of every bank deposit. Directions are given so the proprietor can audit his own cash book "as an easy and pleasant summer recreation": test the cash book additions; look for forced balances, for offsetting errors, for payments on spurious notes payable, and for charges to merchandise of expenses that should go to the bookkeeper's personal account.

G. P. Greer's *Science of Accounts*, published in 1882, contained some significant sections, some of which are summarized below:

> General remarks: Proof should be sought outside the books in the statements of debtors and creditors themselves for comparison with the books; for example, call in the pass books of the depositors in a bank under audit. Watch for omitted postings from the books of original entry; where totals are not passed through the journal, omissions easily occur. When the receipts and disbursements pass through the hands of a treasurer and cashier, and different collecting or disbursing clerks, the accounts should be arranged to check and prove each other. All obligations of the corporation should be authorized by vote of the directors. All payments of large amount should be made by check or draft on a bank of deposit.
> Capital stock: Critically compare the original issue and subsequent issues with the

journal entries and stock ledger. Compare transferred stock with the stock ledger, transfer book, cancelled certificate, and stub outstanding. Compare the stub total with the capital stock account, "great care being taken to detect, if possible, the overissue of stock, if any there be, or any errors in the transfer and cancellation of legitimate shares." Analyze and compare the reserve fund and surplus profits wi.'; the dividend account, the amount of net profit, and the requirements of statutory law.

Cash: Trace receipts to sources, and payments to purposes for which disbursed; count and scrutinize the cash on hand, verify cash on deposit by bank pass book or official statement.

Accounts receivable: Trace to origin and check the valuation estimated; as to accounts past due or long unsettled, inquire regarding the cause, and investigate the parties' standing.

The author also describes procedures to be followed for examination of real property, losses other than regular expenses, accounts and bills payable, and bills receivable. He describes the inter-comparison of ledger, trial balance, closing entries, balance sheet, and profit and loss statement, but does not mention footings and postings. Apparently he does not attempt to describe a "complete audit" as it was known at that time, but it is significant that the procedures suggested involve the securing of evidence outside the books for certain of the assets and liabilities. This outline indicates that something different than a "bookkeeper audit" was being developed.

New York State adopted its first CPA law in August, 1896. A book of unofficial answers to examination questions appeared soon after several examinations had been given. This was *The American Accountant's Manual* by Broaker and Chapman. One of the questions on auditing was this: "In an audit where an exhaustive detailed examination of the books is not stipulated or not practicable, what examination is essential to assure their general correctness?" The authors' answer was:

"An audit under limitations may imply any degree of thoroughness from an exhaustive examination of every detail to a mere cursory review of generalities, the object of each particular audit and the opportunities afforded in each case governing the extent to which it may be carried.

"However, to insure the general correctness of the accounts, the footings of all the books of original entry should be verified, journal entries of an exceptional character scrutinized, and the postings to all nominal, representative and special accounts, both as to aggregate amounts and separate items, should be checked. An audit, to be at all effective, should also include the examination of vouchers for all cash payments and the verification of the final cash balance.

"While such an audit is distinguished by the commission to check the postings to the individual customers' and creditors' accounts throughout, it is practicable where advanced systems of bookkeeping are employed to agree them in the aggregate, and it is advisable in any event to call over a few of the postings to the individual accounts covering a day here and there, and in like manner to examine invoices for purchases, and check extensions for a partial test of their accuracy."

It should be noted that "in an audit where an exhaustive detailed examination of the books is not stipulated or not practicable" it was still considered necessary to foot all books of original entry, to check all postings to the general ledger, and to vouch all cash payments. However, it was considered acceptable procedure to reduce the time required, by omitting or merely testing the postings to the personal accounts, and similarly examining only part of the invoices for purchases, and checking only part of the extensions.

F. S. Tipson, a New York CPA, published his *Auditing* in 1904, in which he used the auditing questions given in New York from 1896 to 1902. Several of the questions involved conditions where it was not feasible to conduct a complete examination. His answers showed some shortening of the program by sampling, but indicated that all books of original entry should be footed, and that the cash book transactions should be vouched completely. Also, "the balance sheet should be taken in hand, to see that it is a fair expression of the Assets and Liabilities of the business as of the date it bears on its face."

By the end of the nineteenth century the literature and practice reflected quite clearly the direction being taken in American auditing as British audit procedures became adapted to American needs. A memorandum of interim work done in advance of a year-end audit, which was copied by permission from the files of one of the oldest firms in this country, probably shows the changes taking place more clearly than does the literature. The work performed covered nine months of the client's business ending September 30, 1900.

> Counted cash on hand.
> Checked bank reconcilements.
> Checked vouchers with cash book, also deposits to bank, and pay roll into cash book to October 23, 1900.
> Checked postings of monthly total from cash book to general ledger from January 1 to September 30—also postings of general ledger column in cash book to general ledger for July, August, and September.
> Checked postings from Journal to General Ledger for July, August, and September, and monthly totals from Journal to General Ledger for nine months ending September 30.
> Checked monthly totals of Invoice Book to General Ledger for nine months ending September 30.
> Checked monthly totals from Returns Book to General Ledger for period.
> Checked Sales Ledger monthly totals to General Ledger for period.
> Checked Settlement Book monthly totals to General Ledger for period.
> Checked entries from Settlement Book to Cash Book for January, February, and March.
> Checked monthly totals of Stock Journal to General Ledger for period.
> Checked footings of monthly summaries in Invoice Book.
> Analysed following accounts:
>> Merchandise account.
>> Manufacturing account.
>> General Expense account.
>> Machinery account.
>> Boston Improvement account.
>> New York Improvement account.
> Verified footings of Pay Roll for July, 1900.
> Checked following trial balances:
>> General Ledger.
>> Sales Ledgers Notes Receivable.
>> Stock Ledger (returned products).
>> Stock Ledger (Consignments).
>> Agencies (product).
>> Accounts Payable and Agents Ledger.

It should be noted that postings were checked completely only for monthly totals to the general ledger; other postings were checked for three months. The only footings checked were the monthly summaries in the invoice book, and the payrolls for one month. A number of important accounts were anlayzed. This technique was not emphasized in contemporary writings, but its use was expanded rapidly in practice.

A book of selected articles under the title of *The Science and Practice of Auditing* was compiled in 1903 by E. H. Beach and W. W. Thorne. This book reproduced some of the few contributions which had been written in this country on auditing but did not present a unified, comprehensive treatment of the subject. Most of the material was very compact and stressed the mechanical details of auditing. For example, the opening paragraph of the "general program or auditing plan" contained in an article by the two authors reads as follows:

> "Check all postings, at least all those in the cash book and nominal and private ledgers. Vouch the cash book and petty cash book; check the additions thereof; verify the balances at bank and on hand. Check the ledger balances and additions of all ledgers; where all postings are not checked, compare the balances of each ledger with the corresponding adjustment account."

The conclusion is inescapable that no important American auditing literature had appeared up to this time. It is obvious however, that the "bookkeeper audits," modeled after British general audits of directors' stewardship and directed toward discovery of defalcations, did not continue to be typical American audits. Frank G. Short, a professional accountant who has had extended experience in auditing practice in the United States, describes this transition as being a change from detailed audits to test audits. Auditors incorporated the idea that "it was not necessary to make a detailed examination of every entry, footing, and posting during the period in order to get the substance of the value which resulted from an audit . . . the second phase of the development of auditing retained the viewpoint of the detailed auditor, but resulted in a less total quantity (and cost) of detailed audit work."[4]

Although the adoption of sampling procedures probably represented the most important development in auditing during this period, other changes were beginning to appear, as indicated in the preceding references. Account analysis was playing a more important part in the audit program. This development also seems to represent no departure from the point of view of the detailed auditors, for it seems to represent originally a substitute for the enormous quantity of detailed audit work formerly done in audits.

A third development during this period does seem to portray the beginning of a difference in point of view by the auditor. Methods adopted for verification of transactions by securing of evidence outside the records of the client implies that auditors were finding it desirable and necessary to consider more than mere clerical accuracy and detection of fraud. Closer examination of the valuations of assets and liabilities also reflects the beginning of the assumption by the profession of broader audit objectives.

4 "Internal Control from the Viewpoint of the Auditor," *The Journal of Accountancy*, Sept., 1940, p. 226.

These developments did not just happen. Although the first audits in the United States were patterned after British audits, changes occurred gradually which represented adaptations of earlier procedures to American business conditions and American needs. Some of the many factors which had an influence on early American auditing are discussed briefly below.

Great Britain had found it desirable to require statutory audits. The United States was a new, expanding country with little industrial history behind it, and with no such requirements. In this country it was necessary that the benefits derived from an audit be apparent to a client in order that he would be willing to incur the cost of such an engagement. The detailed procedures followed in Great Britain soon were found to be too costly to clients who could decide for themselves whether or not an auditor was engaged. Consequently testing or sampling methods for checking footings and postings were introduced and more and more widely adopted as time passed. The necessity of reducing the audit time spent on checking bookkeeping details became more apparent as American businesses increased in size.

The many corporation mergers effected during the last decade of the nineteenth century increased the complexity of business operations in the United States and gave a considerable impetus to the accounting profession. For example, 199 consolidations or mergers were completed between 1885 and 1900; of these 78 were completed in 1899. The separate interests of the several established companies to be combined needed reliable data in order that the combination would be accomplished in an equitable manner. Dependable data on such things as earnings, property values, debts, and financial trends were needed, and professional accountants were called upon to supply this information. A new and broader opportunity for service thus opened up for American public accountants. Not only were they called upon to conduct audits of different scope and purpose than formerly, but also they often installed accounting systems for merged companies, assisted in reorganizations, and prepared statements for concerns in receivership or in bankruptcy.

Another important factor in this early period was the increasingly wide use of single-name paper for short term loans in place of other methods of short-term borrowing such as bills of exchange and trade acceptances. No attempt will be made to examine here the conditions after the Civil War which led to the widespread business practice of granting cash discounts and the resulting use of direct personal loans from banks. It is significant, however, that this method of short-term financing led to the need for credit investigations. The services performed by professional accountants in this connection began to affect the procedures followed.

From this brief survey it will be evident that by the beginning of the twentieth century American auditing was still in an immature stage. Yet growth and change were taking place. Local conditions had brought about some new developments in procedure, most of which reflected the desire and the necessity of reducing the audit time spent on an engagement. Beneath the surface, however, the possibilities of audit services relating to the growing separation of management and owners, to credit granting, to system installations, and to various financial matters, were beginning to transform the detailed examinations of the bookkeeper's work into auditing as we have come to know it.

GOODWILL—THE COMPANY'S 'ULTIMATE ASSET'

Hugh P. Hughes

Hugh P. Hughes

Goodwill –
The Company's 'Ultimate Asset'

This survey—the 701st—is a capsule history for the businessman and accountant of the problems of accounting for goodwill that have perplexed them for the past five centuries and will soon be in the headlines again.

"USE YOUR scientific formulae, yes, but remember, too, that the final result will also be influenced no little by bargaining power, and guess work, for goodwill will ever be like love and the mushroom:—'Something you don't know what you've got until it's too late.' "[1]

That quote sums up better than most of the 700 articles, books, and monographs written in accounting since 1884 the problems associated with goodwill and the exasperation encountered in dealing with the asset. What it is, as well as how it is to be treated has never been completely resolved. Presumably these will

Dr. Hughes is Assistant Professor of Accounting at Georgia State University.

be resolved when love is defined to the satisfaction of psychologists and matter is defined in physics. (Ambrose Bierce has endeavored to enlighten us with his definition of the former: Love, n. A temporary insanity curable by marriage. . . .)[2]

Although definitional problems are a source of trouble, of immediate interest and consequence to businessmen and accountants is the accounting treatment accorded the asset. Six years ago, debate on the subject was climaxed by two important opinions on accounting for goodwill and related considerations, and some thought is currently being given to modifying those accounting standards again. The purpose of this article is to examine for sake of historical perspective the events which culminated in Accounting Principles Board Opinions Nos. 16 and 17 and to offer some reflec-

tions on what the future may hold for accounting for goodwill.

Lest one think goodwill is a new matter of concern to lawyers, businessmen, accountants, economists, and in court, one of the earliest cases involving the asset occurred in 1417. One authority contends that this is the only case in which an English judge is known to have used profanity in his decision.[3] In this case, as in those to follow in the next two centuries, the sale of goodwill was illegal, since it usually involved an agreement calling for the seller not to compete with the buyer for a stipulated period of time. This was viewed by the courts as an unreasonable restriction on the seller's opportunities for making a living at a time when such opportunities were very limited, and both the seller and buyer could be fined and/or imprisoned for making such an agreement.[4] In

1620 such agreements were legalized, and since then British and American courts have broadened the definition and further facilitated the sale of the asset.[5]

The asset appears to have gotten its name from the favorable attitude or "good will" of customers toward a given business, due primarily to the friendly or honest attitude of the proprietor possibly coupled with a good location for his business. Although personal and location goodwill ideas were suitable for proprietary and partnership forms of business, they were inadequate to describe the varied commercial advantages that could be developed in the corporation. As the corporation became more important in business, the meaning of the term goodwill was expanded to include virtually any factor which gave rise to a differential advantage. Such a view may lack precision, but it is implicit in most current discussions of the asset and underlies many technical accounting definitions of goodwill.

In a relative sense, goodwill is not new to accountants either, since accounting articles have been appearing on the subject almost from the beginning of modern accounting literature—the first known study on goodwill being written in 1884.[6] The question of what to do with the asset once it was on the books (permanently retain it or write it off in some manner) had settled into such a familiar pattern that in 1907 two individuals in the course of a discussion were said to have "fairly well exhausted the stock arguments that have from time to time been put forward. . . ."[7]

The arguments for and against various treatments were predictable and, incidentally, were very little different from what was said 70 years later; they also were endless. Until the 1930s, attempts to eliminate alternative treatments for goodwill were generally unsuccessful. In the late twenties, the following treatments for recording goodwill were advocated and practiced.

Initial Valuation
1. Cost—If goodwill is purchased upon acquisition of a going concern, it should be recorded at its cost.
2. Various Advertising Expenditures—Since one way goodwill was created was through advertising, why not capitalize advertising expenditures as goodwill? This was sometimes interpreted to be all advertising outlays or sometimes just extraordinary outlays.

3. Capitalization of Early Losses—When a business is first started, one expects losses to occur which lay the foundation for future profitable operations and ultimately goodwill(?).
4. Developmental Costs—These costs were capitalized as goodwill utilizing much the same argument as that for Early Losses.
5. Arbitrarily Written-Up—If the business has increased in value, shareholders and creditors are being misled if this value is not shown. Therefore goodwill should be debited in the accounts.

remember), various Other Contributed Capital accounts (Capital Surplus), or Appraisal Surplus.

Finally, goodwill came to rest somewhere in the financial statements. The statement user, in light of the limitless possibilities indicated, had to realize that the caption "goodwill" had been used to describe something which could originate almost anywhere, be almost anything, and was treated in virtually every way imaginable.

One practice of writing down goodwill, however, was rather convincingly

---

"Although advertising created goodwill, the subjective measurement problems of recording such goodwill outweighed the conceptual argument in favor of it."

(The problem here, never satisfactorily resolved, was what amount should be credited?)

Subsequent Treatment
1. Permanent Retention—If a business maintains its goodwill, it should not be reduced in the accounts.
2. Amortization—Even if goodwill is maintained, it isn't the *same* goodwill—it is the new goodwill which is replenishing the old as it disappears. Therefore the old goodwill should be amortized.
3. Complete or Partial Lump-Sum Write-Off; immediately or at one's will—This practice was supported on the grounds of conservatism and/or a sudden loss in value.
4. Arbitrarily Written-Up Further—The same argument for arbitrary write-ups expressed earlier applies here.

Once a decision was made to reduce goodwill in the accounts, one still had to decide whether the reduction would be shown in the income statement or whether it would bypass it. The distinction is significant—a charge in the income statement would reduce reported net income and earnings per share, and this could possibly affect the marketability of a company's shares. Bypassing the income statement avoided this problem, but in the opinion of some, the charge was just "buried" elsewhere. One might charge goodwill directly to Retained Earnings (Earned Surplus—for those old enough to

discredited by this time—the practice of writing it down during good times and suspending the practice during bad ones. The obvious paradox was too tempting to some accounting writers who were usually overwhelmingly serious in most of their writings. As Charles Couchman said, "To put it briefly, if you can write it down, you need not; if you cannot, you should!"[8] Or, as an anonymous author noted in *The Accountant*:

"After once placing a value upon your books, if you actually have it, write it off; if not, then continue it and make a showing of having it. If you have a thing, you haven't; if you haven't, you have!"[9]

The twenties represented an era when a maximum number of alternatives existed for dealing with goodwill. The optimism of the twenties, however, gave way to the more pessimistic attitude of the thirties, and emphasis correspondingly shifted from how to get goodwill on the books to how to get it off. Coupled with this was a continuous reduction in alternatives for treating the asset. Over the next 40 years down to the present, the various alternatives were eliminated one by one until finally only one treatment remained for recording goodwill, and for all practical purposes one was left for removing it.

In the conservative mood of the thirties, the cost principle became firmly and quickly established as the basis for recording all assets—a basis from which departures could be made with few exceptions and then were subject to justification. In less than ten years cost thus moved from being an acceptable way for recording goodwill to the only way. Although advertising created goodwill, the subjective measurement problems of recording such goodwill outweighed the conceptual argument in favor of it. From then on, any capitalization of advertising was usually done under some caption such as Prepaid Advertising.

Once on the books, however, there was no assurance of how long goodwill would stay there. In the thirties, the mood of conservatism itself was carried to an extreme, and goodwill was written off for no other reason than the desire not to show it in the balance sheet anymore. Such discretionary write-offs and also those resulting from a sudden decline in value usually bypassed the income statement while systematic amortization of goodwill did not. At that time, the "current operating" concept of reporting income was acceptable as was the present "all-inclusive" approach. Under the current operating concept, only normal, recurring items were reported in the income statement; large, unusual items such as large write-offs in the income statement were felt to detract from year-to-year comparability, and misleading inferences might be drawn from their inclusion.

troversy which ultimately embroiled many segments of the business community.

As were many of the bulletins of that time, Bulletin No. 24 was generally a reflection of what was considered acceptable practice and very much in line with the preceding discussion. Cost was the basis for initial valuation of the asset, and permanent retention was acceptable for goodwill the life of which did not appear to be limited. Amortization also was allowable in this situation. It was advocated for other intangibles, including goodwill, which were known to have limited lives. Lump-sum write-offs directly to Retained Earnings were condoned where the value of goodwill was known to have been reduced. A significant indicator of things to come was the treatment accorded discretionary write-offs of goodwill. They were permitted because of their prior acceptability but were discouraged, particularly when charged to Other Contributed Capital.

The Bulletin apparently was acceptable; at least it drew little criticism in the accounting literature of the time. The remainder of the forties thus represented the last period of relative calm in dealing with the asset. After that, goodwill would be a prime cause of continuous debate for the next 20 years.

Two events occurred early in the next decade which had a significant

values, the various owners' equity elements of the firms would be combined intact, and no new goodwill would be recorded. The pooling treatment was possible if "substantially all of the equity interests in predecessor corporations continued, as such, in a surviving corporation."[12] Important also was the relative size of the constituent companies, continuity of management, and whether or not activities of the companies were similar or complementary. In attaching weight to these characteristics, Bulletin No. 40 stated, "No one of these factors would necessarily be determinative, but their presence or absence would be cumulative in effect."[13]

By comparison to today's pooling criteria, the aforementioned were obviously so subjective that a wide range of business combination transactions could be accounted for as either a purchase or pooling. The lower asset and net worth bases and therefore higher net income and earnings per share computations afforded by the pooling treatment would lead one to believe that this method would almost always be selected. This was not the case at this time, however, for the accounting treatment of a purchase could easily be made to resemble a pooling of interests. For example, an acquiring firm might record the acquired firm's assets at their old book values. Then the excess of cost over book value would be considered goodwill. As previously noted, a treatment available at that time for handling goodwill was an immediate and discretionary write-off to Other Contributed Capital or Retained Earnings. If this were done, a purchase transaction could substantially be given a pooling treatment—all assets recorded at book value and no new goodwill. As indicated previously, discretionary write-offs, particularly when made to Other Contributed Capital, were discouraged, but the option was available for the resolute. The upshot of this situation was that although the subjective criteria offered the opportunity for manipulation, there was no need to take advantage of it at this time.

The second event occurred in 1953 when all existing research bulletins were consolidated in one publication, Accounting Research Bulletin No. 43, *Restatement and Revision of Accounting Research Bulletins*. Bulletin No. 40 was incorporated with very insignificant changes, but old Bulletin No. 24 outlin-

---

"Some of the more imaginative abuses created in this climate of chaos were 'retroactive poolings' and 'part-purchase, part-poolings.' "

From the viewpoint of accounting for goodwill, the "modern era" may be said to have begun with the first pronouncement on intangibles, in December 1944, by the American Institute of Certified Public Accountants (AICPA), before 1957 known as the American Institute of Accountants. The Institute's Committee on Accounting Procedure— the predecessor of the Accounting Principles Board (APB) and the current Financial Accounting Standards Board (FASB)—issued Accounting Research Bulletin No. 24, *Accounting for Intangible Assets*,[10] setting the stage for the purchase versus pooling-of-interests con-

impact on accounting for the asset. The first was in September 1950 when Accounting Research Bulletin (ARB) No. 40, *Business Combinations*, formally introduced the term "pooling of interests" (used in its modern sense) and the criteria for using it.[11] A business combination was either a purchase, whereby assets of the acquired firm were valued at fair market value and any excess was assigned to goodwill, or it was a pooling of interests. Under a pooling, neither firm was viewed as having acquired the other, and therefore no new cost basis would or could arise. All assets would retain their old book ing the treatment of intangibles was modified substantially. Any write-offs of goodwill to Other Contributed Capital, previously discouraged, were now disallowed completely, and the same fate befell discretionary write-offs to Retained Earnings. Therefore, the only time a write-off could occur would be when a substantial decline in the value of goodwill had occurred. As a result, a sharp distinction had been drawn between purchase and pooling accounting treatments with dismaying (from some points of view) clarity; for the first time, pooling-of-interests accounting became important.[14]

The importance stemmed from several factors. This was a significant era of business combinations—an era which began shortly after World War II and ultimately would not slacken until the early seventies. The fifties also were a very inflationary period, and herein lies the significance of the distinction. The pooling treatment, utilizing as it did the old book values of the combining companies, avoided recording the assets at their new and usually greater market values—values which would eventually produce a lower net income figure when charged off through depreciation. And the pooling treatment avoided recording goodwill—which would have to be permanently retained or even amortized. In a majority of cases, therefore, the treatment producing the most favorable net income and earnings per share figure was pooling-of-interests accounting, and the pressure to avoid the purchase treatment became almost irresistible.[15]

To make a long story short, what occurred in the next 17 years until the Accounting Principles Board tackled the problem was pandemonium. The situation was nothing more nor less than a logical follow-through of what one would expect in the circumstances just described—a vague set of criteria distinguishing two treatments one of which offered significant advantages in its use. For the most part, the criteria were brushed aside, abuses flourished, and the accounting profession was criticized.

Four years after Bulletin No. 43 was issued, the Committee on Accounting Procedure gave its last pronouncement on the criteria for a pooling of interests. Bulletin No. 48, issued in 1957, superseded that portion of Bulletin No. 43 dealing with business combinations and was in effect the coup de grace to the old criteria.[16] It did not have far to go

with three of them—continuity of management, continuity of equity interests, and complementary business activities—for they had proven to be either too difficult to define or, as in the case of complementary activities, financially inapplicable.[17] Prior to 1957, however, the size guideline had been followed, but Bulletin No. 48 greatly deemphasized it, and it virtually ceased to exist. Thereafter, almost any combination could be treated as a purchase or pooling at the discretion of the parties involved.[18]

Some of the more imaginative abuses

created in this climate of chaos were "retroactive poolings" and "part-purchase, part-poolings." Retroactive poolings were a result of the relaxed size guidelines promulgated in Bulletin No. 48. Some businesses *retroactively* applied the new and more lenient size criteria to combinations that had been consummated in previous years, and thus changed the transaction from its original status as a purchase to that of a pooling. What appears to be a classic example of abuse through this treatment occurred when one firm treated as a retroactive pooling its combination with another and three years later sold the firm with which it had retroactively pooled.

"Although the concept of pooling does not necessarily prohibit the sale of a previously pooled unit, the cohesive force of the 'corporate marriage' (pooling) may be questioned when one party to the 'marriage' can readily sell of [sic] dispose of the other."[19]

Part-purchase, part-pooling was used where a substantial part of the acquired entity's stock had been obtained by cash and the remainder by the acquiring firm's stock. The purchasing company would then contend that the portion of the absorbed firm's stock obtained by stock was in effect a pooling of interests—albeit only partially. The resulting accounting treatment achieved for the remaining firm the advantages of the

pooling method in proportion to that part of the transaction involving stock for stock. The logical perplexities inherent in such an approach are probably best summed up by the title of one man's study of the subject: "Part Purchase—Part Pooling: The Infusion of Confusion Into Fusion."[20]

The dawn of the sixties witnessed the end of the Committee on Accounting Procedure and the formation of the Accounting Principles Board (APB). The APB inherited several troublesome accounting issues, including accounting for goodwill, and research studies were

commissioned to help solve the various problems.

As the issue moved toward resolution, albeit rather tardily, another related matter was settled which further restricted the existing alternatives for removing goodwill from the books. The great variety of methods available for handling goodwill in the twenties had gradually been whittled down until only cost remained for its initial valuation and permanent retention, amortization (to income), and write-offs (to income or retained earnings) were available for its subsequent treatment. In 1966, the APB—swinging away from its traditional espousal of the current operating approach—virtually adopted the all-inclusive concept of reporting income, and thereafter write-offs of goodwill (those due to a decline in value of the asset) were permissible only in the income statement.[21]

By the mid-sixties, the points of contention thus were well defined: (1) the circumstances under which goodwill would be recognized (criteria for business combinations) and (2) its ultimate disposition (permanent retention vs. elimination in the income statement). The solution, however, was long in coming. Two research projects commissioned by the APB resulted in monographs in 1965 and 1968 on business combinations and goodwill, respectively—neither of which presented proposals acceptable to the APB. Even

"It perhaps is fitting that accounting for this 'ultimate asset' is resulting in a test of the private sector to regulate itself in that regard."

though by 1969 the APB had issued 15 opinions on various subjects in accounting, 16 years had passed since the last substantial pronouncement on business combinations and intangibles (ARB No. 43) had been issued. One of the greatest merger movements in business history had been going on since the end of World War II, and the accounting provisions for such combinations were totally inadequate. Finally, on February 25, 1969, Homer Budge, then chairman of the Securities and Exchange Commission, stated:

"We recognize that this is a highly controversial area of accounting in which many judgment factors are involved, both in the matter of the initial accounting for the acquisition and in the disposition of goodwill when it appears. Consistent with practice ever since 1933, we have supported efforts of the accounting profession to solve these problems. If this does not lead to prompt action, the urgency of the situation may dictate rule-making by the Commission."[22]

In November 1969 the APB concluded that pooling of interests should be abolished, but changed its mind a month later.[23] When the APB issued its exposure draft on the subject in February 1970, pooling was permitted but was severely limited by, among other things, a controversial clause which would have restricted the pooling treatment to companies at least one third as large as the firm with which they were combining.[24] Amid rising debate and threats of lawsuits, the size test was relaxed from three to one to a ratio of nine to one and was finally dropped altogether when APB No. 16 was issued in August 1970.[25] Even so, the remaining criteria were much more specific and very restrictive concerning what combinations could be treated as a pooling of interests.

Legal action against the APB was threatened on the grounds that the APB was attempting to restrict business combinations with mandatory usage of the purchase technique. Furthermore, the size test was attacked because it was arbitrary–a serious criticism which could be leveled at almost all of the criteria. However, part of the problem with less specific provisions, as evidenced in the demise of the old pooling criteria, was that they were very liberally construed and eventually ignored. J.S. Seidman, specifically defending the

size test (with an argument really applicable to many of the other provisions as well), admitted it was arbitrary but felt that guidelines must be established to implement any basic principle.[26]

The size test was not the only casualty in the pooling-purchase controversy. As indicated in the remarks by SEC Chairman Budge, the issue at hand was transcended by the larger issue of the future direction of the accounting profession itself. With such large stakes, coupled with the well-publicized abuses associated with poolings (such as retroactive poolings discussed previously), Leonard Savoie, vice-president of the APB's parent group, the AICPA, stated early in the deliberations that an exposure draft would be forthcoming which would abolish pooling of interests. He went on to say, "Anything less than this solution will mean simply a 'repositioning' of the abuses which have become so rampant in recent years."[27]

When the dust settled, as has been noted, the APB had to accept pooling after all. In retrospect, many of the pooling abuses had been curtailed because of the still nevertheless stringent remaining criteria; the APB had made an important contribution. However, the APB had lost face on possibly what now may be viewed as the most crucial issue it would ultimately have to face–shortly thereafter, a commission was formed to suggest new ways of setting accounting standards. About three years after the pooling opinion in 1970, the APB was superseded by the Financial Accounting Standards Board which has been committed to and is now faced with reviewing the work of its predecessor in the business combination area.

APB No. 16 took care of the recognition of goodwill, but APB No. 17 took care of its ultimate disposition. The primary debate concerned goodwill's permanence or nonpermanence; in an accounting dimension, that boiled down to nonamortization or amortization. The literature on the subject had been voluminous and very repetitive since the early 1900s. Little had changed concerning these arguments except the names of those who espoused each approach as the years went by. Over 40 years ago, one individual indicated his exasperation with the discussion in the following terms:

"The interesting cleavage of opinion . . . is probably quite as much a matter of temperament as of principle,

and whilst one recognises the strength of the arguments both for and against the writing down of goodwill, one is inclined to question whether, after all, it makes any great deal of difference whether it is written off or retained on the books."[28]

In the seventies, however, the effects of the treatments were vastly different. Amortization not only reduced reported net income and earnings per share, but it did so without benefit of a tax deduction. U.S. court precedents set in the twenties precluded treating amortization of goodwill as an expense on tax returns.

The APB did decide, however, on mandatory amortization of goodwill over a period not to exceed 40 years on the grounds that "few, if any, intangible assets last forever."[29] Permanent retention was no longer allowed, and lump-sum write-offs were all but eliminated. Such write-offs were permissible only if a substantial decline in value had occurred and then only in the income statement. The APB further noted that "a single loss year or even a few loss years together do not necessarily justify an extraordinary charge to income for all or a large part of the unamortized cost. . . ."[30]

APB Opinion Nos. 16 and 17 represent the latest and very significant installments in the increasingly restrictive treatment accorded goodwill over the past 50 years. Following the twenties, the great number of alternatives were continuously and gradually whittled away until only cost was acceptable for goodwill's initial valuation and amortization in the income statement was mandatory for its subsequent treatment. Primary causes for this trend were the initial introduction in the thirties and ultimate logical follow-through of the implications of the cost principle, and the switch by the American Institute from espousing a current operating concept to espousing an all-inclusive one in reporting net income. Even the apparently inadvertent loophole created by pooling accounting in the fifties may be viewed as a manifestation of this trend–pooling represented an escape hatch from the narrowing options for recording goodwill until APB No. 16 was issued.

In this setting, the APB's successor–the FASB–is now committed to review and make recommendations concerning business combinations and goodwill. Some significant questions in a historical perspective for the businessman and accountant are: Will the FASB continue the trend or break it? What possible fate may await the FASB with the various courses of action open to it? What effects might these have upon the businessman and accountant?

The task facing the FASB is an unenviable one. The APB was terminated partly in view of its inability to resolve the business combination/goodwill issue; and whether cause and effect can be proven, it is at least historical fact and should be noted that the old Committee on Accounting Procedure went out of existence within three years of its last pronouncement on the subject. Furthermore, some have felt that the FASB may be a last chance before resorting to promulgation of accounting standards by the Securities and Exchange Commission or some such governmental body. Among just some groups—a few of the more important ones of which are financial analysts, accounting practitioners, merger-minded firms, accounting academicians, and the SEC—it is a virtual certainty that someone won't be pleased with the FASB's efforts.

Three broad categories of solutions are evident—with, of course, numerous degrees of variation within and between them: (1) less restrictions on poolings and/or goodwill alternatives, (2) basically the same approach as now exists, and (3) more restrictions on (or elimination of) poolings. The first approach would be acceptable to merger-minded firms but at best would draw very mixed reactions from the other groups. The APB was viewed by many as having yielded to pressure by business. This caused it to lose credibility with much of the remainder of the financial and accounting community.

The second approach might be criticized as "do-nothing," but it does offer the advantage of proven ability to curb earlier abuses associated with pooling of interests. The FASB possibly could offer altered and/or refined criteria to handle any current criticism.

The third alternative probably would result in hostility from merger-oriented businesses, but the FASB would enjoy a boost in prestige if it could sustain its position. Its ability to promulgate accounting standards in a very difficult area would be established, though it might run the risk of a lawsuit.

The evolution of accounting for goodwill, always a crucial area in accounting, thus at present is a crucial issue for the direction of the accounting profession as well. It perhaps is fitting that accounting for this "ultimate asset" is resulting in a test of the private sector to regulate itself in that regard.

---

1. B.J. Sanderson, "Goodwill and Its Valuation," *The Chartered Accountant in Australia*, July 1950, p. 37.

2. Ambrose Bierce, *The Enlarged Devil's Dictionary*, comp. and ed. by Ernest J. Hopkins (Garden City, New York, Doubleday & Co., Inc., 1967), p. 186.

3. John R. Commons, *Legal Foundations of Capitalism* (New York, MacMillan Co., 1924), p. 264.

4. Ibid., p. 22; and Milton Handler, "Restraint of Trade," *Encyclopaedia of the Social Sciences*, vol. 13, 1934, pp. 339-340.

5. Broad v. Jollyfe, Cro. Jac. 596 (1620).

6. William Harris, "Goodwill," *The Accountant*, March 29, 1884, pp. 9-13.

7. "The Treatment of Goodwill in Accounts," *The Accountant*, June 15, 1907, p. 801.

8. Charles B. Couchman, *The Balance-Sheet* (New York, Journal of Accountancy, Inc., 1924), p. 138.

9. "Goodwill: Its Nature, Value and Treatment in the Accounts," *The Accountant*, December 6, 1913, p. 817.

10. American Institute of Accountants, Committee on Accounting Procedure, *Accounting for Intangible Assets*, Accounting Research Bulletin No. 24 (New York, American Institute of Accountants, 1944), pp. 195-201.

11. American Institute of Accountants, Committee on Accounting Procedure, *Business Combinations*, Accounting Research Bulletin No. 40 (New York, American Institute of Accountants, 1950), pp. 299-301.

12. Ibid.

13. Ibid.

14. Dean S. Eiteman, *Pooling and Purchase Accounting* (Ann Arbor, Michigan, University of Michigan Press, 1967), p. 64; and American Institute of Accountants, Committee on Accounting Procedure, *Restatement and Revision of Accounting Research Bulletins*, Accounting Research Bulletin No. 43 (New York, American Institute of Accountants, 1953), pp. 37-40, 55-57.

15. Arthur R. Wyatt, *A Critical Study of Accounting for Business Combinations*, Accounting Research Study No. 5 (New York, American Institute of Certified Public Accountants, 1963), p. 39.

16. American Institute of Accountants, Committee on Accounting Procedure, *Business Combinations*, Accounting Research Bulletin No. 48 (New York, American Institute of Accountants, 1957).

17. For further discussion on this point see Wyatt, *A Critical Study of Accounting for Business Combinations*, pp. 27-28, 36-39; and William C. Suttle and William G. Mecklenburg, "Pooling of Interests," *The Texas CPA*, January 1969, p. 37.

18. Ibid.

19. A. N. Mosich, "Retroactive Poolings in Corporate Mergers," *The Journal of Business*, July 1968, p. 360.

20. Samuel P. Gunther, "Part Purchase-Part Pooling: The Infusion of Confusion Into Fusion," *The New York Certified Public Accountant*, April 1969, pp. 241-249.

21. American Institute of Certified Public Accountants, Accounting Principles Board, *Reporting the Results of Operations*, Opinion of the Accounting Principles Board No. 9 (New York, American Institute of Certified Public Accountants, Inc., 1967), pp. 105-139.

22. "SEC Chief Accountant Speaks Before NYSSCPA," *The Journal of Accountancy*, January 1970, pp. 16, 19.

23. "APB May Abolish Pooling of Interests," *The Journal of Accountancy*, November 1969, p. 19; and "APB: Accounting for Business Combinations," *The Journal of Accountancy*, January 1970, p. 8.

24. American Institute of Certified Public Accountants, Accounting Principles Board, *Exposure Draft: Proposed APB Opinion: Business Combinations and Intangible Assets* (New York, American Institute of Certified Public Accountants, Inc., 1970), p. 11.

25. American Institute of Certified Public Accountants, Accounting Principles Board, *Business Combinations*, Opinion of the Accounting Principles Board No. 16 (New York, American Institute of Certified Public Accountants, Inc., 1970), pp. 279-327.

26. "Accounting Principles Board Proposes 'Merger' Opinion," *The Journal of Accountancy*, April 1970, p. 12.

27. Abraham J. Briloff, "The Accounting Profession at the Hump of the Decades," *Financial Analysts Journal*, May-June 1970, p. 61.

28. A.A. Fitzgerald, "Valuation of Goodwill," *The Chartered Accountant in Australia*, September 1932, p. 379.

29. American Institute of Certified Public Accountants, Accounting Principles Board, *Intangible Assets*, Opinion of the Accounting Principles Board No. 17 (New York, American Institute of Certified Public Accountants, Inc., 1970), pp. 338-341.

30. Ibid.

TABLES AND BIBLIOGRAPHIES

HISTORICAL DATES IN ACCOUNTING

George Abs, et al.

HISTORICAL DATES IN ACCOUNTING*

THE FOLLOWING is a chronological list of dates which appear to be significant in the development of accounting as we know it today. These dates, we believe, through their historical value will give anyone interested in accounting a better understanding of the subject. From the past and from the present, a person has a better appreciation of what may come in the future.

4500 B.C. Taxes were levied and collected in the Babylonian Empire . . . Babylonian influence became the center of commerce and business in its day.

3400 B.C. Early systems of numbering developed in Egypt and Chaldea.

3000 B.C. Early numbering devices such as the Chinese *abacus* and the Peruvian *quipu* appeared.

2300 B.C. Clay tablets were used to record the salary payments for services performed in the temples of Babylon.

2285 B.C. The Hammurabi Code was passed during the reign of Hammurabi in Babylon. This code set the stage for laws of agency and contract and the principle of requiring written evidence for transactions.

2000 B.C. The first record of internal control was used when an Egyptian treasurer's activities in collecting grain were checked by a scribe.

1000 B.C. Records have been found of a banking firm, Egibi and Sons, in Babylon.

549 B.C. A clay tablet was used to record the dissolution of a partnership and division of the stock.

542 B.C. Clay tablets indicated a record of a loan of money, which, if not paid within a month, would bear interest at 20%.

400 B.C. Papyrus (paper) and calamus (pen) as record-keeping devices in Egypt first appeared.

* Prepared by George Abs, Clayton Grimstad, Robert Hay, W. Asquith Howe, William La Place, Francis J. McGurr, and William Serraino.
This project was completed in an accounting seminar under the direction of Professor W. B. Jencks, College of Commerce and Administration, Ohio State University.

400 B.C. Partnerships and companies existed in Greece.

300 B.C. The position of treasurer in the Greek government . . . position was held by Demosthenes . . . was created.

200 B.C. The position of quaestor, a Roman official who examined the accounts of the provincial governors, was created.

200 B.C. Accounting for the Roman Republic was an enlargement of the system used by the family head. Daily receipts and disbursements were entered in a day book, and posted monthly to a register, which was, in effect, a ledger.

200 B.C. The Greeks kept "cash receipts and disbursements" records showing rent and interest as income; sacrifices, wages, and entertainment were recorded as expenditures. Use of drafts, letters of credit and day books was prevalent.

100 B.C. Joint stock companies existed in Rome.

5 A.D. Augustus, a Roman emperor, made the first budget.

292 Diocletian, Roman emperor, created decentralized dioceses, each composed of several provinces, which reported financial information to Rome.

500 The papal treasury at Rome was supervised by a treasurer under whom a paymaster functioned. A decentralized system of accounting for revenues existed. Upon receipt of collections from various church members, representatives sent it to the papal treasury at Rome.

751 Arabs learned the secret of paper making from the Chinese.

800 Charlemagne ordered his famous "Capitulare de Villis" which required an annual inventory of property. Expenses and revenue were recorded in separate books and the balance sent to the king.

831 A deed was executed between the Abbot of St. Ambrose and Senior Donnolo. This deed was signed by an "accountant."

850 A decimal system was used by the Arabs.

1086 William, the Conqueror, made his

Doomesday Book which was a register of all property. From this register revenue and taxes were ascertained.

1096 The Crusades started, which stimulated commerce with the East and which made record keeping by "venture" imperative.

1101–1134 Audits were made during the reign of Henry I.

1130 The compilation of the English Pipe Roll was started. It was a record of taxes, debts, and other liabilities due the crown.

1150 The style of accounting used for estate accounting was the "Charge and Discharge" method, still applicable in estate accounting.

1150 Bills of exchange made their appearance.

1157 The Bank of Venice was established. At this time partnerships were taking the place of individual enterprises.

1164 Italian laws required that accountants help compile General Regulations of Taxable Lands for municipalities.

1200 Guild members were required to keep records.

1202 Arabic numerals were introduced to Europe in book form.

1211 A record was found of "cross entries" in books of accounts of a banking organization in Florence, Italy.

1280 A record in the nature of a journal of cash transactions was kept by Pope Nicholas III.

1285 An auditor was appointed to audit the books of the Commune of Pisa.

1300 Transactions were no longer recorded in narrative form. Similar transactions were grouped together. Pages were totaled, but the totals were not carried forward.

1316 An audit of the accounts of the City of Dublin was made.

1329–1360 German books of account were kept for a Hermann & Johann Wittenborg in the town of Lubeck.

1334 The accounts of the city of London showed greater skill in accountancy than was previously known.

1339 Italian merchant, Peruzzi, used "books" of various colors.

1340 The first record of a complete double entry system of bookkeeping was found at Genoa.

1345 The first of Bonis Brothers (France) used ledgers, journal, deposit book.

1350 In manufacturing plants, the accounting period was the length of time needed to complete a certain quantity of product.

1377 The Bank of Medici used double entry bookkeeping.

1382 Lateral accounts first appeared with debits on the left and credits on the right, replacing the use of vertical accounts.

1400 First evidence of cost accounting appeared in "job order" costing of carding of wool in Italy.

1406 Soranzo Brothers, of Venice, not only kept ledgers but such accounts as "Profit and Loss" and "Capital."

1430 Barbarigo firm of Venice used ledgers with an alphabetical index.

1458 Benedetto Cortrugli's treatise was supposedly the forerunner of Pacioli's manuscript on double entry bookkeeping.

1482 Books were closed and profit calculated on an annual basis in Genoa.

1484 Duke Grandaleozzo Maria Visconti, of Milan, granted to Giovanni Longone, his accountant, the legal right to confer upon his descendants the office of Accountant of Milan.

1494 Pacioli's treatise on bookkeeping, "Summa de Arithmetica, Geometria, Proportioni, et Proportionalita," was published. This publication serves as the basis of many present bookkeeping techniques.

1523 Heinrich Schreiber published the first German book on bookkeeping.

1526 Tagliente, an Italian writer, wrote a book containing *pro forma* entries based upon the principles of Pacioli.

1531 Arabic numerals used in an accounting text by Gottlieb.

1534 Domenico Manzoni, an Italian writer, also wrote a book based on Pacioli's principles.

1543 Hugh Oldcastle, first English bookkeeper, wrote a treatise on bookkeeping.

1543 In Holland, Jan Ympyn Christoffels wrote a book, based on Pacioli and Manzoni, where he first introduced the concept of the trial balance.

1581 The first accounting association was formed in Italy.

1586 Don Pietra, a Benedictine monk, was the first author to think of a business

1588   enterprise as separate and distinct from its owner.

Nicholas Petrie, of Holland, published a treatise in which a compound journal entry first appeared.

1588   John Mellis, of England, first introduced the idea of depreciation as charge to profit and loss.

1594   Passchier-Goessens, of Germany, rearranged the ledger by placing the name of the account at the top of each ledger page.

1595   At this time the accounts of Plantin, a Flemish printer and publisher, contained many elements of a modern job-order cost system. Separate cost accounts were kept for each book published.

1600   The Dutch East Indies Company was formed where "shares" were sold. This is beginning evidence of divorcing of owners from management.

1605   Simon Stevin, of Holland, made a contribution in his book, *Mathematical Traditions;* he started the concept of closing accounts every year; he separated the ledger and set up books in subsidiary ledgers; he laid the foundation for municipal accounting.

1624   The accounts of Merchants' House of Glasgow were audited.

1632   I. Carpenter, of England, wrote a book in which he advocated that all entries appearing in the ledger pass through the journal.

1636   Richard Dafforne (England) wrote "The Merchant's Mirror" which provided illustrative entries to be learned and applied.

1645   George Watson, of Scotland, was the first man to practice accounting as a sole means of livelihood.

1682   The public schools of Boston gave instruction in bookkeeping.

1683   Robert Colinson wrote the first Scotch literature on bookkeeping.

1710   The South Sea Company was organized in England to take over the unfunded national debt. After the company failed, many financially ruined investors demanded an investigation. A public accountant, Charles Snell, was appointed by Parliament to investigate the records. Such is the beginning of public protection of investors by hiring a public accountant.

1717   A book was written by Thomas King (England) illustrating ledgers with debits and credits on separate pages.

1719   John Vernon authored the first Irish bookkeeping text.

1720   In Edinburgh the totals on pages of charge and discharge records were carried forward to the next page.

1721   The Mississippi Bubble, similar to the South Sea escapade, burst.

1740   The need for business instruction in Boston was satisfied by private writing schools which included bookkeeping in the curriculum.

1741   John Mair, of Scotland, wrote the first successful bookkeeping text, which was standard for 50 years.

1742   The Association of Accountants at Milan required a superior knowledge in Latin and law of their members.

1773   The directory of Edinburgh, the first to be published in that city, contained the names of 7 persons who were designated accountants. Thus the accounting profession was being recognized.

1775   Hamilton (Scotland) introduced the concept of accruals in a book that he wrote.

1789   The U. S. Congress passed an act which created the Treasury Department and provided for an auditor and comptroller.

1790   Charles Emmanuel III, of Italy, recognized "chartered" accountants as the only accountants qualified to discharge the duties of public accountants. Such an act is evidence of the beginnings of professional restriction on public practice.

1792   Edward Thomas Jones (England) patented a book and its accounting system for which he charged $5 for every user.

1794   The State of Prussia enacted a bill which required assets to be shown on the balance sheet at the lower of cost or market.

1796   William Mitchell, of Philadelphia, wrote the first American bookkeeping text.

1800   Columnar journals were used for the first time in a book by Degrange.

1805   Napoleon of France stated in a decree that an accountant would not be permitted to practice until he had

	passed a required examination and had served three years with an approved accountant. Such practice restrictions still prevail.
1807	The firm of Cowperthwaite & Son, dealers in furniture, introduced the installment method of merchandising into the United States in New York.
1811	The first general corporation law was passed in New York.
1817	Payen (France) wrote a book on cost accounting.
1817	Accountants began assisting in English bankruptcy cases.
1818	John Bennett conducted double entry bookkeeping instruction in New York.
1825	Uruguay was the first country in the Western hemisphere to legally recognize and regulate accountancy.
1836	Pope Gregory XVI ordered that public accountants concerned with papal activities should pass an examination in technical subjects and should submit a thesis. This was the first time a thesis had been required in the study of accounting.
1836	Argentina enacted legislation regulating the practice of accountancy. The requirements included Argentine citizenship. Only eight accountants were allowed to practice.
1838	Before declaring a dividend, the directors of the Boston and Worcester Railroad reserved $15,000 for deterioration and depreciation of the equipment beyond repair.
1841	Tappan & Company, the Dun & Bradstreet of today, was organized in New York.
1844	The English Companies Act permitted stock companies for the first time since the 18th century frauds.
1845	The English Companies Act of 1845 provided for auditors of all railroads. These auditors were to employ accountants, if needed.
1848	Peter Douff's "North American Accountant" showed an early antecedent of the report form of balance sheet.
1849	The English Bankruptcy Act provided much "winding-up" work for accountants.
1853	The first public accounting society was formed in British Isles at Edinburgh, Scotland.

1854	*Colburn's Railroad Advocate* urged the recognition of depreciation by "setting aside sums each years to cover the replacement."
1857	Inventories were valued at lower of cost or market in Germany.
1860	Price & Waterhouse firm was established in London.
1861	The first income tax law in the United States was passed during the Civil War.
1862	The English Companies Acts of 1862 recommended that all corporations have audits performed by independent auditors.
1867	The Scottish Societies of Glasgow, Edinburgh, & Aberdeen entered into an agreement to standardize examinations and to form a general examining board for Chartered Accountants.
1870	The first English accountants' society, the Incorporated Society of Liverpool Accountants, was established.
1879	Canada was the first British colony to recognize public accountancy (Montreal).
1879	In an English case, *Davidson v. Gillis*, the court gave support to an allowance for depreciation regarding it as replacing the asset.
1880	The English adopted the term, Chartered Accountant, (C.A.), which had been used in Edinburgh since 1853.
1880	Institute of Accountants (London) was incorporated by Royal Charter as The Institute of Chartered Accountants in England and Wales.
1881	Joseph Wharton established the first American collegiate school of business which later became a part of the University of Pennsylvania.
1882	The Institute of Accountants & Bookkeepers was formed in New York.
1882	The first examination was required of chartered accountants in England.
1883	The accounting firm of Barrow, Wade, & Guthrie was founded in New York.
1883	An accounting course was offered as a part of the curriculum at the Wharton School of Finance & Commerce.
1885	The Society of Incorporated Accountants and auditors registered under the Companies Act of 1885.
1887	The American Association of Public Accountants was incorporated in New York.

1891 The accounting firms of Price Waterhouse & Co., and Barrow, Wade, & Guthrie established offices in Chicago, Illinois.

1892 The American Association of Public Accountants started a night school of accounts under the authority of the Regents of New York University. The school failed.

1894 In the case of *Pollock v. the Farmers' Loan & Trust Company*, the Supreme Court ruled that the income tax law was invalid since it was a tax which violated the provision that no tax shall be laid unless in proportion to the census.

1895 The accounting firm of Haskins & Sells was founded in New York.

1895 Netherlands Institute of Accountants was formed.

1896 A commission approved the Uniform Negotiable Instruments Act as it now stands on most state statute books.

1896 The first German Society was formed.

1896 The New York legislature passed a bill to regulate public accounting. The title "C.P.A." was to be obtained by professional examination administered by New York University. Such a bill served as the model for the several state bills to follow.

1897 The first State Society of CPA's was founded in New York.

1898 The Universities of Chicago & California formed Colleges of Commerce.

1899 Pennsylvania passed accounting legislation regulating the practice of accounting.

1899 The first woman CPA in the United States was recognized.

1900 New York University organized the School of Commerce, Accounts, & Finance.

1900 The English Companies Act of 1900 required auditors to audit the books. Auditors were elected by the stockholders.

1902 In England a committee was formed (composed of Chartered Accountants) to standardize terms and accounting principles.

1902 The firm of Lybrand, Ross Bros., & Montgomery was formed in New York.

1902 The Federation of Societies of Public Accountants in U. S. was formed. Its chief purpose was to secure the passage of a federal act regulating accountancy.

1902 The first important consolidated balance sheet was issued by U. S. Steel.

1903 The firm of Ernst & Ernst was formed in Cleveland.

1903 The first Belgian Society was formed.

1904 The first International Congress of Accountants was held in St. Louis.

1904 Cost accounting was being taught in the University of Pennsylvania and New York University.

1904 The first accounting association in Vienna was known as: "College of Expert Accountants in Vienna."

1905 The Federation of Societies of Public Accountants, formed in 1902, merged into the American Association of Public Accountants, formed in 1887. The society advocated federal regulation of public accountancy.

1905 The first issue of the *Journal of Accountancy* was published.

1905 This year marked the beginning of state laws establishing uniform systems of accounts for public utilities.

1906 The Uniform Sales Act was approved by the Commission on Uniform State Laws.

1906 Accounting systems were being taught at New York University.

1907 The Treasury Department changed from single entry to double entry bookkeeping.

1907 The accounting profession started to set up rules of professional conduct.

1908 Sprague wrote *The Philosophy of Accounts.*

1908 Cole wrote *Accounts—Their Construction and Interpretation.* "Where Got—Where Gone" statement was introduced. He advocated setting up sales and purchases net, and showing discounts lost.

1909 Henry Rand Hatfield wrote *Modern Accounting.*

1909 The first U. S. corporation excise tax law, measured by income, was enacted.

1909 Denmark authorized the practice of accounting, reserving the right to prohibit the practice if ethics were violated.

1910 Massachusetts made it compulsory for all savings banks in the state to

	be audited by CPA's once a year.
1910	The University of Pennsylvania offered a bachelor's degree with a major in accounting. New York University offered a master's degree with a major in accounting.
1911	Kansas passed a "Blue Sky" law, requiring the licensing of securities brokers.
1912	Montgomery wrote *Auditing Theory and Practice.*
1913	The Sixteenth Amendment became effective.
1913	The 1913 Revenue Act was passed on October 3, 1913 . . . effective March 1, 1913.
1913	The Federal Reserve banking system was established.
1914	The Uniform Partnership Act was approved by the Commission on Uniform State Laws.
1916	The American Association of University Instructors in Accounting was organized in Columbus, Ohio.
1916	The American Association of Public Accountants changed its name to American Institute of Accountants.
1916	The first estate tax was enacted.
1917	The Revenue Act of 1917 imposed the first excess profits tax.
1917	The American Institute of Accountants and the Federal Reserve Board collaborated to issue the "Approved Methods for Preparation of Balance Sheet Statements," with the objective of standardization of the audit and audit report.
1917	Roy B. Kester wrote *Accounting Theory and Practice.*
1917	The first AIA examination was given.
1918	The Uniform Conditional Sales Act was approved by the Commission on Uniform State laws.
1919	The National Association of Cost Accountants was organized at Buffalo, New York.
1919	The case of *Landell v. Lybrand,* pointed out that the accountant had no liability to third parties unless he was grossly negligent since there was no contract with the third party.
1919	Beta Alpha Psi, an accounting fraternity, was formed at the University of Illinois.
1919	English women were allowed to become Chartered Accountants.

1919	A. C. Littleton wrote *Elementary Accounting.*
1920	The Federal Power Commission Act introduced regulatory accounting.
1921	The American Society of CPA's was organized in Washington.
1921	The Revenue Act of 1921 permitted the use of the lower of cost or market as a means of pricing inventory.
1921	New Mexico was the 48th state to recognize a public accounting statute.
1921	The first *Accountant's Index* was published.
1921	The Government Accounting Office was established.
1922	The federal budget system was inaugurated.
1922	The Puerto Rico Institute of Accountants was formed.
1923	The District of Columbia, Alaska, and Hawaii and the Philippine Islands passed CPA laws.
1923	The American Association of University Instructors in Accounting and the American Institute of Accountants set up committees on education.
1924	The Board of Tax Appeals was set up by the Revenue Act of 1924.
1924	The Alabama CPA law was upheld by the U. S. Supreme Court.
1925	Michigan granted accountants the right of privileged communication with their clients.
1926	The *Accounting Review* was published quarterly.
1926	The Revenue Act of 1926 provided a special method of reporting income from installment sales.
1927	In the case of *Ipswich Mills v. Dillon,* the court held that public accountants were the sole owners of their working papers unless the contract of employment stated otherwise.
1927	Accounting was legally recognized in France.
1927	In Germany, legislation was passed giving accountants of the tax department the right to inspect corporation books for tax purposes.
1928	New York passed a law requiring a CPA candidate to be a college graduate to sit for the examination after January 1, 1938.
1929	The AIA set forth rules of professional conduct.
1930	The NACA "Topical Index" was pub-

lished.

1931 The first chapter of the Controllers' Institute was established in New York.

1931 Accountants were held to be liable to third parties for gross negligence . . . *Ultramares v. Touche.*

1932 The New York Stock Exchange required statements by independent accountants from all listed corporations.

1932 The Revenue Act of 1932 imposed a gift tax.

1933 The federal Securities Act of 1933 compelled the disclosure of pertinent information concerning securities publicly offered and sold in interstate trade or through the mails. Registration statements were required.

1934 The Securities and Exchange Commission was formed.

1934 The Securities and Exchange Act was passed to regulate trade in securities on a national basis and over-the-counter. The Act required registration statements.

1934 Section 77B of the Bankruptcy Act was passed establishing corporate reorganization procedure.

1934 The National Committee on Municipal Accounting was formed.

1935 The Social Security Act was enacted providing for payroll deductions by employer and employee.

1935 The Public Utility Holding Company Act was passed.

1936 The Robinson-Patman Act was passed, prohibiting discriminatory pricing.

1936 The AAA's *Tentative Statement of Accounting Principles Underlying Corporate Financial Statements* was published.

1937 The SEC issued its first accounting release.

1938 The Fair Labor Standards Act required detailed payroll records be kept for five years.

1938 The Chandler Act, an amendment to the Bankruptcy Act, became effective.

1939 The Revenue Act of 1939 permitted the use of the LIFO method of inventory costing.

1939 The McKessons Robbins Case resulted in strengthening auditing procedures.

1939 The American Institute of Account-

ants started publishing Accounting Research Bulletins and Statements on Auditing Procedures.

1939 The Trust Indentures Act was enacted.

1940 The Institute of Internal Auditors was formed.

1940 The Investment Company Act of 1940 brought investment companies under the Securities and Exchange Commission.

1940 The Securities and Exchange Commission issued Regulation S-X.

1940 The Second Revenue Act of 1940 introduced an excess profits tax.

1941 American Accounting Association revised the 1936 *Statement of Accounting Principles Underlying Corporate Financial Statements.*

1941 The first of the New York University Institutes on Federal Taxation was held.

1942 The Board of Tax Appeals was changed to the Tax Court of the United States.

1942 The Federal Reports Act was passed to reduce and simplify reports and questionnaires rendered to the federal government.

1942 Price controls were enacted. Renegotiation laws were passed.

1943 Withholding provisions were included in the income tax law.

1944 The National Conference of Lawyers and Certified Public Accountants was formed to foster better professional relationships.

1945 The excess profits tax was removed.

1945 The George bill provided for comprehensive audits of government corporations. The Corporation Audits Division of the General Accounting office was formed.

1946 The American Institute of Accountants published *Contemporary Accounting*, Thomas Leland, editor.

1947 The American Institute of Accountants and the Rockefeller Foundation sponsored the Business Income Study Group.

1947 Labor Management Relations Act (Taft-Hartley) was passed requiring all labor unions to prepare financial statements.

1947 The American Institute of Accountants began publication of Case Stud-

1948 ies in Auditing Procedure.

1948 The American Association issued *Accounting Concepts and Standards Underlying Corporate Financial Statements.*

1948 The American Association issued a tentative statement of the fundamental concepts of cost accounting.

1948 The American Institute of Accountants began publishing their annual surveys of corporate reports.

1948 The Institute of Internal Auditors issued *Responsibilities of the Internal Auditor.*

1948 The American Institute of Accountants issued Statements on Auditing Procedure No. 23 relative to the accountant's opinion.

1949 The first Inter-American Conference on Accounting was held in San Juan, Puerto Rico.

1950 Another excess profits tax was enacted.

1951 The Securities and Exchange Commission extensively revised Regulation S-X.

1951 The Federal Government Accountants Association was formed.

1951 The Society of Accountants in Edinburgh, The Society of Accountants and Actuaries in Glasgow, and The Society of Accountants in Aberdeen combined to form The Institute of Chartered Accountants of Scotland.

1951 The American Institute of Accountants published a codification of their Statements on Auditing Procedures.

1953 The American Institute of Accountants published the *CPA Handbook*, and also revised and restated their Accounting Research Bulletins.

It is recognized that this list is not all-inclusive. Consequently, we should appreciate any additions which the reader might consider significant. For rather obvious reasons, no text books after 1920 have been listed.

While we realize that these dates may be controversial to some readers, we do think that it is a good "jumping-off place" to list the significant dates in the history of accounting. If some readers have any comments, criticisms, suggestions, or opinions regarding the accuracy, completeness, and significance of these dates, the authors would appreciate receiving them, addressed to the Accounting Department, Ohio State University, Columbus 10, Ohio.

A CHECK-LIST
OF EARLY BOOKKEEPING TEXTS

H. R. Hatfield and A. C. Littleton

A CHECK-LIST OF EARLY BOOKKEEPING TEXTS

H. R. HATFIELD AND A. C. LITTLETON

THE following bibliography of book-keeping textbooks published prior to 1850 is designed to supplement the catalogues of the Montgomery Collection at Columbia University. Taken together these two check lists will afford a rather comprehensive view of the textbook materials of this field which are available in America. No attempt has been made to include old manuscript account books, or treatises on accounting history.

Each entry includes an indication of the present location of the book; if it can be found in several places, several libraries are named. A list of all the libraries mentioned follows. The italic indicates the abbreviations used.

University Libraries:

University of California (*Calif.*); University of Chicago (*Chgo.*); University of Illinois (*Ill.*); Ohio Wesleyan University (*Ohio Wes.*); University of Western Ontario (*Ontario*); Baker Library of Harvard University (*Harvard*); University of Toronto (*Toronto*); University of Wisconsin (*Wis.*); Yale University (*Yale*).

Society Libraries:

American Antiquarian Society, Worcester, Mass. (*Am. Antiq. Soc.*); American Institute of Accountants, New York City (*Am. Inst.*); Library of Congress (*Lib. Cong.*). Henry E. Huntington Library and Art Gallery, San Marino, Calif. (*Huntington*).

Private Collections:

M. I. Fleisher, Philadelphia (*Fleisher*); J. C. Meyer, St. Johns College, Brooklyn (*Meyer*); F. E. Ross, Ann Arbor, Mich. (*Ross*); J. K. Moffit, Piedmont, Calif. (*Moffit*).

ADAMS, DANIEL 1773-1864

Book-keeping, Keen, N.H.: Prentiss [°1849]. *Lib. Cong., Mich., Am. Antiq. Soc.*

AGUCCHIA, LATTANTIO

Il computista pagato. . . . Todi: Galassi, 1671. *Calif.*

ALEXANDER, HENRY

An exposition of book-keeping, by single or double entry. Baltimore: Neilson, 1840. *Lib. Cong.*

ALGER, ISRAEL

Key to book-keeping. . . . Boston: True and Greene, 1823. *Lib. Cong., Am. Antiq. Soc.*

ANDRIESSENS, J. B. P. de

Openbaeringhe van het italiaens boeckhouden op aventeur ter zee. 1724. Calif.

ANONYMOUS

Advice to the women and maidens of London. London: Billingsby, 1678. *Ross*

Einleitung zu einem verbesserten cameral-rechnungsfusse, auf die verwaltung einer herrschaft angewandt. Wien: Trattner, 1764. *Calif.*

Gentleman's and lady's accomptant. London: 1744. *Ross*

Handleyding tot den hollandschen koophandel . . . aentoonende . . . eene schets van het italiaensch boekhouden . . . etc. Brugge: 1784. *Calif.*

Der kaufmann. Prag. 1815. *Calif.*

The merchantile manual, or accountant's guide. New Haven: Steele, 1810. *Am. Antiq. Soc.*

Régie methodique ou la comptabilité du régisseur réduite à les vrais principes. Paris: Chez les auteurs, 1787. *Harvard*

BALUGANI, PELLEGRINO

Instruzione brevissima per formare con metodo qualunque scrittura in un libro doppio . . . Modena: Soliani, 1745. *Calif.*

BARREME, FRANÇOIS BERTRAND 1640-1703
Traite des parties doubles; ou, Methode aisée pour apprendre à tenir en parties doubles les livres du commerce & des finances avec un traité de finance. . . . Paris: 1721. *Calif.*

BATCHELDER, JACOB
The national accountant. . . . Boston: Jewett, 1847. *Lib. Cong.*

BECK, FREDERICK
The young accountant's guide. . . . Boston: Stimpson and Clapp, 1831. *Lib. Cong., Harvard*

BECKER, GEORGE J.
A treatise on the theory and practice of book-keeping by double entry. Philadelphia: Charles, 1847. *Lib. Cong.*

BECKMANN, J.
Anweisungen, die rechnungen kleiner haushaltungen zu führen. —Gross, 1800. *Calif.*

BENNETT, JAMES [ARLINGTON]
The American system of practical book-keeping. . . . New York: Paul, 1820. *Lib. Cong., Ross*
7th ed. New York: Collins, 1824. *Lib. Cong.*
10th ed. New York: Collins, 1828. *Harvard*
14th ed. New York: Collins, 1831. *Mich.*
15th ed. New York: Collins, 1833. *Lib. Cong., Ill.*
19th ed. New York: Collins, 1839. *Ohio Wes., Am. Antiq. Soc.*
21st ed. New York: Collins, 1842. *Am. Antiq. Soc.*
22nd ed. New York: Harper, 1843. *Lib. Cong.*
—ed. New York: Bennet, 1846. *Lib. Cong.*
38th ed. New York: Newman, 1848. Lib. *Cong., Mich., Yale*
41st ed. New York:—1862. *Lib. Cong.*

BERKIN, WILLIAM
[with Francis Walkingame, 1846, q.v.]

BLEIBTREU, LEOPOLD CARL
Lehrbuch der handelswissenschaft. . . . Carlsruhe: Groos, 1830. *Lib. Cong.*
Handbuch der contor-wissenschaft. Karlsruhe: Groos, 1835. *Lib. Cong., Mich.*

BODE, HENRICH [*praeses*]
Dissertatio inauguralis juridico de libris mercatorum suspectis.—1707. *Meyer*

BORNACCINI, GIUSEPPE
Idee teoretiche e pratiche di ragionateria, . . . Rimino: Marsoner, 1818. *Calif.*
2d ed. Rimino: Marsoner, 1838. *Harvard*

BOUCHAIN, LE JEUNE
Traité-pratique de la tenue simplifiée des livres a parties doubles. . . . Rouen: Marie, 1819. *Ill.*

BRENDER A BRANDIS, GERRIT
De handlingen van eenen koopmen. of de gronden van het italiaanisch boekhouden. Amsterdam (?): 1778. *Yale*

BUCHANAN, COLIN
Practical book-keeping. Edinburgh: Muirhead, 1806. *Ill.*

BUCKLIN, ISAAC B.
Bucklin's counting house journal. . . . Troy, N.Y.: Tuttle, 1833. *Lib. Cong.*

BURGESS, N. G.
Colt's Bookkeeping. Cincinnati: 1838. *Yale*

BURN, W. SCOTT
The principles of book-keeping. . . . Toronto: Rowsell, 1844. *Ontario*

CALCULATOR [PSEUD.?]
Counting house manual and introduction to business. London: 1843. *Yale*

CASANOVA, ALUISE
Specchio evcidissimo. Venice: 1558. *Calif.*

CASTRO, J.
A present for young gentlemen on entering the comptinghouse: . . . London: 1750. *Calif.*

CERCHI, LUCIANO
La scrittura doppia mercantile. Mantua:
1847. *Calif.*

CLAPERON, E.
Cours de comptabilité. . . . Paris: Dela-
grave, 1885-86. *Lib. Cong.*

CLARE, [J.] MARTIN
A short and familiar sketch of bookkeeping per double entry in the Italian
manner. London: Birt, 1751. (Also contained in Webster, An essay, q.v.) *Calif.*
Youth's introduction to trade and business. London: 1741. *Toronto*
8th ed. London: 1758. *Yale*

CLARKE, F. G.
A synthetic and inductive system of
book-keeping by double entry. . . . Portland [Me.]: Colesworthy; Boston: B. B.
Mussey, 1840. *Lib. Cong.*
2d ed. [?] Portland: Colesworthy, 1841.
Lib. Cong.

COFFIN, JAMES HENRY 1806-1873
Progressive exercises in book-keeping,
by single and double entry. Greenfield,
Mass.: Phelps, 1836. *Lib. Cong.*

COLINSON, ROBERT
Idea rationaria. . . . Edinburgh: 1683.
Calif.

COLLINS, JOHN
An introduction to merchants' accompts.
London: 1675. (Bound with Malynes.
Consuetudo. . . . 1686 ed.) *Calif., Chgo.*
(1674 ed.), *Ill.*

COLT, JOHN CALDWELL 1810-1842?
The science of double entry bookkeeping. . . . 3d ed. Cincinnati: Burgess,
1838. *Lib. Cong., Mich.*
4th ed. Phila.: Cowperthwait, 1839. *Ross*
7th ed. New York: Foster, 1841. *Harvard*
11th ed. New York: Nafes, 1845. *Ross*
—ed. New York:—1846. *Calif.*

COMER, GEORGE NIXON 1816-1877
A simple method of keeping books. . . .
Boston: Tichnor, 1846. *Lib. Cong., Am.
Antiq. Soc.*

3d ed. Boston: Tichnor, 1847. *Am.
Antiq. Soc.*
6th ed. Boston: Tichnor, 1850. *Am.
Antiq. Soc., Calif.*
A record of the transactions of a mer-
chant. Boston: Damrell, 1853. *Lib.
Cong.*

CORY, ISAAC PRESTON 1802-1842
A practical treatise on accounts. . . . 2d
ed. London: Pickering, 1839. *Lib. Cong.,
Am. Inst.*
—ed. London: Pickering, 1840. *Ill., Am.
Inst.*

COTRUGLI, [RANGEO] BENEDETTO
Della mercatvra et del mercante per-
feto. . . . Brascia: 1602. *Calif.*

COUTREELS, JOHAN, fl. 1603.
Het konstig cyffer-boek. . . . — 1738.
Calif.

CRITTENDEN, A. F. AND S. W.
An inductive and practical system of
double entry bookkeeping. Phila.: Biddle,
1845 *Yale*
2d. ed. [?] Phila.: Biddle, 1850. *Yale*

CRONHELM, F. W.
Double entry by single. London, 1818.
Lib. Cong., Calif.

CRÜGER, CARL 1778-1831 [Langhenie, Ed.]
Der kaufmann . . . 3d ed. Hamburg:
Herald, 1837. *Lib. Cong., Harvard*

DAFFORNE, RICHARD
The merchants mirrour, London: 1635,
bound with Malynes. Consuetudo. . . .
1636 ed. *Yale, Ill.*
The merchants mirrour, London: 1684,
bound with Malynes. Consuetudo. . . .
1686 edition. *Calif., Ill.*

DANDO, JOSEPH
A complete and infallible system of
practical bookkeeping by double entry.
. . . Philadelphia: 1842. *Lib. Cong.,
Mich.*

DEFOE, DANIEL
The complete English tradesman. 2v.
Oxford: Talboys, 1841. *Calif.*

DEGRANGE, EDMOND

La tenue des livres rendue facile. . . .
10*th* ed. Paris: Saintin, 1818. *Calif.*

La tenuduría de libros simplificanda.
13*th* ed. Traducido del francés por Don
José Maria Ruiz Perez. Burdeos: 1826.
Calif.

La tenue des livres ou nouveau traite de
comptabilite generale. Anvers: Froment,
1840. *Calif.*

DESAGULIERS, H.

Grondig onderwijs in het italiaansch
boekhouden. 6. druk. Amsterdam: 1789.
Calif.

DILWORTH, THOMAS

The young bookkeeper's assistant. . . .
London: Kent, 1765. *Mich.*

9*th* ed. London: Causton, 1784. *Ross*

12*th* ed. Phila.: Johnson [°1789]. *Calif.*
12*th* ed. Phila.: — 1790. *Calif., Am.
Inst.*

12*th* ed. London: Wilson, 1792. *Ill.*

12*th* ed. Phila.: Johnson, 1794. *Am.
Antiq. Soc.*

— ed., London, — 1795. *Wis.*

13*th* ed. Wilmington: Brynberg, 1798.
Am. Antiq. Soc.

19*th* ed. London, — 1806. *Calif.*

—ed. London: Wilson, 1822. *Yale, Ill.*

—ed. York: (Engl.), Wilson, 1839. *Lib.
Cong.*

Dilworth's bookkeepers assistant. . . .
New York: Jansen, 1803. *Am. Antiq.
Soc., Ohio Wes.*

Dilworth's bookkeepers assistant. . . .
New York: Totten, 1822. *Lib. Cong.,
Mich.*

DITMAR, WILHELM

Das staatskassen- und rechnungswesen.
Köln: Boisseree, 1844. *Mich.*

DOMENGET, GASPARD

Nouvelle méthode pour la tenue des
livres. Lyon: Ballanche; 1809. *Harvard*

DONN, BENJAMIN

The accountant and geometrician. London: Johnson, 1765. *Calif.*

DÖPLER, JACOB

Der getreue rechnungs-beamte. . . .
Franckfurt: 1680. *Calif.*

Der u n g e t r e u e rechnungs-beamte.
Franckfort: 1697. (Bound with 1697
edition of Der getreue rechnungs-
beamte). *Calif.*

Der getreue rechnungs-beamte. (3 vols.
in 1) Franckfurt: 1697. *Calif.*

DOUBLET, VICTOR

Nouvelle méthode pour apprendre la
tenue des livres en partie simple et en
partie double. Paris: 1848. *Calif.*

DUSSEAU, J. C. G.

Het koopmans boekhouden. Hague:
1825. *Calif.*

EDWARDS, WILLIAM

The book-keeper's atlas. . . . New
York: Harper, 1834. *Lib. Cong.*

EULER, MARTIN

Neues handlungs-lexikon in deutschen,
französichen und italienischen rubriken
für junge kaufleute und contoristen.
Carlsruhe: 1790. *Calif.*

EVERARD, W.

Merchantile bookkeeping. London: 1764.
Wis.

FABRICIUS, GOTTLIEB PAUL

Unterricht zur doppelten buchhaltung.
. . . Regensburg: 1787. *Calif.*

FISHER, ISAAC

[with Francis Walkingame, 1845, *q.v*]

FLASCHIN, SALOMON

Practisches lehrbuch der buchhalterey
nach einer erprobten neuen methode. . . .
Frankfort: Varrentrapp, 1805. *Calif.*

FLEMING, JOHN

The national system of book-keeping. . . .
Pittsburgh: M'Donald, 1846. *Lib. Cong.*

FLORI, LODOVICO

Trattato del mode di tenere il libro doppio domestico. Rome: Varese, 1677.
Calif.

FLUEGEL, GEORG THOMAS

Der getreue und aufrichtige wegweiser zur gründlichen erlernung der hochschätzbaren wissenschaft des buchhaltens. Frankfort: 1741. *Calif.*

Getreuer und aufrichtiger wegweiser zur grundlichen erlernung des doppelten und einfachen buchhaltens. Pest: 1792. *Calif.*

FORT, C. D.

Vollständiges lehrbuch der gesammten buchhaltungs kunde. Leipzig: 1837. *Calif.*

FÖRTSCH, M. F.

Instructie, of grondige onderrichting over het italiaans boekhouden. . . . Amsterdam: 1783. *Calif.*

FOSTER, BENJAMIN FRANKLIN

A concise treatise on commercial book-keeping. Boston: Perkins, 1836. *Lib. Cong., Mich., Yale, Am. Antiq. Soc.*

2d. ed. Boston: Perkins, 1837. *Calif. Am. Antiq. Soc.*

3d ed. Boston: Perkins, 1845. *Am. Antiq. Soc.*

Foster's school bookkeeping. Boston: Perkins, 1840. *Lib. Cong.*

Double entry elucidated. Boston: Marvin, 1852. *Lib. Cong.*

Origin and progress of bookkeeping. London: 1852. *Yale*

FOSTER, B. WOOD

A practical system of bookkeeping. . . . 7th ed. Boston: French, 1848. *Lib. Cong.*

8th ed., Boston: French, 1850. *Lib. Cong.*

FREESE, J. H.

The commercial classbook. London: Longman, 1849. *Yale*

FULTON, LEVI S. [AND EASTMAN, GEO. W.]

A practical system of book-keeping by single entry. . . . 2d ed. New York: Barnes, 1848. *Lib. Cong., Am. Antiq. Soc.*

GAIGNAT DE LAULNAIS, C. F.

Guide du commerce. Paris: Despilly, 1791 [?]. *Harvard*

GALE, EDMUND

An epitome of bookkeeping by singly entry. Nantucket: Tannat, 1817. *Am. Antiq. Soc.*

GERISHER, CHARLES

Modern book-keeping by double entry. New York: Conrad, 1817. *Am. Antiq. Soc.*

GIBSON, JOHN

A new and improved system of practical bookkeeping. . . . Phila: 1826. *Lib. Cong.*

GILBERT, J. W.

A system of banking bookkeeping. London: Clay, 1849. *Havard*

GIRAUDEAU, PIERRE (L'AINE)

L'art de dresser les comptes des banquiers, négocians et marchands. Genève: 1746. *Calif.*

La banque rendue facile aux principales nations de l'Europe. Lyon: 1769. *Yale, Calif.* —ed. Lyon: 1798. *Calif.*

Le flambeau des comptoirs contenant toutes les écritures et opérations du commerce de terre, de mer et de banque. Marseille: Mossy, 1797. *Calif.*

GODDARD, THOMAS H.

The merchant; or, practical accountant. . . . New York: Starr, 1821. *Lib. Cong.*

3d ed. New York: Sleight, 1831. *Lib. Cong.*

4th ed. New York: Moore, 1834. *Yale*

GOODACRE, ROBERT

A treatise on bookkeeping. London: 1811. *Ross*

2d ed. London: 1818. *Ill.*

GORDON, WILLIAM

The universal accountant and complete merchant. Edinburgh: Donaldson, 1763-65. *Lib. Cong.*

5th ed. Edin., 1787. *Calif.*

6th ed. Dublin: Henshall, 1796. *Lib. Cong., Yale*

GOTTLIEB, JOHANN

Zwey künstliche und bestendige buchhalten. 1592. *Calif.*

GOUINLOCK, G. AND J.

A complete system of practical arithmetic. . . . To which are added, a set of book-keeping by single entry. . . . Hamilton [Can.]: Ruthven, 1842. *Ontario*

GRAAF, ABRAHAM DE

Instructie van het italiaans boek-houden. Amsterdam: [17—?] *Calif.*

GREEN, SAMUEL

Daboll's schoolmaster's assistant. . . . Ithaca, N.Y.: 1829. Also 1831. *Ill.*

The practical accountant. . . . New London: Green, 1824 [?] *Mich.*

GRISOGONO, SIMON DA ZARA

Il mercante arricchito del perfetto quaderniere. . . . Venice: Vecchi, 1609. *Calif.*

HABELIUS, ANDREAS

Des buchhaltens neueste und kurtzeste manier. . . . Leipzig: Andream Habelium, 1707. *Calif.*

HAGER, CHRISTOPH ACHATIUS 1584-1624

Buchhalten über proper commission und compagnia handlungen. . . . [Hamburg? 1660?] *Calif.*

HAMILTON, ROBERT

An introduction to merchandize. . . . 3d ed. Edinburgh: Creech, 1797. *Ill.*

HAMILTON, WILLIAM

Bookkeeping—new modelled; or a treatise of merchants' accounts. Edinburgh: 1735. *Ross*

HARRIS, NICHOLAS

A complete system of practical book-keeping. . . . Hartford: Brown, 1838. *Lib. Cong., Am. Antiq. Sac.*

1842. *Ill.*

1845. *Am. Antiq. Soc.*

1846. *Ill.*

1848. *Am. Antiq. Soc., Harvard*

First lessons in book-keeping. . . . Hartford: Brown and Parsons [pref. 1841] *Lib. Cong.*

HATTON, EDWARD

The merchant's magazine or trades-man's treasury. . . . 3d ed. London: 1699. *Ross* 4th ed. London: 1701. *Calif.*

6th ed. London: Knapton, 1712. *Calif., Yale, Harvard*

7th ed. London: 1719. *Harvard*

8th ed. London: 1726. *Harvard*

HAWKINS, JOHN

Clavis commercii. . . . London: 1689. *Calif.*

HAYES, RICHARD

The gentleman's complete book-keeper. London: Noon, 1741. *Ross*

HELWIG, SAMUEL FRIEDRICH

Anweisung zur leichten und gründlichen erlernung der italienischen doppelten buchhaltung. . . . 2d ed. Stettin: 1790. *Calif.*

HERR, GOTTFRIED

Vermehrtes arithmetisches hand-buch. . . . Breslau: 1653. *Calif.*

HITCHCOCK, I. I.

New method of teaching book-keeping. Phila.: 1835. [also 1844] *Am. Antiq. Soc.*

HUDSON, PETER

New introduction to trade and business. 6th ed. London: Johnson, 1786. *Ontario*
—ed. London: Johnson, 1801. *Am. Inst.*

HUTTON, CHARLES

The schoolmaster's guide. . . . 3d ed. Newcastle: Saint, 1771. *Ill.*

A complete treatise on practical arithmetic and book-keeping. [Alexander Ingram, editor] Edinburgh: 1807. *Calif.* [American edition] New York: 1810. *Ill.*

A course of bookkeeping according to the method of single entry. Phila.: Johnson, 1801. *Am. Antiq. Soc.*

1st improved ed. Phila.: 1806, *Yale.*
—ed. Phila.: Bennett, 1809. *Am. Antiq. Soc. Ross*

2d, improved ed. Phila.: Bennett, 1815. *Lib. Cong.*

IMHOOF, JEAN JACQUES

L'art de tenir des livres en parties doubles . . . Vevey: 1786. *Calif.*

INGLIS, W.
Bookkeeping by single and double entry. Edinburgh: 1850. *Calif.*

JACKSON, GEORGE
A new check journal upon the principle of double entry. . . . London: 1826. *Meyer*
2d ed. London: 1928. *Calif.*

JACKSON, [?]
Complete systems of bookkeeping. Dublin: 1840. *Wis.*

JACKSON, WILLIAM
Bookkeeping in the true Italian form of debtor and creditor by way of double entry. Dublin: 1801. *Calif.*
Phila.: Bioren, 1801. *Ross, Am. Ant. Soc.*
New York: Sage, 1804. *Lib. Cong., Am. Antiq. Soc., Am. Inst.*
New York: Smith, 1811. Yale, *Am. Antiq. Soc.*
New York: Brown, 1816. *Ill., Am. Antiq. Soc.*

JONES, EDWARD THOMAS
Jones's English system of bookkeeping, etc. Bristol: Edwards, 1796. *Calif., Harvard, Ill.*
15th ed. London—*Calif.*
1st. Am. ed. New York: Davis, 1796. *Ross, Am. Inst., Am. Antiq. Soc.*
2d Am. ed. New York: Davis, 1797. *Am. Inst.*

JONES, THOMAS
The principles and practice of bookkeeping. New York: Wiley, 1841. *Lib. Cong., Ross*
Bookkeeping and accountantship. New York: Wiley, 1849. *Lib. Cong., Calif.*
—ed. New York: Wiley, 1850. *Calif.*

KELLY, PATRICK
Elements of book-keeping.
Philadelphia: Humphreys, 1803. *Calif., Ill., Am. Antiq. Soc.*
3d. London: Johnson, 1805. *Wis., Ross, Am. Inst.*
4th ed. London: —1811. *Meyer*
5th ed. London: Baldwin, 1815. *Harvard*

7th ed. London: —1821. *Meyer*
10th ed. London: —1833. *Toronto, Ill.*

KING, THOMAS
An exact guide to book-keeping. . . . London: 1717. *Ill.*

KNOWLTON, JOSEPH
A new system of book-keeping by single entry. Boston: Eastburn, 1828. *Am. Antiq. Soc.*

KOCK, DAVID
Kort begrijp van't gantsche italiaens boeck-houden. . . . Amsterdam: 1647. *Calif.*
De luchtende fackel van het italiaens boeck-houden. . . . Amsterdam: 1663. *Calif.*
Kort onderricht van't italiaens boekhouden. . . . Middleburg: 1710. *Calif.*

LA PORTE, [M] DE
Le guide des négocions et teneurs de livres. . . . Amsterdam: Mortier, 1699. *Calif.*
La science des négocions et teneurs de livres. . . . Paris: Nully, 1748. *Calif.*
—ed. Paris:—1753. *Meyer*
—ed. —:—1769. *Calif.*
—ed. Paris: Clouzier, 1741. *Harvard*

LAWES, EDWARD
A practical treatise on naval book-keeping. London: Davidson, 1827. *Harvard*

LEE, CHAUNCEY
The American accomptant. . . . Lansingburgh: Wands, 1797. *Ill.*

LEUCHS, JOHANN MICHAEL
Theorie und praxis des doppelten, des einfachen und des nurnberger buchhaltens.
2d ed. Nurnberg: 1820. *Calif.*

LIDDEL, ROBERT
The seaman's new vade mecum. . . . London: Robinson, 1787. *Yale*

LISET, ABRAHAM
Amphithalamm, or the accountants closet. London: 1684. [Round with

Malynes' Consuetudo, 1668 ed.] *Calif., Ill.*

LONDON, JOHN

An abridgment of Mr. London's complete system of bookkeeping. London: 1757. *Lib. Cong., Yale*

M, J.

Outline of an expeditions method for the daily checking and ultimate balancing of the accounts in extensive savings banks. (Bound with National Security Savings Bank Report, Edinburgh: 1855) Edinburgh: 1845. *Yale*

MACGREGOR, PATRICK

A practical treatise on book-keeping. . . . New York: Newman, 1850. *Lib. Cong.*

M'LAUGHLIN, DANIEL

A treatise on book-keeping. New York: Davis, 1847. *Lib. Cong., Mich.*

MAGINNES, JAMES

The family clerk and students' assistant. . . . Harrisburg: Greer, 1817. *Ill., Am. Antiq. Soc.*

MAIR, JOHN

Bookkeeping methodiz'd. . . .
3d ed. Edinburgh: Sands, 1749. *Lib. Cong.*
4th ed. Edinburgh: Sands, 1752. *Harvard, Am. Inst.*
5th ed. Edinburgh: Sands, 1757. *Lib. Cong., Calif., Ross*
7th ed. Edinburgh: ——, 1763. *Yale*
8th ed. Edinburgh: Sands, 1765. *Ill.*
Bookkeeping Moderniz'd. . . . Edinburgh: Kincaid, 1773. *Calif., Harvard*
2d ed. Edinburgh: Kincaid, 1778. *Ross*
6th ed. Edinburgh: Kincaid, 1793. *Am. Inst., Meyer*
9th ed. Edinburgh: Kincaid, 1807. *Yale*

MALCOLM, ALEXANDER

A new treatise of arithmetick and book-keeping. Edinburgh: 1718. *Calif., Ross*
A treatise of bookkeeping. . . . London: Osborn, 1731. *Lib. Cong., Calif., Meyer, Wis.*

MALYNES, GERARD DE

Consuetudo, vel lex mercatoria. —ed. London: 1636. *Ill.*
3d ed. London: 1686. [includes: Dafforne, Merchants mirrour; Collins, Introduction to merchants accompts; Liset, The accountants closet]. *Calif., Ill.*

MANZONI, DOMENICO DA ODERZO

Libro mercantile. . . . Venice: 1564. *Calif.*

MARSH, CHRISTOPHER C [OLUMBUS]

The art of single-entry book-keeping;. Baltimore: M'Dowell, 1832. *Lib. Cong., Ill.*
—ed. New York: Riker, 1836. *Mich.*
—ed. New York: Riker, 1844. *Am. Inst.*
4th ed. New York: ——1847. *Yale*
The science of double-entry bookkeeping. Phila.: Towar, 1830. *Lib. Cong.*
Phila.: Hogan, 1839. *Am. Antiq. Soc.*
Phila.: Towar, 1841. *Calif.*
La siencia de teneduria de libros. . . . Havana: Charlain, 1849. *Lib. Cong.*

MARSHALL, JOHN J.

The public school account book. . . . Framingham [Mass.]: Boynton, 1835. *Lib. Cong.*
—ed., Framingham [Mass.]: Boynton, 1839, *Am. Antiq. Soc.*

MEISNER, SAM. GLO.

Die kunst in drei stunden ein buchhalter zu werden. Berlin: 1805. *Calif.*

MELLIS, JOHN

A briefe instruction. . . . [This worke . . . the reneuer and reviver of an auncient old copie printed . . . in London . . . 1543 . . . set forth by one Hugh Oldcastle. . . .] *Calif.*

MENNHER, VALENTIN

Practicqve povr brievement. . . . 1565. *Calif.*

MEYER, KOECHLIN, VAL

Esprit de la comptabilite commerciale. Paris et Geneve: 1845. *Yale*

MEYER, JOHANN RUDOLF

. . . Theoretische einleitung in die praktische wechsel- und waaren-handlung. . . . Hanau: 1782. *Calif.*

MIGNERET, P. J.
La science des jeunes négocians et teneurs de livres . . . Paris: [1799]. *Calif.*

MITEAU DE BLAINVILLE
Instruction concernant la tenue des livres en parties doubles. . . . Brussels: 1784. *Calif.*

MITCHELL, WILLIAM
A new and complete system of book-keeping. Philadelphia: Bioren, 1796. *Lib. Cong., Am. Antiq. Soc.*

MONTEAGE, STEPHEN
Debtor and creditor made easie
—ed. London: Billingsley, 1675. *Ross*
2d ed. London: Billingsley, 1682. *Lib. Cong.*
3d ed. London: Billingsley, 1690. *Ill.*

MOODY, PAUL
A practical plan of book-keeping by double entry. Philadelphia: Lippincott, 1845. *Lib. Cong.*

MORISON, B.
Book-keeping improved. . . . Milton, Pa.: Frick, 1831. *Lib. Cong.*

MORRISON, C.
A complete system of practical book-keeping. . . . 3d ed. Glasgow: 1822. *Ill.*
—ed. Glasgow: 1823. *Meyer*
—ed. London: 1843. *Meyer*

MORRISON, JAMES
A complete treatise on practical book-keeping. . . . 3d ed., London: [1808]. *Calif.*
Elements of book-keeping. . . . London: 1810. *Am. Inst.*
2d ed. London: 1813. *Calif.*
3d ed. London: 1818. *Meyer*
New ed. London: 1825. *Meyer, Ill.*

NICHOLAS, ABRAHAM
The young accountant's debitor and creditor. London: 1713. *Yale*

[NORTH, ROGER]
The gentleman accomptant. . . . —ed. London: Curll, 1714. *Ross*
2d ed. London: Curll, 1715. *Lib. Cong.*

NORTHEND, CHARLES
The common school book-keeping. . . . Boston: Reynolds, 1845. *Lib. Cong.*

[OLDCASTLE, HUGH]
A briefe instruction and maner how to keepe bookes of accompts . . . by John Mellis. London: Windet, 1588. *Calif., Huntington*

OUDSHOFF, W.
Volledig theoretisch en praktisch handboek voor het italiaansch of koopmansboekhouden. Rotterdam: 1843. *Calif.*

PACIOLO, LUCA
Summa de arithmetica, etc. . . . [Venetija]: 1494. *Calif., Harvard, Am. Inst. Meyer, Denver, Moffitt*
1523 ed. *Calif., Harvard*

PASINI, GIOVANNI CAVALA
La scuola in practica del banco giro nella serenissima repubblica di Venezia che dimonstra le regole, e le diverse maniere de conteggiare nel banco giro. . . . Venezia: 1741. *Calif.*

PEELE, JAMES
The pathewaye to perfectness. . . . London: Purfoote, 1569. *Lib. Cong. T. E. Ross* (Phila.), *Huntington*

PERCIVAL, RAYMOND
The tradesman's book-keeper. . . . London: Groombridge, 1836. *Lib. Cong.*

PERI, GIOVANNI DOMENICO
Il negotiante. . . . Genova: Calenzano, 1638. *Calif.*

PERRY, WILLIAM
The man of business. 3d ed. Edinburgh: 1777. *Lib. Cong., Calif.*

PETRI, NICOLAUS, fl. 1567-1583
Practicqve, om te leeren, rekenen, cypheren ende boeckhouden. . . . Amsterdam: 1605. *Calif.*

PIETRA, ANGELO

Indrizzo de gli economi. . . . Mantua: 1586. *Calif., Am. Inst.*

POSTLETHWAYT, MALACHY

The universal dictionary of trade and commerce. 2*d* ed. London: 1774. *Calif.*

PRESTON, LYMAN

Treatise on bookkeeping. . . . New York: Sleight, 1831. *Lib Cong., Harvard, Am. Inst.*

New York: Robinson, 1842. *Am. Antiq. Soc.*

New York: Collins, 1844. *Lib Cong.*

New York: Collins, 1849. *Yale*

. . . Manual on bookkeeping. . . . Utica (N.Y.): Danby, 1827. *Lib. Cong., Ill.,*

New York: Elliott, 1829. *Am. Antiq. Soc.*

PUGLIESE, SBERNIA ONOFRIO (DA PALER-MO)

Prattica economica numerale. . . . Palermo: 1671. *Calif.*

RADEMANN, JOACHIM

Der wehrt-geschätzte handels-mann. . . . Hamburg: Neumann, 1714. *Lib. Cong.*

Revidirte und erneuerte rechnungs-in-struction. . . . Stuttgart: 1714. *Calif.*

RICARD, SAMUEL

L'art de bien tenir les livres de comptes. . . . Amsterdam: 1709. *Calif., Harvard, Ill.*

RICHTER, CARL FRIEDRICH

Italienische doppelte buchhaltung oder durch sechs monate geführte fingirte handlung aus freyer hand ausgearbeitet. 2*d* ed. Bremen: 1801. *Calif.*

REYNOLDS, GEORGE

The scholars' introduction to merchants' accounts. . . . 2*d* ed. London: Stouter, 1831. *Lib. Cong.*

ROBINSON, JAMES

A compend of book-keeping by single entry. . . . Boston: Hilliard, 1831. *Lib. Cong.*

—ed., 1838. *Lib. Cong., Am. Antiq. Soc.*

ROCHE, MARTIN

Compendious rules for bookkeeping. . . . Phila.: Garden, 1832. *Lib. Cong.*

The American combined system of book-keeping. Phila.: Town, 1835. *Lib. Cong.*

RODRIGUES, J.

La tenue des livres. Bordeaux: 1810. *Calif.*

ROOSE, RICHARD

An essay to make a compleat accomptant. London: Hannah Roose, 1760? *Calif.*

ROSCOE, D. C.

A new and compendious system of book-keeping. . . . Hagers-town, (Md.): Bell, 1818. *Lib. Cong.*

RÖSENER, ANDREAS CHRISTOPH

Tractatus juridicus de libris mercatorum. . . . Scholvini: [1694] *Lib. Cong.*

ROSS, WILLIAM P. M.

A practical system of double entry book-keeping. . . . Phila.: Zieber, 1847. *Lib. Cong.*

SAVARY, JACQUES 1622-1690

Le parfait négociant. . . .

5*th* ed. Lyon: 1700-01. *Calif.*

6*th* ed. Lyon: 1712. *Harvard, Ill.*

7*th* ed. Paris: Guignard, 1713-15. *Harvard*

—ed. Paris: Guignard, 1736-49. *Calif.*

—ed. Paris: Guignard, 1799-1800. *Harvard*

SAVARY DES BRUSLONS, JACQUES

Dictionnaire universel de commerce. Paris: Estienne, 1723 ["given to the public by Philemon-Louis Savary, 1654-1727"]. *Ill.*

Paris: 1748. *Calif.*

Copenhagen: 1759-65. *Calif.*

Dizionario di commercio dei Signori Fratelli Savary. Venice: Pasquali, 1770. *Ill.*

SCALI, PIETRO PAOLO

Trattato del modo di tenere la scrittura dei mercanti a partite doppie. . . . Leg-horn: 1755. *Calif.*

SCHOAPP, JOHANN GEORG

Buchhalterische belustigung. Nürnberg and Leipzig: 1714. *Calif.*

SCHREIBER, HEINRICH

Eyn new künstlich behend und gewiss rechen büchlin uff alle kauffmanschafft. . . . Frankfurt 1544[?] *Calif.*

SCHUERE, JAKOB VAN DER

Arithmetica, oft reken-konst. . . . Ter Goude: 1634. *Calif.*

SCHULTZE, ANTON

Arithmetica, oder rechenbuch. . . . Lignitz: 1611. *Calif.*

SCHURTZ, GEORG NICOLAUS

General instruction, der arithmetischen und politischen kunst der hochlöblichen wissenschaft der kauff- und handelsleuth des buchhaltens.
Nürnberg: 1662. *Calif.*
Nürnberg: 1695. *Meyer*
Neu- engerichtete material—Kammer. . . . Nürnberg: 1672. *Calif.*

SCRUTON, JAMES

The practical counting house. . . . Glasgow: Duncan, 1777. *Lib. Cong., Calif.*

SHAW, JOHN

Bookkeeping epitomized. . . . 1794. *Fleisher*

SHEA, JOHN H.

Book-keeping, by single and double entry. . . . Baltimore: 1839. *Lib. Cong., Yale*
2d ed. Baltimore: 1841. *Harvard*
—ed. Baltimore: 1848. *Mich.*

SHEPARD, JOHN

The science of double-entry book-keeping. . . . Lansingburgh [N.Y.] Harkness, 1840. *Lib. Cong., Am. Antiq. Soc., Ill.*

SHEYS, B.

The American book-keeper. New York: Van Riper, 1815. *Yale, Am. Antiq. Soc.*
New York: Collins, 1818. *Am. Antiq. Soc.*

SIMON, CHRISTIAN HEINRICH

Kurze beschreibung der bev den kaufleuten gebräuchlichsten handlungsbucher auch hauptbuchsconten zur leichtern erlernung des doppelten buchhaltens für handlungsbeflissene. Frankfort and Leipzig: 1780. *Calif.*

SNELL, CHARLES

The elements of Italian bookkeeping, put into verse 17—*Calif., Wis.*
Accompts for landed-men. . . . London: Baker. *Calif., Yale*
A short and easy method after which shop-keepers may state, post and balance their books of accompts (in Ayres: Arithmetick made Easie; 14th ed. London: 1718, *Am. Inst.* 18th ed. London: *Calif.*

SOLORZANO, BARTOLOME SALVADOR DE

Libro de caxa y manuel de cuentas de mercaderes. . . . Madrid: 1590. *Calif.*

STEEL, DAVID

The ship master's assistant and owner's manual. London: P. Steel, 1803. *Yale*

STEPHENS, HUSTCRAFT

Italian bookkeeping reduced into an art. London: 1735. *Am. Inst.*

STEVIN, SIMON (OF BRUGES)

Mathematica hypomnemata. . . . Leyden: 1605. *Calif.*

STILLIGER, JOHANN

Deutlicher und ausfuehrlicher unterricht zur doppelten oder italienischen buchhaltung. Liebau: 1793. *Calif.*

TAGLIENTE, GIOVANNI ANTONIO

Considerando io Joanni Antonio Taiente, quanto e necessaria cosa a diuersi mercantanti, la regola del tenere conto dei loro libri sempii ne dopii. Venice. 1525. *Calif.*
Considerando io Joanni Taiente quanto e necessaria cosa . . . el laudabile modo de tenere conto de libro dopio cioe. Venice: 1525. *Calif.*

THOMAS, [SIDNEY] A.

A key to first lessons in book-keeping. New York: Clark [1843]. *Lib. Cong., Yale, Am. Antiq. Soc.*

TINWELL, WILLIAM

A treatise of practical arithmetic and book-keeping, by single entry. *5th* ed. Newcastle: Angus, 1805. *Ill.*

TRÉMERY, F.

Nouveau manuel complet du teneur de livres. Paris: 1850. *Calif.*

TURNER, RICHARD LL.D.

A new introduction to bookkeeping. . . . London: 1761. *Yale*

1st Am. ed. Boston: Thomas, 1794. *Harvard Am. Antiq. Soc.*

2nd Am. ed. Salem: Cushing, 1801. *Am. Antiq. Soc., Ill.*

rev. ed. Salem: Cushing, 1820. *Lib. Cong., Harvard, Am. Antiq. Soc.*

rev. ed. Salem: Cushing, 1825. *Calif.*

TURNER, THOMAS

An epitome of book-keeping by double entry. . . . Portland: Jenks, 1804. *Calif., Yale, Harvard, Am. Antiq. Soc.*

VANNIER, HIPPOLYTE

La tenue des livres. . . . Paris: 1844. *Calif.*

VENTURI, BASTIANO

Della scrittura contaggiante di possossioni del Sig. Bastiano Venturi, somputista della serenissima principessa Vittoria d'Urbino, gran duschessa di Toscana. Florence: 1655. *Calif.*

VERGANI, GIUSEPPI

Instruzione della scrittura doppia economica. Milan: 1738. *Calif.*

VERNON, JOHN

The compleat compting house. . . . *5th* ed. Dublin: Grierson, 1719. *Lib. Cong.* [includes: An essay on bookkeeping, by William Webster, 1719]

5th ed. London: Worrall, 1727. *Mich., Yale*

VRETLY, P.

Elements of Bookkeeping, New York: Longman, 1839. *Wis.*

WALKINGAME, FRANCIS

The tutor's assistant. . . . added, A compendium of book-keeping, by Isaac Fisher. Montreal: Armour, 1845. *Ontario*

The tutor's assistant . . . (from the *43rd* Derby ed.); added, A compendium of book-keeping by single entry by William Birkin. Toronto: Brewer, 1846. *Ontario*

WALSH, MICHAEL, A. M., 1763-1840

A new system of mercantile arithmetic. . . . *4th* ed. [to which is annexed a system of book-keeping.] Salem: Cushing, 1825. *Calif.*

A new system of mercantile arithmetic, with forms of accounts. . . . *4th* ed. Newburyport: Little, 1816. *Yale*

Book-keeping. . . . Boston: Carter, 1832. *Lib. Cong., Am. Antiq. Soc.*

WANINGEN, HENDRICK

Le thresor de tenir livre de comptes á l'italienne. . . . Amsterdam: 1615. *Calif.* 't recht gebruyck van 't italiaens boeckhouden Nurnberg: 1672. *Calif.*

WEBSTER, WILLIAM

An essay on bookkeeping, according to the true Italian method of debtor and creditor, by double entry. London: Meere, 1719. *Yale* [also bound with John Vernon, *q.v.*]

An essay on book-keeping according to the true Italian method of debtor and creditor by double entry. . . . *11th* ed. London: Browne, 1752. *Calif., Meyer.* [Contains also Clare, *q.v.*]

Scotch ed. Glasgow: Orr, 1758. *Yale*

WELLS, JOHN C.

Wells's lawyer and book-keeping. . . . New York: Wells, 1847. *Lib. Cong.*

WESTON, WILLIAM

The complete merchant's clerk. . . . London: Rivington, 1754. *Lib. Cong., Calif., Ill.*

WIEDEBURG, JOHANN ERNST BASILIUS, 1733-1789

. . . Anleitung zum rechnungs wesen. Jena: Crokers, 1773. *Lib. Cong.*

WILLSFORD, THOMAS

The scales of commerce and trade. . . . London: Brook, 1660. *Yale*

WILSON, CLEMENT A.

A treatise on book keeping. . . . Phila.: Lindsay, 1848. *Lib. Cong.*

WINCHESTER, GEORGE W.

Winchester's book-keeping . . . Hartford [Conn.]: Mather, 1848. *Lib. Cong.*

WINSLOW, EZRA S.

Winslow's system of book-keeping, by double entry, for retail business. . . . 2d., Woodstock (Vt.): Chase, 1836. *Lib. Cong.*

WOEHNER, PAUL GOTTLIEB

Handbuch über das kassen und rechnungs-wesen. 2d ed. Berlin: Burchhardt, 1824. *Lib. Cong., Mich.*

WOOD, WILLIAM

Bookkeeping familiarised. . . . Birmingham: Pearson, [1778]. *Ross*

WOLF, J. CHRISTIAN

Vollständige anleitung zur kaufmännischen buchführung. Wien: 1774. *Calif.*

WUNDSCHE, JOHANN WILHELM

Neu vermehrt und verbessertes memoriale economico-politico-practicum. . . . Franckfort und Leipzig: [1680]. *Calif.*

THE DEVELOPMENT OF
CONTEMPORARY ACCOUNTING THOUGHT

An Arno Press Collection

Baldwin, H[arry] G[len]. **Accounting for Value As Well as Original Cost** *and* Castenholz, William B. **A Solution to the Appreciation Problem.** 2 Vols. in 1. 1927/1931

Baxter, William. **Collected Papers on Accounting.** 1978

Brief, Richard P., Ed. **Selections from Encyclopaedia of Accounting, 1903.** 1978

Broaker, Frank and Richard M. Chapman. **The American Accountants' Manual.** 1897

Canning, John B. **The Economics of Accountancy.** 1929

Chatfield, Michael, Ed. **The English View of Accountant's Duties and Responsibilities.** 1978

Cole, William Morse. **The Fundamentals of Accounting.** 1921

Congress of Accountants. **Official Record of the Proceedings of the Congress of Accountants.** 1904

Cronhelm, F[rederick] W[illiam]. **Double Entry by Single.** 1818

Davidson, Sidney. **The Plant Accounting Regulations of the Federal Power Commission.** 1952

De Paula, F[rederic] R[udolf] M[ackley]. **Developments in Accounting.** 1948

Epstein, Marc Jay. **The Effect of Scientific Management on the Development of the Standard Cost System** (Doctoral Dissertation, University of Oregon, 1973). 1978

Esquerré, Paul-Joseph. **The Applied Theory of Accounts.** 1914

Fitzgerald, A[dolf] A[lexander]. **Current Accounting Trends.** 1952

Garner, S. Paul and Marilynn Hughes, Eds. **Readings on Accounting Development.** 1978

Haskins, Charles Waldo. **Business Education and Accountancy.** 1904

Hein, Leonard William. **The British Companies Acts and the Practice of Accountancy 1844-1962** (Doctoral Dissertation, University of California, Los Angeles, 1962). 1978

Hendriksen, Eldon S. **Capital Expenditures in the Steel Industry, 1900 to 1953** (Doctoral Dissertation, University of California, Berkeley, 1956). 1978

Holmes, William, Linda H. Kistler and Louis S. Corsini. **Three Centuries of Accounting in Massachusetts.** 1978

Horngren, Charles T. **Implications for Accountants of the Uses of Financial Statements by Security Analysts** (Doctoral Dissertation, University of Chicago, 1955). 1978

Horrigan, James O., Ed. **Financial Ratio Analysis—An Historical Perspective.** 1978

Jones, [Edward Thomas]. **Jones's English System of Book-keeping.** 1796

Lamden, Charles William. **The Securities and Exchange Commission** (Doctoral Dissertation, University of California, Berkeley, 1949). 1978

Langer, Russell Davis. **Accounting As A Variable in Mergers** (Doctoral Dissertation, University of California, Berkeley, 1976). 1978

Lewis, J. Slater. **The Commercial Organisation of Factories.** 1896

Littleton, A[nanias] C[harles] and B[asil] S. Yamey, Eds. **Studies in the History of Accounting.** 1956

Mair, John. **Book-keeping Moderniz'd.** 1793

Mann, Helen Scott. **Charles Ezra Sprague.** 1931

Marsh, C[hristopher] C[olumbus]. **The Theory and Practice of Bank Book-keeping.** 1856

Mitchell, William. **A New and Complete System of Book-keeping by an Improved Method of Double Entry.** 1796

Montgomery, Robert H. **Fifty Years of Accountancy.** 1939

Moonitz, Maurice. **The Entity Theory of Consolidated Statements.** 1951

Moonitz, Maurice, Ed. **Three Contributions to the Development of Accounting Thought.** 1978

Murray, David. **Chapters in the History of Bookkeeping, Accountancy & Commercial Arithmetic.** 1930

Nicholson, J[erome] Lee. **Cost Accounting.** 1913

Paton, William Andrew and Russell Alger Stevenson. **Principles of Accounting.** 1918

Pixley, Francis W[illiam]. **The Profession of a Chartered Accountant and Other Lectures.** 1897

Preinreich, Gabriel A. D. **The Nature of Dividends.** 1935

Previts, Gary John, Ed. **Early 20th Century Developments in American Accounting Thought.** 1978

Ronen, Joshua and George H. Sorter. **Relevant Financial Statements.** 1978

Shenkir, William G., Ed. **Carman G. Blough: His Professional Career and Accounting Thought.** 1978

Simpson, Kemper. **Economics for the Accountant.** 1921

Sneed, Florence R. **Parallelism in Two Disciplines.** (M.A. Thesis, University of Texas, Arlington, 1974). 1978

Sorter, George H. **The Boundaries of the Accounting Universe** (Doctoral Dissertation, University of Chicago, 1963). 1978

Storey, Reed K[arl]. **Matching Revenues with Costs** (Doctoral Dissertation, University of California, Berkeley, 1958). 1978

Sweeney, Henry W[hitcomb]. **Stabilized Accounting.** 1936

Van de Linde, Gérard. **Reminiscences.** 1917

Vatter, William J[oseph]. **The Fund Theory of Accounting and Its Implications for Financial Reports.** 1947

Walker, R. G. **Consolidated Statements.** 1978

Webster, Norman E., Comp. **The American Association of Public Accountants.** 1954

Wells, M. C., Ed. **American Engineers' Contributions to Cost Accounting.** 1978

Worthington, Beresford. **Professional Accountants.** 1895

Yamey, Basil S. **Essays on the History of Accounting.** 1978

Yamey, Basil S., Ed. **The Historical Development of Accounting.** 1978

Yang, J[u] M[ei]. **Goodwill and Other Intangibles.** 1927

Zeff, Stephen Addam. **A Critical Examination of the Orientation Postulate in Accounting, with Particular Attention to its Historical Development** (Doctoral Dissertation, University of Michigan, 1961). 1978

Zeff, Stephen A., Ed. **Selected Dickinson Lectures in Accounting.** 1978